Tawdry Tales and Confessions from Horror's Boy Next Door

By
William Butler

www.DarkInkBooks.com

Copyright © 2021 Dark Ink Books.

All Rights Reserved.

ISBN: 978-1-943201-56-3

Library of Congress Control Number: 2021933362

Cover Photo Credit to Chris Haston
Cover Design Credit to Alicia Mattern
Photograph Credits to Michael Deak, Lance Rider and Jill Rockow

First Published by *Dark Ink Books*, Southwick, MA, 2021

Dark Ink Books is a division of *AM Ink Publishing*. *Dark Ink* and *AM Ink* and its logos are trademarked by *AM Ink Publishing*.

www.AMInkPublishing.com

From the day that I loaded up my pea green Monte Carlo and left for Los Angeles over thirty years ago, I kept journals. Still very young, I truly had no idea if I would ever make it in any capacity. I only knew that the life I was hoping for would require me taking very big chances for someone of my limited capability. Whether I ended up homeless, loaded with cash or somewhere in between, I figured my journals would help me remember the lessons I learned, mistakes I made, and any good stuff I would hopefully experience along the way. Who would've known that I'd have extreme moments of all of the above. This book contains some of the stories from the very best *and* very worst moments of my life as I somehow became horror's "boy next door" and eventually, a working entertainment professional, or "professional adjacent," anyway. I give you now: my dirty laundry.

I dedicate *Tawdry Tales and Confessions from Horror's Boy Next Door* to the best friend I ever knew, a guy who taught me that life is never ever what you expect of it and only what you make of it: the late great "King of all Jackals," Johnny Vulich, and to anyone who is brave enough to throw caution to the wind, ignore the doubts of others, and follow their own bliss.

William Butler and John Vulich

TABLE OF CONTENTS

FOREWORD

By
Greg Nicotero

"This town will eat you alive," I overhead someone saying once.
"God, I hope so," responded Billy Butler, with a raucous laugh in a voice
somewhere between Jerry Lewis and Carol Channing.

Many of us that left the comfort of our childhood homes to move to Los Angeles with dreams and aspirations to make movies in Hollywood share a great many things in common. It is almost like we were separated at birth…..a "Dead Ringers" Cronenberg style scar running across our torsos. Billy moved south to LA from Fresno, California and almost immediately found himself surrounded by friends with the common goal…to make monsters and movies. What many people learn, is that it is all driven by massive passion. If you don't absolutely love it, then you shouldn't be doing it. You can't do it. You love it no matter how difficult it can get. Sometimes you end up working on one of the worst films ever made, but if you have passion, you can always see the good in it.

Billy's love for movies allows us to relish in all things horror and sci-fi related. I have seen it with my own eyes. Whether it was working on the set of LEATHERFACE or just sitting around shooting the shit about the industry, he really cares about his craft and even more importantly the people he surrounds himself with. He's been able to find a path that is very rarely taken, and to this day can call himself an actor, a make-up fx artist, a writer, a producer AND a director. This "Forrest Gump" lifestyle has seen Billy move from genre franchise easily and leaving behind him a trail of bodies….and sometimes even his own. And each time, the people he met, the people he worked with found themselves in the company of someone who not only wanted to scare you….but to make you laugh! And boy has he made me laugh.

I can't help myself being drawn to Billy's unflinching spirit and love of life. He tells it like it is, a trait barely seen in the world today. He doesn't ever care how you respond…he relishes in the sheer audacity of saying it and waits anxiously for what will inevitably be an uncontrollable laugh, gasp or a "no you didn't" eyeroll, but I never want to miss a word.

Trained in a tiny make-up effects studio in North Hollywood, alongside friends like Mike Deak and John Vulich, Bill moved quickly into a position running set in Italy for Charlie Band while absorbing every nuance of what he was learning on set from day to day. Those situations can't help but change you, help you develop a real sense of film-making and a resourcefulness that only "being in the trenches" teaches you. Trust me, I've been there…and many times with Billy. In several instances I was able to hire Billy to accompany me on multiple film sets to puppeteer, engineer an effect, or just drench an actor with Karo syrup and red dye #5. On every occasion I not only found him talented and smart, but kept my spirits high…when so many want the opposite. As we move further into our careers, there are those you can pick up with after many months apart, and Billy is exactly that type of person. I'm grateful to call him my friend and honestly am a little scared to read this book….it's been a crazy ride.

Greg Nicotero
Chatsworth California 2021

HANGIN' AROUND

"I wonder how much longer I have to hang upside down," I whispered to my friend, co-star and then relatively unknown actor Viggo Mortensen as he knelt down next to my head, the one that was currently dangling over a dingy butcher shop blood-drain as the movie crew prepared to roll camera.

"You okay?" he said, nearly laughing at how stupid I looked.

"Terrific, …Would you believe this is a dream come true?" I said to him. I truly meant it. Most performers would take exception to a month's worth of being chased through the woods by a chainsaw-wielding maniac, only to end up with a real bear trap snapped around their ankle and dragged across a filthy, feather-covered kitchen floor. But not William Butler. I was in this for the fun of it, and boy, was I living the dream. My only complaint was about the flying harness that they had me wearing under my costume: it was giving me the granddaddy of all wedgies. Other than that, I was in hog heaven and ironically enough, hanging upside down like a butchered pig, bracing myself to be hit in the head with a prop sledgehammer.

"Look, Mom: I made it!" I joked out loud. I patiently watched the crew from my inverted position, suddenly reminded of the times that my acting teacher told me that my vulnerability was going to be the trait that helped me go far in my movie career. I don't think New Line Cinema's *Leatherface: The Texas Chainsaw Massacre 3* was exactly what she had in mind, but as it turns out, she was correct.

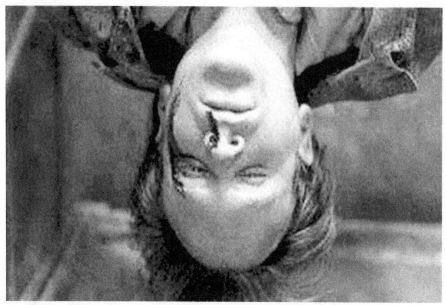

Hanging around on the set of Leatherface: Texas Chainsaw Massacre III

This movie would mark the tenth time that I was asked to have a nervous breakdown and violently meet my maker on screen, and frankly, I was loving every minute of it. At this point in my career, I had been blown-up, beaten, electrocuted, and stabbed with pretty much every gardening tool and cutlery implement available. I'd become what the horror magazines referred to as a "perennial victim," the "Mickey Rooney of horror." I guess maybe I just have the kind of face you want to hit with a butcher knife.

The thing about acting upside down…well, folks, it's tricky. You're only allowed to hang that way for a couple of minutes at a time because eventually, your brain floods with blood. It's also daunting because you're hanging in a room full of testosterone-fueled method actors who are truly ready to bring the scene to life by possibly causing your death. I mean, *really* ready, like wanting to kick your ass ready, and hanging upside down, I had nowhere to run. Acting scared is never a problem when you're being smacked around and mad-dogged by actors who take their jobs very seriously, but then again, it was always something that got a genuine reaction out of me, so I welcomed it.

What a way to be making a living, I thought to myself, dangling there, as a production assistant offered to have a coffee waiting for me when I finally would be lowered back onto the mud-encrusted floor in-between takes. Imagine me laying there in that filth, sipping an artesian-brewed mochaccino while my face was being spritzed with yet another blast of movie blood and fake dirt. Heaven, I tell you; hands down, the absolute most fun, yet most stupid business ever. Working in horror films is the only job on the planet where you get up in the morning, shower, go to set, sit in a make-up chair to be made-up and blow-dried to look terrific, only to then put on filthy clothes and get bloody Q-tips shoved up your nose. Most nights, I would be so tired after filming that I would just change clothes and drive home still encrusted in dirt and dried fake blood.

"Mr. Butler, I have your coffee for you," the pleasant PA said to me as she knelt down beside me, offering me a sip. What a life. I wondered to myself if things were going to get any better or worse for that matter. If I had only known I would run both sides of the spectrum over and over again.

Hangin' Around with Viggo Mortensen on Leatherface: Texas Chainsaw Massacre III

Viggo Mortensen on the set of Leatherface: Texas Chainsaw Massacre III

THE END WAS THE BEGINNING

JUNE 2014

A new beginning started with an unfortunate and abrupt ending as my well-paying gig went away with a single phone call I took while lying on my bed.

"They are ready for a new producer. It's starting to look like I am playing favorites and I just can't do that, Billy." The voice on the phone was very uncomfortable. "I'm getting resistance from a couple of people on the team who want changes, and I have to hear them: that's my job."

"What are you saying…?"

"I'm saying that you are…through here…for a little while."

"I'm fired?!"

There was a very pained pause of silence.

"But my show was just renewed…"

"Something will come up in the future. Just ride it out."

"Please don't do this," I pleaded.

"You *will* find other work, you know?" *CLICK.*

The truth is, I had been miserable for months and my secret prayer to be away from my highly-paying digital short job was about to come true, but not before completely flatlining my life: like, "ground-zero" flat-lining. In the last five years, I had made a deal with the digital-devil and turned my back on the beginnings of a solid movie directing and acting career, all in the name of making big cash and steady employment. I had quickly evolved from hopeful filmmaker to a bitter corporate-TV, digital-shorts guy.

I crawled out of bed, walked over to and stared out the window of the hillside, swimming-pool laden home off of Mulholland Drive that I had been renting. The house was appropriately named "Casa De Mille Putas" or "House of a Thousand Whores" and was everything to me. To say Mille Putas was lavish would be an understatement. Let's just say a lot of very high-class porn had been shot on my patio, people. The realtor thought that was a selling point when she showed it to me, and she was right. Indeed, the joint *was* high-class porn fancy.

When you're raised on the fair and Circus midways of Central California (and we'll get to that), "high-class porn fancy" is a considered a reflection of sheer opulence and tremendous success. I'd evolved from a fat kid from Fresno selling corndogs and cotton candy at the circus into a successful commercial short director with a company that was pulling in a fortune. I had certainly arrived, but it was now clear that the very train that had dropped me off in successville was pulling out of the station for the return trip to broke-town. At moment, everything was ending right where it had started 27 years ago, with me jobless and flat broke. I had turned my back on acting, writing, and feature film directing for a lavish life focusing on work I cared very little about. I'd become a complete whore in the worst way a filmmaker could and that dirty little whore had just contracted a severe case of financial gonorrhea. To add insult to injury, I currently required a fifteen thousand dollar a month overhead to keep my monolithic lifestyle going. I went from making a terrific living to making nothing instantly and what's worse, I had a hundred thousand-dollars-worth of bills on deck.

"Who's ready for a big birthday dinner?!!!" my friend Peter and his friend Joe cheered as I entered the room. Peter Garcia, my forever-faithful, insanely talented, hilarious best friend and partner in crime (sometimes literally) and someone who still, to this day, knows me better than anyone, could instantly see that something was up. "What's wrong?" he said with eyes wide.

"I was just fired off my own show." I could barely form the sentence.
"You always say they're gonna fire you," he said, laughing.
"Well, they just did; so, occasionally I'm right."
"Oh my God, really? I'm so sorry, Billy."
"And...I am flat broke."
Peter raised his eyebrows and let out an exaggerated GULP.
Joe, Peter's vacationing friend who was also staying at my home looked back at me with a shocked, unblinking gaze. I knew he was thinking, *the guy who just bought us a 300-dollar dinner at The Palm last night is flat broke?* Welcome to Hollywood, Joe.
Peter could tell by the look on my expressionless face that I was indeed serious.
"You'll be fine," he said.
"I'm sorry, you guys, but I don't feel like going anywhere," I said.
"I get it. But let's not forget, you have been hating that show for the last couple of years. They did you a favor."
I didn't answer him and instead plopped down on the couch. I didn't care if he was right. "I really just want to be alone," I said quietly.
"We'll give you some space...I'll bring you home some cake," he said, like the true friend he had always been.
They quietly started to leave as I stared forward at the television. Oprah Winfrey was in her last year of production and was recapping coverage of her *Law of Attraction* special. "See it in your mind, know it in your heart!!!" she belted out, beaming in her wide-eyed billionaire bliss. I held back from getting up and putting my foot through the fucking TV screen.
Peter stopped at the door. "Butch (a nickname all of my friends and I have given one another since we were in our teens), you've been in L.A for 30 years and anytime anything like this has ever happened, it has always lit a fire under your ass and you've been okay," he said. "You will be okay, again."
I nodded. Peter closed the door. I remained there a few minutes alone, staring into space.
My three horribly spoiled lap dogs, Gibby, Walter, and Henry jumped up on the couch, curiously eyeballing me. I didn't have it in my heart to tell them that the top-shelf brand of dog food they loved so much was about to go generic. I got up and walked outside into the backyard. The rain had subsided; the sky was now gorgeous and pink. I

walked across the concrete in the massive backyard and looked back at my beautiful home. Memories of all of the family gatherings, wild parties, holidays, and yes, even the multitude of smooth-skinned models, lifeguards, linebackers, and hockey players who resided there on my dime (way too numerous to mention), came to mind. Money very well spent, by the way. I thought to myself, *I am, without a doubt, the stupidest person on the planet.* And I was right.

Casa de Mille Putas

I sat on the edge of my patio and faced the setting sun. Yeah, I know: it sounds like a writer's cliché, but so is going from rags to riches to back to rags again and that happened, too, so get used to it. This story is chock full of Hollywood clichés, because at the time, that's exactly what I was.

The view from my Beverly Ridge home went on forever, easily a hundred miles. It was hands-down, the best place in town to take in the perfect view. It's exactly why we Californians pay so much damn rent. Our magnificent sunlit skies combined with our sickening pea soup-thick smog regularly creates some truly dazzling sunsets. Well, folks, that beautiful view may have been endless, but my whorish lifestyle was no doubt coming to an abrupt and screeching end. I had only ever produced a couple of corporate entertainment companies for the last fifteen years and had pretty much zero other contacts. I didn't know anyone else in town except for the same seven people I had been working with and the hundreds of people I had created jobs for—most of whom had disappeared. I had turned my back on my acting career, screenwriting, and directing. I had no more agent or representation, no more writing partner, and no new prospects for any work. I knew in my gut that I was probably about to lose everything and that's exactly what happened. Dear Oprah, I now understand that the law of attraction" works both ways. I had been wishing for my life to change, and it did just that.

Within two months of being released from my show, I was moving out of "Casa De Mille Putas" and returning my Mercedes back to the dealer. I had to sell much of my furniture and artwork to pay off the massive debt that I had accumulated. Close friends were giving me money to try and ease the hit; some employees told me to just forget what I owed them, and in other cases, people I had given years of work to angrily threatened to take me to the labor board. It was an atrocious, embarrassing, and painful time of my life that I will never ever make the mistake of reliving ever again. Things continued to get worse and eventually, I had to be medicated for the constant panic attacks and deep depression into which I plunged.

Even worse were the passive-aggressive jabs I started getting from a few of my frenemies who, never having approved of my piggish lifestyle, had been waiting for me to take a fall. I got more than a few sugar-coated, venom-laced phone messages from some of my more wicked colleagues: "I'm just checking in on you. I heard you've fallen on hard times. I'm just so shocked about your situation. To think: all this time, I've been so envious of you, but I guess it just goes to show you, you really never know when that rug'll be pulled out from under you. I'm sure you prepared by saving money." This from one of my friends, obviously more entertained than truly concerned by my self-inflicted situation. But I get it, I certainly had it coming. Who knew that so many valuable lessons would be learned so late in life.

Having only produced digital shorts for a couple of companies, I truly didn't have any other contacts and had no idea where to even begin to try to get another job. For now, "Billy, Big Boss Applesauce" was out of a job and completely out of the loop with my past career paths. Forty-six sure seemed like a pretty young age to be cancelled.

Suddenly, I felt like my entire life had blazed right passed me. It felt like it was only a couple of years ago that I was nineteen, just starting out, and now, here I was, by Hollywood's standards, old, washed-up, and jobless. Hard as I tried, I could not find a gig. I'd become so large and in charge, no one wanted to deal with me.

Heavily medicated, I packed up and headed north to my parent's house. I wondered if this was really it. As I drove my beat-up rental car home, I thought back to the time when I first started out and all of the marvelous journeys I'd been on until my unfortunate pause in life. It was truly a miracle that I ever had the nerve to give it whirl to begin with. It seemed that the prophecies constantly whispered to me by the goddamn invisible parrot on my shoulder had finally come true.

Packing Up

Adios Casa de Mille Putas

3

DADDY DEAREST

1980

"Stop procrastinating and just move to L.A.," twenty-something John Vulich's voice droned through the land line at 3 a.m. Doctor Demento was playing on the tinny radio on my desk: the song "Fish Heads," to be exact, a song that, for some reason, has always terrified me.

"I've been seriously considering it," I said. I was lying.

"Stop thinking about it and just do it. You can stay at my place until you're settled. You have nothing to lose," Vulich said.

"Sounds amazing," I said, lying again. Truthfully, the idea terrified me. "Are the people in L.A. nice?"

"No, they're absolute cunts. In other words, you'll fit right in," he laughed. I could always count on Vulich to keep it real. I was a very young seventeen at the time, weighing in at a whopping three-hundred and twenty pounds and sporting a hideously fried green Toni home perm. At that very moment, I was also in my pajamas…at work. I had been working the graveyard shift as a tow truck dispatcher for AAA and quickly realized that I was completely on my own throughout the night. I not only often showed up to work in what was obviously pajamas, but often times, I also brazenly wore a robe and fuzzy slippers. Sometimes, around 4 a.m. when things slowed down, I went as far as to lie down under the dispatch console and read horror novels and *Fangoria* magazine, then sleep until 6 a.m. before my friends on the morning shift started coming in and wake me. If you were stranded on a highway in 1981 and couldn't get AAA to pick up the phone after 2 a.m., it's my fault, as I promise you: I was asleep.

Days passed and John droned on over the phone line once more. "Just pull it together and drive out here. You can survive in L.A. just as easy as anyone else does."

"You're sure I can stay with you?" I asked.

"Of course you can. Get out here!"

I hung up the phone in excitement and fear. Maybe he was right, I thought to myself. Maybe it *was* time for me to stop talking about leaving town and do it. From the day John and I had met when we were just kids, we had planned to move to Hollywood and make films, and for him, that was happening. But for me, well, I wasn't so sure that I was strong enough or frankly, talented enough, to make the commitment.

The truth was, the idea of moving to Los Angeles truly did scare me as I had zero self-confidence that I really could make it. Like none. Unlike my best friend, Vulich, whose artistic talent as a sculptor and FX artist was shockingly obvious from as early as the age of 13, I had no real discernable skills. All of my life, I had grown up pudgy and ordinary; I was reminded time and time again by "Bub," my tyrannical father, that I was a lazy nobody, a "fucking pig" with nothing to offer. And I believed him.

My father was a huge bear of a man, a hardworking beast perpetually dressed in his Pepsi-Cola uniform; his face framed with serial-killer style eyeglasses, his head crowned with a premature combover. He was overworked and pompous, and worst of all, he had zero connection with me, his eldest, oddball son. Despite those less than savory qualities, he was also a generous man, one who provided his three children with piles of Christmas gifts every year but be oddly angry if we spent too much time playing with them. He was an obsessive-compulsive neat freak, a guy with an absolute demand for total order of his house and yard, which was daunting.

We lived on a big farm with a small country house and a yard that was made up of three acres alone. Behind the house was a big metal barn and a saddle house; it was absolute heaven for a kid, especially one with an imagination as big as mine. Chickens, ducks, horses, cattle, and even peacocks were just a few of the animals that resided there with us, and I spent as much time as I could with all of them. It was certainly beautiful, but the daily upkeep was overwhelming for everyone in the family. My father, a rigid taskmaster, expected the place to be immaculately tidy at all times: from the kitchen to the yard, everything had to be in a constant state of order or there were serious problems in store for everyone. If the house was not exactly how he expected it to be when he got home from work, he exploded into a tirade, berating and beating us until things got situated the way he wanted them to be. Back then, that's how some people felt children were to be raised. But even as a young kid, I knew this was not how life was to be spent.

Every day around 5 p.m., my siblings and I scrambled to hide whenever we heard the sound of his Pepsi Cola work truck rambling up the long gravel driveway of our country home. "Stupid fucking pigs," he'd snap at my mother, siblings, and me because somebody had left their socks next to the couch or the lid off the gallon of milk in the refrigerator.

My mother, the prettiest lady on our block, did everything she could to keep peace in the family. I know everyone thinks their mother is beautiful, but my mother truly was. She was petite with a big bleached-blonde bouffant hairdo and sported those pretty, pointy snow-cone boobs that I guess one could chalk up to the bra style of the time period. Unlike most children's parents, my mother was also a good friend and the first person responsible for turning me on to reading books, particularly Edgar Allen Poe and other horror novels.

She watched over her three children like a mother hen and never hesitated to call my father out when he crossed the line...which was often. We were not the only ones that got the tough treatment from him. He also was not easy on her. From a very early age, I can remember him becoming verbally and physically violent with her when he wasn't happy. I also can remember some of those altercations starting after my mother insisted that he lay off of me, the weird son who would rather be sculpting than playing football. I was a true anomaly to him and certainly, he to me.

My mother was a very loving woman who worked very hard to create and maintain her own perfect nuclear family. She yearned for my father and me to be a team, often misfiring when it came to giving me advice on how I could become more appealing to him. Just a few of her ideas to help my PR included me joining a little league team, despite my being completely uninterested and mostly fearful of it, as well as me taking lessons on the coronet, a musical instrument that my father supposedly had played in high school. "Well, he doesn't play it now," I thought to myself as the plan was sprung on me. In the first five minutes after it was out of its case, my brand-new coronet was knocked off the kitchen table and fell onto the linoleum, bending the front bell backwards. As punishment for not taking care of it, my parents made me continue to take classes with that mangled thing. I remember the horrified look on my teacher's face when I pulled it out in class. It was out of a movie, you know, when you see a fat kid in marching band playing a mangled coronet: that was me, except I never learned how to play it. I just pantomimed blowing into the thing during practice, counting the moments until I could get back to my comic books and MAD magazine.

No, friends, I was not the trophy kid a parent would hope for in the least. While most everybody else's children were running with the pack, I was running away from them. But boy, my mom sure tried hard to make me more palatable to my father and peers, sadly, with zero results. I eventually grew into a nervous, chubby bedwetter who'd rather hide in the shadows than interact with people. I was a weird, creative kid, completely consumed with monsters, MAD magazine, acting, Super-8 filmmaking, movies, puppets, music. and live theater. I also lived for any kind of entertainment by the Walt Disney company. From movies and books to the theme park itself, I was deeply drawn to their flawless artistry and style from a very young age. I now realize its Disney's absolute escapism and the message that everything can work out in the end that originally drew me in.

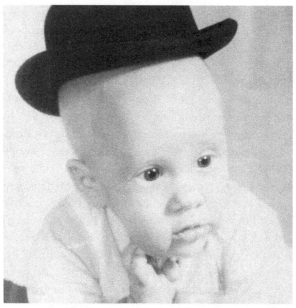

Red carpet ready from day one.

As much as I lived in fear of my father, I also was secretly desperate to be accepted by him. I simply was not who he wanted me to be. It's a very strange and unsettling feeling for a kid to live believing that your own parent wishes you were someone else. Most of our interaction was when he'd take the time to tell me how I wasn't dressed right, was lazy, or was not executing some household task properly. According to my father, there was to be no idle time at home. Unlike most kids, I also dreaded weekends and summer vacation because it meant that he once again would be exploding into my room at seven in the morning, ripping the curtains open, and bellowing his most loathsome and often used phrase, "Get up and get your work clothes on!" It was clear that in his mind that any free time spent having fun was time wasted.

As I got older, my growing skills in the art of sarcasm and total lack of enthusiasm to dive into his daily demands only encouraged his impatient behavior. His consistent disapproval of me eventually made me withdraw from people in general. I started to believe the notion that I *was* indeed a lazy, worthless nobody. It was only the times when I managed to hide in my room surrounded by my books, art supplies, and record player that really ever felt right. I'm still that way. Anyone that knows me will tell you that if I am missing during a holiday family gathering, I can always be found hiding in some bedroom off to the side all by myself. It's a habit that I never lost. It's a habit that still makes me thrive.

The second place you might have found me, especially in the summer, was outside in our big cement well-hole on our farm. It was a huge crusty old concrete vat that held water before it was routed out to our grain fields. I climbed into the well's perfectly clear water and swam every single moment that I was able. It was there where I started to imagine different worlds and a life much different than my own. I remember lying in the pasture next to the well, my chubby, plain self, looking at all of the perfect models and actors in magazines and wondering what life was like for people not perceived as invisible. I guess most kids do that, except when I got older, I eventually had opportunities to meet many of those actors and models and laughed when I realized that only a few of them had much to say.

My parents eventually sent me to therapy as they believed that because I was so introverted, there might be something wrong with me. Some people *still* think that, but I digress. I glared at the cigarette smoking therapist and fired back with one-word answers in my shrink session with him. I drew a hideous monster in crayon when the doctor asked me to draw what was on my mind, for no reason other than I was bored to tears with his attempts to figure out what was going on in my head. I felt like there was nothing wrong with me, everyone else seemed to be following some sort of preconceived notion of how kids were to behave in life. Little boys played baseball and went hunting; little girls baked cookies and played with dolls and both did everything they could to fit into life's pecking order. I did not fit into any of that order and what's worse, I didn't care. I was only transfixed on art, movies, and all things Disney.

Once, when I was entering the sixth grade, I had the audacity to ask my father to take me and my siblings to Disney on Ice. Folks, it was enough to make his head explode.

He just stared at me, his face frozen like he was one of those expressionless statues on Easter Island. Yet I must say, in his defense, despite being completely exasperated by my very unmasculine request, the old man did end up taking us to Disney on Ice and more than once, along with lots of other live shows, so you gotta give him that.

"I'll take you to goddamned Disney on Ice, but you'd better believe me when I tell you that every last one of those male skaters is fruity!" he said, shoveling the hamburger gravy and mashed potatoes into his mouth that my mother had made.

"Fruity?" my young self thought. I had no idea what he was talking about. I thought maybe "fruity" meant insane. Could it be that one of those sequin-encrusted male skaters would execute a flawless triple axel, then suddenly snap, dive off the ice and brutally kill my family and me? I was a very dramatic child, people.

Later, as we sat in the audience at Selland Arena, I felt equal parts terror and elation as I excitedly sat through Disney on Ice, waiting for the skaters to spring into action Charles Manson style, but there was no sign of "fruitiness" that I could detect. On the way back home, I held back from asking my father exactly what "fruity" meant, why it was a bad thing, and most of all, how he could spot it and I couldn't. Bub seemed to have the ability to spot a lot of things I couldn't.

With no father figure in my life that made me feel worthy, I began to yearn for male attention and acceptance, and I mean that in the purest and most innocent of ways. By the time I was in my early twenties, I considered any male adult who treated me kind and worthy to be god-like. I made friends with people who treated me well and then clung to them, often driving them nuts with an over-abundance of attention. I often developed an unhealthy codependence on friends, not wanting them to be around anyone else but me. Like Lenny from the novel *Of Mice and Men*, I latched onto people who I loved and squeezed them until they were completely suffocated by my affections. It was a cycle I am very happy to report has finally, *finally* passed, after much therapy, a few random addictions and twelve-step meetings where I often fell off of the fifth step, and the loss of some very sacred friendships. The ironic part is that nowadays, I love being alone. No one ever has to worry about me overstaying my welcome emotionally, as they can seldom find me. Circle of life, I guess.

Now that I'm older, I realize that both my father and my mother did the best they could back when they were young. I know that sounds laughable, being that my fathers "best" sometimes included dragging me through the house by my hair because he didn't like the way leaves had been raked. I was an unplanned pregnancy. I've always heard that I was conceived in the backseat of an old Thunderbird and I truly hope that is true. My parents had me when they were only seventeen years old, just babies themselves, and I suspect that my father's unsavory behavior was rooted in the fact that my unexpected arrival marked the end of his own childhood; that, combined with the fact that it was obvious from an early age that I would never ever be the kid he expected me to be. I'm on the wrong side of 50 now, and I can still barely keep the laundry done, let alone raise kids, so I get it. My father had been suddenly thrust into the world of young parenting and there was gonna be hell to pay, not only for himself, but for everyone involved, including my mother, who walked a very precarious tightrope trying to balance between being a good wife and a protector of her children.

My father was spawned from hardworking, no-nonsense DNA and the notion of my working in writing, film production or in acting was not only unlikely, it was more so an escape from what he considered to be "real work." "You get a job at Montgomery Ward answering the phones, and in a few years, you could be managing the refrigerator department," he'd knowingly advise.

Bub's explosions into my bedroom to run a system's check came very frequently. Like clockwork, he became irate if he found me doing anything he considered to be a waste of time. Once, when I was around fourteen, Vulich and I were in my room putting together plastic monster model kits. My father burst in and told Vulich to go home. He looked at me in incredulous disgust. "Just look at yourselves, two grown men locked away in here, playing with dolls!" There was no escaping his constant disapproval. Still, although he could easily suck all of the positive air out of a room in an instant, he could not take away my growing interests.

My freshman high school counselor Mr. Henry Silva learned of my growing love of film production and gave me a pamphlet for UCLA. He told me that if I kept my grades up, I could get a scholarship and go to school there, eventually getting a degree in motion picture. When I gave my father the pamphlet, he flipped through it and dropped it on the table in front of him. "We don't go to college in our family, we work," he said. "College is a waste of time. You'll spend every day partying."

That didn't sound so bad to me. I was completely crushed but not shocked by his reaction. He himself had not gone to college and seemed to be doing just fine. "I can learn how to make movies there," I said.

"You need to get your head around the fact that hard work is going to be *your* only chance of survival," he said matter-of-factly. A couple of weeks later, my father asked his friend Mr. Mullins, an agriculture teacher from my high school, to come to our house and spell it out for me Dr. Phil-style.

He showed up in a dusty baseball hat and faded flannel shirt and broke the news to me. "There's no such thing as a pie in the sky. You need to get real about what you're gonna do with yourself or you're gonna be in for a world of hurt." I almost laughed in his face, staring him down and not responding. Mr. Mullins raised his eyebrows, shook his head, and looked over at my parents. "Good luck."

It was at that point that I realized that my life was only ever going to be the way I wanted it to be if I made it entirely on my own. I was clueless but smart enough to know that I had better start focusing if I wanted to make it happen. From that moment forward, I spent every free moment reading books on my interests, completely turning my back on my schooling. Of course, I had never really cared about school, other than for it being a place where I could meet up with my friends so we could collectively ditch it, a habit I now deeply regret, particularly since I eventually became a working writer, one who soars with big creative ideas but also limps along pathetically with tremendously awful grammar. My apologies to the poor dear who is editing my book. *Stay in school, kids!* but then again, never let bad grammar get in the way of a sale of something interesting.

I became driven to succeed in spite of both my father and smug advisors like cow-poke Mullins. Twenty-five years later, I ran into Mr. Mullins at a funeral and jokingly told him that I had made it, despite his advice.

"In case you've ever wondered, that 'pie in the sky' tastes pretty fuckin' good," I said, leaning in with eyebrows raised. Mullins just stared me down like I was still an idiot.

Thus, just so you know, you're wasting your time if you think your haters are ever going to see the light and rethink their judgement of you. If they think you're goofy now, they always will. I am a tremendously goofy guy, just an extremely happy one who's been around the world three times as a result of bleeding for what I wanted in life. It took a whole lifetime to soak in, but I eventually caught on that you must only ever be motivated to tackle goals *for yourself* and never to prove anyone else wrong.

Still, in the beginning, my father's treatment of me actually motivated me to work harder. I sometimes imagine how successful I would have been had he been encouraging. To this day, I still work seven days a week to keep all of the balls in the air. I can safely tell you that I work harder than anyone I know and have pretty much accomplished everything I ever wanted in life as a result of that insane work ethic. Yet, no matter where I am, there is always an imaginary parrot that Bub left perched on my shoulder, one who wickedly whispers to me, "you're not fooling anyone. Stop wasting time and get a real job," especially when the chips are down. And the God's honest truth is <u>this</u>: these days even *I* would never advise a young person to move to a huge city at too young of an age.

The parts of my life in Los Angeles that have worked in my favor have brought me tremendous joy, but the times when things have been tough... well, things have been pretty goddamn grim. My father, no matter how awful his presentation, was not completely wrong about staying planted in the real world.

4

VULICH MAKES HIS FIRST BIG POINT

To the average person, like me, John Vulich was odd upon first glance. Bad rooster haircut, sleeveless rocker shirts, crooked as-all-hell teeth, weird thin moustache, and a wise-ass attitude that gave my biting sarcasm a serious run for its money. He also could drink anyone under the table, spoke several languages, drove like a bat out of hell, and was drawn to chicks of a subservient nature. His Yugoslavian Euro-blood upbringing also gave him a mild homosexual vibe, despite him voraciously banging every girl he ever hit on. John was a lot of things, but gay was not one of them. But the very best thing about John Vulich was his explosive, hyena-like laugh. His magnificent laugh always got everyone in the room laughing, even if you didn't know what he was laughing at. I lived to hear that guy laugh.

"Fuck what your father has to say and get your ass to L.A., dude. We make movies all day and we watch VHS tapes and drink beer every night. It's fuckin' paradise," Vulich said. "You need to get your head around the fact that just because he's your dad, doesn't mean he's always right. And for the record, it's okay for you to tell him that he can't treat you the way he does. If you need someone to tell you the hard truth, I will. The guy is an asshole."

John continued in his matter of fact, hatefully genius tone. "Parents are just people, they don't understand life any better than the rest of us do and sometimes out of practicality, you have to cut unhealthy people out of your life to function. He's got his dick in your brain and he always has. He knows you're afraid of him and he's gonna keep you jumping through hoops until you get out of Dodge. You'd be doing yourself a huge favor by just cutting him out of your life. Go live on your own dime. He doesn't behave like a father should. He can't take anything away from you if you're paying your own way."

I listened, terrified of the hard truth. John was right.

"Your father is very wrong when he suggests you're not worthy just because you aren't who he thinks you should be. He is, in fact, talking about himself."

I sat for a moment without speaking as his point soaked in. And that was it. Vulich had somehow hit pay dirt and broken through to me. If I wanted to fix things, I needed to grow up and go do my own thing. It was time for me to ignore that fucking parrot on my shoulder and find a place where I fit in, and it sure wasn't wearing pajamas reading horror magazines on the floor of the AAA dispatch office. If I didn't like how my life was going, I needed to stop whining about big daddy and go out on my own. I had a lot to consider if I was to finally make my own way.

At that point, having just graduated high school, I had little life experience, and I was still very much a kid in my head. I had never lived on my own steam or been kissed by someone; I'd never smoked a cigarette or a joint, gone on a date or balanced a checkbook; I'd never been in love or had sex. I barely knew that you needed to put oil in a car on a regular basis.

I didn't understand anything about attraction or how coupling worked. As far as I knew, all married people did was lie, fight, and cheat on one another. I chalked up my lack of interest in pairing up as a severe case of arrested development. My brain was completely checked out on the subject. I always figured those feelings would come when they came, but they weren't coming. I was expected to behave like a responsible adult since I was young, so any free time I had to myself, I desperately spent trying to hold onto my adolescence. I positively wanted freedom, but I was too immensely immature to handle it at that moment. It wasn't until years later that I realized that there were many other things going on in my head that were causing me to ignore growing up, shun intimacy and refuse to become an adult. Following my own bliss would certainly be a massive gamble, and I was very nervous about moving out of town, but I needed a big change and getting out from under my father's thumb needed to be the first move. Ironically enough, it was an unexpected gift from my father that introduced me to Vulich in the first place.

Johnny Vulich had been my best friend since way back in the seventies. We first met after I had joined a local Super-8 filmmaking club. I don't have many good memories of my time spent with my father, but after the Christmas that he gave me a small Super-8 movie camera back when I was 12, filmmaking was all I ever thought about, so for that, I owe him a huge degree of thanks. His gift helped nurture my true passion and through that passion, he inadvertently exposed me to a brilliant lifelong friend who would change the trajectory of my entire life. Vulich and I were inseparable from the first day we met.

My good friend and neighbor Brian Reams had started making Super-8 movies in this local film club we'd joined. We were the youngest members of the club, often exposed to film shorts far too adult for kids entering the seventh grade, that we of course found hilarious. Full bush nudity and rape fantasy scenarios were often featured in shorts created by some of the more questionable "filmmakers", men who seemed to be living out their raunchy fantasies and fetishes than actually telling stories.

Despite this, John and I met when Brian and I needed some special effects for one of our films, and we instantly bonded. We had so much in common: our mutual love of films, our wicked sarcasm and sense of humor, our snap-response to question everything in life—particularly parental and non-parental authority—but most of all, we had a common passionate hatred for almost everyone around us. At the time, this was my idea of the very essence of true friendship.

When it came to make-up effects, Vulich was operating at an adult level from a very early age. He strived for total realism, putting raw chicken skin on the roof of his house to study it as it rotted away, and later recreating the texture of its decay. His work methods seemed crazy, but the end result was always flawless. His magnificent brain worked in ways I had never seen, like few had seen in our small town. Later, when Johnny and I started doing our own film shorts, the audience sat in shock at the sight of his special effects gags as our young actor friends seemingly cut themselves with razor blades or had their limbs severed off in one swipe only to be clubbed to death with their own appendages. The two of us choked with laughter in the back of the theater when my

Grandma Butler got up and left at the sight of a rubber baby being thrown off a freeway overpass and run over by an oncoming car. Just good clean teenage fun if you asked us.

John and my friendship continued to grow into very strong bond as we got older. He often invited me over to hide out at his place. Whenever I could manage to steal time for myself and escape, I headed out to his parents' house, which was way out in the wealthy part of our small town of Fresno, California. He lived in a great place. His folks clearly had dough. His mother Franka was a stern, first generation Yugoslavian-American who owned a popular beauty shop in town and his stepfather John, equally stern, worked for the school system. Both were serious and curt, but for the most part nice to me, considering that I stayed at their house until all hours of the night. John was incredibly smart and it was a huge change of pace to sit and watch him question and outwit his parents in virtually every argument I ever saw them get into. I cannot imagine what the outcome would have been had I dared speak to my father the way I saw John dress his folks down. He was as smart as a whip and could talk circles around any argument.

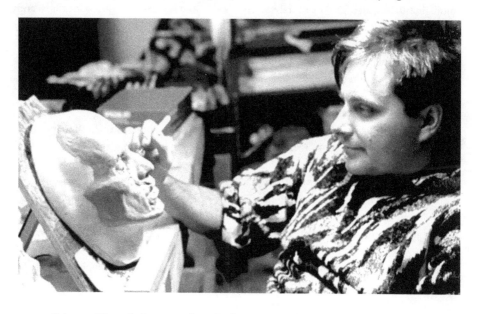

John and I regularly camped out in the art room that his mother and father let him set up in one of the bedrooms of their sprawling home. We'd rent stacks of horror movies like *Phantasm* and *Suspiria* and watch them over and over again while we read *Famous Monsters*, *Fangoria*, and *Starlog* magazines from cover to cover. We wrote, sculpted, and talked endlessly about our hopes of one day becoming a production team.

"You can direct and I'll do all of the creature work, and then later on, I'll direct one every now and then while you produce." John said these things in a way that made me believe that he somehow knew that all of it was going to happen, and sure enough, it eventually did. I believed in him so much and he believed in me. I just knew that somehow, someway it really would come to be.

The art room door flung open at around four in the morning in the middle of our fifth-in-a-row screening of George Romero's *Dawn of the Dead* and Franka squawked. "I cannot sleep vis dat TV on!! You! Go home!" she snapped at me in a thick, angry accent.

I then sulked out of their house and back to my grim reality.

Our regular hangout sessions went on for years, typically ending with our parents bouncing John or me out of the other's house. Usual teenage fare, I guess, but in the process, we became the absolute best of friends. I had finally had a friend who thought I was smart and creative and who genuinely liked me for who I truly was, despite all of my flaws…too numerous to mention. Johnny was a kind person who laughed at what I laughed at, could see through bullshit as easily as I could and understood that there was indeed more to life than working 9 to 5 selling freezers at Montgomery Ward.

We were complete horror hounds and insanely proud of it, neither of us able to get enough of the genre in any form: books, movies, magazines, art supplies, conventions, midnight movies, all of it. We sat talking endlessly about our favorite directors, films, and movie soundtracks. Most of all, we followed our absolute idol, the god of horror, special-effects patriarch Tom Savini's every move religiously. We read everything that we could about him and watch any film or TV show he was involved in over and over again. John even wrote him a letter once, sending Savini photos of his early work, and he somehow ended up on the phone with Tom as only Johnny could. It was clear that film production was where he truly belonged and I wanted to be right in there with him.

Early on when I first started writing, I won an essay contest at a local hamburger place and received free hamburgers for a year (leave it to a fat kid to go after that one and win). John loved the story I had written about my young life thus far and he encouraged me to pursue becoming a writer. It wasn't the first time that I had been encouraged to write. I remember my mother telling me that my sixth-grade teacher told her that writing was something that I would most likely excel in. From that moment, Johnny continually pushed me to write a screenplay so that we could make a film on our own. I desperately wanted to give it a try, but I never thought that it would be possible. My father would not allow me to sit around for hours at a time, typing away and truthfully, I was terrified that I would fail. The two excuses combined were enough for me to procrastinate.

After we got our drivers licenses, Johnny and I became shameless hell raisers. Friday nights were for prowling the city, and he and I sneaked beers from our parents' houses and took his classic Mustang out for boozed-fueled pow-wows we called Jackalfests. The Jackals, as we called ourselves, were an imaginary thug-gang that we drunkenly made up one night during a bonfire down at the river. This rough and tumble (milk-fed veal) "gang" consisted of me, Vulich, and razor-tongued Muffy Bolding, a hilarious, beautiful, and equally brilliant young girl I'd met as a sophomore in high school. From the very first day, we bonded over our love of barbecue chicken sandwiches, reading, writing, and most of all, our deep-seeded mutual obsession with an eccentric local television celebrity, a kid by the name of Tommy "Butch Bond," the son of the original "Butch" from *The Little Rascals* film shorts from the 40s. Butch Jr. had regularly appeared on the *Channel 30 Funtime*, a local TV show for kids, and I watched his every move. In fact, we loved Butch Bond so much that from that very first day I met Muffy to the present day, we still lovingly call each other "Butch." In fact, most of our friends call each other "Butch," as it has somehow entered all of our vernaculars. Some would say that we all *bonded* over Butch Bond. We had a *butch* bond.

I first met Muffy "Butch" Bolding when I was starting a new film project where I needed a pretty girl who could act. My childhood friend Dennis Bolding had recommended his new girlfriend Muffy to me, pointing out that she had been acting in some local theater. As it was with Johnny, I had never met a person with whom I had so very much in common and who I instantly liked so much. Our lives ran in so many parallels: the only moments we were allowed to follow our own interests were mostly stolen ones, and we did everything we could to hang out, including my helping her with her daily list of tasks so she could finish. My father was strict, but her mother was a relentless slave-driver who had Muffy running her parents' entire household, one with eight wild and out of control brothers and sisters who I adored (and still do). Gunfire, drownings, house-robbings and grand theft auto were a part of her family's regular curriculum and I loved every fucking minute of it. There was never a dull moment at Muffy Manson's house. Not *that* Manson by the way.

I had never met anyone like Muffy. She was a smart, insanely intuitive teenager who was quick to verbally assassinate anyone that dared to mess with her. Muffy didn't need booze, drugs, or rowdy high jinx to have fun; her idea of a good time was spending hours in a thrift store or at the library. She was a good kid and by far the most responsible person in her entire clan. She, too, was not impressed by my father's unsavory shenanigans and regularly told me to get the hell out of Dodge. Muffy was the kind of friend you fall madly in love with after the first five minutes of knowing them. Years later, she not only became a creative force of her own but the absolute best mother I have ever known. I mean, how can you not have terrific mothering skills when you're changing diapers and ironing sheets starting at eleven years old? I was and am still so proud to know her, despite my possessiveness sometimes complicating our journey.

Vulich, Muffy, and I built bonfires and watched the river run by as we talked shit all night, listening to cassette tapes of bands like Madness and Journey while drinking beer. Jackalfests usually ended with a "coal walking" ceremony as we drunkenly walked through what was left of the fire at the end of night. The Jackals vowed to live life with their paws to the floorboard, to always throw caution to the wind, to defy and defile others we don't respect, but to never ever defy one another.

We were a dastardly, belly-laughing, mischievous trio who hung out together most weekend nights. Our activities ranged from average Friday night teenage butt-holery to mildly dangerous gags, like the times we "danger game" challenged each other to cruise the fat old truckers who hung outside Fresno's only X-rated adult bookstore. Once, we brazenly flirted with some decrepit old man in a big-rig who was hellbent on hooking up with all three of us at once.

"Oh, we would so hook up with you, but we just remembered we forgot our tit-clamps and Crisco back at the house. We only like to get down when tit-clamps and Crisco are involved," Muffy purred as John and I shamelessly played along.

"Hell, you can always get tit-clamps and Crisco!" the old trucker replied with a toothless smile and a wet smoky cough. Mind you, we were only sixteen.

My mother would have dropped dead on the spot had she known what was unfolding every night that the Jackals rolled into town. Other nights were tamer, but just as entertaining as we held court in Bob's Big Boy on Blackstone Avenue all night, laughing until our sides ached at our friend the waitress who could execute self-induced vaginal farts on command. There was no doubt in any of our minds that we would be friends forever. Stronger bonds were never formed; more beer was never stolen and drank. Muffy, by the way, was also the reason that I was sporting that hideous perm.

One night, after filming on a horror short we were working on, I asked Muffy if she knew how to give home perms. You see, the *Brady Bunch* boys had all gotten perms and I thought they looked really cool. Maybe a perm would help "up" my look? I guess considering losing the additional hundred pounds and fifty pounds I was carrying around wasn't a good start.

"Sure, I can give you a perm!" She said it with such confidence. By now, Muffy had wised up and gotten herself a tiny studio apartment. We met up at her place and pulled out her fold-out bed as it was the only furniture in her place other than her chairless kitchen table. I sat on the edge of the bed while she sat Indian-style behind me. We both watched the *MASH* reruns on her tiny television set as she carefully rolled my hair into each curler. My hair was long then, so Muffy had to put many, many curlers into my brown locks in order to get my entire head covered.

We laughed so hard at how insane I looked with those curlers all over my head, which isn't saying a lot because we could typically find something to laugh about on an hourly basis. Muffy put the chemical solution in, then we lay on our stomachs on her ratty mattress and watched the rest of *MASH* while eating an entire block of cheddar cheese, one bite at a time as we passed it back and forth to one another as if it were a fat orange candy bar. Later that night, directly after *MASH*, we switched the channel to David Letterman and watched all ninety minutes of his show, and then afterwards, completely zoned, tired and very high on cheese, we lay there as we continued watching old reruns of *The Tom Snyder Show*.

We were about halfway through Tom Snyder when all of a sudden, Muffy dove to her feet screaming in absolute terror. I nearly jumped out of my skin, thinking maybe she had seen a prowler looking in the window. "What's wrong???" I asked nervously.

Muffy looked at me with wide, sorrowed-filled eyes as she covered her mouth in fear, backing away from me.

"What? Say it!" I said.

She glared at my curler-covered noggin as I stared back at her, pleading for an answer. "Butch, you've had perm-rods and chemical solution in your hair for the better part of three hours."

"Yeah, I have. Is that bad?" I asked, somewhat afraid of learning the answer.

"They were only supposed to be in for forty minutes!" she screamed.

I wondered if my hair was about to fall out.

"Quick! Get in the shower!" she commanded. I ran into the shower and started tearing my clothes off as she turned on the hot water. I put my head under the running water and one by one, the two of us pried every single curler out of my crispy, tightly-wound and very burnt hair. After twenty minutes of fighting the curlers out of my spring-like locks and three separate shampoos, I finally felt like all the caustic solution was washed out. I chased Muffy out of the bathroom, closed the door, and dried my hair with a blow dryer.

"Are you okay?" she asked.

Ten minutes later, I called out, warning her in fear. "I'm afraid to come out. Because if you laugh, I'm going to burst into tears."

Muffy stifled a laugh from the other side of the door. "I swear on the lives of my future children, I will not laugh."

"Are you sure?"

"Yes, I'm sure, I will not laugh, now let me see!"

"No."

"Get out here, you pussy!" she commanded. I reluctantly stepped out of the bathroom.

Muffy's expression dropped as she burst into laughter.

I turned and looked back in the mirror. I did indeed look like an idiot. The best visual that I can give you is that I looked like I was wearing a large motorcycle helmet made of hair curls. I would say that I looked like Little Orphan Annie, but don't think that her hair was as big as mine. Just think the large, round green bulbous head of the Great Gazoo from *The Flintstones* and that will give you a better idea of what I had going on. If you're not old enough to remember his massive head, google it.

Muffy not only laughed, but she laughed so hard she nearly crapped her pants as she knocked me out of the way and bolted for the bathroom. "Maybe if you sleep with a lot of conditioner in your hair for a few days, it'll relax," she whimpered, trying her best to not burst into further laughter. "Or maybe I could put some salad oil in it."

I looked into the mirror, mortified. There I was. Three hundred and twenty pounds with a head that looked like one of the aliens from *Invasion of the Saucer Men*.

"I could shave your head?" she offered. I thought for a moment, staring into the mirror. After a few beats, I realized there was nothing I could do about it. Long hair was the way to go back in the 80s; the only people who were shaving their heads were neo-Nazis. "Fuck it." I said. "I'll rock this shit like I own the motherfucker." And that's exactly what I did. Folks, for two solid weeks I strutted around with that ridiculous massive perm like I meant for it to look that way, and because I carried my hair like a badge of honor, people treated me accordingly. Thankfully, within a couple of weeks, those spring-loaded locks did relax and I started looking more like Janet from *Three's Company* than the Great Gazoo.

For the record, I never did look like one of the Brady Bunch boys.

Muffy Bolding and I. She was the third in our unholy Jackal trinity.

5

READY TO MAKE THE MOVE, KINDA

I started trying to save money by working several jobs at once. My parents had given me an old column-shift Chevy Nova to get back and forth to my various gigs, one of which was working after school at the Carl's Jr. hamburger restaurant. As you can imagine, my bloated silhouette looked terrific in that ill-fitting orange and brown polyester smock and paper hat that sat precariously on my huge bouffant hairdo. The crew at Carl's Jr. were a wild bunch of scrappy country kids that got into daily salad dressing fights and held deep-fried erotic sculpture contests with the leftover Frispos, the mashed potato substance they used to make the French fries.

After work, I drove myself to Johnny's house, where we hung out at his place until late. We drank beer and watched movies, then grabbed Naugle's Mexican fast food and took insane joyrides in Vulich's car. Johnny often took me to the brink of death with his dangerously reckless driving, all the while cackling his legendary unbridled Jackal laugh. I cursed him out, grasping a Naugle's cheese burrito in one hand and holding on for dear life with the other. No makeshift racetrack was off limits as Johnny careened through the parking lot and blasted up and down the hallways of Fresno High's campus, then exploded out onto their baseball field, spinning donuts until the place was a complete mess.

Every time he headed down those halls, I was terrified we would get caught and locked up. I was a lot of things, but teenage vandal was not one of them. Ever since I had known him, John had so much contempt for that school. I grew to realize he held a boatload of pent-up resentment for the campus, a place where as a teenager, he was bullied so relentlessly for mannerisms the popular kids considered to be "gay" that he eventually dropped out, never to return. As I grew to know John in adulthood, that anger stayed with him when it came to dealing with others who were cruel or treated others poorly. Despite not having a diploma, he still remains the smartest person that I ever have known. High school was only in the way of someone as brilliant as John Vulich, who was a natural born genius, many times too smart for his own good, but also just smart enough to keep me and everyone around him on their toes.

After a series of growing communications with Tom Savini, one day, John just made the leap and left town. I spent weeks depressed that he was gone, but he kept me updated with nightly phone calls about what life on set was like. He had made the move and was instantly flourishing. He got his first break by working for Savini on *Friday the 13th part IV*. John had been invited to the team after Tom saw a handful of Polaroids of John's sculpting work that he had mailed to him. I was mesmerized by the fact that he was working on an actual film, and particularly, with Tom Savini himself. John and I had been such huge fans of Savini's work for so many years.

"Is he nice?" I asked.

"He's hilarious and smart, but also dangerous sometimes," Johnny cackled.

"Dangerous?" I said.

"You'll be standing there working, and then, all of the sudden, a huge bowie knife'll whiz across the room and stick in the wall right next to you."

"He throws knives at you?" I asked, nervous for my friend.

"Yeah, it's like…his thing," John said. "He's constantly doing stunts and rough housing, so you have to really be on your guard, cause he's liable to just sucker punch you out of nowhere. Aside from all of that, he's really a terrific guy."

"He sounds crazy!" I replied, genuinely worried.

"Crazy, yeah, but in a really good way. He's also a huge pussy magnet. Chicks love him."

"Well, yeah, I can see that, he's a rockstar," I replied, totally awed that my friend was in the presence of what I and many considered Hollywood royalty.

Every night, I stayed glued to every word as the calls from John continued. Little by little, I made a list of everything I needed to blow town, while John kept me updated on *Friday the 13th part IV*.

"There's this little kid, a boy named Corey Feldman, from *Gremlins*. The crew hates him. Admittedly, he's kind of a smart-ass, but I like him. I feel sorry for him, too: he's really little. Yesterday, they threw him in a garbage dumpster and I helped get him out. Reminded me of the shit I used to put up with, so…I helped him. His dad's a prick, too." Vulich was always an unflinching fan of the underdog. "The director begged Cory to shave his head for the ending of the film when the character tries to psyche out Jason Voorhees." John said, "He even promised to shave his own head at the same time, but the kid won't do it. We have to try to do a realistic bald cap on him, which isn't going to be easy."

John Vulich on Set of Friday the 13th Part IV

One of John's coolest updates was when he called to tell me how he had helped come up with the way that Jason Voorhees died at the end of part four. "All that it said in the script was that Jason gets a machete to the face, but we brainstormed the idea to have Jason get whacked in the head, then stumble and fall down onto the ground, driving the blade even deeper into his skull." So entirely gross, yet also so entirely engrossing.

I thought to myself, that was it. I wanted in on the action. Yes, I was truly ready. I had to be a part of all the bone-crunching fun, but how? I was so envious of the show business life he was having and getting paid on top of it. I had no earthly idea how I would break into the system, though. I didn't have any special effects skills and no real-world film set knowledge as I was so young. I mean, my thirteen-year-old sister was the grip in the last project I filmed in my backyard. I racked my brain thinking of what I had to offer the film business. I knew I could paint well, but someone like Tom Savini wasn't going to hire me based on photos of the animal ceramics I had recently painted for my mother.

I started looking through the *L.A. Times* for a job that I could set up before I moved, but I found nothing that suited me. I thought to try and transfer to the AAA in Los Angeles, but it turned out, they weren't hiring. So, I went to a quickly improvised Plan B, which was to drive to L.A. myself and apply for work at where else but Disneyland. I mean, why wouldn't they want a fat teenager with a boatload of dreams?

"Welcome to the Disneyland casting office, how may I help you?!" said an overly cheery yet oddly expressionless woman who gazed at me wide-eyed as if she were looking right through me. It was almost as if this overly pleasant being was one of the theme park's very own animatronic figures. I grew to call this undetectable expression "robot-face," a countenance not only utilized by this particularly sweet cast member, but by many other film and TV executives I have had encounters with along my journey. I still to this day utilize the emotionless, mannequin-like trait in all corporate meetings I attend: you should never let them know what you're really thinking by giving them the opportunity to read your face.

"I'd like to fill out an application," I mumbled, nervous beyond belief. Like really nervous.

"I'm sorry, what?" she replied calmly, still not blinking, like a wooden *Shields and Yarnell* robot.

I raised my voice. "Um, I'd like to fill out an application." This time, my voice cracked. What an asshole I must have looked like. All my life I'd been an uber-fan of all things Disney. Being in that Disney office was such a big deal to me. I had finally gained the confidence to drive all the way there on my own, ignoring that goddamn Bub Butler parrot on my shoulder the entire way, and there I was, stammering like an idiot.

I had always been a massive admirer of Walt Disney's ability to manifest virtually anything he could dream of and the park had been by far the greatest escape from the life that I lived as a kid. He had been a massive success just as many times as he was a huge failure, but his will to push onward completely inspired me to never give up.

Robot-face calmly handed me a clipboard with an application. "Do you have any prior work experience?" Boy did I. By the time I was seventeen, I had already carried a boatload of work responsibilities in life. In my family, if you didn't work, you didn't have walking-around money, so we all did indeed work. I also grew up on a farm where hard labor was a regular part of life. The truth was, I had been working at a variety of jobs since I was old enough to do so, and I had acquired a lot of skills, especially after working for my mother, who had juggled a variety of jobs, especially after she finally got brave enough to divorce my father. I had also driven a tractor, flipped burgers, fed chickens and pigs, helped farm worms, sold hot dogs at hockey games, but what could I share with lady robot that would help me to get a job at Disneyland? I doubted my pristine weed-pulling abilities and trash burning skills would come in handy there. I stood there for a moment staring at her, unable to speak as I cracked, suddenly turning around and just bolting out of the office.

6

BYE BYE, BUBBY

By the late seventies, after years of increasingly frequent outbursts, not-so-discreet secretarial encounters and mysterious after dark "golf games" that my father claimed to be venturing out on, my mother had endured enough and got up the courage to leave him. "Do your goddamned balls glow in the dark!!?" I remember her screaming one night as she broke a ceramic ladle over his head when he'd slithered in drunk.

It had been very clear that their marriage was over for some time and it was such a relief when she finally made the move. Gone were the times when she would load us into the car and drive to some run-down hotel where his truck would be parked or the nights when she would sit crying, feeling like she had failed as a wife. When she finally saw the light and got brave enough to shake him, she solemnly sat us three children down to break what she considered very sad news. She braced herself for crocodile tears and broken little hearts but was shocked as two out of three of us bolted up in a child-like cheer of massive relief. We were in no way perfect children, but "Father of the Year" this guy was not.

The day my father left our house was the absolute first day that I ever fully exhaled in my young life. There were going to be no more regular verbal and physical smackdowns, no more constant reminders of my shortcomings or worry that I wasn't executing tasks properly, and best of all, guess who stopped peeing the bed? Yeah. Me.

From that moment on, I did my very best to see my father as little as possible. Minus a brief period when I lived at his house to be closer to my school and after stealing beer money from my mother, I did everything I could to avoid him. As years passed and the occasion arose when I saw him, he continued to point out what he didn't like about me until I finally cut him out of my life entirely: not to be dramatic, but instead out of practicality, just like John Vulich had encouraged me to do for so long. It's been many years since I have seen his face or felt the overwhelming stress I felt when I was around him. Not all people are cut out to be parents. I am much happier now having him out of my life.

Despite divorce having been the right move, it was tremendously difficult for my mother to try and raise us on her own, but we were so much better off. Very poor, mind you, but much better off. My siblings, my mother, and I could now live in peace, making each other laugh and putting on records and dancing in the living room without having to worry about messing up the freshly vacuumed carpeting or wasting what used to be considered "valuable time" by doing crafts and watching old movies. What was even better was we no longer had to see our mother try to hide her crying out of fear, frustration, or betrayal. I will forever admire her for being brave enough to take us away from the living situation we were all in. I am also so very thankful and proud to be her son.

Like a boss, she immediately took on several jobs to make sure that we were okay. She defiantly worked very hard to disprove my father's vomitus brag to his friends that we would all "starve to death and be left living on lawn furniture" after he was gone. We ate a lot of government bread and cheese sandwiches during that time period, but we did not starve, and damn, that waxy cheese was good. You could partially attribute my growing teenage girth to the multiple two-inch-thick sandwiches I made myself from the huge blocks of American cheese my mother brought home. Life went on in a much simpler fashion. We all became a very happy, supportive team, especially once we all started working for my mother at a job that changed my life forever.

My mom worked multiple gigs, but the job that she worked that made the biggest impact on my life was when she helped run a catering company that provided food services for fair midways, traveling circus, ice shows, athletic events, and rock concerts, a company called "Volume Services." Most of the live events that she worked were in the evenings or on weekends, so instead of hiring a babysitter, she brought my siblings and me with her to work and often, we ended up helping her. It was always very hard work, but also insanely fun as the atmosphere was always a party. What better job can a teenager have where you can get paid, eat all of the hot dogs and nachos that you want, and do it all while hanging out with circus elephants and drunken clowns? That's my idea of heaven.

I still, to this day, believe that my unflappable attraction to the underbelly of life comes from all the time that I spent around circus folks and carnies. If I can wake up in the morning and see my face in your gold tooth, you know you're the one for me. Do you have bad tattoos and punch the wall when you're mad? I will positively fall in love with you and try to fix you. (We're still working on that last trait, by the way. Luckily, I have reached the age when rescuing dogs and writing are my main passions and focus.)

The company catered everything from the hot dogs at hockey games to the cotton candy for the Barnum and Bailey circus. I became obsessed with how amazingly organized the traveling circus was, as well as gained an early awareness of the animal cruelty that took place in that setting. Discontinuing the use of animals was a tremendously humanitarian move as none of them ever seemed safe from harm or happy. I saw everything from chimps to tigers being beaten into submission to elephants being prodded with metal hooks in order to get them to perform.

We worked a lot on the fair midway as well as provided backstage catering for the most popular music touring shows including Hall and Oates, Dolly Parton and Kenny Rogers, Van Halen and none other than Prince himself.

7

PLEASING PRINCE

My sister Kim and I had been helping my mother do catering at the Selland Arena in our small hometown of Fresno, California for a few years. In fact, my mother became the employer of most of my young friends during that time period as there was always a need for people to sling hot dogs, swag, or nachos, and—if you were lucky like my sister and I sometimes were—to work the backstage catering during the music concerts. On occasion, she'd even let us run the food to the talent's private dressing room area so we could get a look at the stars and see what life was like for those basking in the limelight. (We got quite an education when we delivered the food cart to David Lee Roth's dressing room once, but that's a whole other book.) I had just turned sixteen and both my sister Kim and I were stoked when we heard that Prince was going to be rolling through town. For weeks leading up to the concert, we begged our mother to allow us to work the dressing room area for the show.

We were massive Prince fans. He was very new on the scene, but thanks to MTV, he had been crammed down all of our throats so much that we were very well aware of him and his high-heeled funk. What was even more exciting to me was that Vanity Six was opening up for him. Vanity Six was a sexy female song trio, famous for their one and only hit "Nasty Girl," written and produced by none other than the purple one himself. I learned years later when I worked with Denise Matthews (Vanity) on the film *52 Pick-Up* that she and Prince were a couple back then.

Everyone working at the company was in a fever, all requesting the gig to work Prince's dressing room, but thankfully and predictably, nepotism ultimately won out and my mother agreed to let us work his private tent. Mind you: I was sixteen and my sister was only thirteen. We were clueless little kids but by then, smart enough to keep our game faces on when it came to dealing with famous folks. Our job was to push the carts and trays of food into the talent tent, set them up on the buffet, and leave. The rule that was pounded into our heads over and over again was crystal clear: WE DO NOT EVER SPEAK TO OR EVEN LOOK AT THE TALENT. This mantra was constantly chanted to everyone, no matter who was performing: Kenny Rogers, The Beach Boys, even Ray Stevens. You were to walk in, drop the food off, and walk away. No starin', no gawkin', most of all, no talkin'. The caterers worked feverishly to prepare Prince's requested menu; an approved list provided to them by what the industry calls a "rider." A rider is a list of requirements that a performer makes as part of his or her deal, things that will make it easier and more comfortable for them to do their job before they go on stage. Riders are iron clad and if anything is amiss, things can go terribly wrong. Most of us have heard the story about the band that destroyed their dressing room because there were multiple colors of M&M's served to them: the caterer had apparently neglected to remove all of the brown ones before serving.

Prince's menu was simple but plentiful: hummus, fresh fruit, pulled pork, mashed potatoes, salads, chicken wings, and finally and most importantly, a silver tray filled with warmed nuts (though no cashews). The staff begin to prepare the menu in the arena kitchen while Prince's crew arrived early in the afternoon. It was amazing to see how stealthy and organized they were as they quickly unloaded the trucks into the loading bay. I quietly watched from the shadows as they swiftly set up a lavish harem tent that was roped off and eventually surrounded by big, burly bodyguards.

The tent—purple of course—somehow smelled of women's perfume; whether it was pumped in or just residue from groupies gone by, I wasn't sure, but it definitely had a "Giorgio of Beverly Hills" kind of a thing going on. Hanging from golden bejeweled posts that surrounded the makeshift structure were smoldering pope incense burners that made the place look like an eerie, purple-bedazzled gypsy tent. I was mesmerized. Prince truly was a prince. There was opulence to the highest degree; anywhere he might set foot was perfectly laid out.

Just before Prince's arrival for sound check, my mother called us back to the service area and dressed my sister and I in white starched shirts and black bow ties. She tied pristine white aprons around our waists and told us to wait for the food carts to be loaded up. The closer it came to serving his royal highness, the more nervous I began to get.

Suddenly, production assistants started chattering to each other through their headsets as people backstage began to scatter. The time had finally come: Prince was in the building. He had arrived unexpectedly early and was swept off into his harem tent. An assistant ran into the kitchen and barked orders at my mother. Prince was starving and wanted to be served right away.

This was it. I held my breath. *No starin', no gawkin', most of all, no talkin'*, I repeated to myself, terrified that I was somehow going to break one of the rules, look directly into Prince's heavily-eyelinered eyes, and instantly be turned to purple stone. My sister Kim was ready to go. She has always been far more fearless than I. Always. As a kid, Kim not only had zero fear of my abusive father when she was growing up, but she bravely dealt with an insane stalker for ten years as a young adult, and later, served papers to the most ruthless tax evaders for the IRS. She has been chased by Pitbulls and had guns waved in her face and not once did she ever break a sweat. She never once flinched at my father's verbal bashings, not one single time.

Little Kim was perfectly confident and ready to rock it with the pint-sized purple one. The chef loaded her little arms with a tray full of raspberry tarts, and after the cue, my sister bravely headed towards the big purple pop-up tent. I watched with eyes wide as sweat beads begin to form on my meat melon of a head. The security guard nodded at her and opened the tent as she disappeared behind the purple silk.

A massive cart full of food slowly wheeled up next to me as my mother's cigarette-smoking, drunken chef looked down with a sneer. "You're on, don't fuck it up," he said. I wiped my forehead and moved into position behind the cart.

Slowly, I pushed the heavy rolling food server towards the tent. As I did, I could see my sister come out and head towards me. She smiled as the security bruiser slapped her a side-five as she exited. Kim closed in on me. "He's in there," she whispered. I dug my heels into the ground and kept pushing as I passed her, growing more and more nervous. She whispered, "He's wearing lady's shoes." I tried not to react as she raised her eyebrows up and down, tormenting me. The security guard must have smelled my fear because his smile began to fade, the closer I got to the tent. By then, my head was soaking wet from nerves.

The guard didn't bother opening the curtain, so when I arrived, I just sort of had to push my way through the hanging fabric doors as he gave me the side-eye. I struggled, trying to get in from a couple of different angles before the cart finally cleared and rolled forward. Once I was finally inside, the tent seemed immense and other worldly: it was truly beautiful. If you didn't know that this place was set up on a cold cement loading bay in Fresno, California, you would think you were in a Beverly Hills poolside cabana. Everywhere you looked, it was purple. Purple candles. Purple flowers. Purple tables and reclining chairs and in the center of the room was a fancy, very long velvet purple couch. There, draped on the couch like Cleopatra in a pencil moustache, was none other than Prince. He was lying there, propped up on one elbow and surrounded by satin pillows, his feet up on the arm of the couch as he lay in a Julius Caesar kind of a pose. My sister was right: he did indeed have on lady's shoes: spiked purple stilettos, to be exact.

He gazed at me with eyes wide but zero acknowledgment. I remember thinking to myself, *Wow, he sure has a lot of eye pencil on.* His eyes looked like they had been completely encircled with a thick Sharpie Pen and false eyelashes. I lowered my head like a clammy, water-retentive Geisha and rolled past him, pushing that heavy cart toward the buffet table. I opened the doors to the server and unloaded the trays of food as the handful of music professionals that also were in the tent swarmed over me as fast as I could pull it out. They were like zombies, snatching the food up as fast as I could set it down, not caring if they were bumping into me as I tried to unload their haul.

Meals go on the buffet, snacks go on the coffee table, I repeated to myself. I nervously looked back at Prince who was talking to someone, but who seemed to somehow know that I was looking over at him as BAM! he eye-bat to the left and caught me gawking.

I looked away terrified and continued to work, desperate to just get the hell out of there. Whoever thought that doing this task was a treat was very wrong. After finally getting all of the main course platters out, I opened the cabinet section of the cart and pulled out a dip and a vegetables platter. Without making eye contact, I crossed the room and set the tray on the coffee table, this time making sure to not look at him. I breathed a sigh of relief as I went back to the cart for the very last dish, the tray of warm nuts with no cashews. I pulled the tray out, took the Saran wrap off, and looked down at the variety of nuts…which *of course* included a boatload of cashews. My stomach sank as my eyes budged in terror. I stared at the platter for a beat, then panicked: should I just shove it back into the cart and take it to the kitchen and tell them to get it right, or would anyone even notice that there were cashews in there? Was he allergic to cashews? What if he ate one? Would his throat close up and the whole show be cancelled? All I knew was I wanted out of there.

At that very tense moment, I made a snap executive decision, one I would deeply regret. I put on a brave face, took a deep breath, and lifted the tray. I slowly turned, but this time, I headed towards the table at the end of the couch, far away from where any one was standing and certainly out of Prince's eyeline. I moved quickly and just as I was about to reach the end table, I heard,

"Put that over here."

I stopped. Then I looked over. The paisley Prince was looking right at me, but this time, a very slight smile was growing on his face. Not a full smile, mind you, but not the cold unblinking glare he had first been giving me. I was so relieved. Could Prince and I be bonding over these nuts? What if we became friends over this chance meeting? What if I ended up moving to Minnesota and traveling with the band as Prince's personal nut warmer? I nodded, smiled back, and slowly crossed to the coffee table in front of him. I carefully set the tray down, looked up at him one last time, then smiled once again and turned to leave. It was over. Mission accomplished. *Good job, Billy! He didn't care if there were cashews after all!* But before I could exhale and take a single step, I heard a word that I could have certainly done without.

"Stop," he commanded out loud. "Wait a minute."

I turned around back towards him. There he was—as God is my witness—staring down into that friggin' tray of nuts…and he was not happy.

"Come here," he motioned for me to come stand in front of the coffee table. The room fell silent as all eyes turned to me. To say I was scared is a massive understatement, but I did exactly what he asked me to do. "Stand right there."

I nodded, taking my position in front of the table. I stood there stiff with fear as Prince reached down, and one by one, flicked each cashew with his finger. You know that kind of flick where you latch your middle finger into your thumb and really get a trajectory when you release it? That's exactly what he did: he flicked each one off of the tray, sending it hurling into my pudgy little man titties. Cashews were bouncing off of my chest and face as I flinched with each hit. A couple of people in the tent started laughing at me as they gathered around to watch. I didn't dare move. I had broken all the rules including having served the forbidden cashews. My face was beet red with embarrassment. I was completely humiliated.

Just as he got to flicking the sixth cashew at me, a voice suddenly rang out from across the room. "Prince, stop!" Everyone in the room looked over to the entrance of the tent. There, standing in white lingerie and high heels and looking like an absolute love-goddess was none other than the lead singer of Vanity Six, Vanity herself. "Don't do that!!!" she barked at him. Prince shot Vanity a playful girlish side-glance as he smiled and honored her request.

She crossed to me, taking my fat face in her hands. "What's your name?" she asked. I swear, she was the most beautiful woman I had ever seen. Her make-up was heavily applied for the stage, so perfect; her hair was massive with glitter sprayed all over it, and all of this beauty was amplified by the fact that she was only wearing panties and a bra. Vanity was an absolute goddess whose pussy clearly controlled all.

"Billy," I mumbled. I could barely get the word out.

"Well, you listen to me, Billy. Don't you ever let anyone treat you like that. Ever. Do you understand me?" I nervously nodded, about to burst into tears, praying she would just let me go so I could dash out of there. I was very, very close to shitting my pants.

Just as I finished nodding, Vanity bent down, pulled me close, and placed a full, open-mouthed kiss on me. Full tongue. Well, folks, you could have knocked me over with a feather: I went completely limp as she finished the deed by going in deep. Very deep. Was this really happening? Was I finally getting my first kiss and from none other than Denise Matthews, *Vanity herself*, the absolute personification of unbridled sexuality, a strong woman of the 80s with a face that had single-handedly inspired so many beauty shop Nagle paintings. Vanity was a woman that so many men would have killed to be with, and for that brief shining moment, right in front of Prince himself, she was all mine. Vanity smiled as she pulled away from me, leaving my lips lightly smeared with her candy apple red lipstick.

"Now go get my chicken wings," she said as I bolted for the exit, terrified.

Therefore, whenever someone asks me if I have work experience, the answer is a resounding YES.

8

THE SECOND ATTEMPT

"Yes, ma'am, I do have work experience," I confidently told the Disneyland Head of H.R. after I went back a second time; this time, not shaking in my shoes nearly as badly. Robot lady was there again and had me fill out an application as she told me to wait in a bland beige waiting room with several others.

We all sat there for a couple of hours, nearly driven into madness by the constant roar of the Tyrannosaurus Rex animatronic that was clearly on the other side of the wall. I realized that the casting office must have been nestled somewhere inside the same building as the Disneyland railroad's "dinorama," as they still call it. I was finally called in and interviewed by yet another bright-eyed personnel woman, this one slightly older but just as calm and unblinking. I told the pleasant lady that I was a huge fan of the company and would do anything to work there. She nodded and smiled as I further explained that I had lots of local theater experience back home and that I really wanted to be placed in the character or live show department: that's the department where if you don't end up performing as yourself, you get dressed up like Pluto or Mickey and run around the park taking pictures. It seemed easy enough, and I just needed a gig to get a place before I transitioned into working in film.

The woman pursed her lips. "I'm so sorry, but we have very strict height and weight restrictions in that department," she said, glancing at my ample gut. "It could be dangerous for a *person of size* to spend too much time in one of our costumes. They can be quite taxing." She wrote "P.O.S." at the top of my resume.

Person of size?? I thought to myself. *Why, you rotten robot bitch...*

I started to change the subject, telling her that any department would be fine, but she cut me off. "Thank you so much for coming in, but at this time, we aren't hiring. On behalf of the Walt Disney Company, we truly appreciate you reaching out." And with that, my interview was over.

They aren't hiring for any other departments? I thought to myself. There must be two thousand jobs to consistently fill in that company. I smelled a fat rat. A *R.O.S.* Regardless, I dragged myself back through the Disneyland parking lot and drove the drive of shame back to Fresno, but not before sneaking into the park and riding all the rides.

My mother tried to hide her disappointment when I walked in the door with the bad news that I had been turned down. This was before cellphones and computers, so both good and bad news had to wait until you met in person or had enough change for a payphone, and at that point in my life, I barely had enough gas in my car to get to Anaheim and back, let alone make a three-dollar phone call. Always my biggest supporter, my mother pasted on a smile and gave me a hug, reminding me that Disneyland wasn't the only place in L.A. where one could find a job. But she didn't need to convince me to look elsewhere. While I was away on my trip to interview at the Magic Kingdom, I looked up some of the Los Angeles-based make-up effects labs that Vulich had been talking about and quietly drove past them. They all were so much dingier than I had imagined and all of them were tucked away in some of the most unsavory parts of Los Angeles.

All my life, I had grown up reading *Famous Monsters* magazine. All of the FX make-up artists I'd ever seen were old guys with pencil thin moustaches, wearing white lab coats while they applied make-up. As far as I could tell, all of these shops were nothing more than industrial warehouses inhabited by young guys that looked like metal-hair band members and not the high-tech scientists that I was used to seeing in books. If anything, the sight of seeing people my own age working in the business alleviated the intimidation that I had grown up feeling. Even if I didn't have a mullet, I could easily fit in. Maybe Vulich was right. Maybe everybody in the business was just a bunch of goofy hopefuls like myself.

Disneyland

It was the 80s. Ronald Reagan was President, MTV was on fire, TV series like *Dallas* and *Dynasty* were the shows to watch, and The Go-Go's, J. Geils Band, and John Cougar Mellencamp were the must-have audio cassettes for your portable tape player. It was a happy, pink pastel and aqua blue world with no such thing as school shootings, no worry of pandemics or people crashing airplanes into skyscrapers. Not unlike the 50s, the 80s were a much happier time and I was so ready to take a bite out of the juicy peach that was life.

Upon the invention of the home video player, the VHS tape market was booming, and there was movie production work everywhere in Hollywood. There was a movie crew filming on every other street corner in town. Big budget films as well as micro-budget productions were rolling. The possibilities seemed endless and they were.

On my explorative trips to L.A., I sneaked onto all of the movie lots many times. Back before 9/11, you could easily walk right onto a studio lot if you acted like you had somewhere to be. They wouldn't even check your I.D. before you breezed in, especially if you kept a grim look on your face that challenged the guards to ask why you were there. I quietly sneaked in and visited the sound stages that were open and even had lunch in the Paramount commissary one day. I saw Ted Danson and Steve Guttenberg sitting together and almost fainted, I was so star-struck.

During that trip, I was able finally to see an entirely different perspective of life, and on the four-hour ride back home, I realized that something had changed in me. Being away from home and on my own felt good, it felt right, even if it was only for a few days. I liked being in charge of my own life and having my independence. Something clicked in my head. I was truly ready for something new. For once, I could see that things could unfold in a way that I wanted them to. Fuck being a loser P.O.S.! I was ready for an entire new life from beginning to end. I was ready to change everything about myself, and that's exactly what I did.

I'd been heavy or fighting being heavy most of my life (okay, *fat*). My grandmother used to think saying "heavy" had less of a blow than just telling someone they are a lard-ass, but to me, it always sounded worse. "You're not fat, you're just heavy," she would say, God love her, but to hear to my face that I was a "person of size" from a total stranger, someone that worked at Disneyland no less, was finally too much. I was deeply embarrassed and bothered by her and frankly, *everyone's* growing chubby perception of me; so much so, in fact, that I reached a solid turning point. But it wasn't just that. It was clear that a fire had been lit under my ass to start making changes. I liked what I saw in Los Angeles and I was going to figure out how to get there.

The Monday after returning home with no job but with a much clear perspective, I started changing my way of living. For starters, I finally realized that no one was going to believe in me if I didn't believe in myself. If I wanted to act I could. Anything seemed possible in Los Angeles. My issues weren't just about how I looked, but more so about how I felt. What I did to show people I was serious, my confidence, my self-worth, all of it had to change and it was changing. I doubled my workload at AAA, started acting at the local dinner theater, and saved every penny I could. I also cut all my food intake in half, stopped drinking soda and beer, and I started running: if you could call hobbling forward with a fat side-ache running. I was so fat in the beginning that I could barely move, but I stuck with it.

I started going to the gym, drank tons of water, and for the first time in my life, started weighing myself. Somehow, I didn't once lose focus during this process and the weight started falling off of me. In a month's time, I lost thirty pounds. The more I lost, the harder I tried. The moment that parrot of self-doubt tried to land on my shoulder I swatted him away and carried on. For months, I continued working and saving, acting locally, and taking theater arts and film courses at the City College. I was finally beginning to grow up, as much as an immature person such as myself could. Within just a few months I had lost 65 pounds and had evolved into nobody's fat joke.

"*Disneyland* passed on you?" Vulich laughed. "What the fuck are you doing applying for work at Disneyland? Just go to any of the FX make-up labs and offer to dump the garbage for a couple of weeks. Once they realize you're not a total fuck-up, they'll hire you. Then you can get an agent and start auditioning."

"I know, I'm still trying to get my ducks in a row. I'm finally ready to do this," I told him. "I really appreciate you letting me stay with you until I get a place."

"It's no problem. Just get here," he said. "The VHS business is booming, man: there is work everywhere!" I could feel that this was going to unfold.

John had just finished work on *Friday the 13th Part IV: The Final Chapter* and had moved on to George Romero's *Day of the Dead*. This time, he was filming in Pittsburg as part of Tom Savini's special effects team, and once again, he was as entertained by working with Savini as he was proud to be associated with him. I felt like I was in the film business by proxy. My friend was killing it and so could I.

I could hear in John's tone that he was becoming more confident as he began to make his way up the food chain—maybe a little too confident, some would dare say. John was quickly realizing he was good; no, he was realizing that he was *great*, and he already seemed to be butting heads with some of his young co-workers. Anyone that was competition with him suddenly became a target. Still, he had been operating at a professional level since he was thirteen, so who was I to question his ballooning ego.

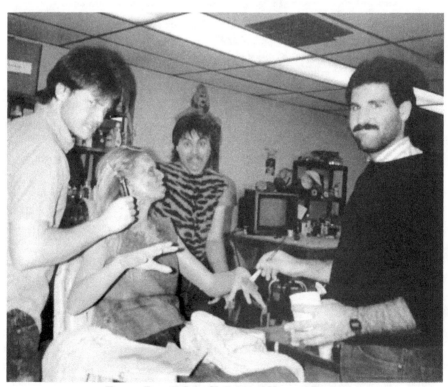

Everett Burrell, John Vulich and Howard Berger

He was working side-by-side with other young newbies like Everett Burrell, Howard Berger, and Greg Nicotero, just a few of the young team members who helped Savini create those insanely realistic effects on *Day of the Dead*. Back then, they were just skilled, hopeful fanboys. Today, most of them are some of the most revered artists and Oscar and Emmy Award winners in the business. I'm very happy to report all of them are still my friends because as you will read in the pages ahead, my path eventually crossed with all of them at different points in my own insane career.

John Vulich with Bub

John Vulich Working on Day of the Dead

Mike Deak and John Vulich

John Vulich Working on Day of the Dead

One night, while I was tucked in snuggly on the floor at work, John told me they were filming scenes of *Day of the Dead* in the massive Wampum underground Limestone mines outside of Pittsburg and were creating dozens of zombies and lots of gory effects. He explained that they had just finished filming a scene where the character Miguel, played by Antone DiLeo, was torn apart by zombies. Vulich laughed at what a horrific fiasco the day was. He told me that they had put the actor on a table that they had a hole cut in; his body went beneath the table while a fake torso was glued onto Antone's neck. The plan was to have a mob of crazed zombies furiously rip him in half as George Romero called *"Action!"*

Apparently, Savini was striving for absolute realness on this project and had the idea of using real animal innards for the guts: they would be exposed as the foam latex chest was ripped apart. John told me he sent the boys to a local Pittsburg butcher shop before they left for location and to buy more than enough entrails to fill the rubber body cavity, enough for multiple takes. After the guts were purchased and taken back to the shop, they were put in a mini-fridge that was to be transported to the location. When the day came to transport everything out to the mines, the fridge got moved but was never plugged in. Those pig guts sat unrefrigerated in those plastic bags for two days before the gang got around to using them. Vulich said everyone was gagging as they opened the bags and brought the innards to set: they had begun to decompose. Because they were too far away to replace them, the crew was forced to use them in the scene. He told me people were puking and running off the set in droves. The FX guys were gagging, the zombies were gagging, but the actor himself—who was in absolute hell—never said a peep. He was a total professional. To this day, if you watch George Romero's *Day or the Dead*, you can still see poor Antone DiLeo choking and nearly hurling at the smell of those rotting pig guts as they were revealed. The lesson learned here is obvious. Anyone who thinks it doesn't take guts to work with Tom Savini is gravely mistaken. *Goodnight, Pittsburgh! Try the shrimp-puffs!*

Months passed and my savings account grew to a couple of thousand dollars, and while my bank account got bigger, my fat ass continued to get smaller. A very strange occurrence and eye-opening event was unfolding, something that I would've never thought was possible. I started to realize that underneath all of that fat was a decent looking kid. Okay, folks I will come out and say it: I was okay-looking. Who knew? In hindsight, aren't we all good-looking at twenty?

Okay, so truthfully, I looked like Jamie Lee Curtis when she was in that aerobics movie *Perfect*, but I for sure had finally become fuckable. Before you roll your eyes and think I'm being arrogant, just keep in mind that I spent most of my life being an ordinary fat kid who was ignored and bullied his entire life, one who spent every single Friday night alone as a high schooler because I was different. I spent most of my teen years invisible to everyone around me. Suddenly, I was coming into my own and feeling great being accepted and looked at as something other than fat. I was so proud of how hard I had worked to change the way I looked that my self-confidence tripled in a matter of a year.

For the first time in my entire life, people were paying attention to me, wanting to speak to me, finally looking me in the eye when they spoke to me, and most of all, wanting to connect with me on more than a social level. Still, I was so inexperienced in that department that it often went over my head. I was very unaware of what it was like to even have a person flirt with you. It had never happened, so I never saw the signs. I would always have to be told by a friend afterward that someone was hitting on me or making a pass. Though I was becoming an adult, I was still very naïve.

Even stranger, at that point, was that I still felt zero attraction to anyone. "I'm just a late bloomer, I guess," is what I said to people when they asked me why I wasn't going on dates. I constantly wondered why I wasn't interested in people, men or women. But one thing was for sure, the thinner I got, the more disciplined I became. In no time, I had lost a hundred pounds. Family members noticed my physical change and started treating me different, too, but not all of it was in a complimentary fashion.

"Are you sure you don't have AIDS?" my aunt brazenly asked me. "You're becoming painfully thin."

"Are you using coke?" other family members asked. Some still, to this day, believe that's how I lost all of my weight, not taking into consideration the countless hours that I spent starving myself and working out. To me, it's the ultimate disrespect when someone asks me that. For the record, I didn't start carrying on with drugs until way after I started getting asked to the party. But as you will read, once I was at the party, boy, did I dive in head first.

100 pounds lighter and without a clue.

9

SIX TOUCANS EQUAL A SIX PACK

Months later, I was in the best shape I had ever been.

"You got some mail today," my mother said as she curiously watched me take the envelope from her hand. It was a nicely crisp, business-sized envelope with a teal blue moniker on it that read "Disneyland." It was the kind of chalky aqua-blue color that only the Magic Kingdom seems to utilize. My mother waited while I ripped the envelope open.

I read the contents aloud. "We are pleased to tell you that you have been hired by the Walt Disney Company. Please report this coming Monday the 28th to the Disneyland Park for your training. The attraction you have been hired to perform on is The Jungle Cruise." We jumped up and hugged one another. I had been hired after all. I was so proud to be taking this massive step. The cherry on the icing of this big marvelous Disneyland cake? I was no longer a fucking person of size. Boy, was ole robot-face who called me a P.O.S. in for a surprise! The Jungle Cruise? How did she come to that conclusion? Finally, my shticky personality was going to pay off. I hugged my mother as reality hit me. I was hired. I was going to be working in Anaheim. That meant I would have to move to Los Angeles. I felt equal measures of elation and horror at the same time.

"You can do this Bill," my mother reassured me. "You've already made so many positive changes in your life. You can do this."

I was scared as hell, but it truly was now or never, and I was so ready for it.

"I have great news! I'm coming down there next week!" I told Vulich, excited to finally be joining him and starting my own journey.

"Good for you! I'll talk to my roommate and let him know you're coming down," he said. "I'll be in Pittsburg to work on another film for Savini after *Day of the Dead*, but then I should be back."

"Okay. Thank you so much, John," I told him. "I'm so excited to be doing this move. I couldn't do it without you."

And that was it. I was officially moving to Los Angeles. All that week, I packed a bunch of my things into my huge, pea-green Monte Carlo. The faded car had been given to me by my mother and father for my seventeenth birthday, and even though it was a huge gas guzzler, it was a very reliable ride and a much-appreciated part of my life. It was a massive car with a huge backseat: I could haul five of my friends around in that big tank, and I crammed all of my belongings into it for the trip. Grandpa Butler bought me a new set of tires. My mother threw me a going away party with all of my friends and family in attendance, and the morning after, I gassed up the Monte Carlo, took every penny I had out of the bank—about $2,400—and finally drove away to start the life that I had prayed for my entire life.

My journey had officially begun. I had no idea what would lie ahead, but I was sure excited to find out. Would I become an actor right away? Would I be able to afford acting classes? Would I continue to make small films? I pictured myself in John's apartment, kicking back on the couch with his friends and roommates, all of us drinking beer and watching horror films after we'd all had a long day working on a movie together, one just like he'd been describing for months. I was surely headed for the good life that I had been hearing so much about. Ironically enough, Prince had just released his *Purple Rain* album, so I listened to the cassette over and over while I made my way down the five-freeway. As I passed Magic Mountain theme park on the five freeway, I felt different. That night, I was going to eat dinner when I wanted to eat it, go to bed and wake up when I felt like it. I was officially an adult, for once in my life, out on my own and barely closing in on twenty.

It was still early in the day when I finally reached the edge of Los Angeles, so I took an excursion through Hollywood via Highland Avenue. I parked my car and walked up and down Hollywood Boulevard, thinking that I was going to run into a movie star or accidentally meet a casting director who would discover me on the spot. But instead of movie stars and casting directors, I was met by a mob of prostitutes, tourists, and homeless punk rockers who lined the streets panhandling, and then there was that overwhelming stench of urine that has never faded even to this day.

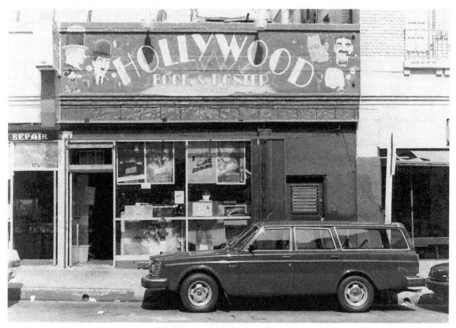

Hollywood Book and Poster

I came upon Hollywood Book and Poster and remembered the time back when I was sixteen and my parents first took me to visit LA. While my family and I strolled the main drag, I was mesmerized by the fact that I was in the very town that most of my favorite films had been produced. A trip to the Universal Studios tour had only reinforced that I knew exactly what I wanted to do with my life. At that age, I was completely obsessed with going to the movies and all I wanted to do was learn how to act in them and to eventually create them myself. My family and I had just visited the footprints at Mann's Chinese Theater when we spotted the famed bookstore. Hollywood Book and Poster was a well-known shop that stocked hundreds of movie posters and lobby cards both old and new. The owner was a glasses-and ponytail-laden man by the name of Eric Caiden. He was a mellow but helpful guy and pretty much an expert on film promotional art and posters. I asked my parents if I could go inside to look at the photos as they went next door to order pizza. I spent the better part of an hour looking through Eric's endless file cabinets full of movie memories.

I was about halfway done pouring through the movie photo stills when I came upon a folder for the horror movie *The Howling*. I had seen the movie at the drive-in with John Vulich and we were huge fans of both the film and its director, Joe Dante. I pulled out a still photo of one of the werewolves from the movie and was studying it when a man stepped up beside me.

"Do you like that movie?" the man asked.

"I love it. Joe Dante is my favorite director," I told him. I grasped the picture with both hands and stared at it with a calm smile, ignoring the guy until he finally stepped away. The photo was six dollars, but I had to have it.

I went to the register, reached into my pocket, and pulled out a wad of money. I only had three bucks. "It's okay," Eric said to me from across the room. "He bought it for you." He motioned toward the door.

"Really?" I looked around the room to find that the guy had left.

"Yeah, kid. That was Joe Dante," Eric laughed.

I froze in my tracks. "What?!" I gasped.

He handed me a pen. "Go get him to sign it." I snatched the pen from his hand and dashed out. I skid back out onto the walk of fame, desperately searching for him before he got too far down the block. About two blocks away, I spotted him about to cross the street at Ivar.

"Mr. Dante!" I yelled. He turned around, only slightly startled, and I ran over as fast as I could. "Will you please sign this?" I asked, completely out of breath and handing him the photo.

He started laughing. "Yes, if you promise me you that you will take a breath, please." He smiled as he signed my souvenir. *Beast Wishes, Joe Dante.*

"Beast Wishes: that's cool," I said, elated that I had just met my idol.

"I stole it from Forry Ackerman," he replied with a smile. Forry Ackerman was the longtime editor of *Famous Monsters of Filmland* magazine, which was pretty much every horror film nerd's bible.

"Thank you," I said. "I want to be a director as good as you one day."

"You'll do it. You can do anything you want. Just keep your eye on the ball." He was still smiling as he turned and continued down the street. I stood there staring and didn't move from my spot until he was completely out of sight. Joe Dante had just said I could do anything I wanted.

Just seven years later, I was standing in the same spot I'd chased Joe Dante down, now trying to give it a shot myself. Little did I know that twenty-five years later after that, I'd be sitting right next to him, signing autographs at the Dark Delicacies bookstore. I recently asked him if he remembered the little fat kid chasing him down. To me, it was odd that he didn't recall it, because the moment changed me forever.

For the record, I, too, now sign everything with "Beast Wishes."

I continued my tour of Hollywood Boulevard as I spotted a flickering neon sign that read *Stella Adler Theater*. Stella Adler was a renowned acting teacher that I had read and heard about for many years. After having a successful acting and directing career of her own, she had moved to teach hundreds of performers on both coasts, many of whom had made it to the big time, including Warren Beatty, Marlon Brando, Robert DeNiro, and Harvey Keitel. It took my breath away to see that I was standing there in front of her actual studio. I walked in, past the empty box office, and stuck my head into the theater. There, standing in all of her puffy flamboyance, was none other than Stella Adler herself, who at that moment was dressing down a young actor as if he had just taken a crap on stage.

"You will never get this right if you remain closed," she bemoaned. "As long as you remain closed, it will never appear to be so!"

The actor nodded and hung his head in shame as she whipped around and spotted me standing there. "We're closed!" she yelled at me. I nervously backed out of the room and got the hell out of there. I thought to myself that I would never survive that kind of berating. She was, well, so overly dramatic, which seemed odd for an acting teacher. It was like she was acting while teaching acting. Maybe taking classes wasn't going to be for me.

I had a quick lunch at the Snow White Café next door to the Hollywood Wax Museum, avoided a bevy of teenage panhandlers, and found a payphone. I put a few coins into the phone and dialed John's number. He wasn't in his hotel room, so I left a message that I was in town and that I would try to call him back once I got into Anaheim. I figured I could go stay in a hotel there for my first couple of days of orientation. I hung up, got back into my Monte Carlo, and headed towards Disneyland.

I got into town and rented a tiny motel room at a novelty motel, the Peter Pan Motor Lodge. It was within walking distance of the Disneyland park and appeared safe enough. Most of all, it was only sixty-eight dollars a night. The room was spotlessly clean, smelled of cheap motel soap which I loved, and had two sturdy locks on the door, just what the doctor ordered for a young punk like me. It also had an overly chlorinated pool swarming with tourists and kids, yet it was still welcoming enough. I cranked down the A/C in the room to 60 degrees, pulled out my journal, and flopped onto the bed. It was that very day that I began writing down entries, and every night thereafter, it is an activity that I continue to do until this day. I had no idea that many years later, the stack of journals that built up would lead to this book.

Each night after I journaled, I called to check in with my mother, letting her know that I was still alive. I'd call her from the red neon illuminated payphone in the parking lot at the Peter Pan, and of course, I'd call collect. We'd talk about my Disney training, whether I was eating enough, and ways to keep from being murdered in a rough and tumble town such as Anaheim. Because there were no cell phones or computers at that time, I slowly lost touch with John as I trained for those two weeks. He was constantly working during the nights and I never seemed to have enough change to call all the way to Pittsburgh when our schedules meshed. I figured I would ride it out in the motel for a few days and then make a plan to move into his place when I could finally get ahold of him.

Peter Pan Lodge

My training continued at Disneyland and I quickly grew to love the place. It was everything I had admired and so much more. I was so proud to be a part of the company and what's more, I didn't look fat in that godforsaken skipper costume, thankfully. It was a total blast learning how to drive the Jungle Cruise boat as I floated around and around and around that plastic jungle for hours. I loved every minute of it. There was not one uncomfortable moment with any of my interactions in that park. I was so happy to see for myself that Disneyland truly is the happiest place on earth, and I was happy to be starting my new life there.

There was one sobering and growing reality that I couldn't ignore, however: it was becoming very clear that living out of town was going to be very expensive. I was not in Fresno anymore, my room was five hundred and twenty-five dollars a week, and eating two meals a day out was costing about another hundred dollars. In two-weeks' time, I had already burned through half of the money that I had brought with me. It was a serious situation to consider, but I wasn't worried. After all, I was going to be working at the park and staying at Vulich's place rent free until I saved up enough money to get a room of my own. Things were going to be really tight, but all seemed to be going according to plan. I felt fearless and accomplished as I ever had.

Two weeks of training quickly came and went, and I was finally ready to make the move from the hotel to Vulich's place. I left a message with my mother to tell John to call the payphone at midnight Friday. Friday morning at the Disneyland park, my training manager informed me I was fully trained and ready to work. It was time for me to go backstage to get my first schedule. I had accomplished exactly what I prayed for. I had moved to L.A. and already had a steady job to fall back on.

The View from My Jungle Cruise Boat

"Welcome to the cast!!" The beaming scheduling woman at Disneyland grinned as she enthusiastically handed me my first schedule. My jaw dropped as my stomach sank.

"Oh, think there is a mistake," I said, handing it back to her. "I'm only scheduled to work Saturday and Sunday every week for the next month."

"Yes?" she replied, having moved onto her next order of business.

"I was under the impression I was working full time," I said.

"Oh, no: everyone starts out on a part time basis and only during peak days." She smiled, slipping into that robot face that I instantly recognized, and asked me to step aside so the person behind me could get their schedule.

I'm working two days a week at 68 dollars a day? I thought to myself. I did the math in my head in a panic. I had just moved my entire life to Los Angeles and was only going to be making 136 dollars a week, minus taxes. I tried not to panic. Maybe they would see what a hard worker I was and give me more hours. I caught my breath as I remembered that I had that free place to stay with Vulich, so I told myself I could pull it off until I saved up money or got a second job. It was going to take some figuring, but I was confident that it was going to work out.

It wasn't.

10

GREETINGS FROM THE HOTEL MONTE CARLO

"My roommate doesn't think there is enough room for you to stay with us," Vulich droned over the phoneline.

"What?!" I responded from the payphone at the Peter Pan Motor Lodge.

"He can be pretty uptight if he doesn't know a person. He said doesn't want any other people there unless I'm back in town."

"When are you getting back?" I choked the words out in terror.

"Like in three months," he said.

"Three months? I don't have a place to stay, John. I moved here because you said it was all good for me to stay with you!" I said in an absolute panic.

"I don't know what to tell you, Billy, I tried. Besides, you have a job now. You'll be able to save up and get a place pretty fast."

"What am I supposed to do in the meantime? I don't know anyone else here."

"I dunno," he yawned audibly into the receiver. "Have your parents keep you in a cheap motel room for a month."

"That's not going to happen. You've really fucked me. I hope you realize that!" I barked into the phone causing a fat family at the pool to look up from their chicken strips.

"I didn't tell you to move to L.A. with no money," John said, completely disconnected from the urgency of my situation.

"Thanks a lot, John, I'll figure it out." I hung up the phone in an absolute fury. Suddenly, my outlook went from being sunny and wondrous to instantly ominous. In less than four days, I would not only be completely out of money, but I would also be living on the streets unless I went home, and just two days shy of my twentieth birthday. Happiest place on earth, my ass. I either had to head back to Fresno and face everyone seeing me fail in only three weeks or come up with a plan.

The next morning, I packed all of my things from the Peter Pan Motor Lodge and went to work at the park. I figured I'd better find a cheaper motel room off of the Harbor Boulevard strip in order to make do with what little money I had left. I wasn't going to be paid for another two weeks from the first day that I started working, so there was definitely going to be a few days where I had no cash.

I didn't know the area at all, but I figured Buena Park would be cheaper than Anaheim, so after my shift ended, I headed over in that direction. I managed to find a run-down motel way down Beach Boulevard about five miles east of Knott's Berry Farm. The place was dingy and sagging but was only forty dollars a night, so I got a room there for three days. There were prostitutes and junkies wandering around the parking lot, a drooping, gray colored bed, a flickering television, no phone, and worst of all, no coffee maker. I kept the door locked and curtains drawn as I plotted my next goals; number one on my list was to stay alive.

Since I was only working at Disneyland on Fridays, Saturdays and Sundays, I planned to drive home Sunday nights for my days off and then come back each week. It was not the most ideal plan, but at least I would be safe. The night before, I had woken up in the middle of that night and watched out the window as two men beat the living daylights out of each other in the parking lot. I was beginning to get worn down and I had only been there for four weeks. Things could not stay the way they were, but the idea of moving home was not an option. I wanted so badly to pull it off on my own. I prayed every single night for something good to happen.

The next morning, I stopped for breakfast at Denny's on the five freeway as I headed to Disneyland. While seated in a booth and writing in my journal, I overheard the manager in a panic. Someone on the graveyard shift had just quit and she was in a panicked bind to try and replace them quickly. It was instant good fortune, right out of a movie, and exactly what I needed. Being raised as a workhorse, I was certainly used to working two jobs, especially if it got me out of the growing bind of impending homelessness. The manager told me that she needed someone to work from midnight to eight. I quickly filled out an application and was hired right there on the spot: I was to start that night.

My plan was that I would wait on tables from midnight to eight, show up early to my morning shift at Disneyland, shower and dress there, then stay at the motel after I was off at three, sleep until ten o'clock in the evening and then do it all over again. It was going to be a nearly impossible, brutal schedule, but I only had four hundred dollars left and the hustle would eventually fix my situation. I had just enough money to keep a roof over my head and for food once a day until I was eventually paid for either of my two jobs. The manager at Denny's handed me a stiff polyester smock and nametag. She told me to be there at eleven-thirty and that I needed to wear brown slacks and black dress shoes.

"No problem," I smiled as I shook her hand. *Shit!* I thought to myself as I headed outside. I opened my trunk and rummaged through my suitcase. I had, of course, no black dress shoes or brown slacks. I pulled out a pair of old white tennis shoes, they weren't even close to dress shoes.

I was going to have to break down and buy the stuff that I needed for work there, expenses that I positively could not afford. I walked to the phonebooth and looked up Kmart, wrote down the address, and headed in that direction.

The Buena Park Kmart was bustling as I made my way to the men's department, finding the only pair of brown slacks that they sold. They were hideous and baggy but only fifteen bucks. The black dress shoes they had were suitable enough but were thirty dollars. There had to be another way to pull this off; I just could not spend that much money. Up on a shelf next to the shoestrings, I spotted a bottle of Kiwi Liquid Shoe Polish, black. It was only a couple of bucks. I grabbed it, went through the cashier, and headed to my car. I pulled out that ratty pair of white sneakers, cranked on my Prince tape and sat in my Monte Carlo, coloring those old shoes with the black shoe polish. These were in no way shape or form dress shoes, but when I was done, they were at least black. If you looked close enough you could still see the Adidas stripes on the side and the sole pulling away from the bottom of the left shoe. I also only had white athletic socks, not thinking enough to pack a pair of black dress socks before I left.

My only saving grace was when I finally put on those awful brown slacks, they were so long that they mostly covered my shoes and white sock-covered ankles. I looked like I was wearing brown polyester bell bottoms, and I can't even describe how awful I looked in that orange Denny's smock.

"Don't use that toaster. Yesterday, a rat jumped out of it when I was dropping toast," said Trina, a frazzled twenty-one-year-old divorced mother of two.

"What?!" I asked incredulously, wondering why the contraption hadn't been taken out to the parking lot and burned.

"You're going to start by running food to the bar tonight."

"There's a *bar* in a Denny's?" I asked.

"There is in this one. It's so wrong," she whispered, shaking her head shamefully. "I pray for every single person that sets foot in there."

I pictured sad lost diners wearing Mickey Mouse hats drunkenly pouring bourbon over their pancakes. Trina also warned me that there was an annoying regular who came into the bar every night. He was a shabbily dressed elderly man named Ronald. No one knew for sure who he was or anything about his past. Some of the waiters thought they heard he was a Vietnam vet, while others said that he was secretly a lonely billionaire.

"You have to really take charge when you're stationed in there; otherwise, Ronald will run the place like he's the mayor. He'll also play the theme song from *Cheers* on the jukebox over and over until you go insane. God bless him. He's so lonely," she said in a tone of overly-concerned sadness. I didn't buy it for a minute. I timidly poked my head into the bar dining room, but found it empty.

I then quietly walked over to the jukebox, pulled it away from the wall, and yanked its plug out of the socket. I looked around the restaurant's crappy orange décor and hanging resin lamps. It was official: Hollywood's next big thing was a waiter at Denny's. I wasn't anywhere near the bright new show business discovery I had hoped to instantly become, but at least I could breathe a slight sigh of relief. I was working two jobs and had a roof over my head, no matter how leaky it was. If I could just make that last four hundred dollars last until I got my first paycheck.

I went into the walk-in freezer to restock the sliced lemons and spotted my next improvised survival tactic. There, on the shelves, were several containers of sliced roast beef, turkey, cheese, onions and tomato. Without hesitation, I moved to the tubs and made myself the world's fastest "breadless sandwich," stuffing it all into my face in an astonishing thirty seconds. Maybe that four hundred bucks would last me after all. I walked back into the diner as Trina met me at the counter.

"You got company in the bar," she said in a sing-song way that made me nervous.

I looked over her shoulder towards the lounge as the scratchy record of the theme song from *Cheers* began to blast. Someone had plugged the jukebox back in.

"Ronald?" I asked.

She nodded. "I'm going to pray for you," she said with sad, dead eyes.

The rest of the night was an insane blur of pancakes, irritating drunks, and Mayor Ronald himself who held court in the lounge all the way until my shift ended. I went to the men's room at seven in the morning and changed back into my street clothes to head to Disneyland. This sure wasn't going to be easy, but it looked like I was going to be able to pull it off.

I looked at my exhausted self in the mirror and smiled. "Good job, Billy. Looks like you're gonna make it after all."

I think it was around 8:15am when my car tire blew out on the freeway.

I guess Grandpa had opted for the retreads instead of new Firestones. I was on the five freeway, heading south towards Disneyland, when it blew. This wasn't just any blowout: the entire tire had come apart and the rubber tread and steel lining was beating against the side of the car in a thunderous cacophony. I was in the far-left lane when it happened, so I did my best to "thread the needle" across four lanes of traffic and get to the side of the road. Because there was no shoulder, I had to keep driving for several minutes until I reached the offramp. The tire was slamming into the side of my car so hard that it had dented in the entire body above the wheel.

I rolled into the McDonald's parking lot like a lopsided jalopy and nervously got out. The tire was completely destroyed and that side of my car was mangled. The metal was munched and the edge of the rim was rippled like a potato chip. I searched for a payphone, dug up some change, and called Disneyland to tell them I was going to be late. Then I called AAA roadside service. It would go without saying that a person who'd spent the last four years as a AAA dispatcher would have an up-to-date membership card with the company, wouldn't it? Imagine my surprise when the operator advised me that my card had recently expired. Not having any other alternative, I agreed to pay for the truck to come out to help me change the tire, and an hour later, the tow truck driver finally showed up.

The driver and I had to completely unpack all of my stuff from the Monte Carlo onto the ground to get to the spare, which we eventually discovered did not exist. "Don't worry, we have tires at our shop," the porn-star mustached Armenian driver reassured me.

Completely broken at this point, I agreed for him to load my car up onto his truck. Three hundred and eighty-four dollars later, I had a beautiful new rim and tire and was left with a whole twenty dollars to spare for myself. *I now had no money left.* What's worse, I hadn't paid for my motel room for the night. I raced to Disneyland and worked my shift on the Jungle Cruise and then headed back to Buena Park. I needed to figure out where the hell I was going to sleep. In the pop of one tire, I suddenly had no money, no place to stay, and no friends or family anywhere in the area.

I desperately needed to sleep before my graveyard shift at the diner. I called my mother collect and told her what had happened. This was the first of many times in the next month where my mother begged me to just forget everything and come back home, but I was hell-bent on trying to make it and didn't want to make the shameful drive home in defeat. She offered to put some money in the bank for me, but it was a Saturday at three in the afternoon by the time I spoke to her, and the bank was closed. This was way before computers, so nothing was going to instantly happen. She wouldn't be able to make any kind of deposit until Monday. Plus, truthfully, my mother was in no financial position to fund her son's wild career experiment, even though throughout the next few months, she did as often as she could when times got rough. Even my father stepped up on occasion when I finally got up the stomach-turning nerve to hit him up out of sheer desperation.

It killed me to think my mother would even offer to do such a thing, but that day, I was going to have to come up with a solution of my own and quickly. I had been awake for nearly twenty hours and now, thanks to an unexpected turn of events and a blown tire, I was flat broke. I sat in my car in silence for a moment, trying to keep it together. This was the first time that I started to feel afraid and alone. I didn't even have enough gas to hang it up and just drive home.

I eventually came up with the only solution I could muster. I went into the gas station bathroom, put on a bathing suit, slathered on sunscreen, and headed to Newport Beach. There, I spread my blanket out on the sand, took my pillow from my trunk, and laid down for a desperately needed six-hours of sleep. I woke up hours later to find a family of German tourists lying on towels not far away from me. The way they were all looking at me made me wonder if I had been snoring in my unflinching slumber. I realized later on it was because I was beet red with sunburn on my back from not turning over for six hours. I packed up my stuff, washed off at the beach shower, and headed to my graveyard shift at the diner. While working that night, I was told I was off from the diner on Sunday but scheduled to work the next evening. My plan to drive back to Fresno on Monday to keep a roof over my head for a few days was not going to work. I was going to have to find somewhere to sleep Sunday night, and it certainly wasn't going to be in a motel room, as I had only twenty dollars to my name.

Morning rolled around and I headed to Disneyland, worked my shift, then once again headed out to Newport Beach to sleep. This time, I just dropped the guise of pretending to be a beach goer and just laid down on my blanket fully clothed. I slept for hours, and when I finally woke up, I once again felt the horrible sting of sunburn on my neck, arms, and face. At this point, my skin was nearly purple it was so burnt. Sleeping outside during the day wasn't going to be the answer unless I invested in a very big beach umbrella.

"Maybe you should just come home," my mother suggested once again.

I didn't want to leave. I didn't feel like I had fully arrived there yet. There were horror films to watch, beers to drink, movies to act in, and friends to be had when Vulich finally got back to L.A.: these are the things I'd tell myself, even as I was starting to question why I was there. Things were not unfolding as planned. I took my last twenty dollars and bought some apples, leaving me ten dollars. My plan was to eat an apple every three hours until I fell asleep. If I could make it until Monday, maybe my mother would make a deposit and I could eat and possibly get a room. That, or I could try to wait until I could help myself to my makeshift sandwiches in the Denny's walk-in freezer. It was certainly going to be a long two weeks until I was paid.

Reality was soaking in hard. It became obvious to me that I was going to be sleeping in my car that night. I tried to plot where the safest place would be for a teenager to sleep in the backseat of his car without danger. I didn't know the area but was really too stupid to be scared. I decided to drive back to Buena Park and see if I couldn't find a place around there. I thought maybe you could pull a car into a KOA campground. I was wrong: I found out that I'd have to pay for a space. I had become familiar with the area after staying at the fleabag motel there and had seen how busy the Ralph's was on Beach Boulevard. Not only was the parking lot massive and illuminated, but there was a twenty-four-hour security guard standing at the entrance. I figured I could call for help if anything unsavory happened.

At around nine-thirty, I pulled into the parking lot. I covertly opened my trunk and took out my towels, blanket, pillow, and coat. I rolled up the windows, tucking the towels into the top of the glass as it closed, creating makeshift curtains so that no one could see inside. I made my bed in the backseat by laying a sleeping bag down and spreading out my blanket. I locked the Monte Carlo up and climbed into the backseat. There I was, a kid with ten dollars to his name and a bag of apples, sleeping in the backseat of his car 300 miles from the nearest friend or family member. I still wasn't willing to walk away from any of it; I was positive something good was going to eventually unfold. I lay in my car, listening to my cassette tapes: Aretha Franklin, James Brown, Springsteen's *Born in the U.S.A.*, and of course, Prince. I wrote in my journal until I could no longer keep my eyes open and eventually fell asleep. I didn't feel scared at all.

My eyes bolted awake at about three in the morning.

There was a loud and urgent tapping on the glass of my car's rear window. I nearly leaped out of my skin as I sprung awake and yanked the towel down to find the Ralph's security guard hitting the glass with his flashlight.

"You can't stay here," the man said.

I nervously nodded and scrambled to the front seat, still very much asleep. I can still remember how weird it felt to try and drive with no shoes on. I sped out of the parking lot and headed down the street, circling around with a U-turn and heading back to the general area as it was well lit.

Why in the world I thought heading into the alley behind Ralph's was a good idea I could never say, but that's just what I did. The alley was cluttered with trash bins and boxes, and no other cars, and it was totally dark. The only light source was a streetlamp way at the far end of the alley and it illuminated nothing around me. I was so exhausted, all I could think about was going back to sleep, so I parked there. To this day, I cannot believe how brave, or rather, foolish, I was to park back there as it was about as unwelcoming as you can get. I thought that certainly, I wouldn't be caught by security as there wasn't a soul in sight and nobody with a brain in their head would walk back there out of fear of being murdered, except of course for my nineteen-year-old self. I re-hung my towels over all of the windows. I said a nervous prayer and climbed into the back seat to lie down once again. Within a matter of minutes, I had fallen back to sleep.

Just so you know, if you ever find yourself sleeping in an alley in your car, as the air cools off in the middle of the night, your car upholstery gets quite cold and hard, so when I shifted awake at a sound I heard an hour and a half later, I figured it was because the car's vinyl seat had crunched as I rolled over. I lay there for a minute trying to go back to sleep until I heard another sound; this time, it wasn't my car seat. It was the sound of the handle to my car door trying to open. Someone outside, less than a foot away from where my head was laying, was trying to open the rear door. I bolted up and whipped the towel open as I came face to face with a dirty, greasy-looking guy with a glazed look. I yelled at the top of my lungs as I dived up to the driver's seat and started the car. He reacted by violently yanking on the door handle, determined to get the car open. I lay on the horn, not letting up as I threw the Monte Carlo into gear and sped off, not concerned if I was going to run him over in the process. As I raced to the end of the alley, I looked back in the rearview mirror to see my clearly drunken intruder staggering around in circles as he attempted to relocate my car.

By now, it was nearly six in the morning and the sun was rising. I drove to Huntington Beach, slathered sunblock on and hit the sack on my beautiful bed in the sand. Once again, I slept like a baby, albeit a very sunburned one. Later, I sat in my car and took a picture of my reddened face. I never wanted to forget what I was going through to make things happen for myself. I was sad and exhausted. I just felt in my gut that things were eventually going to be okay.

My Monte Carlo

I quickly got the hang of living in my car. The next night, I found another illuminated parking lot and managed to sleep through the whole night. In fact, the entire week after that when I wasn't working at night, I managed to sleep in my car without anyone harassing me. I was getting pretty good at being homeless. I even found an area in the Ralph's parking lot where the security guard couldn't see my car parked, so I stayed there for a few nights. Aside from the possibility of being mugged or murdered, the hardest part of sleeping in your car is waking up in the middle of the night and having to go to the bathroom. I became skilled at the mind control it takes to hold it all until dawn. I got up at sunrise, drove to a secure gas station, used the facility, washed my face, and brushed my teeth. At that point in my life, I knew where every single safe gas station bathroom was in Buena Park and where every public shower was in Huntington Beach. At work, I'd stuff my face in the Denny's walk-in freezer and call my distressed mother every three days. She continued to beg me to come home, not having enough money to send me much more support than a hundred bucks here and there. Every time she did, I was wrought with guilt.

Living in my car. Deeply sunburned from sleeping on the beach.

Two weeks passed and I *finally* got my first paycheck. It was a whopping one hundred and eighteen dollars. I was able to get myself a couple of motel rooms which cut the nights of sleeping in my car down to two a week. Even better, I was able to eat like a king once a day. I preferred eating a massive breakfast and trying to not think of food for the rest of the day and night. I lay in bed (or in the backseat, depending on the day) and told myself that I had just eaten a huge dinner and was full in order to forget about how hungry I was. The good news was, I had no problem staying thin as I was getting painfully thinner with each passing week, but my god, what a pretty skeleton man I was.

It had been weeks since I had been in touch with John Vulich, so I reached out to him and finally got him on the phone.

"What the hell are you doing living in Buena Park?" Vulich bemoaned.

"Like I have a choice, John!" I snapped back at him. "I'm in this shitstorm because of you."

"If you were gonna move to L.A. to be homeless, at least you could have done it in an interesting city," he snickered. John told me to calm down, that he would be home in a couple of weeks and that he would try to help me solve my unfortunate homeless condition. I didn't hold up much hope that he would come through, but at least I would know someone else in town. Of course, that also meant I would have to move to Hollywood, which was sounding more and more appealing, as working Denny's graveyard shift was beginning to grate on my nerves. Still to this day, if I ever hear the song "Where Everyone Knows Your Name," I feel like taking hostages.

One morning, I woke up in my car, went through my gas station bathroom routine, and headed to Ralph's for my coffee. *Greetings from the Hotel Monte Carlo!* I wrote on a postcard that I mailed to Muffy Bolding. I spent the rest of the morning writing in my journal and trying to not think of how hungry I was. I finally decided to break down and get something to eat at a pizza place a few businesses down in the mall. It was a tiny restaurant named Lampost Pizza. I went inside, sat at a table, and ordered from a very bubbly young blonde waitress.

The place was very "mom and pop" and packed with customers. Everyone seemed to know each other and there was a tremendous feeling of family and togetherness, a feeling that I hadn't felt in a couple of months. One might say, ironically enough, that it was indeed a place where everybody knows your name. The most notable thing about the joint was that the young beautiful girls that worked in the place seemed to be having the time of their lives. They were laughing and playing music, and most of all, they were very friendly. I hadn't been there more than thirty minutes when a couple of them were sitting at my table with me, asking me about myself. Waitress Linda was a tall, beautiful girl and an aspiring model around my age, and Gina was a smaller one, equally as pretty, who proudly showed me how loud she could burp on command.

Linda leaned forward and whispered to me, "You're the guy that sleeps in his car."

I was mortified that someone had seen me set up camp in the parking lot.

"We see you out there, we've been wondering who you are," one of them whispered.

I shamefully admitted that it was indeed me out there and explained what had happened to put me in the position. I described how I was desperately trying to save money to get a place to live but was having to spend every dime I made just to survive. I simply was not making enough money to get on my feet. Linda disappeared into the back of the restaurant and moments later, emerged with the owner. His name was Ed and he was a very quiet, no-nonsense fellow with a big mustache and an icy blue-eyed glare. The girls gathered around him like he was a protective father and explained my situation to him.

"Can you please give him work, Ed? He can't be sleeping in his car." The girls pleaded with him as he listened without speaking. As it turned out, the stern-looking fellow was, in fact, a very kind and compassionate guy, just one with a very gruff delivery.

"I need someone to scrub the floors when we close. If you think you can pull that off without fucking it up, I'll give you thirty bucks a night. If you steal from me, I'll kill you," he said with zero humor. I eagerly agreed to scrub and not steal. Thirty bucks was much more than I was making at my shrinking hours that Denny's was giving me and I wouldn't have to stay awake through the entire night. Even better, I would no longer have to hear that damned theme song from *Cheers* anymore. I turned in my Denny's smock and within a couple of days of serious floor scrubbing, Ed asked me to also help out waiting on tables. I became full time and was suddenly both eating and making great money. More importantly, for the first time in a couple of months, I felt like I had friends. The other waiters quickly welcomed me as part of their pack. We laughed, sang, drank Ed's beer, and created some of the most awesome customized after-hours pizzas you've ever eaten. It was in no way like working a job, more like hanging out in a clubhouse.

After I had been there for a couple of weeks and become fast friends with her, Linda quietly pulled me aside and handed me a key. "No one should ever have to sleep in their car. My mother and father have a camper in the driveway that they never use," she said. "If you think you can be gone by 7 a.m. every morning when my dad goes to work, you can sneak in after ten at night and sleep in there until you save up enough money to get a place."

I hugged her, holding back tears. I was so blown away by her kindness as truthfully, I was at my breaking point when it came to my public sleeping. I could never tell you how grateful and relived I was at her offer. Young Linda, pretty much a stranger, gave me a place where I would be perfectly safe, provided her old man didn't find out I was out there. I stayed in that camper for nearly two weeks but I felt like I was kicking it at the Four Seasons Hotel. I am still grateful for her kindness and know her to this day. Linda will always be a person I regard with tremendous decency, and her act is part of the reason I reached out to people in need when I was finally able.

11

THE MIRTH AND MAYHEM OF MMI

"You gotta come check out this make-up effects shop I'm working at," John Vulich said as if he had never left.

"Wait…you're back?!" I said from the Ralph's payphone.

"I would have called, but I didn't have your phone booth's number," he sarcastically quipped. "It's a place called Magical Media Industries. This guy, John Buechler, owns the shop and is hiring a bunch of entry-level people," he explained.

"In other words, he's cheap?" I said.

"Yeah, but it's a fun place to work and you got no skills, so get your ass over here and I'll hook you up."

"Good point, I'll be right there," I agreed.

I reorganized my car, said a heartfelt goodbye to the girls at Lampost Pizza, and headed to North Hollywood.

Special effects artist John Buechler was a true anomaly. Certainly not the top special effects artist in Hollywood, but indeed, he was a man who tackled his work with an enthusiastic smile, a genuine love for his craft, and a good sense of humor. One needs a sense of humor if they plan on navigating the entertainment business. He was a chubby, funny, generous fellow, forever clad in blue P.E. coach shorts, flip-flops, and a yellow tank top. When I write that this was his chosen uniform, I mean that he wore the exact same thing every day, even years later when we were shooting movies in freezing cold temperatures. One could always expect John to come flip-flopping onto the soundstage in shorts on even the coldest of days.

I first met him at his tiny effects shop near Van Nuys. It was a long and narrow, girly-magazine-littered, bowling alley lane-shaped make-up lab. There were piles of dusty half-sculpted creatures tossed onto shelves and bizarre paintings of wizard-like sorcerers and full-bodied pig-beasts everywhere you looked. John also had a thing for creatures with massive foreheads, some of which actually resembled himself, a physical quality he brandished like a badge of honor. This guy had a head like a cinderblock accentuated with the kindest eyes and the most impish smile. He was truly a good guy.

Early in his career, Buechler had gotten some attention after creating the monsters for a low budget, Saturday morning TV show called *Jason of Star Command*, and though most of the creatures were less than stellar, esthetically speaking, they managed to fit perfectly with the series' limited budget and had garnered him a mild level of notoriety. Most of the *Star Command* monsters were fashioned from soft mattress foam covered in garish fun-fur or old shag carpeting pieces and found objects like ping-pong balls for eyes.

I myself was a huge fan of the kooky beasts he'd been cranking out, and I was starstruck at the opportunity to meet him.

John Buechler Behind the Scenes of Sorceress

To some, John's creations were laughable; to Buechler, they were works of art that perfectly suited the show's needs, and he was right. The stuff looked pretty cool in a kooky, post-70's kind of way. Not all of John's work was wacky, though. The work coming out of his shop often straddled the line between goofy and high-quality from show to show as he was always smart enough to keep himself surrounded by talented and hungry young artists who helped raise the bar with beautiful sculpting.

John was a lovely man with some very interesting ways of executing his own art. It was a regular occurrence to walk into his shop and find him standing at his work bench, joyously sculpting with an actual hammer as he pounded clay into monstrous shapes. It was very easy to see just how much Buechler truly loved his craft and it was that very passion that made everything he created somehow work. Hilarious and impromptu, he was also a man with a very unique sense of humor, one who'd never hesitate to announce when he was about to make a bowel movement or that he was going to build a space-shuttle and only let his true friends fly off into space with him when the world ended. Anyone who had the privilege of knowing John loved him and no one more than me. He was at his very core, a smart, creative, and kind man who was always willing to give anyone a chance.

The afternoon that I met him, he sat listening to everything I had recently been through, then gave me a shot as his new shop runner with no hesitation. After three months of sleeping in my car with no friends, slinging both pizza and pancakes, I had a real job working on a real movie. Well, sort of a real movie. I called Disneyland and told them I had sailed my last jungle expedition and reported for duty at MMI.

The movie they were currently wrapping shooting was Empire Picture's *Ghoulies*, a low-budget horror film starring a bunch of unknowns, including Jane Mansfield's daughter Mariska Hargitay now of *Law and Order* fame. The movie was filled with a variety of slimy hand puppets, each resembling a demonic animal: a fish, a cat, a bat, and a rat. Was the movie goofy? God, yes. But I was loving every minute of it. There was no task I was not willing to do as I soaked in as much about the movie business as I could. In my time off, I did everything I could do to save money and stay thin while looking for a decent acting class to get into.

From day one, Buechler encouraged me, telling me that he'd help me break into acting and that's exactly what he did. I wasn't the only one he helped. John was quickly gaining a reputation for giving people their first start. The young artists working for Buechler on *Ghoulies* were a talented, rowdy, and hilarious young bunch that kept each other on their toes in between bouts of clay ball wars and demonstrations of their insanely impressive artistic skills. They were all kids just like me, all from different walks of life, but who'd all grown up with an insatiable passion for cinema and special effects. Everett Burrell, Howard Berger, Mitch Devane, and of course, Johnny Vulich were just a few of Buechler's original motley crew. Every single one of these guys eventually went on to become celebrated and respected Emmy and Oscar award-winning FX artists. But back then, they were mostly beer-drinking, girl-crazy, movie-loving, mullet-sporting dudes who were just as likely to fire a wet clay ball into the side of your head as they were to deliver brilliant effects work.

Working on Journey to the Center of the Earth

Passionate and heated debates on whose turn it was play their favorite music cassette or audio porn tapes occurred regularly. The laughs were continuous; the bonds we all formed were fast and true. Visitors or potential new productions came into the FX make-up shop often and always with the same laughable questions and comments. It was the same shtick from "civilians" over and over again.

"Looks like my ex-wife," a producer stated upon spotting a monster sculpture.

"Do you get your ideas from your nightmares?" was a frequent quip.

"Looks like me before my first cup of coffee in the morning!" some guy chuckled as we stared him down.

"Are you ever afraid this stuff is going to come to life and kill you?"

"I bet you have fun on Halloween." (The truth was, we hid on Halloween.)

"Is that the color it's going to be?" This, upon seeing a green clay sculpture of a monster sitting on a table.

"When you're done sculpting the monster, you peel the clay off the plaster head base and put it on your face?" To this, we retorted with a resounding, *yes*!

It was an insanely busy time in Hollywood and there was pretty much work for anyone who wanted it. At that point in the mid-eighties, the VHS home video market was booming and there was a huge demand for films, particularly those of a niche market such as horror. It was the Gold Rush of the movie business and I was in heaven. The movie jobs came one right after the other as Buechler's growing in-house team quickly became a big, dysfunctional, albeit very close-knit, family.

Just as Vulich had predicted a year prior, we spent our days working on movies and our nights drinking beer and watching old films. I am happy to report I was finally invited to sleep on John's apartment floor until I was able to figure out a place to rent. Once more, it looked like I was going to be okay after all.

I was having an absolute blast. Then I met this guy named Mike Deak.

"An actor? What kind of loser occupation is that?" Deak said, sneering at me as he stared me down, taking a drag of his cigarette.

"Who is that asshole?" I incredulously asked Vulich from his tiny kitchen.

"That's Deak. That's his way of being funny," John snickered.

"I'm not laughing," I told him, staring Mike down from across the room.

"Trust me, you're gonna love him. He's a hilarious genius," John said dismissively. As much as I couldn't see it at that moment, it turned out, Vulich was right.

Mike Deak was a tall, funny kid in dressed perpetually in a red Hawaiian shirt and jeans. He was a dude with a bona fide New Jersey accent and an encyclopedia-like knowledge of Godzilla movies and films in which things explode. He had also recently started working at MMI and was quickly becoming a very valued crew member. Mike had a hilarious vernacular, using words like *cones* when describing a woman's chest and *broads* like he really meant it. His charm and good heart always took away any possibility of anyone ever being offended by his hilarious brashness. Mike Deak was and is to this day a person you can rely on. As much as I was terrified of him, I was equally fascinated. He was way cooler than me, way more confident—or so it seemed anyway—and at that time, he was sleeping on John's couch, which I considered my potential bed.

I didn't talk to Deak for the first few days after I met him because he intimidated the hell out of me, but as a few days passed, I realized I was wrong about him. Way wrong. Vulich was right: Mike's abrasiveness was indeed part of ongoing shtick. He was, in fact, very smart—brilliant—and yes, a hilarious genius. In a matter of weeks, Deak and I had gotten to know one another and were making each other laugh, constantly busting each other's chops and finding many things in common: mostly, as it with Vulich, our mutual hatred for most everyone around us. He evolved into someone who I had complete respect and heartfelt friendship with and that remains to this day. Mike Deak is someone who I consider part of my family.

Kane Hodder, Greg Nicotero and I

As we all started hanging out, John Vulich, Mitch Devane, Mike Deak, Gino Crognale, and the new kid, Robert Kurtzman, (a hot-headed but massively creative artist from Ohio), we found many things that we had in common beyond making movies, things like Tommy Burgers, home of the chili-burger, chili-fry and the chilly-Coke, beer, going to female mud-wrestling clubs and appreciation for a little film called *Orgy of the Dead*. I can't remember who discovered the movie first or whether we just randomly rented it at Odyssey Video in the valley, perhaps the coolest video store in Los Angeles at that time, maybe the world. *Orgy of the Dead* was written and directed by Ed Wood, the same guy that did *Plan Nine from Outer Space* and many other films that hurt so good to watch.

Orgy of the Dead follows the terrifying tale of "Shirley" and her bloated writer-boyfriend as a car accident leaves them stranded and eventually captured in a fog-enveloped, cardboard cemetery where they are forced to watch a variety of horribly bad strippers perform for a grandiose psychic vampire known as Criswell, a character portrayed by the actual real-world 60s psychic Criswell, the man who predicted such gems as the total destruction of Denver, Colorado ("I predict in 1968 that this catastrophe will take place during the tourist season and the fun-loving people in an amusement zone will suddenly find their day of pleasure turned into one of sheer horror as the state implodes and comes to an end!") and Las Vegas, Nevada ("March 10, 1990: The very first Interplanetary Convention will be held in the new Convention Center on the famed strip with colony citizens of Mars, Venus, Neptune, and the moon in full representation.") Criswell also once claimed that on a certain date, the entire state of New Jersey would turn to jelly and when that date finally came and it didn't happen, he said "Well, it *did* happen, but it turned to jelly and then solidified so quickly that no one noticed." The movie is unintentionally hilarious and me and the boys gathered around John's clunky VHS machine weekly to re-watch it over and over every Friday night, drunkenly laughing until we finally passed out. I had finally learned to laugh harder than I ever had and I loved every minute I could spend with them. I was quickly realizing that I was indeed right where I belonged. I was amongst new friends with whom I had things in common, even though admittedly, most of those things were beer and our mutual love of bad movies. The bottom line is, my life had indeed completely rebooted and I was headed in an all-new direction.

I once again stuck my head in the door at Stella Adler's acting studio, this time finding a bored-looking stick of a woman sitting in the empty theater. "Can I help you?" she said, seemingly exhausted.

"I wanted to ask about taking some acting classes here," I said.

The bored woman exhaled as if I had asked her to loan me money. She got up and sauntered to the office, then returned, handing me a flyer that featured a bunch of classes and prices. It was very expensive, but the real deal. "Classes are Monday, Wednesday, and Friday. We also have weekend classes, but you have to audition to be involved in any of them."

I nodded, telling the unimpressed assistant that I had wanted to study with Stella for a long time.

"Oh, you're the one," she said, as if it were a regular part of her grouchy comedy repertoire.

I pasted on a smile and made the long walk back to Franklin and Gower. I was starting to get the picture that nothing in Hollywood was going to come easy. It looked like I was going to be focusing on sweeping the floors of Buechler's shop instead of studying for now.

The Stella Adler Theatre

The insanely fun days working at Buechler's shop with Vulich and the guys continued. I quickly worked my way up the ranks at MMI, graduating from dumping garbage and sweeping floors to full-on shop monkey. At night, I spent every free moment reading every book I could on acting, writing, and filmmaking. Eventually, I had saved enough money to audit and take acting classes and even better? My close friend from Fresno, Peter Garcia, decided to make the move to Los Angeles and we got ourselves an apartment. I finally had a bedroom of my own and an actual roof over that bedroom. I was finally working and living in Hollywood, safe and sound right there on the corner of Franklin and Gower, a corner that is now a dingy mecca for two dozen homeless folks. Back then, it was right in the center of all the action.

One day, Buechler called the team into his office and told us that Charlie Band had a *Ghoulies* emergency that he needed our help in solving. The television ads for the theatrical release original *Ghoulies* movie had started to run and the parents of America were flipping out. For those of you who haven't seen the trailer, the content of the teaser pretty much follows the movie's storyline of how the Ghoulies came to be and the havoc they eventually cause, all buttoned up with the film's logo and an astonishing shot of the fish Ghoulie popping up out of the toilet. The funniest part of the kooky toilet gimmick was that it wasn't even in the original film but was instead added into the trailer by a genius marketing guy and longtime friend of Charlie in the hopes of getting the movie attention, and boy, did it.

Ghoulies, they'll get you in the end! the voice-over announced as the fish Ghoulie popped up out of a commode covered in muck. Effective yes, but equally catastrophic when it came to the children of America spotting the shot of a demon from hell popping up from the toilet. To many kids, the commode instantly became a portal to hell and hundreds of children became terrified of going into the bathroom. As you can imagine, all sorts of messy unpleasantries immediately unfolded thereafter, and parents went berserk filing complaints to their local television stations to pull the ads and boycott the movie. To make matters worse, a well-known pro-life foundation attacked Charlie, accusing him of glorifying women who abort or lose babies in toilets. As insane as the thought was, Charlie scrambled to accommodate them by reshooting the *Ghoulies* poster to make the creature look less like a newborn baby.

Buechler explained to us that Charlie wanted us to grab a fish Ghoulie out of storage and take it to a photography studio that he had rented. Charlie's idea was to dress the fish Ghoulie in clothing so that it looked more like a character than a naked human baby. John told us to stop by the drugstore and buy a cheap baby doll and take its clothes off, then put them on the Ghoulie, pose him in the toilet, and have new pictures taken. We did as he asked and went up to John's storage. Unfortunately, the only Ghoulie that we had left from the first shoot was beat to hell: it was dirty, cracked, and ripped up; the paint had wiped off in many places and the hands were caked with big chunks of old super-glue from the original shoot. We did our best to patch and retouch the puppet, but since none of us knew how the original paint scheme was done, the little bugger ended up a lot brighter shade of green than he appeared in the film.

Afterwards, we went to the drugstore and bought a doll that was roughly the same size as the puppet. We opted for a baby blue crop top and bloomers, but when we got to the set, we realized that the bottom half of the creature would be hidden inside the toilet bowl. Thinking that it looked odd wearing a crop-top and potentially nothing else below, I decided to make the little guy look like he was wearing suspenders that connected to his unseen pants, helping sell the idea that he was indeed dressed below the waist. We scrambled around the photo studio, looking for elastics or something that could double as suspenders. I wandered into the kitchen area of the studio, where someone in the office had clearly just celebrated a birthday. There was a half-eaten birthday cake and red and white streamers strung all over the table. Thinking quickly, I grabbed a length of streamer and took it back to the studio. Five minutes later, with the help of a little super-glue and duct tape, the fish Ghoulie was wearing a pair of festive suspenders.

If you look closely at the new poster, you can see that the suspenders he is wearing has a red stripe, but both of them are on the same side. That's because it was just cheap paper garland that we threw together and not real suspenders. Fifteen minutes later and three days beyond that, the all-new toilet baby-friendly *Ghoulies* poster was hanging all over Hollywood. Anyone who doesn't think that Charlie Band is a guy who can make things happen is terrifically misinformed. The movie went on to make a small fortune and helped fund Empire Pictures' next few films.

12

ROBOTS, NINJAS AND KILLER CRABS

"How would you like to go to Spain?" Buechler asked me one day as we ate lunch at the dingy Lamplighter diner in Laurel Canyon.

I stopped mid-bite into my chicken salad. "Say what?"

Buechler explained to me that he was about to send most of the team to Rome to work on Empire Picture's latest pictures, *Troll*, directed by John himself, and *Dolls*, directed by *Re-Animator*'s Stuart Gordon, and he desperately needed more hands on-set in Madrid. The film shooting in Spain was *Eliminators*, which had been shooting for a month and yet was somehow already a month over schedule.

According to John Buechler, for every day *Eliminators* shot, it was already two days behind. How was that even possible? The film followed the character "Mandroid," a half-man, half-droid, all-*Terminator* rip-off, a comic book style rebel who was hellbent on saving the world from Dr. Abbott Reeves, a power-hungry madman portrayed by Tony Award-winning English actor Roy Dotrice. (Dotrice's daughter had played little Jane Banks from Disney's original *Mary Poppins*). The project also starred Denise Crosby, Andrew Prine, and Patrick Reynolds as the Mandroid, all directed by Peter Manoogian. John explained that he needed two assistants to fly out and help dress the actor playing the lead robot. By then, I knew my way around a make-up effects shop and had even helped paint parts of the costume, so I was very familiar with its many, many various pieces. Most of them were fashioned from plastic toys and beach shovels we bought at Kmart. Helping put the actor into the suit would be very easy for Mike and me.

I gladly accepted my mission and not long after, Mike Deak and I headed to Spain. I was supposed to be there for two weeks while they caught up and wrapped shooting. Little did I know, I'd end up staying for nearly three months as the production dragged on in complete disaster. Empire had put the crew up at the marvelous Apartamentos Villa Magna, a beautiful hotel in Madrid filled with well-to-do tourists, traveling business-people, and many Americans working on films in the area.

Apartmentos Villa Magna in Spain

This was the mid-eighties, when the dollar was very strong, so a lot of movies were shooting there including *Marine Issue*, starring Michael Pare and Tawny Kitaen, and *Solarbabies*, starring Jamie Gertz, Lucas Haas, and James Legros. This officially marked my first time working on set and other than having boatloads of enthusiasm, I had zero idea of any operation or protocol. Mike, artist Desiree Soto, David Kindlon, Mitch

Devane, Michael Hood, and me were picked up in a van and taken to set as the driver filled us in on why the production was such a mess: literally. He explained that aside from the Spanish crew being incredibly laid back, most everyone on the crew had taken a turn catching a brutal stomach virus. Out of nowhere, people were suddenly doubling over in cramps, fever, and worst of all, explosive diarrhea.

As you might imagine, this was a real problem, especially since the film was shooting in what Deak referred to as the "Jungles of Madrid," a very overgrown and secluded "lake" in the middle of nowhere. It wasn't really a lake, but instead a raw sewage treatment reservoir. A literal river of shit flowed from the city into this massive body of water that was set far outside of town where it was to be recycled. If one drop from this murk flew into your mouth or eyes, you became violently ill within a matter of hours. Since the film featured a lot of boat chase scenes, there was always a fine mist of water everywhere, so it was only a matter of time before you got sick. To make matters worse, we were often ten minutes from the shore and any form of bathroom. It wasn't *if* you were eventually going to crap yourself, but *when*, and if you were lucky enough to get to dry land before the floodgates opened, the only bathroom available was a five-gallon bucket with a toilet seat duct-taped to it. The dingy bucket sat under a tree out in broad daylight with no partition for privacy.

The Sewer Reservoir Where We Shot Eliminators

People piled off of the boat as it hit the sand and made a hasty run for that makeshift lavatory, nearly always filled to the brim with human waste and with no toilet paper in sight. Unless you remembered to bring paper with you, your only option was a clump of faded wet hemp that was hung on a hook screwed into the tree. You were expected to use the hemp to clean up afterwards, then rinse it out in a bucket of murky water and hang it up for the next person to use. In a moment of desperate improvisation, I opted to use one of my socks. It was a far cry from the glamorous life of film production that I had always dreamt of. One day, as I was walking back to the effects trailer, I suddenly heard the star of the movie, actress Denise Crosby, later of *Star Trek* fame, cry out "Billy! Quick! *Please* bring me some toilet paper!" as she made a mad dash for her trailer, holding onto the seat of her pants. This bug was truly relentless, as well as a non-stop source of laughs.

As the month passed, each member of the crew took turns being out of commission; if you didn't get sick from the water, it was from the vile set food. *Bocadillos* were served daily by the Marquis de Sade of catering for nearly every meal during the production. The sandwiches consisted of rock-hard bread rolls stuffed with cold scrambled egg and boiled potato or slices of meat that we referred to as "stained glass ham," a thinly sliced pork that after sitting in the sun for days at a time eventually became red and translucent. Day after day, the very same fly-covered bocadillos came out at both breakfast and lunchtime and *kept coming out* if we hadn't previously eaten them.

One day, Mike and I took two of the awful sandwiches and threw them off the boat into shit lake, only to spot them floating in the water three days later, still not saturated or eaten by the birds or fish. They were *that* awful. The caterer also served platters of peas and asparagus, slathered in room temperature mayonnaise. Whatever wasn't eaten that day was scraped off plates with the caterer's bare hands and right back into plastic jars to be served the next day. I learned very early on that a nightly plate of French fries back at the hotel was going to be the extent of my daily eating there. I have since then heard from many people that the food in Spain is actually marvelous, but certainly, it was not on that movie set.

MMI Crew on Eliminators

Mac Alberg and Patrick Reynolds, Eliminators

Our director, Peter Manoogian, was completely frazzled by the misfiring production but not without a sense of humor. It was a regular occurrence for us all to break into laughter as impending hells unfolded, one after another. The Spanish crew was very laid back, mildly unmotivated, and mostly hungover. Back then, the party in Spain did not even begin until after two in the morning and most of the crew went out at least a couple of nights during the work week. They came crawling in bleary-eyed, quickly reporting to the set "doctor," a chain-smoking Spaniard who sat around high from smoking hash all day. He dispensed a speed-like *aspirina* that turbo-charged your heart and spun you into a tooth-grinding state of complete sobriety. Because it was so incredibly hot during the days, many of the male crew members showed up to work in a Speedo and a tool-belt and nothing else. It didn't make any difference how fat you were or how much you should not be seen in a Speedo; if it was hot, that's exactly what you wore. And the fatter you were, the smaller your Speedo was.

The star of the movie, Patrick Reynolds, was a very nice guy. He was a big, strapping athletic fellow, who was very well-read and smart. He was also the heir to the vast Reynolds Tobacco fortune, a very wealthy young guy and ironically enough, also a staunch anti-smoking proponent. Patrick's claim to fame was that he was one of the sexy "after" workout guys in Olivia Newton John's legendary "Let's Get Physical" music video, where he transformed from fat to fit. Every morning after he came out of make-up, it was our job to dress him in his robot suit.

The foundation garment of the robot suit was black spandex and the "droid" armor pieces slid on one by one and were all snapped into place. The job should have been easy enough, but getting Patrick to stand still in order for us to dress him was an antagonizing daily task. We quickly went from total on-set professionalism to "Patrick! Stand fucking still!" in just a matter of days. You couldn't blame the guy for not wanting to wear it. The suit was heavy, cast in prickly rigid fiberglass, and what's worse, the poor dear had to wear a resin robotic plate on half of his face that covered one of his eyeballs. Because one of his eyes was covered, he had zero depth perception, so his falling down and running into the walls was a constant occurrence. It was as hilarious as it was concerning to see him tumbling over boulders and tripping and rolling around in the dirt, when he was in fact, portraying a stealth-killing machine. He fell off the back of the boat into shit lake, he fell down the mountain, down a set of stairs, and somehow, he lived through all of it and with a huge smile and a lot of humor.

Patrick Reynolds, Mandroid in Eliminators

Patrick Reynolds and Crew, Eliminators

Patrick Reynolds in Eliminators

One day we were dressing Patrick and as usual, he was shifting around and trying to walk away, but this time was different as he could not sit still. He was huffing and puffing and scratching at his loins. Mike had one of the upper thigh pieces on one side and I had the other on his right leg and we were both tugging them upward into place.

"Hold still, will ya Patrick?!" Mike barked as he leaned into Patrick's leg, struggling with the leg piece.

"I'm sorry: I am having a hard time this morning. My crotch is very itchy," he explained.

Mike and I shot each other horrified looks. "Dare we ask why?" I asked in fear.

"Well, I've come down with a very bad case of crab-lice," he said.

Our screams echoed through the makeshift jungles of Spain as Mike, Desiree, and I simultaneously flew backward ten feet. The shoot was halted, and we lost yet another day of filming as our leading actor went off to be deloused. While Patrick was out getting his bits and pieces shaved and disinfected, we decided to move on to the scenes that didn't require any actors—well, not living ones, anyway.

One of the other characters in the film was S.P.O.T., or the Search Patrol Operation Tactician, a tiny robot that looked like he could be R2D2's baby, a high-tech droid supposedly created by Denise Crosby's scientist character. The robot was a resin and fiberglass, radio-controlled, articulated puppet that supposedly flew on its own. It sported a digital readout screen, had right and left head turning ability and working hand pinchers (none of which ever worked). We took the stupid thing to set and switched it on, holding our breath as its lights started blinking out of control and its head started rotating in a circle and not stop as it began to smolder. Director Manoogian ripped his headphones off and begged us to get S.P.O.T. to work, but it never ever worked the way it was supposed to. To give the illusion that it was flying, Mike Deak had to resort to stringing it up with fishing line and swinging it into frame with a bamboo stick, often slamming the thing into Patrick Reynold's head or a nearby wall. To say we all hated S.P.O.T would be a huge understatement. Betsy Magruder, the first assistant director, fresh out of the hospital and her twenty-pound weight loss from the bug going around, went from blowing her colon to blowing her stack every time the little droid ruined a take by malfunctioning and spiraling out of control.

None of us had any experience with electronics, so we had no choice but to power the thing off to keep it from spinning out of control. If it couldn't be fixed with duct tape and a prayer, we had no earthly idea how remedy the issues we were having. Mike lay on the ground behind the little robot and manually turned its head with his hand whenever he could be hidden away. The puppet was a total bust. To make matters worse, the FX artist who built the little shit and who may have known how to fix the thing, a guy named Michael Hood (a hilarious and hugely talented artist) was nowhere to be found. About a week after everyone had arrived in Spain, Michael had just disappeared. He didn't leave a message or call: he was just suddenly gone. No one had any idea of where he went or why he left. After a week had passed and we had all but forgotten about him, he showed up on set again one day with the excuse that he needed some time alone. Years later, Hood told me that he didn't come to work because he didn't want to miss the opportunity to see Spain. Remember, people: we were all young and stupid back then, but this kid had big brass balls. It was hilarious. When we finally wrapped the movie three months later, the crew gathered around S.P.O.T., attached him to a stick of dynamite, and blew him up into a million pieces.

Eliminators - SPOT

Back in L.A., Buechler's make-up effects lab was as busy as it ever was. The crew was enormous. Gino Crognale, Howard Berger, Jeff Farley, Joe Dolinich, Eryn Krueger, and John Criswell were just a few of the many amazing artists now employed at MMI and believe me, it was one big party. Charlie Band was now cranking out a movie every couple of months. He was dominating the sci-fi/horror home video market and I was very much in love with working for the company. I had never been happier at that point in my life.

As we hustled our way into the system at Empire, Mike Deak and I took regular production meetings at Charlie's office on La Brea Avenue. We schmoozed anyone that would listen and quickly became well-liked around the office for our jackassery. Charlie Band, the owner of the company, was a bright-eyed, ever-optimistic dude with a Beatles-like haircut and endless energy. He was a prolific film producer-director who was an unflappable creative force with a genuine love for genre entertainment. Charlie had grown up on movie sets as his father Albert Band had been in the film business for many years. Marilyn Monroe was Charlie Band's babysitter at one point: that's how connected the Band family truly was. Charlie's temper was always cool and patient. In all the time that I have known him, which is now going on almost 35 years, I have never once seen Charlie lose his cool. He is, to this day, a very smart, funny, kind, and extremely generous person. He always has the uncanny ability to make you feel important, no matter who you are in the pecking order. As a result of his hugely gratuitous nature, I still work with him whenever I can. Charles Band helped me embark on a lifetime of having fun.

The next project Empire was producing was a film called *From Beyond*, a horror sci-fi picture inspired by the short story of the same name originally written by H.P. Lovecraft. The film was to be directed by horror fan favorite Stuart Gordon. Stuart had previously directed *Re-Animator*, starring Barbara Crampton and Jeffrey Combs, which was an instant classic. I first knew of Stuart Gordon as a director-writer from his insanely cool theater background. In 1968, while still in college, he had brazenly directed a psychedelic adaptation of *Peter Pan* and was immediately arrested on obscenity charges for gratuitous nudity and disrespect of local officials. Eventually, he and his wife Carolyn weren't charged because no one in the community would stand up and file a formal complaint, except for one man, a guy later revealed to be a convicted child molester, so the case was dismissed. Afterward, Stuart dropped out of his university and formed the Organic Theater group in Chicago where he and his wife Carolyn Purdy Gordon produced the first incarnation of David Mamet's *Sexual Perversity in Chicago* as well as *Bleacher Bums*, which ran in Los Angeles for over ten years and is still to this day a revered piece of theater. Anytime you were in Stuart Gordon's glorious presence, you never once forgot the idea that you were working with a true artist, a brilliant man whose talent was only surpassed by his massive kindness and quick wit. I loved the guy.

From Beyond was jammed with wall-to-wall creatures and complicated, elaborate make-up effects. The film was shooting in Rome at the newly purchased Empire Studios. Charlie had recently acquired the place from Dino De Laurentiis and planned on filming several other movies there for the next ten years. In the past, the studio had produced productions like *The Bible, Barbarella, Man of La Mancha, Red Sonja*, and many more. Like in Spain, the American dollar was stronger than ever and shooting overseas was a very wise decision for low budget filmmakers. In order to build the multitude of monsters in *From Beyond*, the special effects gags and creatures were broken up and designated to several different make-up effects companies, with Buechler's gang handling the majority of the gooey fun.

My friend John Vulich, along with a couple of other make-up artists, were still in Rome finishing the horror film *Dolls* for Stuart Gordon. The boys were to originally stay there and be joined by the MMI team for *From Beyond*. Mike Deak and I were supposed to stay in the U.S and help prep for the for next project, which was most likely going to be the sequel to *Ghoulies*. I was happy to stay home in the U.S., balancing my time between acting, improv classes, and working at Buechler's shop. My life was never better. Truly, I was completely happy for the first time ever. But the notion of staying in the U.S. didn't last for long.

13

WHEN IN ROME

"Things are very bad on the set of *Dolls*! Very, very bad!" John Buechler huffed as he flip-flopped his way out of his office into the shop. "The cast and crew partying is out of control." Buechler cringed as he explained that actors Stephen Lee, Bunty Bailey, and Cassie Stuart had gotten so drunk that they had "thrown the mattress out of their fifth-floor hotel room window down into the street."

"Even worse." Buechler said with eyes wide. "The MMI guys are at each other's throats! The Italians are furious. The production no longer wants any of them in Italy. They're flying home Friday and I need you and Deak to go help out on the set of *From Beyond*." The film followed the story of two young scientists and their bodyguard friend who accidently discover a madman-created machine that stimulates the pineal gland, a gland in the center of your brain. They find that stimulating this gland brings tremendous pleasure, but sadly also realize that it rips open a hole to another dimension allowing all sorts of unsavory beasts in the process. Deak and I jumped at the chance. Our responsibility was to help ship all the puppets to Rome, coordinate MMI's designated effects for the project, and be slime jockies on set. "Slime jocky" is a special make-up effects term for those of us who stand behind the camera with a bucket of clear goo, ready to run in to freshen up the creatures with a new coat of drippy slime before each take. The "slime" in this case was a goopy, colored mixture created from something called methylcellulose, normally used as the thick base for McDonald's milkshakes.

"I'll go, but I just paid for my acting classes, I will have to come right back," I told John. I was so determined to get the acting ball rolling.

John thought for a moment. "I'll make sure you get acting parts while you're there. Just stay." I couldn't believe what I was hearing. "I'll set you up with a meeting with Charlie, I'll send him your picture and resume. I'm positive he will give you acting parts because you'll be able to do double-duty for him, both acting and coordinating. Just please go."

I was already going to go, but that made the trip to Italy all the sweeter. I thanked Buechler and agreed that I would leave Friday.

The next day I went to Charlie Band's office on La Brea with my photo and resume. "Dude!" Charlie called out as he finished his meeting with his marketing assistant, an eager newcomer by the name of Greg Kinnear, now an Oscar-nominated actor. I had quickly learned that "Dude!" was Charlie's go-to greeting (and has remained so for the last thirty-five years). He told me that John Buechler had called him, looked at my picture and resume, and gave me his stamp of approval. "Dude, there'll be lots of cool acting parts there at the studio. If you can act, they are all yours! We will for sure try to make something happen." He sent me downstairs to his casting director's office, a guy by the name of Anthony Barnao.

The casting office was directly across the street from the Empire offices on La Brea. His assistant Lisa buzzed me in and I sat in the lobby with two handsome young actors who were about my age. We sat and talked as we waited. The two guys introduced themselves as Brad and Robert; they were there to audition for one of Charlie's other upcoming movies. Brad was fresh off the boat and on one of his first auditions, and Robert was a distracted but nice local kid who told me he had grown up around the business. I nervously waited until they finished their appointments and then went in to meet with Anthony Barnao.

Anthony was a big, kind, gregarious bear of a man with a serious mullet. He asked me where I was from and gave me a few pages from one of the scripts on his desk. I didn't know what the scene was from, other than the character seemed extremely nerdy. I read the copy, slightly nervous, but I managed to pull it off for not ever having seen it before.

"Great!" he grinned after I read for him. He scribbled something on my picture and dropped it into a basket on his desk. "I have something for you to do in *Ghoulies 2*. I'll send you the script. Do you have an agent?" he said, hustling me out of his office.

Not only did I not have an agent, but I barely had a picture and resume. "Did I just book this?" I laughed.

"Yes! Good job," Anthony said, explaining that I shouldn't worry about having no representation: he would help me put my deal together. He shuffled me out the door.

Ghoulies 2 was of course the sequel to *Ghoulies*. The film was not exactly *Gone with the Wind*, then again, I was no Scarlett O'Hara, but it was a start and my very first paid film acting role. I was thrilled. I had gone from sleeping in my car to landing my break, and the movie was filming in Rome of all places. It happened that fast. John Buechler had back-doored me into the acting business, just like he said he was going to.

I was later told that handsome Brad and Robert didn't book the gigs they were auditioning for; I realized sometime after that it was Brad Pitt and Robert Downey, Jr. I had shared that waiting room with. I'm sure they were okay with that: they seemed to have eventually found their own way into the system.

That night, I walked from my new apartment to the acting studio to tell my new coach that I was going to be gone on location for a couple of months. Her look of total elation at the news of my booking a movie role instantly faded into one that was what I can only describe as "disturbed" after I told her the title.

"*Ghoulies 2*?" She stared at me with incredulous, overly made-up eyes. "Was there a *Ghoulies 1*? Or did they go right to the sequel?"

I did my best to explain the movie to her as she zoned out with a pasted-on smile.

"Well, it's a start, isn't it?" she said as she immediately turned away and began squawking at another performer who walked through the door. I didn't care. She had, in her own way, given me the thumbs up, and it meant everything. I walked back home to Franklin and Gower, excitedly stepping over the piss-drenched stars on the Hollywood Walk of Fame.

To me, things couldn't be any more perfect. After only just a couple of acting classes, I was already on my way to becoming an actor.

"Let's do some coke and celebrate your first booking!" my roommate Roger said to me with wicked glee in his eyes.

"Coke? What? No!" At that point in my life, I had never done a drug of any kind and was terrified of the idea of ever starting. By then, I was a seasoned drinker; in fact, at that age, I was probably already drinking more than I should, but drugs like coke or pills were not an option for me. I was way too scared of the unknown. "Where the hell does that crap even come from?" I asked.

"The jungle. That means it's natural," he said.

"It does? No way. I'm too afraid," I said.

When I was a kid, I was afraid of everything. Everything. Halloween masks terrified me; I was horrified of big dogs and meeting new people and other children. I was horribly shy and was prone to run out of the room whenever I was subjected to anything new in life, particularly anything scary. I had also grown up in the late 60s, back when it was a regular occurrence for schools to terrorize children on the dangers of illicit drugs. One hit and we would be instantly transformed into addicts, forced to walk the streets, selling our young bodies for the next fix.

Once, when I was ten, I was so terrified when I caught my thirteen-year-old babysitter Lori sneaking a cigarette in my parent's bathroom that I called the operator and asked her to send the police to my house because I had been left alone with someone who was breaking the law. I was anything but a cool child; instead, a nervous wreck scared by a variety of the silliest of subjects. As a little one who dreaded any time that I was home when my father was around, I cherished the moments that I was allowed to spend the weekends at my Grandma Butler's house. She was my father's mother, a very Southern, very helpless, extremely kind and deeply religious woman who lived in absolute mortal fear of most everything in the world, and I listened closely to her every word. She constantly warned me of what she considered the many "overlooked terrors in life," things like: you should never forget that you could drown in a teaspoon of water, or you should never lie on the floor in front of the TV set as it may explode in your face at any moment, you should remain terrified and untrusting of all hippies (really, any people with long hair and beards), and most of all, you should never forget that drinking a glass of milk with a tuna fish sandwich would cause instant death. Apparently, she'd had a family member who'd died after eating the same combination and since then, the family never took its chances.

"Billy, please watch Jim and Tammy Baker with me: they've got puppets," my Grandma Butler would plead, hoping that I would somehow be infected with the stupidity that those two religious morons spewed. From a very young age, I easily could spot the Bakers' horse shit, but it was a huge source of peace for my grandmother, who was hyper aware of everything that could go wrong in life and would be the first to warn you. One time, she told me that if I didn't embrace Jesus that Satan would look in my bedroom window in the middle of the night.

"Good! I want him to. I want to see what he looks like," I said back, giving her the treatment. Moments later, my grandfather made me lick a bar of Lava soap. Lesson learned, but truthfully, I'm still kind of curious as to what Satan looks like; I just don't want to meet him firsthand.

For years, both my grandmother and grandfather gave a percentage of their income to the P.T.L. religious organization; that is, until Jim Baker eventually got busted for his indiscretions. After that, it was as if they both erased any knowledge of Jim and Tammy from their memory. Grandma Butler never mentioned Jim Baker ever again.

She was also very nervous around anyone who wasn't white. One time, my grandmother and I were walking down the sidewalk when just ahead of us, an African-American man was on the same side of the street, heading in our direction. She quickly pasted on an all-too-obvious smile, tightly took ahold of her purse strap and headed across the street through oncoming traffic, just to keep from walking past the guy. The most humorous part of her fear of minorities was that I know, in fact, that she truly never wished a single person any ill-will. She was so kind, just very naive when it came to being around anyone unlike herself as a lot of older people from that generation were. It's all very ironic: years later, after my grandfather had passed, it was revealed that Grandma Ora Lee Butler's husband Claude Butler was, most-likely, part black. Talk about facing your fear. The universe has such a lovely way with its various ironies.

My Grandpa Butler's Mother, Clearly a Woman of Color

Yes, Grandma Butler was indeed afraid of everything, and she passed that gene down to her chicken grandson. I rarely took chances, other than stupidly living in my car in the pursuit of happiness. I never took big risks when it came to my own health or safety, especially when it came to ingesting things of unknown origin. Pretty much anything other than beer and margaritas were strictly out of the question. That night, however, my hilarious roommate continued to push and push me, daring me to loosen up and just give coke a try, and as the booze soaked in, I eventually started to listen. After all, he was years my elder, a dear friend, and a seasoned party professional, not to mention the fact that the Cuervo poppers we were all slamming were doing their job.

Roger was a great friend who never did me any harm. He was a belly-laughing, artistic man's man. I'd met him in Fresno back when we both worked at a local theater where I started performing. He was a fast friend who always had a witty answer for most of life's problems. Roger was a multi-talented actor, a set designer, and a guy who always seemed to do the right thing, except for when it came to paying his car tags. For whatever reason, Roger refused to ever pay them.

When I met him in 1980, he drove this beat-up, faded 1972 red van that was a rolling construction shop. It had everything you needed to build a complete theater set: a skill saw, tools of all kinds, lumber, dry wall, and even a dirty mattress in back that he used for God only knows what, but the one thing the van didn't ever have was its car tags. Not long after I'd met him, he proudly showed me his license plate. The last time Roger had paid his car tags was back in 1977, back when he'd first bought the thing. It had been four years since he had paid to register his rig and he'd never been pulled over. "The money from car tags is supposed to be used for filling potholes in the streets. They're all over the place. I'm not giving 'em my money until they fill the damn potholes!" he comedically growled.

Riding in that beat-up van with him was a true adventure as he worked the constant miracle of keeping one eye on the road and the other eye in the rear-view mirror at all times, always looking for the cops. We spent three times as much time getting to places we were headed to as he was always forced to take a bizarre triangulation of tiny side streets to keep off the main routes in fear of getting pulled over. Still, knowing Roger was one of life's greatest joys. He later moved to L.A. and ended up being my roommate; he also worked at John Buechler's shop, finally doing construction on high-end television commercials. Many years later, after we were both older, greyer, and certainly much wiser especially when it came to imbibing in things that we should not have, he suddenly passed away; he had not detected prostate cancer in time. Ironically enough, as he passed, it was reported to me the tags on his latest car were up to date. But back in the day, we had nothing to lose.

Roger smiled as he put the coke in front of me and handed me a straw. "You're going to love it. Just do it!" he said.

"I don't do this stuff," I said, taking a huge swig of Cuervo and staring down at the chalky line, scared out of my wits.

"Oh, yes you do," he said, pushing it closer.

"I can't believe you expect me to do this," I laughed, nervously nabbing the straw out of his hand.

"And I can't believe you've already killed a half bottle of Cuervo, but who's counting. You're no angel, Butch," he laughed back.

I was so ill-informed on the art of drug taking that I didn't even know how to plug my opposite nostril before taking the snort, nearly blowing the stuff off the mirror as I made a half-attempt.

"Give me that!" he said, snatching the straw and showing me how to do it like a boss. Like a Hoover vacuum. Roger handed the mirror back to me, and I nervously leaned forward and snorted the line.

I sat up in my chair and looked at him for a few beats.

The chemical melt going down my throat was vile.

The rush was instant and well...*absolutely marvelous*, if I'm to be honest.

Roger smiled at me with his eyebrows raised in anticipation as he waited for my reaction.

I instantly felt sober, alert, and very, *very* much alive.

"Where do we get more?" I said, like the Jackal I clearly was.

He was right: I did like it. Actually, no, I didn't like it. I loved it. All at once, I wanted to talk, sing, dance, fold laundry, alphabetize video tapes, all of it. Roger burst into his brilliant gregarious belly laugh. "I'll make a call."

That was it. I was on board. I was off to the races and in an instant love affair with the ol' Peruvian Dance Powder, the demon dust known as cocaine.

The phone rang in my apartment as I was packing for my flight to Rome. It was my mother and she was very worried. She often worried about my new life in the big city. She told me that she had just seen the news and that there had been a big terrorist attack in the airport that I was going to be landing in. Four Arab gunmen had walked into the Leonardo da Vinci International Airport with grenades and machine guns and had killed 16 and wounded 99, including American diplomat Wes Wessels. I was still very young and even more green when it came to traveling, so I was instantly worried if flying out was going to be a mistake or if there were even going to be flights at all.

"Dude, it's Europe. That's just another day over there," Vulich said to me, taking a bored drag of his cigarette. He had just gotten home, fresh from being fired from *Dolls*. Of course, he had bounced right back with an even bigger job helping with the FX build on *The Lost Boys* over at Greg Cannom's shop. "Stuff like that happens all the time overseas," he said.

"And I want to go there because?" I asked.

"Look at it this way. That airport is going to be crawling with the Italian military. There's no safer place in Rome than Da Vinci right now. You'll be fine. Just get on the plane and don't be a pussy." He said it in a way that made me think he was right. Again.

The Saturday morning after we flew out from LAX, Mike Deak and I flew into Da Vinci. We were to report to the studio on Monday morning to start working on *From*

Beyond. Mike and I made our way through customs to meet our ride, walking right past the area where dozens of people had just been mowed down with bullets, and sure enough, John was right: there were Italian military police everywhere, all donning lethal-looking machine guns with their fingers on the triggers. Vicious-looking police dogs sniffed and stared everyone down as we sauntered in with caution. We were safe alright. I tried to not show how shaken I felt as we walked past the Sbarra Pizza where nine people had just died.

We were taken to our hotel by a funny Italian dude named Emanuele, a forever-unshaven, forever-smiling guy who had been assigned to drive us around. It would be the first, but certainly not that last time an Italian would pronounce my name Beely. He jokingly told Mike that he looked like a *Pennello Alto* or *Pennelone*, which translated into English means "tall paintbrush" a nickname for him that stuck to Deak from that moment on.

Being in Italy was like being in another world: a beautiful, marvelous new world. Every American on the planet should have the pleasure of experiencing that beautiful country for a period of time. Everything was jaw-droppingly beautiful and different than life in the U.S. in such a good way. We drove past vast fields of trees and vineyards and dozens of old stone structures, many of which were still standing from ancient times. I was completely overwhelmed by everything I was seeing. I could not believe that some kid who had never been out of Fresno was suddenly in another country.

The driver took us to the Hotel Corsettimare, which was about an hour and a half away from the airport. It was located in a tiny beach town called Torvaianica, a subdivision of the town of Pomezia, named after an old coastal watch tower, *Torre del Vajanico*, which was built in 1580 to defend against the Barbary pirate attacks. The town was founded in the 1940s and by 1985, it had become a busy and popular tourist destination, during the summer, that is. During the winter when *we* first got there, there was no one in the hotel but us; there was only a few people in the entire town other than us.

Hotel Corsettimare

The Hotel Corsettimare was big and rustic and sat right on the beach. Dotting the street that the hotel sat on were several tiny mini-markets, all filled with magazines, freezers full of gelato, and outdoor courtyards framed by chunky, salt-air rusted rod-iron fences where you could sit and drink the best coffee you've ever had in your life. This was back when music videos were a huge deal and most of these patios featured mounted TV sets that played the top-ten videos on a never-ending loop. It was hilarious to see groups of eighty-year-old Italian men sitting bundled up on these patios, all smoking cigarettes and sipping coffee while watching videos of songs like The Mary Jane Girls' "My House" or Cameo's song "Word Up."

Hotel Corsettimare

Each of us from MMI were given our own little beach bungalow. The rooms were small and rustic with a bed, steam wall heater, TV, bathroom, and bidet. It was my first experience with a bidet; at first, I thought it was what you used to wash your socks at the end of the day. Both breakfast and dinner were eaten in a huge empty dining room. The image of the group of us sitting there in that vast empty restaurant was something right out of *The Shining*. There was no one staying in that big hotel but us.

Hotel Corsettimare Dining Room

Make-up artists and FX technicians John Criswell, Mike Deak, John Buechler, Dave Kindlon, Jeff Farley, Robert Kurtzman, Tony Doublin and me, along with a few others, took over the place and quickly made it our rowdy playground. Our mornings were filled with Italian coffee and pastries, fresh fruit and American-style eggs and bacon, and at night, we were served some of the best Italian food I've ever eaten in my life. A variety of handmade pastas served with either white and red sauces were made for us daily and we ate them out of house and home. Roasted fish, beef and chicken, dozens of bottles of red wine and a huge antipasto with peppers, European cheeses and vegetables were laid out by the most kind and loving staff you would ever meet. In particular, Sondro, a bushy-browed older gentleman in a red vest tended to our every request and always with a huge laugh. Sondro did not speak much English, but that fact nurtured how fast we all learned to speak Italian, if you wanted to eat, you had to learn the lingo, so it was perfect motivation. I quickly realized that if you can speak Spanish, you can learn Italian, as many of the words are the same, just pronounced differently. I can't imagine what he must have thought of us boisterous, obnoxious Americans, but regardless, he sure made us feel loved and welcome, as most Italians did.

Hotel Corsettimare – Mr Tony

Standing off in the shadows, constantly wringing his hands, was the hotel manager, Mr. Tony, a seventy-something-year-old guy who always wore the exact same dinner jacket and who also didn't speak a word of English. Running the front desk surrounded in a perpetual cloud of cigarette smoke and sitting behind an ever-full ashtray was a nearly toothless, gregarious old guy in a cabbie hat that we all nicknamed "Leatherface" as his thick, wrinkled mug looked like he'd been smoking cigars since the age of six. Not only did Leatherface not speak English, he barely spoke at all, not in words you could understand anyway. Every now and then he'd slowly make his way from behind the 1930s-style switchboard in the front of the hotel to our table and attempt to tell a story in a raspy, incomprehensible Italian dialect that even the other locals could barely understand. His animated attempts to tell a story that no one could follow were a constant source of entertainment.

The hotel's only housekeeper was a woman named Rita, an older Italian mother right out of central casting. Rita spoke perfect English as she had spent time living in the States; she was a lady who continually found joy in the strangest of items. Once she found a colored paper clip in my room's trash can and asked if she could give to her son to "play with." Soon enough, we were buying small toys from the gift store and giving them to her to share with her little boy. The hotel felt like home right away and still, to this day, leaves me filled with tremendously happy feelings whenever I think about it. I would love to go back there and often wonder if it's still standing.

Charlie's studio was appropriately named Empire Studios. It was a sprawling movie lot filled with massive soundstages, dozens of offices, a plaster and set-building shop and a costume stage that housed hundreds of costumes from every period of time. There was also a fully set-up bar and coffee barista there where everyone converged. Unlike in the United States where drinking at work was not okay, day drinking in Italy was not only tolerated, it was celebrated and encouraged. Wine was always served at lunch, frozen limoncello or Campari was acceptable at four when you needed a pick me up, and whiskey flowed whenever it felt right, which was most of the time.

The studio was originally built by Dino De Laurentiis and was once known as Dinocitta, a tongue-in-cheek nod to the legendary Cinecitta Studios where Fellini had made most of his films. De Laurentiis had produced a hundred films there including Franco Zeffirelli's 1967 adaptation of *The Taming of the Shrew* starring Elizabeth Taylor, *The Man of La Mancha,* and *Barbarella* starring Jane Fonda. After falling on hard times due to high operating costs, De Laurentiis closed the studio and Charlie Band took it over. Band immediately put it to use producing his own movies and we got there right in the middle of his heyday. The American dollar had never been stronger, and Empire could easily double their budgets by shooting overseas.

There were dozens of empty offices in the main studio building; there were only fifteen people working on the entire massive movie lot. When we first arrived, we explored the whole place, heading up to Dino's old office to see what it was like. It was a lavishly big office with expensive Italian post-fifties design and a huge desk. The rest of the place looked like someone just walked in one day and asked everyone to get up from their desks and leave. There were papers, pens, and even coffee cups with dried coffee in the bottom of them just sitting there covered in dust. The place was a complete ghost town that we all continued to explore in most our down time. De Laurentiis' office was astonishingly unlocked for anyone to just walk in and check out. Early on, I also discovered that the phone at his desk was still connected, and that came in handy for late-night, long-distance phone calls back to the States. Every day, after we wrapped shooting and everyone was in the bar, I slipped up to Dino's office and sat in his chair with my feet propped up on the desk while I called virtually everyone in my phonebook. (Sorry for the phone bills, Charlie, if you're reading this.)

Empire Pictures Stages

The MMI special effects workshop was on the backlot next to a long-rotting Styrofoam castle and set pieces leftover from the movie *Red Sonja* starring Brigitte Nielsen. There was a big moat filled with murky old water and a huge miniature foam mountainside behind it. Behind the soundstages were rows of wrecked cars and many large, slumping set pieces from *Barbarella* (including the "sex organ" that the villain in the film tried to kill her with by making her orgasm to death). The place was a film nerd's playground to the hundredth degree.

The workshop itself was located inside a row of buildings where the exterior had been dressed to look like a gas station and a grocery store for the film *Troll*, but as with many times in Italy, a lot is lost in translation, especially when it comes to Italian to English, and the sign that hung above our shop didn't say "Grocery Store" but "Eating Supplies." The workspace they gave us was completely empty on our first day of work, so we did some quick thinking and turned the crates we had built to ship the *From Beyond* monsters into makeshift work-tables. We poured all of the packing peanuts into one massive crate that was dubbed "the Jacuzzi," a place we later sat in during meetings or whenever there was time for a stolen nap. The shop was also absolutely freezing at all times year round.

"We need to bring some of the crew to the airport." Emanuele said as he came into the shop frazzled.

"What's wrong?" I asked, scared that a late arriving crew member had been detained by immigration. Most of us were working there without work permits.

"The largest shipping crate fell off of the forklift while being unloaded off the airplane. The monster is laying on the Da Vinci runway." The monster he was referring to was the giant flying chicken-shrimp monster, or so we called it: a 400-pound rubber puppet that was easily over ten feet long, with a wing-span of twelve feet. Some of the more eager and able-bodied guys in our crew went with Emanuele to go collect the wayward beast. We were later told that the entire runway was covered in packing peanuts as if it had snowed.

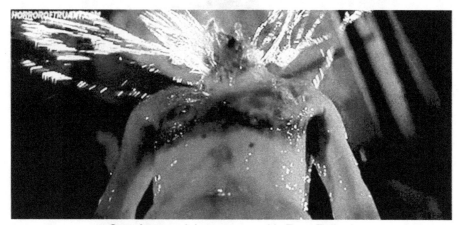

One of many miniatures we used in From Beyond

While we were shooting, we were told we were going to utilize over 200 gallons of methylcellulose slime during the shooting of *From Beyond*. It was the most goop that any of us ever had dealt with. Since our schedule was tight and our workdays long, we had the brilliant idea of mixing all 200 gallons of slime at once. We took four fifty-gallon barrels, mixed the methylcellulose powder and water together, and within just a couple of hours, it had thickened to its proper gooey consistency. What we didn't take into consideration was that the stuff goes sour after only a couple of days, and it quickly began to stink to high hell. The longer it sat in that shop, the worse it smelled over the following few weeks. It was truly awful. There were many days on set where the MMI FX team members nearly came to blows over who was going to puppeteer lying under a platform that a monster was standing on, as the spoiled slime concoction poured down on the unlucky one's head throughout the entire day. "It smells like rotten coochie down here" was a phrase that was often heard coming from beneath the saturated set floorboards.

The first day on set for me was an effects-free scene. I met the leading actors Barbara Crampton, Jeff Combs, and Ken Foree, who were shooting a scene where their characters were eating breakfast. I was completely star-struck by meeting Ken, who had previously starred in George Romero's *Dawn of the Dead*, one of my favorite movies, one that Johnny and I had watched over and over again. He was funny and nice, easing my shaky fandom. Little did I know, less than ten years later, I would be acting alongside him in *Leatherface: The Texas Chainsaw Massacre 3*. The house set was huge and solid; most of the rooms were reconfigured set pieces originally built for the film *Dolls*, also directed by Stuart Gordon. The actors were terrific performers: they made us all feel very welcome, but by far, the coolest person on set was the film's brilliant director Stuart Gordon. Watching him direct was inspiring, and his hilarious sense of humor made him not only accessible to anyone involved, but a good audience for our own MMI jackass brand of comedy. This was especially true for Mike Deak and I.

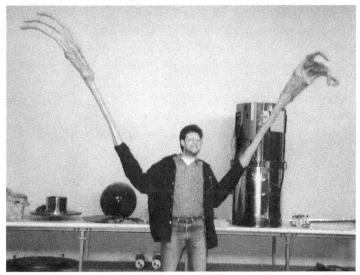

From Beyond – Mike Deak

From Beyond - Make Up Test

Stuart, Mike, and I sat on set every day, talking endlessly about our favorite movies as well as about a few that didn't even exist but truly should, including *Queen of Crisco Mountain*, a fake film that the three of us pretended to be writing. As each day of shooting passed, we discussed the next scene we were supposedly writing as our imaginary film continued to grow. Our epic took place in the future and involved a group of wrongly convicted female prisoners who found themselves locked up in an intergalactic prison spaceship. In this made-up movie, the beautiful lady prisoners began to plot together to break out of their spaceship hell and finally return to a life of interstellar freedom. The whole point of our dumb movie was to get to the finale where a hundred hot women in black and white striped prison-issue bikinis had to fight their way up a giant mountain of Crisco, the very tip of which led up to a tiny escape hatch.

We killed time in between shots, belly laughing at the thought of a butch robot prison matron played by old actress Martha Raye and justifying the giant pyramid of Crisco existing in space by deciding that the ship's slave work detail was for the women to machine stamp foil serving trays in the prison ship's TV dinner factory. For many years after, whenever we had dinner together, Deak, Stuart and I threatened to write *Queen of Crisco Mountain* into a 100-million-dollar movie starring Scarlett Johansson and Nicole Kidman. Because of Stuart Gordon's untimely passing, I very well may one day write the movie in tribute to him.

Working on *From Beyond* entailed an insane amount of work, but for every day that we sweat it out, we also balanced things by the amount of fun we had. We were a bunch of fearless kids playing in a giant movie-making sandbox that we ruled and loved.

Working with the Italian crew members took a little figuring out. The best way I can describe working with Italians is the treatment that you get when you go to a car repair shop and the owner tells you, "this car can't be fixed, you'd be better off junking it" only to call you two hours later to tell you that your car is ready to be picked up. Exchanges like this were a daily, sometimes hourly, occurrence in Rome:

"Hey Tino, can you ask someone to pick us up a can of red spray paint?"

"We do not have this," the crew member said apologetically.

"You mean locally?"

"No. We do not use red spray paint in Italy."

"There's no red spray paint in the entire country?"

"No. I am sorry, Beely" he said, shaking his head.

"Are you sure about that?" I said, hoping it would soak in and he would realize what I was talking about.

"We do not have."

"Uh, okay...thank you anyway." And just as I started to walk away:

"Oh... Beely..."

"Yes, Tino?"

"We do have a type of paint...she comes in a pressurized metal can and...uh, when you push the button on the top, a mist of red paint will fly out of its nozzle in a fine spray."

"Yes! Yes! I need that. That's the mist I need. Red. Please!"

"Okay, no problem. I bring it for you Thursday."

"Thursday??? It's Monday…"

"Yes, but the pressurized metal paint can store is only open on Thursday from 11 to 2."

"What? Oh, never mind."

Two hours, later after I'd given up hope, Tino showed up with a can of red spray paint. "Beely! I find-a de red spray paint!"

We celebrated.

Working with those lovely, beautiful people sometimes involved taking a long, precarious road and a lot of tail chasing, but they always seemed to get there and with so much damn charm and earnest enthusiasm that I could only love them for their efforts. Some of the most brilliant artists I have ever worked with have come out of Italy. Italians also did not work one minute past their ten hours; we were in the middle of a shot and suddenly the entire stage went dark because it was officially quitting time. No amount of cajoling, paying, or flat-out begging got them to work overtime. They worked to live and never the other way around.

One day, while we were shooting, there was a shot where actor Ted Sorel who played Dr. Edward Pretorius was to rip his own head from his neck as it split in two gooey halves. Buechler and the gang had created this horrifically bloody head, complete with life-like eyes and mechanics to make it split into two pieces. It was an impressive bit of disgusting art. As we were about to shoot it, Mike and I thought it would be funny to make a shoddy-looking fake head to reveal on set in the hope of getting a big laugh before we shot the real one. We took a beat-up old Styrofoam head we found in the shop and spray painted it, then took ping-pong balls and drew crazy black dots on them for eyes; we glued them in a crossed-eyed position and created a huge bouffant of messy hair out of spray-painted packing hemp. The thing looked absolutely ridiculous and we were positive that no one would ever mistake it for the real thing.

The time came for us to shoot the head gag and Mike and I covered it with a plastic sack and took it to set. The film's cinematographer was Mac Ahlberg, a very gentle, regal and, polite Swedish man who was fast becoming Empire Pictures' main director of photography. He was a well-spoken guy, always donning a stiffly-ironed white shirt and often peering through his monocle lens. He spoke fluent Italian and worked very fast, introducing the most brilliant, saturated color pallets for each film he DP'ed. He never ever complained or cursed and was nothing but a refined gentleman until that morning.

Mike and I set the fake head we made, still covered by the plastic bag, on a stack of apple boxes in the middle of set as Mac began to aim lights in its direction. After everything was in position, Mac politely asked if we could remove the bag from the mechanical head so he could finish lighting it. With completely straight faces, we removed the sack, revealing that insane looking mess with crossed eyes. But instead of everyone instantly bursting into uproarious laughter, the room fell dead silent as everyone suddenly lost all expression. Mac Ahlberg's smile faded and his eyes bulged as his face went from flesh-colored to bright red to purple as he completely blew his stack, turning to Stuart in absolute fury.

"Stuart! Vat is dis? I cannot possibly shoot zis piece of shit!! Zere is no amount of fucking lighting in ze vorld that can save zis bullshit!!" Mac started to storm off set as Mike and I scrambled to pull the real head out, explaining that we were only joking. Everyone caught their breath and regrouped as our dumb attempt at humor became the Italian crew members must-have photo op. All through the years that we spent in Rome, that goofy cross-eyed, hemp-haired head remained the shop mascot, until one day when it became a makeshift soccer ball and was punted into the trash where it belonged. So much for using bait and switch gags for laughs.

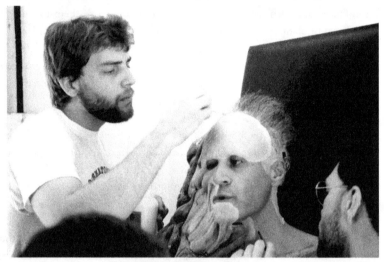
From Beyond - Robert Kurtzman

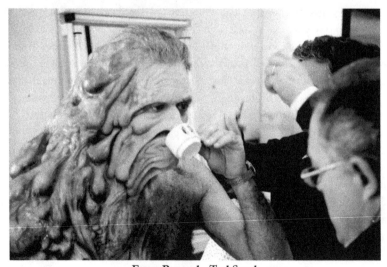
From Beyond - Ted Sorel

By the third week of shooting, Barbara Crampton and I were slowly becoming friendly. She had a good sense of humor and we bonded over the fact that we were both raised around the fair circuit and our shared focus on working out and staying in shape. She was very encouraging that I keep up my dieting and pursuit of becoming an actor. I was inspired by how beautiful, talented, and gracious she was. Barbara was and still is the kind of woman you really liked to hang out with; she always holds her own and fits in with pretty much anyone she chooses. By now, I was becoming a lot more confident in life and her approval and encouragement meant everything to me. We made plans to go work out together when we got back to the states as she was preparing for a big shoot she was going to do for *Playboy* magazine. Even though there was no gym around for me to work out in, I took long walks through Pomezia, listening to cassette tapes that Babs lent me. One of the first cassettes she lent me was a young new singer named Janet Jackson. I had never heard of her up until then.

From Beyond - Jeffrey Combs, Barbara Crampton and Mac Ahlberg

Every day after wrap, the MMI gang and I headed to the studio bar to throw back a few frozen lemon vodkas and then headed to the screening room where we were allowed to watch dailies. After you're done shooting each day, the department heads view the footage from the previous day's shooting. In retrospect, I can't believe that Stuart Gordon even let us wise-crackers in the place, as all we did was laugh and make goofy comments at any of the mistakes we spotted, most of which were made by us. Many times, when you are puppeteering in a film, there are takes where the operators are accidentally spotted or where the puppet isn't moving properly before you get it one hundred percent. It can end in very funny results, especially with some of the complicated puppets and the ungodly amounts of slime we were dealing with. Still to this day, there's a shot that somehow made it into *From Beyond* where you can clearly see me standing next to one of the creatures as I am puppeteering it. It's a close second to the legendary shot where you can see Everett Burrell's finger inside the fish ghoulie's mouth as he puppeteers it in *Ghoulies*. Still, good natured Stuart sat there, laughing along with us, so we always managed to escape being bounced out of the room.

Overall, it was clear that *From Beyond* was turning out to be a great movie. It was beautifully shot, terrifically acted and directed, very colorful, and filled with great make-up effects gags. Everyone involved let out a collective exhale. Stuart was truly a special director.

For the next few weeks, everything went fairly smoothly, minus special effects make-up artist John Naulin cutting his finger off when he accidentally closed his hand in a heavy soundstage door, but who's counting. That was just another day at the office when filming in Italy.

From Beyond - Stuart Gordon and William Butler, Prepping Ken Foree

Days before we wrapped, we shot a huge scene where the leads in the movie were surrounded by flying beetles that materialized when the machine known as the "Resonator" turned on and short-circuited. To achieve the effect of the flying bugs, the Italian physical effects guy painted thousands of Styrofoam beads the color grey. Boxes of these beads were then placed on the sides of the set as bored, cigarette-smoking grips poured them in front of blasting effects fans and sent them hurling at the actors. It was a hilarious mess that required thirty minutes of reset with each take that we did. What the production didn't consider was that the tiny beads would also end up flying into the actor's eyes, ears, nose, and mouth. Pretty much any of our exposed cracks instantly filled with these annoying pellets upon the start of the action. At one point, we had to stop shooting to get one of the tiny beads out of Ken Foree's ear canal as it had wedged its way deep inside his head. He never complained: not once. He just sat there patiently as the set medic removed the plastic bug with a spirit gum coated Q-Tip and we went back to work.

The scene ended with the slightly laughable shot of Ken's character's obliterated skeleton as it lay on the floor moaning in pain and reaching out for help. Apparently, there was a miscommunication in exactly how tall and large Ken was and the meatless skeleton they created was literally half his height and girth. Apparently, not only did the bugs eat him, they also shaved inches off his legs and arms. It wasn't a stellar moment for our team, but it was one of few true snafus in the movie. The rest of the shoot was a complete pleasure as the MMI team and I became closer and each of us found our strengths and how we all could better keep things on track.

That year, Thanksgiving fell on a weekday and the Italian set caterer threw us the best Thanksgiving feast they could muster. We all gathered around the tables in the rustic old cafeteria as they lovingly served us pan-fried packaged turkey slices, boiled potatoes, Panettone cake, the most delicious pasta you've ever eaten in your life and of course, bottles and bottles of red wine to wash it all down. It was not the most traditional of Thanksgivings, but that day, I was truly so thankful for the new direction my life had taken and the marvelous new friends that I was so lucky to be surrounded by.

We were all very grateful for the Italians' kindness and their loving attempt to give us our holiday. We all toasted John Buechler, who sat at the head of the table, dressed in his finest Thanksgiving tank-top, shorts, and flip-flops. John had happily brought us all together; he was a guy who never hesitated to see the good that each of us were capable of. We were genuinely thankful for the opportunity he had laid before us. That whole first trip to Italy was such a blessing. Being in Rome truly changed my entire life for the better.

One of the many things I really loved about living there was the appreciation and respect I gained when I watched the Italians taking their time when eating a meal, being good friends, and finding time for themselves and family members. I was beaming with happiness. The kid from Fresno had not only somehow gang-busted his way into the movie-making business, he was also doing it in Italy of all places, and with friends who loved and accepted him.

14

THEY'LL GET YOU IN THE END

The Christmas break arrived and we all headed back to the States to spend time with our families and prepare for *Ghoulies 2*. I was so excited to finally start doing on-camera work for my part in the movie. I was going to be playing "Merle" a nerdy dude who meets an early fate from the hands of the Ghoulies. The character was not sizeable or pivotal, but it was all mine. Charlie's father Albert Band was directing the film and I couldn't wait to work with him. Albert was a hilarious older guy who after escaping France during World War II, had gotten his start working in movies, having assistant directed for John Huston's *The Asphalt Jungle*. He later went on to write the adaptation of *The Red Badge of Courage* and direct many films including some of the old Steve Reeves *Hercules* movies in which Charlie Band himself played Hercules' son. He's also the guy who directed *Dracula's Dog*.

I met with the *Ghoulies 2* wardrobe person and loathed what she was dressing me in but said nothing. For some reason, she saw Merle the nerd dressed in ill-fitting clothes and leather go-go fringe.

By now, Buechler was also trusting me to do more creative things in his shop and he decided to give me a shot designing the paint schemes for a couple of the Ghoulie puppets. The crew had continued to grow and shift as Howard Berger and Robert Kurtzman left the team to go work on several higher profile freelance projects of their own. They eventually teamed up with the future Executive Producer of *The Walking Dead* and *Creepshow* series, Greg Nicotero, and founded the Oscar-winning KNB Effects group. One day, Kurtzman came by MMI after hours to do a head cast mold of someone for a film that he was freelancing on. He asked me if I would lend him a hand and I agreed. A young African American actor came in about an hour later and we molded the guy's head in dental alginate and plaster bandages. I had no idea who he was or what the movie was about, but later, after he left, Kurtzman mentioned that the head cast was for an old age make-up in an upcoming Steven Spielberg movie.

"It's an adaptation of a book that was really popular about an abused woman living in the south," Bob said. "Spielberg is going to get an Oscar nomination for it, for sure." I later realized that the actor was Willard E. Pugh who played the character Harpo and the film was *The Color Purple*. In the same month, I not only worked on a massive Spielberg movie inspired by a Pulitzer Prize-winning novel, but also a film where tiny hell-spawn beasts climb out of the toilet to kill you. Just another day at the office in the world of 80s filmmaking.

"Bob Villard is coming by the shop today for another photoshoot with one of his clients," Buechler told us. The MMI crew shot each other uncomfortable looks, as Bob's visits were always strange. Bob Villard was a friendly-enough but guarded, well-established publicist and manager for kids, mostly young boys, including Tobey Maguire, Leonardo DiCaprio and Noah Hathaway, long before they were famous. Bob strolled into the shop about once a month, usually with a twelve-year-old male in tow. He often had the young performer pose with the various monster displays in John's shop as he snapped publicity pictures. It was only a matter of minutes before the kid was typically taking his shirt off for a more extensive session.

"Am I the only one aware that this guy is a complete chicken-hawk?" I brazenly blurted out once after he left.

Most everyone on the crew looked at me with terrified, knowing eyes. Some heads secretly nodded in agreement, but no one ever saw anything beyond shirtless pics, so there was no proof. That didn't stop my loudmouth. "Bob has short-eyes," I told Buechler, who laughed at my suspicion, telling me I was crazy, though I could see his wheels turning. *Short-eyes* is a prison term for a pedophile, if you've lived your life without picking up that lingo. From that moment on, Villard was quietly referred to as "Chicken-Hawk Villard" as he continued to appear at the shop with a bevy of tween boys who always ended up shirtless and draped across one of our dusty old monster suits.

Referring to Bob as a chicken-hawk without knowing what his situation was would have been incredibly mean-spirited, unfair, and in fact, illegal had Bob not eventually been busted for trying to get teens drunk at his house and taking sexually provocative pictures of them. Sure enough, the guy did have short-eyes. Not long after that, he was also arrested for possessing child porn and when he got out of that, he was arrested for committing a lewd act upon a child. It was revealed years later in the "deeply underground," very hard to find, whistle-blowing documentary *An Open Secret* that he had for many years been taking sexually suggestive pictures of kids and selling them online without the performers or their parents' knowledge. Where there is smoke, there's a perv, people. Keep your kids close to home.

The latest MMI crew continued to evolve including a core group that remained the same for the better part of a year. It included John Criswell, Mike Deak, Jeff Farley, Eryn Krueger, Thom Floutz, and Kenneth J. Hall. By then, Criswell and Deak were veterans when it came to working on films in Rome. Eryn was just eighteen at the time, an eager, talented young girl who started out as an assistant but later progressed so much in the make-up world that she eventually accrued thirty-eight Emmy nominations and eight wins. She is now one of the Executive Producers of *American Horror Story*. Everyone else also moved on to do very well for themselves after the good old days. Deak worked on several Michael Bay productions, Criswell runs the Jim Henson Company FX mechanics shop, and Kenneth Hall helped shape and write the first *Puppet Master* screenplay as well as ran his own busy costume company.

But back in the day, the MMI gang were pretty much just a bunch of hopeful, fun-loving punks. We were young, thin, long-haired, talented, cocky and—need I mention—gorgeous. "Are you guys in a rock band?" The stewardesses often asked as we loaded onto our plane flights to Rome.

"Sort of," John Criswell answered, jokingly asking her to not bring attention to us.

The gang and I arrived in Rome and we hit the ground running. We were going to be working on several movies at once: *Ghoulies 2*, then another movie, *The Caller*. Since

I was going to be acting in *Ghoulies*, I asked Buechler if I could do effects work on *The Caller* so I could remain focused on my acting part for the other film. He agreed and made me the key effect make-up artist on the movie. There wasn't much to do, anyway. The picture starred Madolyn Smith from *Urban Cowboy* and Malcolm McDowell from…well, pretty much everything, including *Cat People*, *Caligula*, and a little film titled *A Clockwork Orange*, directed by Stanley Kubrick.

JUST WHEN YOU TOUGHT
IT WAS SAFE TO GO BACK
INTO THE BATHROOM…

GHOULIES
II

Ken Hall, John Criswell, William Butler and Mike Deak at Empire Studios

Once again, the house set used in Empire Picture's *Dolls* and *From Beyond* was put to use as the reeking slime from the last project was mopped up and the place reconfigured into a different layout. By that time, I had been around the make-up room long enough that I could be trusted to adequately, but certainly not expertly, apply the special effects make-up appliances. Since most of the time the gags I was doing were covered in blood or slime, I couldn't really screw it up. I was assigned to apply the wounds and the surprise-ending make-up on Malcolm himself.

We spent hours a day with Malcolm, and I grew to love him as he regaled us with stories from his fascinating movie-making past. He told us all about doing the film *Caligula* which upon first reading was not the shocking XXX porn film as it was eventually released. Malcolm explained how he and the other cast members (including Sir John Gielgud, Peter O'Toole, and Helen Mirren) had shot what they believed to be a high-end period piece about the tragic fall of Rome's most infamous Caesar, Gaius Germanicus Caligula, but what was released turned out to essentially be the most expensive porn film ever made.

The film was originally written by Gore Vidal and directed by Italian filmmaker Tinto Brass, but Vidal headed for the hills and bailed on the project after Brass polished the script and omitted much of his original work. What's worse, after the main actors wrapped shooting, *Penthouse* magazine executive Bob Guccione, who was also one of the producers of the film, went back and shot several real sex scenes featuring his favorite *Penthouse* pets and cut them into the movie. Apparently, Malcolm and the other actors nearly fell out of their theater seats as random scenes featuring hardcore, up-close love-making popped-up in between the narrative. Regardless of how raunchy the end result was, McDowell clearly survived the film's scathing reception. The movie ended up making millions and is still considered to be a cult favorite. Just don't watch it with your grandmother unless she's a whore.

The Caller - John Criswell

The Caller was a thriller produced by Frank Yablans, the producer who went on to produce the popular gorilla movie *Congo*. The story followed a mysterious woman and an even more mysterious stranger who comes to her home after his car has supposedly broken down. After a twisted game of mental cat and mouse, it's revealed that no one is who they really seem. We eventually learn in a twist that comes out of nowhere that Malcolm is, in fact, an android who's been sent to track Smith down and exterminate her. Before he gets the chance, she outsmarts and short circuits him by throwing boiling water in his face. John Criswell had built a flawless mechanical arm and robotic head for the final reveal and make-up had been created by Buechler for Malcolm to wear for the close-ups of his final monologue.

Though Malcolm and I were really getting to know one another, I was very nervous about applying the "robot face" appliance that Buechler had cranked out. It did not look up to snub at all. Also, Malcolm was an actor of tremendous experience and I could tell that he was very quick to point out if something was, in his opinion, substandard. Early on, he told me about the hours he had spent in the make-up chair on *Cat People* being transformed into a man-panther hybrid only to later watch the movie and find himself hidden in the shadows. He grew to trust me and the last thing I wanted to do was piss him off, and I knew he was going to hate that goofy-looking robot make-up. Since the movie itself was a complete afterthought and not on our original schedule, Buechler had gone into the shop and quickly pounded out (literally with a hammer, I assume) a very sloppy *Terminator* rip-off. It looked very rushed, more like a buck-toothed Mortimer Snerd puppet than a high-tech killer robot.

For days, I kept the appliance hidden under the make-up table so Malcolm couldn't see it. Whenever he asked to check it out, I made up off the cuff excuses like "Oh, it's still baking," or "I put it on the roof so the paint would dry faster," or "It's still clearing customs," anything to keep from showing him what I was certain was going to make him blow his stack. The gang from MMI laughed at me as I grew more nervous the closer it came to pasting the stupid thing onto his face. Malcolm was such a great guy, and the last thing I wanted to do was let him down by making him look goofy.

One night, he picked us all up in his town car after shooting and took us on a whirlwind tour of Rome's very best nightclubs. To say the evening was magical would be a vast understatement as everywhere we went, we were subjected to the best treatment possible. The Italian public gushed over him. It was clear we were not only working with a movie star, but a very decent and generous person.

Finally, the night before I was to apply the ill-fated make-up, Malcolm and I found out that we had a four a.m. make-up call so I could be finished applying it in time for us to shoot by nine. Since I normally rode to work with the rest of the gang and their call wasn't until eight, Malcolm offered me a ride to the studio in his car. Around three in the morning, his driver showed up to pick me up and then proceeded to the center of Rome to pick up Malcolm at the Excelsior Hotel. It was still dark as we drove the hour half back into town and up to the Empire Studios, where we were surprised to find the place sitting in total darkness. There was not only no one at the unlit studio, there was also no one at the guard gate.

I sat quietly as Malcolm calmly asked the driver to see if the gate was unlocked. It wasn't. There was no one in sight. What's worse was we had no way of calling anyone to get an ETA. Malcolm and I sat there patiently as four-thirty a.m. rolled by, then five a.m. I think it was at about five-forty-five a.m. when he calmly said with a smile. "Well, we're giving them five more minutes and then we're going back into Rome to get a proper breakfast and some coffee."

I didn't know what to say, I knew I would be in big trouble if he wasn't ready in time to shoot, but before I could object, we were already on our way back to Rome. One hour later, I was at the bottom of the Spanish Steps in Piazza di Spagna, having a huge American Breakfast at Babington's Tea Room. Malcolm sat calmly sipping coffee with his eyebrows pleasantly raised in satisfaction as he read the *New York Times* from cover to cover. Never once did he even glance at his watch. After my last bite of bacon and the very last page of his newspaper was turned, Malcolm glanced over to me and casually asked if I were ready to go to work. I nodded. After all, it was well after ten o'clock in the morning and the shit had surely hit the fan. We were six hours past our call time. Another hour later, our car rolled up to the guard gate where the guard had been joined by three bickering Italians.

Malcolm calmly rolled down his window and smiled as one frazzled Italian producer ran up. "Where have you been?!" he sharply asked.

"Oh, I'm sorry. I thought perhaps the shoot had been cancelled this morning, since we sat here for close to two hours waiting for someone to open the gate." The Italian swallowed as he backed off. Malcolm added, "I suppose tonight the guard will double-check his alarm clock?"

The producer sheepishly nodded as the gates creaked open. We finally made our way into the make-up room as I nervously glued that damn Mortimer Snerd-looking make-up appliance on Malcolm's face. After the morning he'd had, I fully expected him to dive out of the chair and punch me, but he didn't. He just sat there and let me do my thing. I could tell by the way he was watching me that he knew I wasn't liking what I was seeing as I pasted on a forced smile. When all else fails in film, utilize robot-face. Never ever let anyone ever see you panic or ever show signs of worry. Every now and then he had me stop what I was doing so he could turn his head and check out all of the make-up's angles. After a few beats, he nodded for me to continue my work. The biggest problem with the design of the make-up was that the fake teeth that were part of the appliance rested on his own lips, causing him to look like a buck-toothed jackass. I snuck downstairs and did a huge shot of frozen limoncello to calm my trembling hands. (Truthfully, my hands were trembling from the previous night's drinking, but who's counting?) I was sweating profusely from nerves. After I had finally gotten the appliance fully glued down and colored, Malcolm said only "thank you." He just got up, turned his head, looking at the angles, and went to his dressing room.

We walked together to the soundstage as I hung my head in low shame, waiting for everyone to burst into laughter upon the sight of him and for me to get fired. But as soon as we walked into the stage, Malcolm crossed to the director of photography before anyone else even had a chance to see it. "It's best if this make-up is shot from this angle," he said and turned his head to a certain position where, low and behold, it didn't look awful. The D.P. agreed and Malcolm looked over at me with a wink. "It's going to be great, thank you very much," he said.

From that point on, no one questioned if the thing looked goofy or not. The star of the movie had given it a thumbs-up and that was good enough. I guess I should have considered that an actor with twenty-years more experience than me might have an idea how to sell something on film. And that he did. Take after take, Malcolm McDowell held his head at the perfect angle for each shot and somehow helped us sell that goofy gag. The end result on film was very cool. I really lucked out that he was such a team player. We got through the day and shot the entire sequence without fail. Criswell's mechanical arm and head went off without a hitch and I finally left the studio that night in total relief; *The Caller* was officially done shooting and I was to start acting in *Ghoulies 2* the very next day. I never got a chance to say goodbye to Malcolm, but I was very pleased to work with him a few more times over the years. He has always been a consummate professional and approachable guy.

As I said earlier, I am the luckiest movie nerd on the planet.

Finishing the Paint Jobs on the Ghoulies

The first day of shooting on *Ghoulies 2* was a major event for me. Early in the morning, I went into hair and make-up where I met the some of the other actors. Starr Andreff (who had just finished acting in the television series *Falcon Crest*), Jon Pennell, Sasha Jenson, and Kerry Remsen, a sweet young girl and the daughter of actor Burt Remsen, were all friendly and as eager as I was to get started. This was, however, to be my very first, but certainly not my last, experience where a few of the actors on set postured to try and pull rank on each other.

"Who's your agent?" one of them said in a slightly condescending tone.

"No one," I replied shamefully, feeling like the Charlie Brown who'd been handed a rock on Halloween.

"You got that dork thing down, man: you must really be one," another one of the actors said to me with a snide sneer.

I quickly learned to be quiet and keep to myself, a practice that I continued through most of the time that I was an actor.

By far, the coolest actor in the film for me was a man by the name of Royal Dano. Aside from his vast body of amazing film and television work including *The Rifleman*, *Bonanza*, and *Gunsmoke*, he was also well-known in the "Disney-nerd" world for performing the voice of Abraham Lincoln in the "Great Moments with Mr. Lincoln" attraction in all of the Disney parks.

Ghoulies 2 was a horror-comedy that took place as a traveling carnival stops in a small town and is unexpectedly put under attack by the mischievous and most often murderous Ghoulies. The sequel was designed to be more of a comedy than the original with loads of slapstick gags and lots of bloody fun. Since a lot of the movie took place at night, the production had completely blacked out one of the studios' biggest soundstages with massive runners of black fabric and had created an entire carnival inside it. A fully functioning Ferris wheel, bumper cars, carnival games, and many other attractions were set up as the makeshift playground where the Ghoulies would unleash their playfully murderous wrath. You felt like you were outside as the production even went as far to put twinkling star lights on the black tarps to create a night sky. It was a magnificent set, and it wasn't until years later that I ever worked on another as huge or elaborate. Much of the story revolved around "Satan's Den," a seemingly endless haunted house attraction at the carnival that was somehow supposed to fit on the back of a single semi-truck bed. The place featured room after room of different horror-themed areas, including a pit and pendulum set, which for some reason had an actual, working pit and pendulum torture device in it.

I got to the set and met up with our director Albert Band. I was so nervous. I had waited for a cool moment like this to unfold forever and all I wanted to do was please him and experience it all. Albert and the director of photography finally got to my first shot. In the scene, I was supposed to climb a set of stairs at the "Satan's Den" attraction and give the leading man a hard time before entering the place. He was a nice enough actor named Damon Martin, a kid whose claim to fame was his role as the motocross kid in *Pee-wee's Big Adventure*. I looked around the place. All eyes were on me. This was it. My very first shot and the chance to finally put my studying to use. Albert climbed up onto a crane and was lifted into the air. A man stepped in front of me with the clapper in front of my face.

"*Ghoulies 2*, Scene 4, take one!"

I flinched as he clacked it hard and stepped away, and Albert looked down at me and yelled, "Action!"

The crane lowered and pushed forward, I took a breath, made my way up the stairs, delivered my lines, and entered the haunted house set.

"Cut, moving on!" Albert yelled as he was lowered back down onto the sand.

He climbed off the crane and lit a cigar.

I poked my head around the corner of the set, looking over at him as he spoke Italian to the D.P. The assistant director crossed over to me and asked for me to get ready for my next shot. "We're only doing one take?" I asked, confused.

The A.D. shrugged as he moved onto his next order of business.

I stepped off the platform and crossed over to Albert.

"Mr. Band?" I sheepishly said, trying to get his attention.

Albert turned to me with a pleasant smile. "Yes, dear?"

"Was...that...good? Was that...what you wanted?" I nervously asked. I could barely get the words out.

"Was that good?" he said to himself, taking a puff of his cigar. "Hmm... was that what I wanted?" He rubbed his chin, then turned to the director of photography. "Was it in focus?" he asked.

"Yep," the D.P. replied.

"Kid, you were fucking brilliant," he said to me with a smile.

And with that, Ladies and Gentlemen, I officially learned my first lesson in how not to fish for a compliment on a low budget movie. I realized that filmmaking of that nature was seldom high art but more so, a task. I also learned that Albert Band had a hell of a sense of humor. One take was the norm from that moment on. We shot so fast that sometimes that I thought we were rehearsing only to realize that we had just filmed the rehearsal.

Ghoulies 2 - Dude! Your Tunes!

Ghoulies 2 – Hitting the High Note for the Cat Ghoulie

Ghoulies 2

The days on set began to drag, however, as we soon began to fall behind schedule. The insane amount of puppetry the movie called for really slowed things down as it took loads of time to find places to hide the operators, especially when there were three and four puppets performing in the same scene. Often times, everyone lay crammed on top of one another, wedged under a false floor as they tried to get the Ghoulies moving just right, which was no easy task.

A second unit director was brought in from the States, a meek and mildly clueless older guy. Word was that he had been second unit director on the 1976 version of *King Kong* and was supposedly going to get us all caught up. Frankly, he was mostly lost when it came to dealing with the Ghoulie puppets. Because weeks were being added on a daily basis and Ken Hall had to go back to the States due to schedule conflicts, I was asked to do double-duty and rejoin the puppet unit to lend an extra hand.

One day on the second unit was particularly hilarious when the director began calling out direction to Ken, despite the latter having been gone for two weeks. We were all under a platform and out of view with puppets on our arms as the director yelled out "Okay, Ken?"

"Yes?" one of us yelled out in Ken Hall's legendary and unmistakable vernacular.

"Okay, Ken, wiggle the ears. Very good!" (This, despite the fact that the fish Ghoulie's ears had no ear wiggling mechanism.)

"Yes," another one of us shouted back.

"Now, Ken? Wiggle the eyes...very good!"

"Yes!"

"Now, Ken? Wiggle the nose..."

"Yes." (There was no nose mechanism either.) The exchange was a constant source of hilarious entertainment. The director had countless conversations with Ken Hall as each of us took a turn doing Ken's voice.

We had regular meetings on how to execute some of the more complicated puppet gags when it came to the Ghoulies themselves. Producer Frank Hildebrand held court in the studio conference room and we all brainstormed ideas on how to better execute the upcoming gags.

"Okay, in this next scene, the fish Ghoulie peeks in the window, climbs inside, hops down, and runs across the room. After finding a big butcher knife, he cartwheels across the floor, jumps up into the air in an impressive karate kick and then splits a man's face in two with his steely blade. What can you do for me in that scene?" he asked the MMI puppet patrol.

After a solid beat of quiet, "We can make him peek around the corner," we replied. The concrete floors in the soundstage where the carnival was built were solid, so there were very few places to puppeteer the way we wished that we could. For certain, there would be no cartwheeling.

Ghoulies 2 - William Butler, Thom Floutz and Mike Deak

Ghoulies 2 - Puppeteering the Flying Ghoulie

The days were fun, but the nights were a blast as the actors and FX guys got closer. We closed the studio bar and then headed to the center of Rome or back to our hotel where we kept the party going late into the night. Being so young, it was no problem for any of us to party all night and bounce back into action by morning. One night, Mike

Deak and a couple others raced the rental car on the backlot and flipped it into the *Red Sonja* moat. Everyone drunkenly headed out and helped flip the car upright again.

We continued our daily production meetings. All of the lead producers on the film became frazzled as things continued to drag at a snail's pace. The number of puppets in each shot were slowing production more and more each day. The producers started to do everything in their power to try and keep the movie in order. After watching the dailies of a scene where Deak played a grouchy clown who gets knocked into a dunk tank, one producer sat up in his theater chair. He noticed that one of the extras was completely checked out in the scene and was blankly staring at the camera front and center in an important reverse shot. The extra, was a beard stubble-sporting drag-queen who was not a convincing lady in the least. We all watched laughing as she divided her attention between the action of the scene and staring directly into the lens.

"Just look at that drag queen!" the producer yelled. "He's laughing in every shot! He's looking right down the barrel of the lens! Look at him: he's a fucking disaster! He's made this footage completely unusable!"

At that moment, the drag queen glanced right back down the lens as if to defy him. The producer pointed his finger at the screen. "Cunt!" he shouted.

Another day, we were shooting a scene in which Royal Dano was supposedly electrocuted and falls to the floor in death. Mike Deak and I were operating Ghoulie puppets from below, so we were lying right at his feet just out of frame. The crew set up spark squibs on an electric chair that Royal was standing next to and after a few lines, they ignited them as he pretended to be shocked and then fall down. For some reason, every time he fell to the floor, he farted uncontrollably. When I say fart, I mean the kind of blast that echoes through the entire room like the screeches of a furious duck. Mike and I stared at each other, afraid to breathe as we were not only about to burst into laughter, but we were also enveloped in a huge cloud of gas.

Royal never said a word: each time, he smiled as if he didn't hear anything, brushed himself off, and got up to reset for the scene, only to fall to the floor and once again rip another huge unbridled fart as he fell. This happened over and over again to the point where you really had to wonder where the gas was all coming from. At a certain point, he surely must have crapped himself. Still, he was nothing but smiles. To this day, I bet Mike Deak and I are the only two guys ever farted on by Abraham Lincoln.

When the shoot was nearly over, after another night of heavy debauchery in Rome with the actors, I decided to crash at Jon Pennell's hotel room as opposed to taking a cab all the way back to the beach. The phone in his room rang at about 4 a.m. We were both still hammered.

"It's for you," Pennel said to me, drunkenly handing me the phone.

"For me?" I said as my eyes sprung open.

"Dude, it's your mom," he laughed.

"My mom?" I took the phone in shock. Sure enough, it was my mother.

"I'm sorry to be calling so late, but I am phoning you to ask permission to have what's left of your car towed away."

"What?" I answered.

"Apparently, your Monte Carlo has been stripped and is sitting on cinder blocks somewhere in North Hollywood," she explained. "The police looked my name up on the registration and called to tell me that there is hardly anything left and that you need to get it off the road."

A million questions popped into my head. For one, how the hell did my mother figure out how to find me in a random hotel room in Rome? I didn't ask. Although I was heartbroken at the idea of my car being a thing of my past, I agreed to have what was left of it towed away. She said she would arrange it and I flopped back into bed, staring at the ceiling.

My beloved Hotel Monte Carlo was not only a great ride, but was at one time, also my temporary housing. Going home to no car was sure going to be interesting while living in Los Angeles.

You Know You've Made Your Mark When Your Face Hawks Ghoulie Toys

A month later, we finally got to the last shot of *Ghoulies 2*, when the giant fish Ghoulie gets blown up after being tricked into eating a bomb disguised as one of the little demons. Effects team member Thom Floutz brought the full-sized fishy beast to life with his high-stepping, wiggly-monster suit strut and the time had come for the beastie to meet his maker. The Italian physical effect crew had us cut the suit into pieces. We then lightly glued it onto a wooden skeleton covered in rubber innards. The Italians not only loaded the suit with sticks of dynamite, but also wrapped its legs and arms with primer cord. The hope was to blow the fish Ghoulie up enough to bring him to his knees as he fell dead, but when the Italians finally threw the detonator switch, the suit blew up so intensely that it was instantly vaporized. Everyone ducked as chunks of burning polyfoam rained down all around us.

"He blew up real good," Deak said with a satisfied smile.

It was a fine finish to an amazing trip.

15

ACTING BUG-BITES

We headed back to the United States to start prepping the next few projects at MMI which included *The Garbage Pail Kids Movie*, *Spellcaster*, *Transformations*, and something coming up called *Cellar Dweller* that Buechler was going to direct. We were going to be busier than ever, but my interest in make-up effects was waning as acting was all I could think about. I planned on getting an agent just as soon as I got back in town and starting the process of changing all of my focus onto becoming a working actor.

As soon as I was back, actress Barbara Crampton and I got on a solid schedule of workouts. She had her *Playboy* shoot coming up and I was hellbent on keeping my weight off. We took two aerobic classes a day, one in the morning and one at night. The classes were held at the legendary Sports Connection on Santa Monica Boulevard, the location of the infamous workout movie *Perfect* and the place was packed for every class. It was the 80s and we were all decked out in garish workout gear that certainly reflected the time. Headbands and leg warmers were required attire.

Two weeks after that, I somehow landed an agent interview with Flo Joseph of the Flo Joseph Talent Agency. Her office was upstairs in a run-down mini-mall on Ventura Boulevard that's now a weed store. Flo was a gregarious woman who had a small but impressive roster of actors that had been with her since they first started out, including Frederic Forrest, Forest Whitaker, and Herta Ware. Flo and I had instant chemistry as she signed me on the spot and sent me to her friend to have my first pictures shot. I was thrilled to finally have an agent and get into the auditioning pool.

Selected
Artists
Congratulates

WILLIAM BUTLER

on the completion of his
leading role in
New Line Cinemas

THE TEXAS CHAINSAW MASSACRE III

Opening November 3, 1989
INQUIRES 818·905·5744

Postcard Sent Out by My First Agent, Flo Joseph

WILLIAM BUTLER

My First 8 x 10 Headshot, If David Hasselhoff and Martina Navratilova had a Baby

At home, my roommates and I started to go out on Friday nights. I had never gotten any attention as a fat teenager, but boy, was I popular as a thin adult. My drug use had also graduated from once a year to most Friday nights a month as my friends and I headed out to the bars and party the night away. I drank myself silly and then staggered over to the gas station on the corner of Franklin and Gower at 5 a.m. to get myself aspirin and bottled water. I was slowly evolving into an L.A. cliché and I was proud of it.

Yes, I know I looked like a hot lesbian

I was also figuring out that I was more interested in men than in women. Despite having solid hang-ups about connecting, it was becoming very clear what side of the fence I was going to end up on. Because it was the eighties and I was an actor, I played my cards very close to the vest in hopes of not sinking my career before it even left the dock.

All the new developments in my life kept me very distracted while I was working at MMI this time around. Instead of paying attention to what I was doing, I was constantly checking my machine for audition appointments, pow-wowing with Flo Joseph, and daydreaming about the new direction my life was heading in, as well as doing a mild amount of quiet whoring. At work, I became more trusted artistically as Buechler asked me to paint all of the mechanical heads for *The Garbage Pail Kids Movie* for what ended up being an abysmal and excruciating film to work on. Thanks to me, there almost wasn't a movie at all.

After painting all of the completed mechanical Garbage Pail Kid heads, meticulous creations that took months to put together, the MMI crew and I made our way onto the set. The movie was so low budget that they weren't even filming on a soundstage but rather in an old warehouse in the valley off of Sherman Way. The building was easily a hundred degrees as there was no air conditioning and the little people playing the Garbage Pail Kids were dropping like flies. The mechanical heads were huge and heavy with zero visibility or ventilation. Two minutes after the little actors were suited up, they started staggering around, running into one another and often overheating to the point of fainting.

The shit really hit the fan on the first scene where the little buggers had to talk. All of the voices had been pre-recorded and puppeteers littered the floor around each of the characters as they all tugged on cables, animating the faces while the actor strutted around and danced. On the very first word of the very first song, the mouths of the Garbage Pail Kids opened and huge rips suddenly tore in the foam latex from each corner of their smiling faces. Every single one of them looked as if they had been sliced a new grin, mafia-style. I remember seeing John Criswell's expression drop as the director called cut in a complete panic. Shooting for the day was cancelled as the producers lost their shit, chewing us all out. No one had an answer as to why this happened. We had tested the heads for weeks before I painted them and they were all working just fine. We took all of the foam rubber masks back to the shop and scrambled for a solution to our huge problem. The heads were now a complete disaster.

"Why do you think that happened?" I asked a very distraught John Criswell.

"I have no idea," he said, looking at me as if he were thinking otherwise.

"Maybe it's the heat in that place?" I said.

"Yeah...no..." Criswell waited for me to come up with the correct answer. "Out of curiosity," he said, unblinking, "how much medical adhesive did you put in the paint when you painted the heads?" Back in the day, when you painted foam latex, you had to do it with a mixture of perfectly measured parts of acrylic paint and a flexible medical adhesive that kept the paint soft. PAX paint it was called. Using acrylic paint on its own wouldn't work because it would dry stiff and cause the foam latex to tear the moment there was any flex or movement to it. It was at that very moment that I realized that in my distracted daydreaming of becoming an actor, I had forgotten to put any adhesive at all into the paints. None at all. I hesitated for a beat, trying my best not to flinch or indicate my internal terror.

"Um...I put in the usual amount," I said, lying through my teeth.

"Hmm, weird," John said looking at me as if he knew the rotten truth.

I had fucked up royally.

The crew and I spent the next two days puttying the cuts in the heads' destroyed mouths with a mixture of cotton and latex. Instead of fixing the problem, it only made the situation worse as the rubbery mixture ended up looking like scar tissue when the mouths stretched open and closed. All through the shoot, I never admitted that it was all my fault. All through the years, I kept it to myself until now. But come on, Criswell: you knew, didn't you?

The Garbage Pail Kids Movie

The Garbage Pail Kids Movie

"I have something for you to audition for," Ken Hall said to me over lunch at the Creole restaurant at the Farmer's Market. Ken had been writing a lot as a screenwriter for the home video market and was quickly working his way up the food chain. The picture was a horror film called *Terror Night* and was produced by a guy by the name of Nick Marino. Marino had previously executive produced *Hollywood Chainsaw Hookers*, a successful cult film by home video entrepreneur legend Fred Olen Ray, and was ready to branch out on his own and give producing a try.

Marino was grouchy and most-likely mafia-adjacent (or wanted to be perceived that way, anyway). He was a stern guy who lived in a bungalow in Studio City where he housed an entire family of misfits and runaways. Ken had been hired to write and direct the project and I was just happy to have a shot at auditioning for one of the leads. He called me in to his offices on Gower and I read a few pages of the script for him and Marino. The part was once again for another nerdy teen, but it was a big part and I was happy to have a shot at a project where I was in pretty much every scene. *Terror Night* followed a group of kids who decide to break into the sprawling manor of a long dead silent movie star and one by one are all taken out by murderous characters from his most popular movies. After several auditions and a chemistry read with actress Staci Greason, Ken Hall called me to tell me that I got the part. I was elated to be acting on a film where I wasn't also expected to have my hand crammed up a puppet's ass, for once. In a week's time, the other actors were also cast including a good-looking kid named John Wildman. Rumors of several celebrity stunt castings were also a buzz as we prepared for the film. That was right about the time that Ken called me to tell me that he had quit.

According to Ken, he and Marino had a huge altercation that was beyond repair and he had abruptly left the production. I was so glad when Ken assured me that he didn't expect me to quit as a result of his departing as I really wanted to stay on board. I was really going to miss Ken on the ride: he had given me one of my first cool breaks. We all were also very surprised to hear that a hardcore porn film director named Fred Lincoln had been chosen as Ken's replacement.

Fred Lincoln was a funny, older, long-haired man who had not only directed several triple-x porn films but had apparently appeared in a few as well. Most of the cast was so young that the idea of a porn director taking the helm was shocking, but once we got to know Fred, we quickly realized that he not only was a terrific guy, but he also really understood actors and knew how to communicate as a director. We quickly grew to respect the guy. It was one of life's early lessons to never judge a book by its cover.

We started shooting our first scenes in a Sisters of the Immaculate Heart Convent in Los Feliz. The place was a sprawling mansion estate owned by a bunch of nuns who hilariously stood around eating our craft services snacks while watching us actors run up and down the halls covered in blood and screaming bloody murder. The convent is the same building that has been in the news a lot lately as it's the property that Katy Perry has been in a legal war over after she bought it amid much protest from the nuns who now feel they are entitled to a cut of the sales profits. It's funny to me that their argument for not wanting Katy Perry to buy the property is that "she has joked about selling her soul to devil" when they themselves were standing in the room laughing and eating fried chicken as they watched actor John Wildman be brutally dismembered. The Lord works in mysterious ways, indeed.

As the filming progressed, we were surprised to see what famous person was going to show up and make a cameo in the movie. One day, I was sitting on set in the convent when I realized a person had taken the seat next to me. I turned to see who it was only to find actor Allen Hale Jr. also known as "The Skipper" from *Gilligan's Island*, sitting there. I almost fell out of my chair as I did a complete double-take. He was pretty much wearing his exact costume from *Gilligan's Island*, including his skipper cap, and instead of smiling and bumbling like everyone was used to seeing him, he simply sat there, scowling at me. I was still very new to being on a movie set in an acting capacity only and I was very nervous about appearing like I didn't fit in or looking like I didn't know what I was doing as, let's face it: I barely did know what I was doing. I tried to open my mouth and say "hello," but I was so nervous at the sight of him that nothing came out. My eyes just went wide as my entire childhood spent in front of the TV set watching him flashed before me.

Hale stared at me disapprovingly as he waited for me to spit it out, but I just couldn't form a sentence. Instead, I played it cool and nodded to him as I put my Walkman headphones on and looked away. From that moment on, we remained completely alienated from one another. Allen refused to talk to me and I didn't look at him in between shots even as we stood no more than a couple of feet apart. The more he glared at me, the quieter I got. It was my first, but certainly not last, experience when you meet someone famous and they aren't anything like you hoped or expected they would be. Never meet your idols, people. It can seriously blow up in your face and working with this guy was certainly no three-hour tour. It felt instead like a few days of total tension that you could cut with a knife.

As the day progressed, I constantly caught Hale glaring at me over and over. I put my Walkman earphones on each time and stared into space. Later, before he left, I heard him talking to the publicity lady, telling her that his biggest disappointment with young actors in the new Hollywood was how completely rude and disrespectful they were. He finally finished and left, making sure to shoot one last dagger in my direction.

Not long after we wrapped, Hale sadly passed away. It's a bitter, albeit hilarious pill to swallow, knowing that the Skipper from *Gilligan's Island* died hating you. I often think of how different things would've been if I had just regrouped and been brave enough to say "hello." Sadly, I had seen how some of the actors in *Ghoulies 2* were behaving and thought that nervousness should be covered with cold and arrogant posturing. I was very wrong, very wrong indeed. I wish I had been friendlier and I still very much regret my attitude towards him to this day.

Working with and completely hating actor Cameron Mitchell is a different story altogether.

Mitchell had been a huge star in his career, having gotten his start on Broadway, eventually moving to tinsel-town to appear in many major films featuring some of Hollywood's biggest stars including Clark Gable and Lana Turner. This guy had been in everything, including originating the role of "Willy Loman" in *Death of a Salesman* and starring opposite Marilyn Monroe and Lauren Bacall in *How to Marry a Millionaire*. He was a revered actor throughout his youth and well into his 50s. Sadly, by the time that Mitchell had worked his way to *Terror Night,* he was clearly over it all. By then, director Fred Lincoln was also out of the picture, suddenly and abruptly replaced by our third director, the completely cantankerous 1953 *House of Wax* helmer, Andre De Toth. Andre was, at one time, a very well-known Hollywood commodity himself, having been nominated for an Oscar for outstanding writing on the film *The Gunfighter* among working on many films that are still considered classics. He was a brilliant talent and would be the first one to tell you so. Just like Cameron Mitchell's, Andre De Toth's joy-train had apparently left the station for the very last time.

I was so excited to meet De Toth, having been a huge fan of *House of Wax*, but I found out very quickly that the feeling was in no way mutual. Andre had been dragged into the production by Marino who knew him through a friend of a friend and he was not happy about it. De Toth was a very old guy who sported a faded eyepatch and a thick Hungarian accent. Nearly all of his limbs were covered in medical braces of some sort, including his neck, which was bound with a thick plastic support to help him hold his head upright. He could barely walk around. We were never really sure of what had happened to him, but never got a chance to ask, being that he mostly bitched and complained to us all day. He'd yell, "You act like a fucking wooden puppet!" (which was probably true but hurtful nonetheless). The less praise I got, the worse I was in a scene. Working with a mean director guaranteed a full day of me nervously sweating, questioning my choices, stumbling through scenes, and sometimes forgetting my lines.

On the subject of stumbling, Andre also spent a lot of time falling and tumbling into the set. Being that he wore that eyepatch, the poor old guy seemed to not see very well. We would be waiting to go on only to hear a thunderous crash as Andre came bursting through one of the wall flats or knocking over a massive light. At one point, he fell and cut his head open after crashing down onto the corner of a coffee table. The actors and I sat in shock as he berated everyone around him. "Who put that fucking coffee table there?" or "I told you, no chair!" he'd squawk while having his latest head wound dressed. We were all so disappointed that someone who we all idolized as kids had turned out to be so damn mean and abrasive when we finally got the chance to work with him.

Just as we thought the tone on set couldn't get any worse, Cameron Mitchell arrived. As with Andre DeToth, Mitchell would have gotten an insane amount of respect from us young actors, but from the moment he showed up, he strutted around, mad-dogging and bullying everyone.

I certainly knew who he was, but I didn't give him the pleasure after he boisterously dropped names of ancient movie stars and start mocking everyone around him for "lowering himself" to work with newbies.

"Who the fuck is this scrub?" he motioned to me, trying to get a laugh at my expense. "I go from working with Marilyn Monroe to this clown?"

He said trying to get a laugh from the crew, which worked.

"I'm glad to see you've finally booked something else since then," I said, throwing shade before shade was shade. Mitchell glared at me, furious that I dared to fire snark back. "Shall we?" I said, glaring back at him as I stood on my mark.

In between scenes, he sat at a table with me, staring me down. One time, he did so while pulling a piece of paper from his coat pocket. "I've taken the liberty to punch up your dialogue for the next scene," he said with a challenging gaze.

I didn't pick the paper up as he slid it over to me.

"The dialogue is shit; young people don't talk that way," said the sixty-something actor who had just bragged about working with a twenty-five-year-long-dead movie star.

'Yeah…no, thanks," I said, pushing the paper back to him.

Mitchell glared at me like he was going to slap my face. "You disrespectful piece of garbage," he whispered out of the corner of his mouth as we waited for the camera to roll.

It was a very long two days. After a few last, painfully awkward scenes, Cameron Mitchell finally wrapped shooting and left without saying a word.

The rest of the shoot was a breeze. We worked with very nice, very drunk, Golden Globe nominee Aldo Ray and the *Grizzly Adams* star Dan Haggerty, who I brazenly did coke with in the bathroom at the sisters' convent. By then, I was not shy about using cocaine, especially when it came to film night shoots. At that point in the eighties, it wasn't considered a party drug on a film set as much as it was a regular part of the all-night movie making process. Or that's what I told myself anyway. It's humorous to me how very anti-drug I am now. I am as terrified at the thought of using drugs now as I was when I was a scared little kid finding my babysitter smoking a cigarette. But back then, I sure took tremendous pleasure in doing the secret baggy hand-off with none other than Grizzly Adams himself. He was really funny and nice while I worked with him—aside from having the booger-sugar in common. I heard that very same year he went on to clean up his act. For me, though, I was certainly using more drugs than I should have back then. It was noticed and brought up by my co-stars, who kindly didn't judge me but certainly let me know that they were well aware that the reason I couldn't sit still was not because I had too much coffee like I was telling them.

"Butler, are you a faggot?" The meat-headed actor playing the meat-headed character in the movie asked me in front of everyone on set.

"What? No!" I answered defensively. Making a vicious comment like that would end someone's career these days, but back then, bullies were allowed to spew whatever hateful thing that they wanted to in the name of getting a laugh.

The fact is, I still truly did not know where I fit in. For some reason, other than exploratory random hookups, I made it to my early twenties without having any heartfelt feelings for anyone. I easily developed massive crushes on people, mostly for their talents or admittedly, their power, but the subject of seriously pairing up with someone still made no sense to me. I just kept figuring that I was still a slow-learner or that I had a form of arrested development as a result of my upbringing. I mean, I was a person who didn't even have body hair when I graduated high school, let alone know what it was like to be attracted to someone on a seriously intimate level. I was so obsessed with my goals and making something of myself, I didn't think much about any of that stuff. The subject of love was still one that was a total mystery to me. Obsession and love seemed to be one in the same. I wasn't comfortable thinking about it…and I had no idea why.

It was during the last week of *Terror Night* that I started acting in another film that I booked: *Lady Avenger*, directed by legendary genre director David DeCoteau. I played the boyfriend to a machine-gun toting Playboy bunny named Peggy Sanders. After that film was done, I knew that acting was becoming the only thing I wanted to focus on. I made the easy decision to quit effects altogether and went to Buechler's shop to thank him for the amazing start in L.A. and tell him about my plans to pass the make-up baton.

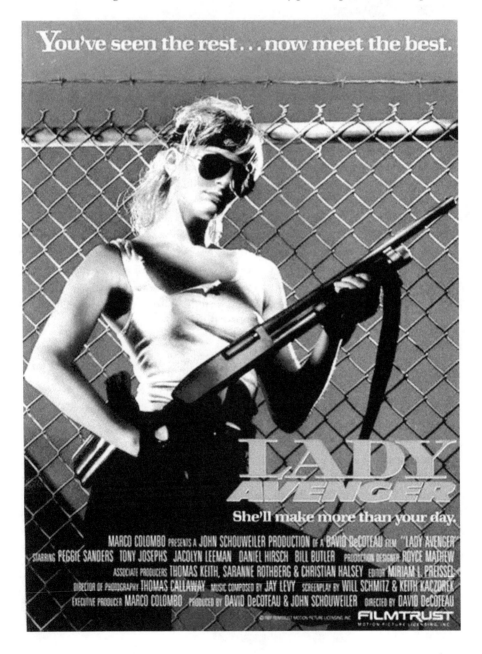

On Set of Lady Avenger

Deep inside, I still believed I was the fattest, ugliest person in the room

16

ALL ROADS LEAD BACK TO ROME

Before I could finish the sentence, *I quit*, Buechler cut me off. "Charlie Band has a bunch of stuff for you to do in Rome and elsewhere."

"What?" I replied, knowing where this was headed.

"If you are still willing to do double-duty, I know there's at least three more parts for you to do over the next six months." That's all he had to say, and I was still an eager part of the MMI effects team. After all, I was still learning how to act and behave on set; I couldn't say no as I was so thrilled at the idea of getting more chances to get better at something I truly loved. Plus, by now, I adored living in Rome.

The next film we were doing at Empire Studios was a horror-mystery called *Spellcaster* directed by Rafal Zielinski. The story was a *Ten Little Indians*-inspired tale about a group of young contest winners who get a chance to stay in an Italian castle. While they are all there, they embark on a scavenger hunt that leads the winner to finding a million-dollar check. Mike Deak and I were really excited as we got cast as a team on this one. By now, we were not only good friends but also the "Heckle and Jeckle" of Empire Pictures production team, providing everyone with as many laughs as we did hard work with our own moronic brand of comedy. Mike and I were class-one hustlers or schmoozers if you want to keep it real and we loved every minute of the time spent working for the company.

The film was being shot in the Castel Bracciano, a massive castle in a small province of Rome. It's also the same castle in which Tom Cruise married Katie Holmes. Mike and I excitedly learned our parts. They were small but really fun: we played two dopey MTV cameramen who ultimately get blown up in a car. The film starred Gail O'Grady, who back in the day was a very young, very funny and talented model who was transitioning into a serious actress and who has since then had a huge acting career. It also starred Bunty Bailey (the girl not only from Empire Picture's horror film *Dolls*, but also the female lead in Ah-Ha's "Take On Me" music video), the late Harold P. Pruett, a former child actor, Traci Lind, a ravishing model turned actress, Richard Blade, a kind and popular Los Angeles based D.J., as well as the actors Kim Ulrich, Michael Zorek, and Martha Demson. We all got along well and were so excited at the news that legendary English punk rocker Adam Ant would also be joining the cast.

This time Buechler was flying in with the MMI usual suspects to oversee the effects. Right before I boarded my flight, one of the Empire Pictures coordinators asked me to stop by the office and take an envelope with me to give to the Italian production. While on the long flight overseas, I got curious as to what was inside the heavy envelope and took it into the bathroom. I carefully opened the big manila package and found over a hundred thousand dollars in one hundred-dollar bills stashed inside it. I nervously bundled it back up and poked it into my backpack. Thankfully, I was able to disconnect and go to my happy place when the immigration agent asked me if I was bringing any money into the country.

"No, sir. I'm just a tourist," I said, like a good little unwitting money runner should.

From that moment on, I was out of the courier business.

Spellcaster - Adam Ant and Gail O'Grady

Spellcaster - Kim Ulrich Getting the Treatment

We all got situated at the Hotel Corsettimare once again and headed to the castle on Monday morning. I was really excited to be starting another acting job. We spotted director Rafal Zielinski as he made himself a coffee at the craft services table. Zielinski was a Polish filmmaker who had previously directed the film *Valet Girls* for Charlie Band and the raunchy teen comedy *Screwballs*, a film where a teenage boy gets his boner stuck in the finger hole of a bowling ball.

Mike Deak and I walked over to introduce ourselves.

"Oh, hello," he said in his thick Polish accent. "I'm so very sorry you won't be appearing in my movie," he continued, flashing a phony smile. Apparently, Zielinski had taken offense that Mike and I had been cast in the film with no one clearing it with him, and he'd made the decision to ditch us and replace us with Italian actors. In hindsight, I can't really blame the guy: they should have at least had us audition for him, but I was crushed to get the news, as it was the only reason I had agreed to come there.

"That decision is not going to stick!" Buechler angrily assured us. He swore that he was going to call Band himself and fix things.

Sure enough, that night at dinner, we all sat surrounding Rafal as he held court in an amazing restaurant in the center of Rome. He looked over at Mike and I, then forced an irritated smile and said, "Congratulations on it working out for you two." His deadpan gaze certainly communicated that he felt otherwise. I guess Charlie had put his foot down and the American rookies were staying in the picture.

That night, we had a great dinner as one by one, Zielinski tried to make moves on each actress only to be shot down.

"I bet you thought I'd have tits," Bunty Bailey said to Zielinski, who went blank, not knowing how to respond. I bet he did, too. She didn't.

That night, the cast really got to know one another as we all bonded. Shooting started, the days moved along smoothly, and the nights were filled with even more rowdy fun. We ate, drank, and danced most of the nights away, only to turn around and do it all over again.

Spellcaster - William Butler and Bunty Bailey

The day finally came when Mike and I were going to shoot our acting parts. I had started to get nervous both from anticipating filming with my new friends and impressing them as well as dreading how Rafal was going to treat us as we had clearly been forced back into the film. Sure enough, when the moment came for me to do my thing, I ended up choking.

Rafal was clearly unhappy that we were still in the movie and barely spoke to us. Take after take, I got quieter and shyer, not focusing on the scene at all as I felt his unimpressed resentment. I was a distracted mess through all of my scenes. Still, the movie makes for fun party watching should the question *What is your worst performance?* ever come up. I sucked so bad in that movie that I can only own it.

One day, my assignment was to dress Mike Deak in a suit of armor so that he could attack one of the actors in a scene where the furnishings in the castle come to life. The armor was real but the body suit underneath it was a tight-fitting, hand-knit foundation that was spray-painted silver made to look like chainmail. All day long we went back and forth between Mike wearing the suit for the acting part of the character and the stunt man wearing it for any hardcore stunt stuff. A couple of days later, a Friday to be exact, Mike and I were shooting a scene with a puppet that we referred to as the "Flying Birthday Cake." It was a brightly-colored, foam-fabricated flying demon with a vagina-like mouth that Ken Hall had fabricated. In the scene, the head is knocked off of the suit of armor and the flying birthday cake bursts out of it, attacking one of the kids. While we were setting the shot up, Mike became very antsy.

"What is wrong with you?" I laughed.

"I don't know...I think I have jock itch from all of that jumping around I did on Wednesday."

"Why? What's wrong?" I asked.

"My crotch is on fire! It's burning!" he snapped.

"Did you bang a hooker and get V.D.?" I laughed.

"No!" he said, scratching away.

We continued working throughout the day and every now and then, I found Mike away from set, furiously scratching his loins. "I have to go back to my hotel room! This is nuts! I feel like taking a fork and scratching myself: it's driving me crazy!" he said. The guy was losing it.

I agreed to take over and laughed it off, because that's what me and my friends do: hysterically laugh at each other's misfortunes. I just chalked it up to him coming down with a nasty case of jungle heat rash from that rough crochet jumpsuit he had worn the previous days. That day, we wrapped early and I went back to my room to find the light on the phone blinking.

"For fuck's sake, I have fucking crabs!" is all Mike said before he slammed the phone down. Sure enough, it was Mike Deak's turn to come down with a case of overseas crabs. Moments later, I was down the hallway at his room as he answered the door in sheer terror, wearing only a bath towel and holding a disposable razor.

"What are you doing?!" I asked.

"What do you think I'm doing? I'm about to shave myself! These little pricks are biting the hell out of me!" he said furiously. "That fucking stunt man who wore my body stocking must have had crabs!" Mike barked, about to slam the door shut as he furiously scratched at himself.

"Wait!" I said, grabbing the door laughing until I almost wet myself.

"What?" Mike snapped back. "I don't know what I am going to do, man. This is killing me!" he said.

"Fuck…" I continued, knowing what I had to do. I inhaled and stared him down. "I will go buy you the fucking crab medicine."

"Really? Seriously?"

I nodded, rolling my eyes. I was earning "awesome friend" points for this one. "Yes. Just stay here and don't shave your bits and pieces just yet. Let me try to figure out where to get it." I zipped up my coat.

"Okay, thank you so much, man," he said, dancing around as he continued scratching and slamming the door.

"Yeah, yeah," I replied as I walked back down the hall and out onto the street.

By then, my Italian was getting pretty good. I would say I was chattering at about a nine-year-old kid's level. I understood pretty much everything and though I struggled with verbs and what versions of words I should use, I could converse and people understood me. For the most part, that is. What I didn't take into consideration was all of the rough Italian street slang that also had soaked into my head from hearing my Italian friends talk at the studio. Things like *va'a fare in cul* or *vafangool*, as you often hear it in the States, which translated means "Go fuck yourself in your own ass," was a regular part of casual conversation. As with English, there are lots of vulgar slang words for private parts, most of which no one would ever use in a conversation with a stranger. I finally figured out where the Pomezia Pharmacia was and nervously made my way there, trying to rehearse the conversation with the pharmacist ahead of time, just in case the medicine wasn't sitting out on the shelf, and of course, it wasn't.

I looked up and down the aisles for about thirty minutes but found nothing that looked like crab lice medicine. I don't know if you have ever been to a pharmacy out of your own country, but the boxed items like that on the shelves may as well be written in a language from Mars, because you don't recognize a single thing.

"May I help you?" the older, chubby, female pharmacist asked me in Italian.

"Uh…*Si. Per favorie… mi scusi, ill mio italiano non e' molto buono* (Please excuse me, my Italian is not very good)," I said to her sheepishly in my terrible Italian.

She smiled at me, kindly patting my cheek with her hand, replying in Italian, "It's no problem, my child. What can I get for you today?"

"Well," I nervously said, "*mi scusi, senorina*, but…well…*ma devo compare per il mio amico qualcosa.*" (I need to buy something for my friend)

"Yes? What thing?" she smiled and replied in Italian.

"Well…*per mi amico.*" (It's for my friend)

"*Si, Che cossa, mi amore?*" (What thing, my love?)

"*Quello di cui ho bisogon'e...*" (What I need is) And here's where the conversation went haywire: "...*una medicina...per...*" (A medicine for)

"*Che?*" (What?)

"Uh...well...*una medicina per insectos di cazzo.*"

Her face went blank. "*Che?!*" She was completely shocked.

It wasn't until later that night that I realized what I had said to her was "a medicine for bugs of the cock." The term *cazzo* is a very dirty slang term that would in no way ever be used when you're talking to your doctor and certainly not your local pharmacist. It's the same as if you walked in and asked for some "antibiotic cream for my cunt."

The woman held back her laughter as she replied, "*Mi scusi, un momento per favore.*" (Excuse me, me one moment please) As she made her way to the back of the pharmacy, I could hear her rattling in Italian and then the explosive laughter of others. She composed herself and emerged with two other Italians, both of whom had shit-eating grins on their faces.

"*Per favore...repeata.*" (Please repeat) She was trying her best to look serious.

"Uh...*questo es per mi amichi...*" (This is for my friend) I was breaking into a sweat.

"Uh-huh," she nodded in doubtful glee.

"*Una medicina per insectos di cazzo.*" I repeated.

All three pharmacists burst into laughter. "*Insectos di cazzo?!*"

"*Si,*" I quietly whispered as they exploded into laughter once again. The lady pharmacist rattled off some more Italian as she made her way behind the counter and motioned me over. I sulked over in complete terror. By now, I was drawing a crowd of giggling locals as well. She pulled out a small box from behind the counter.

"*Dillon al 'tuo amico',*" (Tell "your friend") she began, suppressing a laugh and making quotations with her fingers, "*dovrebbe pettinare questo medicinale attaverso i peli del corpo.*" (Tell him to comb the medicine through his body hair) "*Per di...insectos di... cazzo.*" (For insects of the cock)

Once again, everyone in the place exploded into laughter as I sank further.

"*Tra un'ora il suo cazzo dovrebbe andare perfettamente bene.*" (In a hour, his cock should be perfect)

Everyone burst into laughter a final time as I hung my head in sheer horror. I paid for the medicine and walked out, turning around one last time as every eye in the house watched me exit.

"*Di 'al 'tuo amico' di smettere di dormire con le scifoza puttane!*" (Tell "your friend" to stop sleeping with dirty whores!) an old man yelled as I began to run down the road back towards the hotel.

Moments later, Mike swung the door open, catching his breath. Without saying a word, he nabbed the pharmacy bag out of my hands and disappeared back into his hotel room. Later that night, he emerged into the dining room, finally able to sit straight. Deak hoisted a drink in my name and thanked me for saving his loins. That night, we all dined on crabs to celebrate both our victory and the death of *insectos de cazzo.*

Just when I didn't think it could get any busier at the studio in Italy, we noticed that Charlie suddenly had a movie filming on every soundstage. It was non-stop for a few months as pictures would crew up, shoot, ship out, and start all over again. Films like *Crawlspace* starring Talia Balsam and Klaus Kinski, *Robot Jox* directed by Stuart Gordon, *Arena* by Peter Manoogian, *Catacombs* starring Timmy Van Patten, and *Transformations* starring Rex Smith from *Pirates of Penzance* were just a few of the films shooting there. By then, a lot of us were just staying in Rome in between films because we had so little time off in between, and I was loving every minute of my time spent there.

Stuart Gordon and I were officially friends. Anytime I could get a chance to spend time with him were minutes well spent. I was inspired and entertained by his every word. One day while he was prepping *Robot Jox*, he met up with me in the bar and asked if I could do a Russian accent.

"Can I do a Russian accent? Boy, can I!" I said, suspecting he was going to ask me to audition for something, which he did. We finished our coffee and he invited me to his office to read for him.

"Just so you know, you cannot do a Russian accent at all," Stuart said, laughing at my eager but failed attempt to sound Slavic. I guessed my sure thing part in *Robot Jox* had just sailed off into space.

It wasn't long after that I would be heading out way beyond the ol' Milky Way after I was cast in Charlie's futuristic kickboxing film set in space, *Arena*. I played the role of Skull, a shifty, butt-headed space-alien hell bent on executing a variety of murderous get rich quick schemes. The director, Peter Manoogian, was a great guy with a terrific sense of humor. We had all known him since *Eliminators* and were really excited about working with him again. The film followed a handsome, albeit orphaned young boxer who was recruited to fight aliens from around the universe in an intergalactic boxing competition known as the Arena.

This was Empire's largest production to date as it featured a dozen massive monsters and many prosthetic make-up creatures of which I was one. Every make-up artist in town worked on the film in some capacity, including the now legendary Steve Wang, who had just come off of the original *Predator* movie. My extensive make-up required me to sit in the chair for three hours a day and featured full scleral contact lenses that covered my eyes. I could see very little while I had the lenses in and had to be led around to where they wanted me to stand.

The make-up wasn't bad but wasn't much fun to wear for ten hours a day, particularly after I began to sweat through the sponge appliance pieces. Every day for a month, at around three o'clock, I started feeling like I had a wet dish sponge glued to my face, but I never said a peep. I was having the time of my life acting with such a great group of character actors, guys like Hamilton Camp and Armin Shimerman. It was a great time...until I ended up being treated by the set medic.

We finally had gotten to the scene where my character dies. In the film, Skull, who has a powerful computer embedded into his head, taps into the Arena's odds-making computer and messes with the handicap beam, which weakens the lead to the point where the bad guy can beat him down. Instead of just throwing the odds off and bailing, my character gets greedy and ultimately gets his head blown off as his computer explodes. To achieve the effect, a mechanical head of the Skull character was built so that the pyro people could blow it up after I screamed in horror while supposedly shorting out. Before they got to the money shot where the puppet explodes, the Italian effects guys asked me if they could wire my helmet to spark for the very first part of the action. They brought me to their truck and showed me what the spark squibs looked like and how big the flash was. I agreed wholeheartedly, not considering the idea that something might go wrong. I stood in the truck while they wired my helmet up with about a dozen squibs then led me to set afterwards.

When the time came to shoot, I stood on my mark as the effects guys hooked a bunch of wires that trailed down my back onto a big car battery. Manoogian walked me through the action, and once everyone cleared the set, I got into place to start the pyro shot. At the precise moment I was to scream and shake my body, the effects guy threw the switch to ignite the sparks. They were supposed to fly up into the air directly behind me, but instead of flying upward, the sparks and fire sprayed directly down into the collar of my costume as the guy threw the switch. My flesh sizzled as the flaming sparks burned deep through my costume and into my skin. I fell down to the ground holding my neck as the second assistant director poured a bottle of water on me and put out the sparks with a towel. Everyone was quick to get me to the set medic as they ripped off my costume. I had been burned pretty badly, but it wasn't anything that needed outside medical attention. I was able to work my way through the rest of the day. He put some aloe vera all over the back of my neck and bandaged me up. Twenty minutes later, I was back on set; toastier, but happier nonetheless.

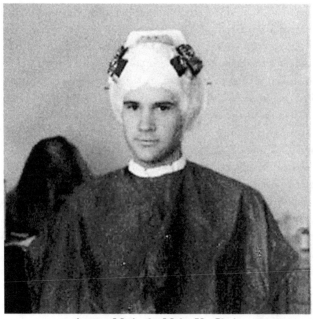

Arena - Me in the Make-Up Chair

Arena - Me as Skull

Arena - Paul Saterfield

Arena - Skull and Armin Shimmerman

One morning at some point during all of this insane journey, the studio was a buzz that legendarily crazy actor Klaus Kinski was back on the lot shooting pick-ups for an Italian film called "Vampire in Venice". Apparently, he had harassed the Italian crew so much while they were filming that they had rushed through the shoot and many of his close-ups were unusable. Klaus was only there for two days and was already raising hell. I ran into to Stuart Gordon in the hall as we passed Klaus' dressing room and he told me a great story about the last time Kinski was on the lot. Gordon said that Klaus was filming an Empire film called *Crawlspace*, the story about a beautiful young girl who moves into an apartment building only to slowly realize that the creepy landlord of the place is a peeping Tom who watches the tenants from within the crawlspace of the building. Murder and mayhem eventually unfold for everyone involved.

Klaus Kinski was a well-known German actor who was as brilliant a performer as he was a legendary madman. He starred in dozens of films, including *Dr. Zhivago* and *Gulag* and had worked on many well-known films with Werner Herzog, including *Nosferatu*. Kinski had a reputation for throwing tantrums, getting directors fired, and spelling it out for anyone within earshot, including the time he told Steven Spielberg that the script for *Raiders of the Lost Ark* was a "yawn-making, boring pile of shit." Apparently, Kinski was offended by the portrayal of the Nazis in the film and called the character that Spielberg offered him "moronically shitty."

Some of Klaus' other interesting traits involved the time he tried to strangle his girlfriend, the molestation accusations from his own kids, and his good old-fashioned, diagnosed psychopathy. Stuart said he was really giving the director David Schmoeller a horrible time, having gotten himself into fist-fights with various members of the crew only one week into production. Kinski also forbade Schmoeller from ever calling both "Action" or "Cut," saying that he would instead start and finish whenever he felt like it. After losing many days of production when Kinski continued throwing tantrums and just disappeared, Schmoeller made the plea to have the actor fired, but the executive producers were intent on keeping him in the film, so he had to deal with him.

Vulich, who also worked on the film once told me that, Kinski stopped in the middle of one scene, suddenly grabbed his skull, fell to his knees, and screamed, "My dear God! The pounding in my head! It won't go away! Please, God! Stop the pounding in my head!"

The funny part is that there was actually real hammering just outside the soundstage and when it was pointed out to him Klaus just stared everyone down with greasy, crazed eyeballs and his signature toothy smirk.

Stuart said they were filming a scene where Kinski was trying to climb his way through a metal air-conditioning vent set. In the film, his character uses the air ducts as a way of getting around in the building undetected.

Kinski crawled on his hands and knees inside the metal shaft, hatefully staring into the lens like he was about to blow his stack. He was sweating profusely as four 10,000-watt Tungsten spotlights were aimed at the shaft to illuminate the vent's metal grating covers but were also heating the shaft up to sweltering temperatures.

Growing angry, Stuart said that Klaus suddenly started to moan and pant like a dog. He then threw his head back like an animal and hollered, "I am not a fucking hamburger!"

He continued to scream in horror as crew members scrambled to pull him out of the metal shaft. Kinski swatted at everyone on the crew, cursing them out in a variety of languages, then stormed off the set and ran all the way to his dressing room.

Apparently, at one point, the Italian producers went over to Schmoeller, pleading, "David, please: please have Mr Kinski killed."

"We don't have people killed just because we don't like them, that's not how it works," Schmoeller answered.

"That is exactly how it works here: we can take money from the production and have him killed, and then the executive producers can file an insurance claim and get the money back." Thankfully, everyone came to their senses and no death hit needed to be ordered. Watching Stuart Gordon describe the entire scene was completely entertaining, I had not laughed that hard in a very long time. We finished our coffee and that was the end of that...or so I thought.

Later that afternoon, Stuart and I ran into each other again. This time as we passed Klaus's dressing room, I grabbed my skull and screamed...

"I am not a Hamburger!"

Stuart and I burst into laughter as suddenly, the door to Klaus's dressing room exploded open. There he was, in all his crazy glory. He had heard every word. Klaus whipped around towards me with those crazy eyes and immediately started chasing me. I ran as fast as I could, but he quickly and easily gained on me. I luckily made it inside a one-way employee exit door as one of the crew members exited the main building. I slammed the door shut just as Kinski nearly grabbed the back of my hoodie. I stood there for a moment catching my breath as he pounded on the door, furiously trying to get it open. Thinking quickly, I jumped into the elevator that went up to Dino's old office and disappeared until later that night. Finally, at about eight that evening, I slipped back out and asked for a ride to the hotel.

The next morning, I was so nervous to go to work. Surely I would run into this guy again, and then what? I did everything I could to look different, wearing a baseball hat, sunglasses, and a different coat to try and throw him off. Everyone taunted me as I pulled up to work that next morning and we headed to the studio bar for coffee. After everything I had been through in life, was I to eventually die at the hands of none other than Klaus Kinski? This was not how I wish to be remembered. Later, I was mixing artificial sweetener into my coffee when someone next to me whispered, "You've got an admirer."

I froze, slowly turning around...only to find Klaus standing directly beside me. Our eyes locked as my cohorts nervously stared down into their java. I forced a smile, not knowing what to say as he glared as me for a minute- which felt like forever. Klaus sneered, reading my face with his eyes as if he were picking the spot that he was about to slap.

"Good morning, Mr. Kinski." I said terrified.

His eyes bulged at my audacity.

And then...without explanation...

...Klaus started laughing a huge insanely boisterous laugh as he hugged me in a friendly headlock featuring the most pungent rotten armpits I have ever experienced in my life.

He stepped away from me and shook his finger in my face with his eyebrows raised.

"Hamburger, indeed." He said, then grabbed his coffee and floated out of the bar like Nosferatu himself.

I exhaled a massive breath. It seemed that I had survived the wrath of Klaus Kinski...but just to be certain I stayed out of his line of fire for the next day until he was gone. Not only was he not a hamburger, he was also not without a sense of humor.

Another small quick movie that Charlie squeezed in out of nowhere was a bizarre film that took place in space, a picture called *Transformations*, directed by a man known by the name of "Uncle" Jay Kamen. The film was shot on what was left of the old *Robot Jox* set and starred Broadway and television actor Rex Smith. Rex was very well known for his Broadway debut and long run in *The Pirates of Penzance* and a popular TV show called *Street Hawk*. Both Kamen and Smith were absolute joys to work with; Rex, in particular was a very funny guy and complete team player. Often times working in film, you'll meet someone that you get along with so much that you're certain they'll be your best friend when you get back home, yet somehow, after you wrap shooting, you never see them ever again. Rex was no exception to that occurrence. He disappeared right after that shoot and I never saw him again, but while were working together, we all got along like a house on fire. We all sat around the spaceship set, making each other laugh, playing stupid games like "would you rather" or asking each other completely inappropriate questions. Rex was always down to play and gave answers that kept everyone laughing out loud.

"Would you rather eat a vomit popsicle or slide down a fifty-foot razor blade into a pool of iodine?" were just a few of the questions asked between takes.

"Vomit," I answered without a beat.

"Where's the weirdest place you've ever had sex?" I brazenly asked the former Broadway star that I barely knew.

"Oh, I don't know if I can share that one…it's out there, man," he said, laughing.

"Go!" I said, begging him for the story. Smith leaned close and proceeded to tell us in a whispered hush that many years ago when he was a young man starring on the television series *Street Hawk*, he had to go to the studio for a gathering where all of the company's current stars were making an appearance. According to Smith, he and one of the original *Solid Gold* dancers ended up hitting it off at the party. The two of them slammed a few drinks and then snuck onto *The People's Court* soundstage where they proceeded to make insanely passionate love on Judge Wapner's desk.

We all cheered him on with huge belly laughs as he explained that the two of them were all over that desk and in every position in the book until late that night, somehow never being caught. After they were done with their wild relations session, they cleaned up the scene with Judge Wapner's robe that they had spotted hanging on the back of his chair. "Still to this day, I can never watch reruns of that show without wondering if Judge Wapner sat down the next morning and smelled the remaining stench of sex," Rex said in ponderous retrospect.

Six days later, *Transformations* was in the can, and I never saw Smith ever again.

We finally got another break from shooting, and I went back to L.A. for two weeks. By then, Bunty Bailey from *Spellcaster* had moved in with Peter Garcia and me in our apartment on Franklin and Gower. During that time period, my drinking got heavier. One night, Vulich and I went out drinking and he decided it was time for a heart to heart.

"I know you aren't into guys, but if by chance you were, it wouldn't affect our friendship in the least," John said to me, taking a drag off of his cigarette as we stood outside Residual's Bar in North Hollywood. We were both buzzed.

"I'm not," I said. I started to change the subject.

"I know you're not," John said, "but I just wanted to let you know, if you were, it would be okay." Vulich had continued to excel in the effects business while I was in Rome and had just opened his own make-up effects lab, a busy new company called Optic Nerve he founded with make-up artist Everett Burrell. John and I were never closer friends, but I wasn't ready to talk about my private life and certainly not the lack thereof.

"I know that, John, but I'm not."

"I know. But if you were—"

"I'm not."

"But if you were—"

"I'm not!" I said, cutting him off as he started to speak once more. "Stop," I snapped.

"Sure, man," he said with a smile. "We can talk about it another time." He looked at me as if he already knew what time it was.

I was starting to get this treatment a lot from people. Everyone wanted to know what was up with me personally. The truth was, I *had* quietly been in a relationship with a good friend I had met on a set. He was an insanely smart, funny, creative guy, and oh yeah, "straight." It was complicated enough for me to get through it all, let alone be ready to start discussing my situation. Very few people knew of what my home life truly was like.

It was also the 80s. Alternative lifestyles were not totally accepted at the time. The AIDs epidemic had spread a lot of fear and had further alienated a lot of gay people. Being that a good measure of my friends and family were straight, I was terrified of losing people that I cherished, foolishly thinking that just being myself would somehow let them down. I know now that I was wrong. There was also the unspoken rule in Hollywood that if you were an openly gay or bi actor, your career was over unless you were willing to play a sassy hairdresser or nelly uncle. If you planned on playing straight roles, you'd better pass as straight. I just wanted to act and figure out who I was on my own time. The friends I did have that were gay were a hilarious, supportive, and wild bunch. They always accepted me and my decision to keep to myself. Especially Peter Garcia and my dear friend Craig Newman. Not only did they invite me to the party, be the most reliable people I knew and laugh with me for hours, but they would also on occasion feed me when I was broke and in between jobs. They will never know how much I will never forget those times.

My work life continued to grow and I was very much at peace with what I was doing in that department, but at home, I was slowly growing to hate myself as I slowly realized that I was never going to live the life that I grew up thinking I would. I had always imagined that I would end up married with a wife, kids, and a dog or two, all of us living in some beautiful craftsman home in Martha's Vineyard somewhere, but the opportunity for any of that never unfolded. I thought maybe I was just a slow learner and that everything would eventually figure itself out, but it was becoming very clear to me that the wife scenario was never going to happen. Very clear.

There was something more going on beyond my taste in a partner, something was not right with me. I was still very much a kid in that department despite my first (by then, ended) relationship having been a pleasant one. I found it impossible to fully connect with either men or women on an intimate level. I had no idea of what was wrong with me. I was developing a tremendous anxiety on the subject of sex and it was not getting better. I had to be completely blacked out drunk to participate and never with anyone I knew more than a few hours. I desperately wanted to be happy in that department, but for some reason, I just couldn't fully go with it. For years, I kept mum with even my closest of friends.

"You vo-dee-o-doe," my roommate Peter Garcia said to me, indicating that I was hooking up with men.

"No, I don't," I replied.

"Oh, you vo-dee-o-doe, alright," he purred with knowing eyes.

"No, I don't."

"Well, you vo-dee-o."

"Well, yeah, I…vo-dee-o," I fessed up, shrugging, trying to make him laugh.

On the odd occasion that I started to date someone male, it always seemed to be a person who I knew would ultimately leave me or eventually dismantle the relationship. I had a deep-seated shame burned into my brain and it was not going away. I also didn't have a lot of belief in relationships. As far as I knew, having a significant other mostly involved screaming, cheating, and throwing things at one another. I knew there must be a bigger reason why I was so closed up; I just didn't know what it was. To keep myself distracted, I continued to bury myself in my work and when work ended, I struggled with an inescapable depression that I could not shake. I began to hate myself in between jobs no matter how short the amount of time it was in between gigs.

In regard to work, I did very well; life, not so much. I started to develop serious codependency issues on anyone that gave me the attention that I prayed for, to the point of becoming so possessive that I ultimately drove them away. Again, I now believe it's because I ultimately didn't feel I was worthy and secretly wanted to dismantle any relationship I had, both with friends and beyond. My drinking and drug intake started to increase as I tried to mask how I was feeling at the end of the day. I was very lonely at home and slowly gaining the reputation of being the ultimate one-man party. If I wasn't working, I was drunk or high.

17

GET OFF MY FUCKING BLANKET

The call to come back to Rome happened just in the nick of time. It was once again time to get cracking and away from self-medicating. I flew back to the studio in Italy and dove into my work headfirst. This time, Buechler was directing a film for Charlie Band called *Cellar Dweller*. At this point, my attention was completely checked out of the effects scene and I was focusing mostly on acting. I hustled on set when it came down to helping out and then went back to my hotel room and read one of a huge stack of books on acting that I had bought at Samuel French.

Cellar Dweller was the story of a beautiful young artist played by Debrah Farentino, a woman who gets a scholarship to study in an immersive institute where art students can live while they explore their craft. The project was co-produced by a coke-fueled, fiery-tempered Italian by the name of Pino Brutti. This was the first time we had ever worked with him and it was certainly a different experience than on all of the other films. He screamed at the crew in between puffs of non-filter cigarettes and spoke in an Italian accent from a part of Italy that I struggled to put my finger on. Pino also didn't hide the fact that he hated the American crew and did everything he could to negate any request that we made. From the minute we started, we knew he was someone that was going to make the shoot tough, and he did just that.

In the film, Farentino finds herself unraveling a mystery as the students begin to disappear, ultimately realizing they've all met their fate by being eaten by a werewolf creature conjured up out of an old comic book. The film was a virtual who's who of television past, as all of the actors in it had starred on huge television shows at a certain point in their career (way back when). Vince Edwards, who played Dr. Ben Casey on the 1960s hit TV series was there, as was Pamela Bellwood from *Dynasty*, an actress who seemed completely unaware that she was not in real-life the snobby debutant from her defunct series, a lovely soap opera star Miranda Wilson, and a nice guy named Brian Robbins from *Head of the Class* who is now a huge film and television Executive Producer. But by far, the person who I could not take my eyes off of was the legendary actress Yvonne DeCarlo, TV's own Lily Munster from *The Munsters*.

Yvonne was a quiet woman who sat on set in between takes, speaking to no one. I remember being mesmerized by the fact that after all this time, she still had the same Lily Munster style make-up on: tons of blue eye shadow, thick liner, and false eye-lashes surrounded her striking blue eyes. Yvonne carried herself like she was a boss and let's face it, she was. One glance from her and you were clear that she was in full judgement of you. Though a very odd and mismatched bunch, every single one of them was a top-notch performer, but you positively got the "what the fuck am I doing on this film" vibe from everyone…including me. The movie was weird and it was freezing that winter. It was obvious that everyone's goal was simply to get a free trip to Rome and not one of creating cinematic brilliance.

My job on this project was to dress Mike Deak who played the werewolf monster. The suit was unlike anything I had ever experienced. Buechler had the crew make the thing out of five-inch-thick polyfoam and sealed latex instead of the usual lightweight foam latex material that was industry standard. The result was a costume that was like a stiff brick oven. Make-up artist Chet Zar and I put Mike in the suit and in a matter of minutes, he became soaking wet. What's worse was that the hair we used to cover the polyfoam costume on the outside was a real yak fur, which once the suit was wet made it smell like a wet yak. We unzipped the costume and the entire room filled with a wretched dead animal smell. I can't imagine how Deak must have felt inside that thing as it had to have climbed to over 100 degrees.

Cellar Dwellar - Myself, Mike Deak and Chet Czar with Werewolf Costume

The schedule was insanely tight this time around, but Buechler approached each directing day with a huge smile and sense of humor despite the obstacles he was facing, which was mostly dealing with his performers. Vince Edwards was a grouchy, humorless guy and he only got worse after he caught his wife shamelessly flirting with Mike Deak in the bar. Brian Robbins and Miranda Wilson were fun to work with and Pamela Bellwood seemed to still be in a bubble of self-imposed famousness. She didn't really speak to anyone, which was fine, and all I could see when I looked at her was the bizarre pictorial spread she'd done in *Playboy* magazine. A couple of years before, she posed for photos of herself running naked through Africa. There were shots where she was dressed like a Nigerian princess as black natives lifted her high above their heads as if she were some sort of white hope that had dropped in via plane wreck. In her defense, they were very pretty photos though no matter how completely un-PC they were. Of course, this was sadly back when *politically correct* wasn't a thing yet.

By far, though, my number one source of entertainment on set was watching Yvonne DeCarlo work. I checked out the call sheet and went into the studio even if I wasn't called just to get a look at her in action. I was a huge fan of *The Munsters* and seeing her in person was the ultimate thrill. One of the many fascinating things about Yvonne was that she could not remember any of her lines: none. She was older by then, and a lot of actors use cue cards, but she was an absolute master at it. At the beginning of each scene, Yvonne showed up with her script pages cut into tiny thin strips. Each sentence was a separate slip of paper. She meticulously taped lines all over the set, depending on where her blocking had her standing or moving. Then, once the director called action, she did this incredible dance where she somehow pulled off reading each line without the viewer ever detecting it.

"Well, well, well," she said as she opened her desk drawer, pretending to look for a pencil, but was in fact really just reading the next line.

"You think you can just come in here…" She picked up her coffee cup where another line was pasted on the side facing away from camera. "And tell me…" She took a sip and looked inside the rim of the cup. "How to run my school?"

She picked up a piece of paper and crumpled it, but not before reading the next line. "Well, *you* can pack your things…" She threw the wad of paper into the trash, reading another line taped inside the waste can. "….and get out."

She pulled it off like a pro. You would never know she was reading every single line, but one thing was for absolute certain: Yvonne DeCarlo did not give a fuck if you did. We were lucky to have her on the movie and she knew it.

One of the other main quirks she had was the fact that she constantly carried around a crocheted blanket with her. It looked kind of like the one that lays over the couch on the *Roseanne* TV show. She carried this ratty thing around with her wherever she went and wherever she sat, and before she sat, she took five minutes carefully spreading it out and making sure it was perfectly smooth beforehand, picking all the fabric pills and dust flecks off of it. She put the blanket on her set chair, on the barstool in the bar, and even on set pieces in the actual movie if John would allow it, and of course he did. One day, she was in a scene that was going on; I had been wandering in and out of the soundstage all day, dividing my time between the set and exploring through the massive costume warehouse that the studio housed. Towards the end of the day, I went back to the set where I could hear Yvonne doing her last shot as she did her usual dance, walking around reading her lines off the furniture and props. I sat on a bed in an adjoining set and watched them film, eventually getting sleepy from our over-indulgence of lunchtime wine and lay back onto the mattress, drifting off to sleep.

I was in a deep slumber when a screeching voice jerked me back to reality.

"My blanket! What the fuck are you doing on my blanket?!"

My eyes sprung open as I found Yvonne DeCarlo standing directly over me. She was not happy. "Get the fuck off my fucking blanket!" she snapped.

I dove to my feet, scrambling to apologize. I hadn't realized that she had spread her blanket out on the bed. The crew ran onto the set to watch the action as I fumbled, apologizing profusely. "I'm sorry, Ms. DeCarlo, I didn't realize…"

"Just go!" she screamed, pointing at the door as I ran in no particular direction.

It was official: I had just had my ass served to me by Lily Munster. First the Skipper, then Klaus Kinski, now this. Was I fated to be dressed down by all of the film and TV stars of yesteryear?

I went to the studio bar and pulled it together, bellying up for a whiskey with Deak and Chet as we laughed in total shock. "What in the fuck was that all about?" I asked as we slammed one. "Only I could get yelled at for doing nothing," I said.

How in the world was I going to face her the next day? The woman was furious.

I spotted Yvonne walking into the bar. She saw me and gazed over at me with a cold glare as her eyes went down to my whiskey glass.

"We are so busted," I said hanging my head as she ordered a hot tea, giving us one more side-eye in her usual full judgement.

"Who's watching her fuckin' blanket?" Mike jokingly whispered. Yvonne got her tea, shot me one more look of disgust and headed to her dressing room.

I was crushed. She was such an icon and for her to not think I was cool was a huge blow to my ego. Anyone who knows me knows that thousands of people can love me but I will positively become obsessed with getting the approval of the one person who doesn't like me and this one really cut to the bone.

The next day, I got to the studio and of course, the first scene called for Yvonne and the *Cellar Dweller* character to work which meant we were going to be in the same room all day. I sheepishly made my way onto set and found Yvonne sitting at her desk. She stared me down as Chet Zar and I saddled Mike up in that stinking yak costume. All day long we worked side by side and I had to look away to avoid Miss DeCarlo's disapproving icy daggers, but at about three o'clock that afternoon, things took a huge change for the better.

We were told we had twenty minutes for the crew to execute a new lighting set up, so the boys and I decided to go to the bar for a coffee. I walked into the bedroom set to get my coat and found Yvonne sitting in her chair, and more importantly, on her sacred blanket. I ignored her as I put my jacket on and started to walk out.

"Young man—" Yvonne said to me as I paused and cautiously turned back towards her.

"Yes, Miss DeCarlo?" I mumbled in fear.

For a moment, I stupidly thought she was going to apologize.

"I overheard that you're going to the bar…"

Oh shit, here comes the lecture.

"Yes, ma'am." I could barely get the words out.

She motioned for me to come closer, which I did.

"Would you be so kind as to ask the bartender to pour me," Yvonne held up two fingers indicating about half an inch, "this much gin."

I lit up. Thank God: she was one of us. Maybe my chance for redemption had arrived. "Why, it would be my pleasure, Miss DeCarlo."

She smiled, but only slightly. "And, dear—" Yvonne leaned forward and whispered to me. "Put it in a coffee cup. One must keep up professional appearances, you see," she said.

"You read my mind," I said to her, giving her a reassuring wink. She slightly smiled again, shooting me a knowing glance that told me my blanket crime was forgiven.

Ah-ha! I thought to myself as I trucked it over to the bar. Not only was Yvonne DeCarlo a master of pasting her lines all over the set, but she was an expert day-drinker. A coffee cup? Brilliant move! We were going to get along just fine. I went into the bar and asked Andrina the bartender to not only pour gin in a coffee cup but to fill it all the way to the rim.

I walked back onto the stage, careful not the spill any of Yvonne's sweet nectar of the gods. Her usual serious expression changed to that of a child's face on Christmas morning when I handed her the cup and she realized how full it was.

"Thank you very much, young man," she said to me. For the first time, Yvonne full on smiled at me. It was official, all was good with Lily Munster. Pleased with myself that I had finally done something right in her eyes, I exhaled. "What is your name, young man?" she asked, sipping on that room temperature gin like a boss.

"My name is Billy, Miss DeCarlo," I said.

"Well, thank you again, Bobby. I'm getting over a cold, and this helps clear the congestion in my chest."

"Anything I can do to help is my pleasure," I said.

And that was it. From that moment on, Yvonne DeCarlo and I were as right as rain.

I made many, *many* more trips to the bar for her the next couple of weeks.

"Bobby!" She called out to me from the other room. I never corrected that she wasn't getting my name right. "Bobby, would you be a darling and bring me my coffee mug? I'm feeling more chest congestion coming on," Yvonne said with those beautiful sparkling blue eyes and eyebrows raised like she and I had a dirty secret.

"Would you like a twist of lemon this time or maybe a pearl onion? That also might help clear the mucus," I said, getting courageous. "Some vermouth?"

"Just my usual cup please, Bobby," she said. "For medicinal purposes." Within three days, "Bobby" and Yvonne had a full-on secret language going on, all of it of course involving me bringing her booze. I never bothered to ask how her cold was coming along because it was clearly one of a long-lingering variety: I'd guess for the last forty years.

Finally, the last day of shooting came and Yvonne was wrapped. I was in the middle of spraying Lysol in that awful stinking werewolf costume when I heard someone behind me.

"Bobby...?" a voiced called out. I turned around and there was Yvonne herself, all dressed up and ready to travel home. She was, of course, carrying her beloved blanket. I got up and crossed to her. She was there to say goodbye. For one brief moment, I had the instant internal fantasy that she had decided to give the stupid thing to me, but no.

"I just wanted to say it was very nice meeting you, Bobby," she said.

"It was an absolute pleasure, Miss DeCarlo, *an absolute pleasure* and you take care of that cold, now," I said to her, reaching out to pat her blanket covered arm as she yanked it away from me before I made contact. And with that, Yvonne DeCarlo left.

All was good between me and the mother from *The Munsters*, star of *The Ten Commandments* and *The Greatest Show on Earth*. She was, indeed, a genuine star. Not only did I get to know her, she came around to say goodbye, even if it was to call me by the wrong name one last time. It's one of the coolest things that ever happened to me.

The shoot wound down and one by one, all of the other actors left. One day, I was sitting on set reading and waiting to be called to shoot inserts when a grip accidentally got his tool belt hooked onto one of the big lights illuminating the windows. The lamp went crashing to the ground right beside me, breaking in a huge *pop*. Before I had a moment to react, Pino Brutti ran from behind the flats, saw me sitting next to the broken light and punched me right in the face. I flew backwards off the apple box I was sitting on and down onto the concrete. After a moment of seeing stars, I pulled myself together as the Italians converged on Brutti, cursing him out and explaining that it wasn't me who had broken the light.

I walked out of the stage rubbing my jaw and went up to Dino's office. I picked up the phone and called Charlie Band's office back in the U.S. "I want to go home," I told him.

I explained what had happened and after a moment of shock on his behalf, Charlie said, "I'm very sorry, we will fix this."

"It's not just that. Thank you so much for everything you have done for everyone, but I think I've had my fill of Rome. I'm gonna make the leap to acting only. I'm done here," I told him.

"Well, just ride this week out," Charlie told me. "You only have a few more days. Then, come see me when you get back. I will see what I can do to help you."

I agreed to stay for the last week. Five days later, after almost five years of production in Rome, I left for the U.S., not realizing I would never go back to the Empire Studio ever again. It was snowing the day I flew out, just like it had been the first day I had arrived.

Today, the studio still stands, but as an amusement park. I still think about my wonderful time spent there almost every day. Italians are some of the most magnificent people on earth.

Me and Chet Czar on the Beach at the Hotel Corsettimare

Cellar Dwellar - John Buechler on Set

Cellar Dwellar - Deborah Farentino, John Buechler and Brian Robbins on Set

Cellar Dwellar - Mike Deak and Deb Farentino

Cellar Dwellar - John Buechler

It Takes Guts to Work with John Buechler

Cellar Dwellar - Jeff Combs and William Butler

Cellar Dwellar - Jeff Combs Meeting His Fate

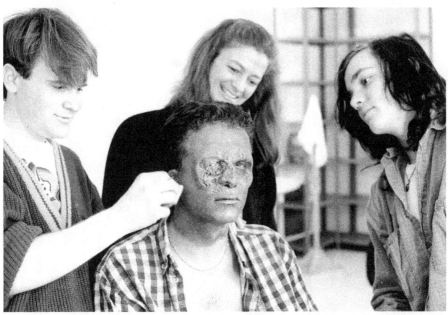

Cellar Dwellar - Completely Posed Shot in the Makeup Lab

Cellar Dwellar - Me Making Up the Jeffrey Combs Zombie Double

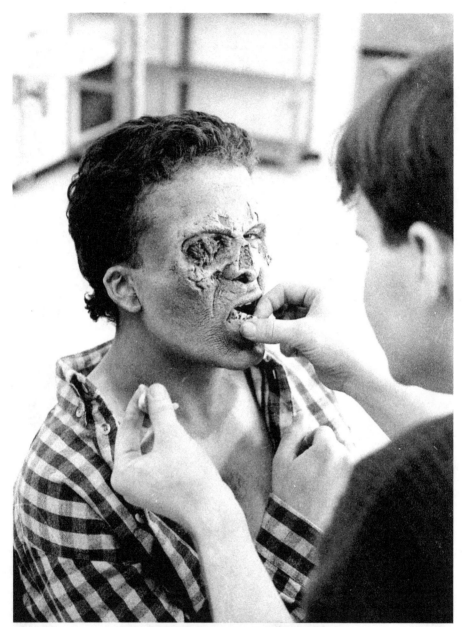

Cellar Dwellar - Fitting the Zombie with Teeth

18

OH, THAT'S WHAT'S WRONG WITH ME

I went back to my hometown to visit my mother for Christmas. Missing my old friends from the past, I spent a lot of time with my old pal Muffy Bolding and John Vulich, who had also come back for a visit. One day, Muffy and I went to the big mall on Blackstone Avenue to spend the day shopping for the holiday. I had no idea that moment would have such an impact on me, a day that was going to change me forever.

Muffy and I were in Sears department store wandering the aisles for Christmas gifts when we made our way into the appliances department. We were joking around and checking everything out as the two of us split into two different sections. I was browsing the refrigerators as I moved past the displays and over to the boxed items when something suddenly came over me. Something was instantly not right.

I felt hot and flushed, like I had forgotten how to breathe, and I started to get dizzy. I called out to Muffy who came around the corner. She could clearly see something was wrong with me as my knees buckled.

"What's wrong?" she called out, panicked.

"I have to go outside," I said as I burst into tears in a full-blown panic attack.

"What happened?" she said in shock. Behaving like this was way out of character for me. The term "panic-attack" was completely out of my vernacular. I had no idea how to explain what I was feeling, other than to say I felt like I was dying. I ran through the store and out the front entry way doors. Sitting down on the curb, I began sobbing my eyes out.

"What's wrong with you?" she asked again as I buried my face in my hands. Overwhelming feelings of shame and sadness were coming over me and I was terrified to speak the words that were about to come out of my mouth.

"I know what's wrong with me, sexually," I said, choking back tears.

"What?" she said, totally confused. We had barely ever spoken about the subject.

Suddenly everything was clear. "I was molested when I was little," I said.

There was dead silence for a few moments as I began to fall into instant exhaustion. Muffy hugged me as she and I sat on the curb crying our eyes out, laughing about the insanely random revelation one minute and becoming completely distraught and shaken up the next.

"The refrigerator section of Sears brought you to *that* revelation?" she laughed.

I laughed too. I suddenly felt like a six-year-old kid again. I was completely wrought with sadness as the locked file cabinet in my brain finally opened after all this time. Floods of horrible memories began to come back to me. All of my confusion on the subject of sexuality and my lack of interest in being my genuine self suddenly became instantly clear. All of the questions as to why I was constantly investing in doomed relationships were answered, and all of these revelations had been triggered by the sight of a stupid refrigerator box. The fact was, I never wanted anything real on the subject of coupling because the subject terrified me. I pulled it together as best I could and began to tell Muffy a story that I myself felt like I was hearing for the very first time. Finally, I was able to realize my own awful secret.

It all happened back during a time period when my parents bought their first house. I was around seven years old. It was a time when they both were working full time jobs and I was often left in the care of babysitters both young and old. As I mentioned previously, my father worked as a Pepsi Cola bottle delivery person and my mother was a medical assistant. Both worked long, arduous hours that often kept them busy until well into the evening. They had no choice but to leave us in the care of others, and I certainly don't blame them for what happened to me. I was a very good little liar, just like my molester taught me to be. I got very good at keeping secrets at a very young age, no matter how dark they were. I'm not going to name the beast who demolished my innocence, but I will say that *she* was a female who is now long gone out of my life. Hopefully she's dead and rotting in hell, right where she belongs.

One day, as my parents were getting settled, they bought a new refrigerator, and I made a fort out of the leftover box that it had come in. My father laid the box on its side and cut windows in it so I could play inside it. I stayed out in there with the neighborhood kids after school every day, decorating it with colored markers as my babysitter sat in the garage eating canned nuts and watching.

One day, after all of the other kids had left for home, this hideous person decided to go somewhere with me that she never had gone before. "Do you want to play house like grown-ups do?" she asked me. "I'll show you."

I was curious as to what she was getting at. She had previously gained my trust by allowing some household rules to be broken without consequences and my parents trusted her enough to leave me with her, so I agreed. I had no reason to believe she would do anything to hurt me. She told me to go into the box as she kneeled down beside me. She explained that she was going to show me what Mommies and Daddies did while little children were asleep. I can't bring myself to write into words all of the insidious things that this beast made me do, but it was bad enough to not only scar me as a kid and cause me to block out part of my own life, but later, also to ruin intimacy for me for many years in my adult life.

I now understood why I spent years battling all sorts of unsavory growing addictions as I self-medicated my personal pain and tried to build a barrier between myself and the people in the real world. I had started out a very quiet, hopeful, loving kid, but from the very first day she did such unspeakable things, my life changed. I lived in absolute fear of most people around me as I secretly believed that no one was truly who they seemed to be. The subject of sex became something that was bad and never to be spoken about.

My molester told me that I could never tell anyone what had happened and what continued to happen or I would get into trouble and what's worse, I would be taken away from my family. She also convinced me that I was an active participant in what was unfolding, so I was just as much at fault, and I believed her. Still to this day, I fight a tremendous amount of anxiety when it comes to the subject of sex, and I now understand why, for many years, I could never be with anyone without being completely plastered drunk.

This person had changed me forever. I can still clearly see the inside roof of that cardboard box as I lay there staring at it, completely checked out while she manipulated me. I can still smell the cardboard and have to fight having flashbacks of what happened anytime I smell it now. I can remember my thoroughly confused mother trying to figure out why I would desperately cry and beg for her not to leave me at home with this person. My parents couldn't imagine what I could be so distraught about, and I never gave them a single clue until I was finally able to completely block all of it out and it went away. Writing this and remembering this has been the single most difficult thing I have ever done in my life. In writing about it, I know I will be forced to talk about it with others and that prospect terrifies me still.

Feeling drained and embarrassed, Muffy and I went on with our day. Though I was worn out by it all, it felt good to get it out. Little by little, I began to tell other people about my terrible revelation. Some cried for me, some hugged me tightly, some said that they had been through the same thing, but some suggested that I had made it all up for attention. I can't blame them. It's a hard and horrible thing to get your head around: I know this more than any of them. I wish I could say none of it happened, but it sure did.

"You don't pee the bed until you're in seventh grade without a bunch of rotten things going on in your head," John Vulich calmly said as he hugged me. "I figured you must've had something along those lines goin' on. The good news is, it's all just a memory now and you can finally accept the fact that it's just something that happened, something that wasn't your idea. Getting it out of your head was the most important step and you made it. You *will* get better."

I could always count on John Vulich to have the answer and he was right. The sooner I got my head around the idea that yesterday no longer existed, the faster I started coping with and dismantling the destruction my abuser caused me. I put drinking and partying on hold and quietly went to a counselor that I met at the codependence anonymous meetings I had started to attend, and he pretty much said the same thing. We can choose to be screwed up over our past or we can remember that the past no longer exists, and that's just what I did. It was up to me to look at it all as something that happened but is no more.

Joking with my jackass friends has also tremendously deflated the impact of my situation. Still to this day, they never hesitate to ask me if going into a Box City cardboard store makes me horny. Assholes. I love them all. I will say that I sure feel sorry for anyone that I find out has taken the innocence of a child.

19

DOING TIME ON PRISON

"I think I can get you your Screen Actors Guild union card," John Buechler told me as he padded through his shop in his dusty flip-flops. He explained to me that since the value of the dollar was beginning to drop, Empire Pictures was going to start doing productions in the United States again. Having a union acting card was a game changer back then, but I also knew what it meant. Buechler wanted me to jockey slime and apply make-ups if I wanted to be in the next movie Charlie was doing.

The truth was, I had really grown to enjoy doing monster make-ups, and with a SAG card, I could audition for more legitimate work, qualify for health and dental insurance, and eventually have a pension. Besides all of that, the movie was filming in Wyoming and I had never been, so I agreed. Once again, I teamed up with the brilliant Mike Deak on a trip that ended up being the trip of a lifetime.

The picture was a film called *Prison* and was written by one of my favorite screen writers, C. Courtney Joyner. The director was a newbie, a big tall blonde Nordic looking man by the named of Renny Harlin. You might know him as the well-known director that he evolved into after directing such cool movies as *Nightmare on Elm Street 4*, *Die Hard 2*, *The Long Kiss Goodnight*, and *Deep Blue Sea*, but back then, he was just a young scrub filmmaker like the rest of us. I had been told that Renny was a passionate and kind guy who was very approachable, and he certainly didn't disappoint as he was just that. He still is, in fact, as he and I have remained in touch all these years.

Even more impressive was the fact that none other than Irwin Yablans was producing the film. Irwin is the legendary producer responsible for John Carpenter's original *Halloween*. I was so excited to be meeting him.

The movie's story took place in an old dilapidated prison in Rawlins, Wyoming. It was at one time a real functional prison that had been recently closed down due to its size and lack of functionality. Mike Deak and I arrived and checked into our rooms at the Holiday Inn. Rawlins was a very small and quaint town surrounded by endless wilderness and beauty. That's one of the magnificent things about working in film: the opportunity to work and live in places you would normally never go. Rawlins had one small main strip that ran through town, dotted with many old bars and restaurants and even an old timey "dime store."

We arrived in the morning and visited the prison. It was a spectacular structure that was castle-like and surrounded by twisted and rusty barbed wire. As usual, we were given another cold, empty room inside the prison for our effects shop and quickly made it our own. There were tons of special make-up effects in this film so we had a lot to prepare for. The story followed a vengeful ghost that returns to haunt the place after unjustly being put to death in the electric chair.

According to Buechler, I was going to be playing the role of Brian Young, a baby-faced kid who ends up in jail on a third strike and eventually become the submissive punk to a ruthless convict named Rhino, a character played by a real-life prisoner the production had found in Rawlins. I was so happy to be acting again and more importantly, finally getting myself into the acting union. I knew the part front ways and back.

However, it was only a matter of a few hours after we had arrived when I was unpacking that Buechler called me in my hotel room. "Uh, I have something uncomfortable to talk to you about," he said.

"What?" I said, worried that one of my team members had fallen ill and we would be short-handed.

"I spoke too soon. Irwin Yablans' son Mickey was cast in the role that Charlie said you could play. You've been replaced."

I was crushed.

"The good news is, Charlie still wants to give you your SAG card."

I thought for a moment. There was a ton of special make-up effects work ahead of me on *Prison* and the truth is, it would have been hard for me to balance both jobs. I told Buechler it wasn't a big deal and was thrilled that I would still be getting my union card. My disappointment was further alleviated after I met Mickey Yablans in the lobby. He was such a terrific guy and truly excited about the opportunity to be in the movie. If I had to lose an acting gig to someone, I was sure happy it was him. He ended up doing a terrific job and the guy who played Rhino was not only a pussycat, but a terrific actor as well.

The Sunday before we started shooting, Deak and I finished setting up the effects lab at the prison and headed back to the hotel. I hadn't met any of the actors yet, but word was, the casting director Anthony Barnao had assembled a very strong cast. I unpacked my bags and went to the hotel restaurant to eat lunch by myself. I was sitting alone in one of the booths when suddenly, this strikingly handsome young dude came into the room. He was an unassuming blonde with a fresh crewcut, wearing a faded green t-shirt, torn-up old blue jeans, but no shoes or socks. Every eye in the room fell upon him as he made his way to a table.

Who is this weirdo? I thought to myself. Barefoot in a restaurant in Rawlins, Wyoming of all places? Maybe this was some kind of local custom I was unaware of. His massive presence was undeniable. There was something about him that was very special, and he wasn't even trying. He sat there politely, quietly chatting with the old people seated at the table next to him, completely unaware that virtually everyone in the room was watching him.

I did my best to not get caught as I stole glances of him graciously giving the waitress his full attention while she took his order. Whoever he was, he sure was very considerate and kind. After ordering, he pulled out a pile of rumpled, half-drawn drawings and pastel sticks he'd brought with him and proceeded to sketch. I divided my attention between my salad and watching him busy at work with his drawings until he caught me staring at him and gave me a friendly nod. Embarrassed, I stared back down into my food and didn't look up anymore until he was gone. I figured he must have worked in the hotel as he looked very much at home.

The call time the next morning was six a.m. The sun was just rising as I made my way through the hotel lobby, grabbed coffee, and went out to the valet area where a van was waiting to transport a bunch of us to the set. I climbed into the warm van and low and behold, there sat the mysterious blonde kid with the crewcut.

"Hey there. I'm Viggo Mortensen," he said extending his hand.

"Of course you are." I said shaking it. A person who looked and behaved like him could have only been named *Viggo Mortensen*, I thought to myself.

"Are you one of the actors?" he asked as the van rambled towards set.

"No…yes…well, not on this one, I mean, *I am an actor*, but I'm only helping in the effects department on this project. It's just something I do to help my friend." I stumbled through my response, feeling embarrassed as I turned back towards the road, clamming up. *My God, Butler, you are such an idiot!* I thought to myself. *Can you ever play it cool?*

"I saw you yesterday in the restaurant," Viggo said to me. "I figured you were an actor. There's something going on behind your eyes."

I slowly turned back around, slack-jawed and instantly charmed. He kindly smiled at me, giving me his full attention, just like he did with the waitress the previous day. "By the way, there's no shame in being an actor and being able to work in the special effects department," he added. "You're very lucky that you're multi-talented. I wish I had several skills like that."

Well, ladies and gentlemen, that's all it took. I was off to the races. From that moment on, I was 100% pure "Team Viggo." Suddenly, walking around in public with no shoes on and doing pastel drawings in hotel restaurants made perfect sense to me. He proceeded to humbly tell me he was one of the characters in the film. I later learned he was, in fact, the lead, but at the time, he played it down and was more interested in my history than in the fact that he was the actual star, and clearly a huge star in the making. Viggo was a person that I instantly liked and aspired to be more like. In fact, everyone that met him that day liked the guy. To this day, he remains one of the kindest, funniest, most talented, and smartest people I have ever had the pleasure of meeting and a person who will forever have my respect. He is a true artist across the board.

Most of the scenes in the film involved action with lots of actors and prison extras, some of whom were real prisoners allowed to appear in the film for their good behavior. Many of them were terrific and extremely talented. Arlen Dean Snyder from Clint Eastwood's *Heartbreak Ridge*, Tony Award nominee André De Shields, Lincoln Kilpatrick from the original cast of *A Raisin in the Sun*, and Lane Smith from many movies and television shows were just a few of the top-notch performers who appeared in the project alongside Viggo.

In a matter of days, the crew had quickly bonded and become a cohesive and well-oiled machine. The weather was perfect and we stayed on schedule right from the start. I think part of the reason that things ran so smoothly was that the production heads were very gracious. They consistently had fantastic on set meals and treats and created amazing activities for the crew to do together on the weekends. Irwin Yablans generously organized barbeques, white water rafting, and fishing trips, and even took us all horseback riding through miles of beautiful empty riverbeds. I remember holding on for dear life trying to look like I knew what I was doing as the cast ran the horses over the rocky cobblestone terrain. Irwin also regaled us with fascinating stories about when he first produced *Halloween*: the movie originally had been inspired by an old radio show. It was honestly the most fun I've ever had filming a movie.

On set, I was fascinated by watching Viggo act. He was a consummate professional who clearly took his job seriously and someone who dove into his part with everything he had. I couldn't wait to have the chance to use many of the tricks I learned from him, including creating character scrapbooks and listening to music in between takes. He also was the first actor that I ever witnessed being so well-behaved and respectful. There was also none of the usual actor shenanigans I had grown accustomed to and thought was acceptable. There was no complaining about his hotel room or participating in feuds with other fussy cast mates. He was clearly there to give a kick ass performance and that's just what he did. In between moments of gawking at this fascinating creature and new friend, Mike Deak and I headed out with a second unit camera and shot the countless special effects shots that the film required.

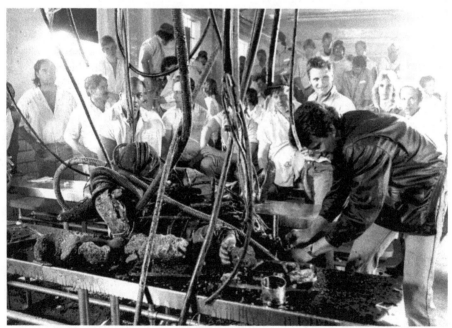

On Set of Prison

Deak and I pretty much ran second unit on that movie, shooting everything from dropping a dead body dummy from the cafeteria ceiling to burning a head puppet of Larry Flash Jenkins. We shot dozens of reverse shots where one of the prison guards, played by Hal Landon Jr., was wrapped up like a mummy in lethal-looking barbed wire that was in fact just speaker wire spray-painted silver. Mike Deak was a genius at figuring things out on set and kept things moving with his constant proven theory that "any special effect in film can be accomplished with the aid of duct tape, super glue, and fishing line."

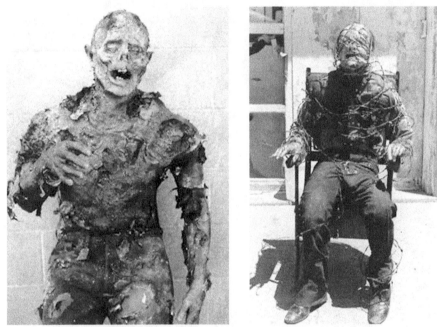

Left - Burned body I created for the Hershey character on Prison
Right - The dummy Mike Deak and I made of a prison guard on Prison

After about the second week of shooting, I woke up to find a test make-up for the film's main ghost on the schedule. I was taken to set and met up with a stunt man by the name of Kane Hodder. My job was to make him up from head to toe in pre-painted make-up appliances that made him look long dead from electrocution. The quality of the sculptures and design of the make-up was as good at it ever was from John's shop, created by artist Jeff Farley among others. I followed the sounds of uproarious laughter to the make-up room and found Kane already there, making everyone in the room laugh. He was a hilarious guy with a tremendous sense of humor, one who was instantly burping and farting on command within five minutes of meeting him. Kane was also a person who proudly could vomit on command and did not hesitate to show you his vile skill. I was as repulsed as I was completely entertained by him.

One of the other things I immediately noticed about Kane was his severe burn scars running along his arms and neck. He vaguely explained to me that he had been burned in a stunt accident years before and was hoping to skip some of the arm make-up appliances and just use his own scars. I told him I thought it was a great idea if he didn't mind, and I didn't ask any more details about how he was burned as it was obviously something that was personal to him. It wouldn't be until many years later, when I saw the documentary about his life, *To Hell and Back,* that I would realize just how traumatic

169

the experience was. If you haven't seen the film, you really owe it to yourself to watch it, as it's a true testament to his amazing willpower and perseverance.

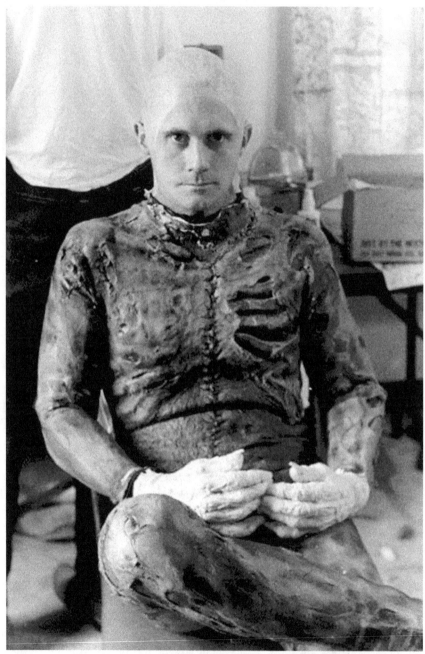

Kane Hodder getting ready for make-up on set of Prison.
This make-up inspired the Jason Vorhees make-up he later wore in Friday the 13th VII.

When he was young, Kane was being interviewed for a local news channel segment and when a fire stunt he was demonstrating went wrong, he was ignited from head to toe, the result of which was a series of horrible, body altering burns. After that, he spent months in the hospital, healing without any pain medication because his father, worried he'd become addicted to opiates, instructed to the hospital staff not to give him any. The story is heartbreaking. How Kane is such a solid decent person after living through all of that I will never figure out. Despite the horrific experience, Kane was one of the strongest, most optimistic and hilarious co-workers you could ever hope for. We spent the day together bonding and making each other laugh as I glued him into his ghoulish monster suit and we became friends. I had no idea that the make-up that I did on him would eventually be the very selling point for Kane to take over the title role of Jason Voorhees in many of the *Friday the 13th* films, and even more mind-blowing would be the fact that I myself would end up acting in *Friday the 13th Part VII: The New Blood* and become his very first victim on set.

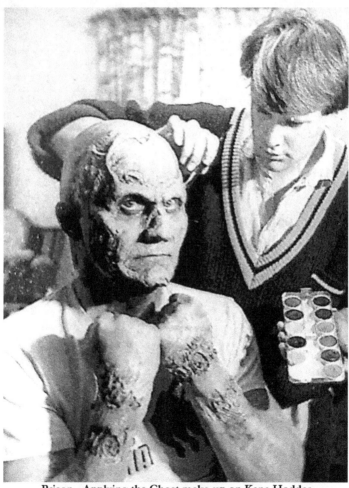

Prison - Applying the Ghost make-up on Kane Hodder

Prison - Kane Hodder

We were a wild bunch on that movie. Every night after work, the crew headed to the hotel bar where we all drank, hung out, and got rowdy. Playing opposite Viggo in the film was a beautiful young girl by the name of Chelsea Field. She was low-key, funny, and friendly and really great to be around. She had just finished shooting the movie version of *He-Man, Masters of the Universe* and was a terrific actress who easily fit in with an all-male cast. She was far more disciplined than the rest of us when it came to partying. I remember sitting watching the new George Michael "Faith" music video on a pull-down screen that hung in front of the bar's tiny dance floor as Chelsea sat with me, sipping herbal tea then wisely heading to her room as the rest of us raged on.

Chelsea Field and I on Set of Prison

As the shooting days passed, my friendship with Viggo grew and I began to develop a genuine liking for his talent and amazing sense of humor. I followed him around like a wide-eyed puppy whenever I had the chance. For once in my life, the coolest person on earth seemed to genuinely enjoy spending time with me, and I cherished that attention and acceptance. Like John Vulich, Viggo never hesitated to remind me that I was worthy. These boys were clearly the daddy that Billy boy never had and I grew to be as attached to him as I was Vulich. It was one of the few times in my life that an older male chose to not only see the good in me, but to constantly remind me that I was worthy. I know that he had no idea what a huge impact his acceptance was having on me because he was kind and respectful to everyone he interacted with.

Friday rolled around once more and we all closed the bar. Viggo and I, still very much young dudes who enjoyed an occasional taste, invented a cocktail that quickly became the crew's signature drink. We called it the "Aqua Velvis." It was a lethal booze concoction consisting of Pineapple Juice, Blue Curacao, Rum, two shots of Bacardi 151, cherries, and splash of soda water. You have to remember we were very young then, way back at a time in our lives when our livers could easily survive drinking such dastardly things. Still, having more than one of these babies always led to all sorts of misbehaving.

One night in particular, just before we had two days off for the weekend, the gang and I headed to the bar and closed it down as usual. Viggo and actor Arlen Dean Snyder were going fly fishing first thing in the morning and we all ended up in his room as the two prepared for their trip. We sat in a circle, talking and passing a bottle of Jack Daniels around as the two men tied their fly hooks. It felt so good to be included with the two of them. Arlen was a seasoned acting professional and had many stories that spawned from his long journey in the business. Viggo was equally entertaining as he shared his history in the theater performing and in his studies with actress and teacher Sandy Dennis. I finally figured out that actors and film folk were the people I felt most comfortable with. It was just as the last sip of Jack Daniels was imbibed that things took a hilarious but humorously terrifying turn. Arlen suddenly glazed over and looked over at me with a smile.

"We gonna catch us some big fish tomorrow, Viggo?" he said.

"Yes, sir," Viggo concurred.

"Well, then, I think we might need to get some practice." Arlen mad-dogged me as he said this.

"Oh, yeah?" Viggo continued.

"I think we might have us a real big bass sitting right here," Arlen said as he raised his fishing rod.

"No!" I said laughing. They couldn't be serious.

Arlen smiled, raised his eyebrows, and then suddenly cast the fly hook in my direction. It landed in the carpeting, snagging as all three of us burst into laughter. My laughter came to an abrupt stop as Arlen crossed and yanked his hook out of the rug, reeled it back in and whipped the rod back, ready for another shot.

"Very funny. Don't you dare," I nervously laughed as Viggo raised his own rod with a wicked grin.

I knew he was just giving me the treatment, but I'm sure it was fun watching me squirm, as I am the world's biggest chicken. Arlen, on the other hand, I didn't really know very well at that point, so while I was laughing along with the shtick, I was also wondering if I was going to end up catch of the day. "I say we give this big bass to the count of five before we hook that little son of bitch," he said.

Viggo burst into laughter, nodding. "Uh, huh."

"No!" I laughed as the two of them smiled with wicked glee in their eyes. "You guys, no!" I begged as I backed up towards the door.

The men snapped their poles and both of their feathered fishhooks flew across the room and snagged into the carpet on either side of me. Thinking quickly, I bolted out of the room as the two pried their hooks out of the faded hotel carpeting. I sprinted down the hallway just as Arlen exploded out of the room. "Get that son of a bitch!!!" Arlen yelled as Viggo and he chased after me, laughing like drunken hyenas. I knew they were only kidding around…mostly, but just to be sure, I got the hell out of there.

Since my room was upstairs and I was nowhere near the elevator, I dashed out the door and into the pool area as the boys flung their hooks at me once more. I ran out to the pool gate and around to the front of the hotel as I heard Arlen's voice echo, "Here fishy, fishy!!!"

I bolted into the lobby, trying my best to not overreact. The last thing I wanted was to piss off the production. I ducked down behind the front desk, begging the puzzled clerk to not expose me as Viggo and Arlen crossed into the room and continued down the hall.

Once they were out of sight, I quietly ran behind them and took a sharp right to the east wing of the hotel. I made my way to Chelsea Field's room and pounded on the door, begging for her to let me in. She answered, frazzled in her pajamas, and let me in. We sat there laughing as we listened to Arlen bellow and continue to call out for me. Eventually, the echoes of laughter died down as I hid there in her room until the boys' midnight fishing expedition ended and I was able to sneak back to my room.

That night *I* was indeed the one that got away.

Mickey Yablans, Viggo Mortenson and I taking a break from the set of Prison

The rest of the shoot went terrific as we rolled down to the very last shot with Kane Hodder. We put Kane in the zombie suit and he sat seated in a rigged electric chair that violently shot up from the ground on strong pneumatic rods. By now, everyone had learned that Kane was fearless and a top-rate stunt man, and he pulled the stunt off perfectly in one single take. Ironically enough, if you look at the debris as the chair lands, you will see that two shattered sticks form a cross that sticks up in front of him. It was a perfect accident as most of the film features an old crucifix that the angry ghost left behind. It was a fitting ending to a marvelous journey.

Viggo Mortensen and Kane Hodder on the set of Prison

Viggo and I decided to drive home from Wyoming via Route 66 as opposed to flying. He had bought himself an old faded Ford truck while he was in Rawlins and while it was insanely cool to look at, it also broke down a lot. Still, we were both still at the age where nothing bothered us, not even the possibility of getting stranded. The truck breaking down just offered us a few hours to check out an unexpected little town, plus Viggo always managed to get the rig patched up no matter what went wrong. Along the way, we vowed to stop and play a game of pool in every bar where we saw a "Pool" sign hanging, and there were a lot.

One of the first of many stops we made was at an old cowboy bar that was just outside Rawlins. Not only was there a sign that let the world know they had pool tables, but the place also boasted the claim that legendary Wild West gunslinger Annie Oakley had shot a hole in the wall there. We parked along a row of motorcycles and other beat-up trucks and went inside. The place was a rough and tumble bar, mostly filled with older locals, and the room pretty much fell silent as we sauntered in.

The place was beautiful without trying. It was a huge, all-wooden saloon-type bar constructed in 1862. A line of dusty old men sat on bar stools drinking and chatting with each other. They coldly eyeballed us as Viggo and I bellied up to the bar. Sure enough, hanging right above the booze-bottle filled shelves was a picture frame that hung near the ceiling. Instead of a framing a painting, though, the frame surrounded a huge bullet hole that had been shot in the old adobe brick.

We ordered whiskey as one does. No one was too eager to be friendly to us as I put money in the jukebox and played Hank Williams followed by Jody Watley's "New Love" (which, in hindsight, I may have thought through a little better). Truthfully, I looked completely out of place, but I did my best to play it cool. There were six pool tables, all of them occupied. Viggo and I sat at the bar drinking as we waited for a table to open up. Across the way, a craggy-looking old cowboy who was playing a game by himself was about to finish. Viggo grabbed his drink and sauntered all the way across the bar and over to the old man.

"Mornin', sir," he said politely to the grim-faced geezer who didn't answer as he took another shot, sinking the ball with zero effort.

"My friend and I, we were wondering…"

Another ball went flawlessly into the pocket.

"if you would like to play us…"

And another ball was sunk.

"a game of pool."

And another.

The man sized up the eight ball, not once looking up at Viggo. "I don't care to," he said in the coldest, more unimpressed tone possible just as Jody Watley began to echo through the bar. With that, he sunk the final ball in the corner pocket.

Viggo sheepishly nodded and made the painful trek of rejection back to his barstool. The old man re-racked the balls, glancing up at us only once to shoot us a disapproving look as he nodded his head, chuckling to himself in full judgement.

We slammed our drinks and were back on the road before all of my horrible song choices had finished playing. We both laughed as we rolled back out onto Route 66.

Viggo & I Breaking Down Yet Again Along Route 66

20

HIS NAME WAS JASON

After a marvelous two-day road trip, Viggo and I were back in Los Angeles. I had not only seen a part of the United States that I never had before, but I also had gotten to know Viggo better and officially considered him a good friend. When we got back into action, he offered to introduce me to his acting agent. After a couple of interviews and watching my reel, she picked me up for representation. I was finally ready to hit the ground running and give it a go solely as an actor. Even more awesome was the fact that a section of the house that Viggo and his wife Exene Cervenka (from the L.A. punk band X) were renting had opened up while we were away. Viggo encouraged me to take the place and I did just that. Within a week of being back in town, I had once again changed my life in a huge way. I was never happier or more content.

The following Monday, I got back home from the gym and turned on my answering machine. It was my friend John Buechler's voice. "Come by the shop tomorrow. I have some good news for you."

The next day, I pulled it together and made my way out to Buechler's shop. In the middle of the room stood Kane Hodder's plaster body cast and it was covered in clay. Buechler, as usual, was standing next to it, pounding the clay into place with a mallet while listening to the soundtrack album of the play and film *Camelot*.

"I got a cool acting gig for you, buddy" he said to me. "One you're really going to like." As he continued his work, he told me it was a big horror film and sent me into his office to read the script on his desk. "I want you to play the role of Rocky. He's a loser rock star wanna-be."

I whole-heartedly agreed, not having any idea of what I was getting myself into. I was also not sure I was right for the role of a wanna-be rock star, but I was willing to check it out. John told me if I liked the part, I would have to come to read for the executive producers, reinforcing that I was really going to have to earn it this time.

I went into John's dusty office and sat at his desk. Sitting there was a screenplay titled *Birthday Bash*. I read the entire thing from beginning to end. My part was small, but because I returned as a ghostly vision a few times throughout the story, there was enough to do, and I was frankly glad to be invited to try out for it. The story revolved around a group of young kids who make their way to the mountains to throw a surprise birthday party for my character and each of us are eventually taken out by the hands of a ruthless and unstoppable masked killer. The script was well-written but painfully familiar. I finished reading and went back into the shop as John continued to sculpt. By now, he had made his way to the sculpture's head and he had spread clay all over and was beginning to carve away at it.

"Is this for the movie?" I asked him.

"Yep. Do you like the script?" he asked.

"I do, it's incredible, except—" I hesitated.

"Except what?" he asked, looking at me with a knowing smile.

"Well, it's a really good script, and I'm so thankful you're giving me the opportunity to audition, but it seems a lot like a *Friday the 13th* rip-off." I said.

"A lot. Like, exactly. I mean, the killer in the movie wears a hockey mask." I thought maybe John was losing his marbles.

"Well, there's a reason for that," John said as he carefully carved grooves of rotting flesh into Kane's clay-covered body-form. "That's because it *is* a *Friday the 13th* film".

"What? Are you kidding?" I said, completely stunned and overjoyed.

"Nope," he said, pulling out his hammer, then slamming it into his growing sculpture. John explained to me that Paramount was trying to avoid the film going union, so they're flying under the radar as a low budget, non-union horror film instead of a studio picture.

"Wait: I'm auditioning to be in a *Friday the 13th* movie?" I asked again, completely shocked.

"Yep. So, if I were you, I would get my buns home and start studying. You have a big audition tomorrow and I don't have the final say, so don't screw it up."

I couldn't believe it. As long as I had been in Los Angeles, John Buechler had been my biggest support system and advocate. He was and remains the only person I that I ever met while I lived in Los Angeles who kept his word with me one-hundred-percent of the time, and one of the few males who wanted to help my career without boinking me first. I was so happy and thankful. The biggest horror nerd in the world had just scored the experience of a lifetime.

I was auditioning for a sequel in one of horror's biggest franchises, *Friday the 13th Part VII: The New Blood.* Even better news was the fact that Kane Hodder had been cast as the new Jason Voorhees based on his performance in the movie *Prison*, the very film I had just finished working on. According to John, the footage of Kane wearing the zombie make-up I did, combined with his fearless stunt and great acting abilities, had sealed the deal. I was so happy to have been a small part of what helped propel him forward. Kane was the new Jason, and I knew he would excel at it. And as you certainly know, dear reader, he certainly did.

I got my *Friday the 13th* audition material that night, and the next morning, I headed to casting director Anthony Barnao's office. Since I still hadn't gotten a new car after mine had been stripped and towed, I walked from Hancock Park to the audition which was easily five miles. By then, Anthony and I knew one another well as I had done several movies for Charlie Band at Empire Pictures. In fact, Anthony's casting office was still in the old Empire building which was located right on La Brea Avenue, just south of Sunset Boulevard.

Sadly, by then, the film production department of Empire Pictures had closed its doors after a very long run, and the home video market was flooded with excess product. Everyone in town had figured out how to create a low budget film and the competition was stiff. Making independent films for a million dollars no longer made sense, since the small films seldom got any theatrical run. Charles closed the company and restructured as a much smaller operation: a new, financially conservative version of Empire Pictures known as Full Moon Features. It is a company that still thrives today with a small crew of brilliant young filmmakers, producers, and marketing people.

I went into the lobby at Barnao Casting and was shocked when I found several other guys that looked like me sitting there with the same material. John was right: this one wasn't going to just be handed to me. I nervously kept quiet as I waited my turn. Not only did I really want the part, but I had additional pressure of actors I knew being in the audition room with me as I waited, actors that worked a lot more than I did. What's worse, they were all beautiful. Ten handsome brown-haired dudes sat around shooting the shit as one by one they were called in. Self-doubt began to fill my head as I could hear them chatting about the recent acting gigs that they had done during their meeting with John. I began to wonder if the only reason I had done so well in the last five years was because I was willing to work in virtually every department to reach my goal. I suppose there was some truth to it, actually, but I had gotten where I wanted to be regardless.

I told the receptionist that I was going to the bathroom and went down the hall to be alone for a few moments. I nodded to a smiling man in one of the offices next to the men's room. He looked up at me like he knew me as I passed. When I came out of the bathroom, he called out to me, introducing himself as director Jeff Burr. I instantly knew who he was, as Jeff had directed a horror film I was a huge fan of a picture called *From a Whisper to a Scream* starring Vincent Price. Jeff told me that he recognized me from some of the work I had done for Empire and wanted to say hello. We instantly got along as we talked about our love of film and all things horror. I told him that I would love to audition for him sometime. We shook hands and I went back to the lobby just as my name was called.

There in the office, eating lunch, was John Buechler, Anthony Barnao, and Barbara Sachs, the associate producer of the film. My audition sides, which are pages they give you from the script, were mostly laughable. In the scene, my girlfriend and I break down in our car out in the woods; I decide to go pee and eventually get whacked by Jason. It was pretty much your usual *Friday the 13th* fare, but I was thrilled at the idea of potentially being *that* guy. Who doesn't want to be killed by Jason? To think I had seen the first *Friday the 13th* in the drive-in and here I was, in Hollywood, taking a shot at being in one of the sequels myself.

At that point in my career, my acting skills were rigid at best, but after spending so many years working on horror films behind the scenes, I knew how to give a good nervous breakdown performance just by proxy of watching all the other actors I had worked with in the past. I did my scene, pretended to pee against Anthony's office wall and hurled myself across the room as I pretended that Jason Voorhees was stabbing me over and over. I got so into it that I used all of my air and started gagging, nearly throwing up. Everyone laughed and applauded as I dropped to the carpeting choking and gasping for air. Little did they know, I had just given myself a complete head rush to the point of passing out. The gang thanked me and I walked all the way back home in what felt like five minutes as I knew I had done the very best I could. I asked the universe to please give me this chance and promised I would make the most of it.

That night, Viggo, Exene, and I had just turned on a VHS movie in my furniture-less living room when the phone rang.

"You got the part," my agent said. "They're changing the character from wild rocker to white-boy yuppie for obvious reasons that I don't think I need to explain to you, but you got it. You start work next Monday here in town, then leave for Alabama the following week for a month."

I was so happy. I had finally gotten an acting part from auditioning and not because of my willingness to do double-duty painting slime on hand puppets. I guess it's true when they say it doesn't matter how you get there, just as long as you get there, and I had arrived.

Suddenly, I realized that I was in a feature film that was going to be seen by millions. I wanted to put my very best foot forward and that meant not only knowing the material but looking the very best I could. That night, I didn't eat again out of fear that I was going to gain some of my weight back before we shot. Controlling my weight was still a huge issue for me. I had finally lost all of the fat that I had carried around for years and I was terrified of going back. I didn't realize at the time that I was starting to develop a seriously unhealthy issue with my relationship with food. I simply would not eat. Before I had gotten it together, I was eating everything in sight to mask my feelings, and at that time, I was virtually starving myself to stay in control.

By then, I was eating pretty much no food, maybe one small meal a day at around two o'clock. It had been many years since I had eaten a hamburger or a single French fry. I had learned from living with Bunty Bailey that you need very little food to get by and that's just what I was doing. The week before I filmed, I ate only a quarter can of cream of mushroom soup a day, while also going to the gym, once in the morning and once at night. I lay in bed every night hungry, telling myself that I had overeaten and that I needed to be more careful the next day, despite having eaten less than 200 calories. I was burning so many calories from working out that weight was now falling off of me, even when I no longer needed it to. I was beginning to look too thin.

Since I had finally gotten my looks together, as well as I could anyway, I also started to getting invited to go out with my new friends more often. It was weird to me how I was suddenly getting the attention of others since I was the exact same person I was when I was a hundred and twenty pounds heavier. We hit the bars and drank until we closed the place nearly every weekend. I quickly realized I had a particular knack for raising hell. Two drinks in, I was hilariously funny or thought I was anyway. Three drinks in, I was a little quieter, but one sip into the fourth drink, I was fully capable of turning on you. If I wasn't rudely dressing anyone down who gave me what I perceived as attitude, I was positively up for a fistfight. It was during many of these drunken weekend nights that my love affair with drugs began to flourish. I went from only using on Friday nights to using pretty much whenever anyone had it (which was often), to having my own dealer deliver a gram to me once a week. Having a delivering drug dealer that not only brought the crap to you but also brought it to you when he actually said he would was like finding a unicorn in Los Angeles. For those of you who are smart enough to not have a full-time drug runner, there is no one on the planet more unreliable than a drug dealer. I mean, let's face it, if they were fine upstanding and citizens, they wouldn't be dealing drugs to begin with.

My dealer or "witch doctor," as I called him, was a guy named Bobby, a motorcycle-driving, tattooed bad boy and longtime boyfriend of my pal, actor Leslie Jordan. Leslie's best known these days for his Emmy award-winning appearances on the television show *Will and Grace* and is a revered stage performer and brilliant comedian. He is currently the darling of YouTube with over five million followers and shooting a new television series *Call Me Kat*, but back then, we were just two young actors constantly looking for work and well frankly…trouble.

Leslie and I first met at a coffee shop in West Hollywood and became fast friends. We had a lot in common: our love of acting, our deep-seated fascination for the underbelly of life and all things dangerous, but mainly the fact that we were both absolute masters of self-medication. This is many years ago, mind you, before Leslie became a pillar of sobriety. He's now a man who refuses to go to parties, he is so uninterested in being drunk or high or being around others who are…but back then, we redefined the art of misbehaving.

On a slow week when auditions were few, we headed to our favorite dive bar to drink the day away, only to sober up in the later afternoon with whatever drug we could get our hands on and from a variety of nefarious sources. How we were not murdered in our relentless pursuit of seedy fun I will never fully understand. My love of coke and being distracted from everything going on in my head led me to try other drugs. *Many other drugs.* Mushrooms, speed, acid, ketamine (which is used as a cat tranquilizer believe it or not) and a new drug that had just arrived in town from the East Coast called ecstasy. I spent many weekends on ecstasy getting really high then coming down really hard. The crash from all of this stuff was legendarily horrendous, especially for someone with depression issues like myself, but since I was young, the turnaround was quick so I started constantly putting my braincells to the test.

"You know that crap you're doing messes with your dopamine when you come down right?" Viggo told me as I sat on the steps of our Handcock Park house, ready to hang myself after a three-night drug-fueled bender.

I foolishly figured the best way to avoid a crash was just to stay high. Lots of times, my drug friends and I partied all night, took a day nap or tanned by the pool, then woke up, did another gigantic rail, or six, and then did it all over again. I can't tell you how many times we went out dancing all night only to emerge from the club in broad daylight. These days, I'd be dead from such scandalous activities. There isn't a day that goes by where I don't acknowledge that I am probably living on borrowed time for all of the synthetic fun I had back in the day. The fact that I am such a snob on the subject of drugs these days is completely laughable. Thank God I don't have kids. It would be very hard for me to keep a straight face while I asked them "Just say no," when I spent the better part of fifteen years shouting a resounding "YES!"

These days, I am highly against doing drugs of any kind and I measure my drinking as best as I can, but I was only able to make that wise life choice after trying everything under the sun over and over again. Seriously, kids: don't even try any of it. It's a slippery slope that never ends well, but damn, I sure did my best to try and climb that slope, didn't I?

I was called in to meet with the *Friday the 13th* wardrobe designer Jackie Johnson, who later moved on to become a highly regarded costumer, creating costumes for shows like *Breaking Bad* and the *High School Musical* TV series. Jackie took me to LL Bean and dressed me in what I like to refer to as my Katharine Hepburn from *On Golden Pond* look. I was head to toe in rustic cozy, brand-spanking-new mountain wear. (For whatever reason, this started a trend with me as I was dressed pretty much the same way in most of the other acting gigs I booked throughout my career.) The next day, a new shooting script was messengered to me and I read it. It was wildly different than the original draft I had been given, particularly my part, which had gone from heavy metal wanna-be to annoying cracker yuppie, and the part was half the size it was in draft one. It's really amazing how sometimes you audition for one project and by the time you get to set, it's an entirely different movie. It just goes to show you how much of show business is a huge crap shoot based on luck and good hair.

This *Friday the 13th* sequel, *The New Blood*, was an homage to the movie *Carrie* where the leading character and final girl Tina was a person endowed with the power of telekinesis. The story follows Tina as she and her mother meet up with her wicked mental health doctor as he plans to take her back to the mountain town where her father died in the hopes of bringing out her powers so he can document proof of it. Of course, that town is Crystal Lake and all sorts of mayhem breaks loose as she accidentally brings the killer Jason Voorhees back to life. The cabin they are staying in also just so happens to be next door to the place where my character Michael is heading to for a surprise birthday party thrown by all of his friends.

Although my character had been changed from wild rocker to pasty nerd, many of the original characters and dialogue remained in the script from the previous drafts. More than once the characters in the story refer to Michael as an insane party animal, despite my looking more like a milquetoast mannequin from LL Bean. After my contract was signed, Buechler asked me to come in and do a chemistry read with some of the girls they were auditioning to play my girlfriend in the film. I went in and read with a variety of actresses including Staci Greason, who had previously played my friend in the film *Terror Night*. John loved Staci and her funny, positive disposition, and she was quickly booked. I was so happy to be working with her again. She would be meeting us in Alabama in a week.

The first week was shot in Los Angeles in a stage near Culver City. We shot most of the interiors in cabin sets the production had built in a huge sound stage. I was scheduled on the very first day of shooting and I was in the very first shot that was filmed. I am also proud to boast that I was also the very first person to appear and be killed on camera by Kane Hodder as Jason. For a fan boy like me, this was massive.

In between shots, I sat with actress Lar Park Lincoln, a beautiful young girl and great performer who was playing the leading role of Tina along with Larry Cox who played the conservative yuppie of the bunch. Lar had previously starred in a film called *The Princess Academy*, and on the film *House 2,* she was funny and kind and I was really looking forward to getting to know her better. She seemed to know how to carry herself on set while I was strictly faking it. I was a nervous wreck.

Years later, Lar Park Lincoln is still a dear friend

Buechler called me in to shoot my very first shot with Kane; it was footage that was to be used for one of Tina's psychic visions she had of me throughout the story. The effects guys had me stand on an apple box and squat down. They filled my mouth with a huge mouthful of stage blood, a goopy concoction of Karo syrup and red food coloring. It tasted so awful. Then Kane, in his Jason costume, stepped up behind me. One of the interesting and somewhat terrifying facts about Kane Hodder is that when he is wearing the Jason costume and hockey mask, he is always in character. If he is supposed to chase you, he really chases you. If he is supposed to choke you, he really chokes you, and in this case, he was supposed to stab me and lift me up off the ground.

Kane glared at me as he took his position. "Are you ready to do this buddy?" I nervously chuckled as the hulking monster stared me down with no reply.

I turned back towards the camera white as a ghost, having flashback visions of the misguided time I tried to play Pop Warner football and the other kids massacred me because they could smell my fear. On action, Kane grabbed the fake camping tent spike that had been glued to my back and jammed it into me with all of his force. There was no acting required as my eyes bulged and I coughed the fake blood up. I did my best to pay tribute to Janet Leigh in *Psycho* by reaching out to the camera as I got shanked, but the shanking was feeling all too real, so my expression was strictly real.

Kane Hodder's very first kill as Jason

Everyone on set clapped when we were done after only one take. What no one noticed was my reaction to the pain was no performance: Kane had grabbed the handle so tightly as I backed into it with all of my force that we both ended up jamming it into the meat of my back and into my spine. The next day, I had a huge bruise on my back. Talk about your method acting. From that moment on, I knew that Kane Hodder meant business when he was in that Jason costume. Every time he had the suit and mask on, he stayed firmly in character and I stayed as far away as possible.

The first week of shooting seemed to fly by and the next thing I knew, we were about to film the finale when the character Tina burns Jason in the basement. The set was slowly becoming very tense as little by little the upper management of the production began to hassle Buechler. John told me that management was endlessly questioning his every move to the point where his focus was beginning to split between trying to make a good movie and appeasing those around him who seemed to be under the impression that they know how to do things better than him. Every single day, new script pages were being generated and polished by John's assistant David Ronan. Dialogue was changing, action was changing, page by page and from day to day. This was not a good sign, as it was hard to keep track of exactly what was staying and what was going.

One of the other main things that Buechler insisted on was that the film be filled with lots of blood and gore effects. After all, if you go to see a movie called *Friday the 13th*, you know what you're in for, but from day one, there was major push back on how much gore was going to end up in the final film. This was a time where the Motion Picture Association of America was really censoring films, horror films in particular. If you wanted your film to have a theatrical release, it needed to be rated by the MPAA. Even more pressing was the fact that since the film was coming out within just a few months, it was also being edited by editor Barry Zetlin as we went along. Usually a film is shot completely out of sequence due to scheduling and actor availability, but in the case of *Friday the 13th Part VII: The New Blood*, the film was shot mostly in sequence so that it could quickly be finished as we ended principal photography. The last shot that we shot was the last scene of the movie, and as the film was developed and cut in, the rough cut was finished the next day. This is generally unheard of, but Barry somehow pulled it off as he cut the movie feverishly in his hotel room in Alabama. Not six months from the time we started pre-production, the rough cut was already completed.

This was my first time acting in a bigger studio picture and I was nervous about fitting in. The crew was huge, the food was better, the equipment was top-rate, and most of all, the cocaine was plentiful. For the most part, all of the main actors were squeaky clean and drug free, which is exactly why an out of control wildcat such as myself made fast friends with the scallywag crew members on the production. As much as I love directing actors these days, back then, I found hanging with the crew much more comfortable than with the other performers. This was the eighties, and doing coke on set was *not* considered scandalous in any way, but rather a way of life. A big baggie of "Peruvian Dance Powder," as they called it, was continually handed from person to person, particularly when we were shooting late nights. This was ironic as there was no one on the planet more against doing drugs than John Buechler himself. He would have chewed me out had he any notion that this activity was unfolding, and in hindsight, I wish he had. I was developing a pattern and a resistance for things I truly had no business dabbling in. As I have pointed out, that way of life is long behind me, but at the time, I was right in the middle of it.

The day before the burning basement sequence finale in the film, the character Tina supposedly whammies Jason so bad that his hockey mask magically cracks off and falls to the ground, giving us a long-anticipated look at that hideous face of his. You would think that pulling this stunt off would require a lot of high-tech effects gadgetry, but in fact, the make-up guys were applying another make-up in the next room, so Buechler asked me if I could help him figure out how to pull it off. Thinking quickly, Buechler and I had one of the construction grips cut the hockey mask in half, then slightly tack it back together with super glue. Then, we carefully placed it back on Kane's head. Right before we shot, I kneeled down behind him. I reached up and grabbed ahold of the back of the mask. On action, we yanked back as Kane leaned forward and somehow, the mask broke in two perfectly. If you watch closely, you can kind of tell that he is helping it along as he leans forward and it cracks off. It's funny how sometimes thousands of dollars are spent creating special effect gags, and other times, you just pull it off on your knees with super glue.

Everyone in the rest of the cast was friendly and awesome in their own way. We really had zero complainers acting-wise on that set. Kevin Blair (now Kevin Spirtas) played the male lead and my cousin in the film; he had a great career going and was an established Broadway professional. Susan Blu, Diana Barrows, Liz Kaitan, Heidi Kozak, Jeff Bennett, Jon Renfield, Diane Almedia, and veteran actor Terry Kiser were some of the others that made up the majority of the cast. They were all really good and seasoned performers. I did my best to fit in as we all quickly bonded.

Actor Larry Cox and I clicked over our love of theater, writing, and improv, and he invited me to come see a show that he was in called *Theatersports* that had been running in Hollywood for a long time. Little did I know that I would eventually be taking classes with the comedy troop and end up in the show myself. That show is ultimately what got me into the *National Lampoon Live* show and eventually elevated my writing career.

By far, the light of the *Friday the 13th* set was the actors' make-up artist, Jerrie Werkman. She was a hilarious, beautiful, smart, rodeo-haired young girl who somehow managed to keep all of us looking good and laughing and who, along with her longtime boyfriend Kenny Meriedeth, has remained my one of my closest and most cherished friends for the better part of 35 years. Jerrie has stuck with me through all of my journeys: rich, poor, fat, thin, working, not working, sober, high as a kite, and sometimes even higher than that. Her friendship has remained unflinching for many years and *Friday the 13th Part VII: The New Blood* was where that friendship all started. The film changed my life for the better in so many ways, but Jerrie Werkman was my most prized get.

Key make-up artist Jerrie Werkman and I on the set of Friday the 13th, Part 7

The last day of shooting in Los Angeles before we left for Point Clear, Alabama for the exteriors was upon us, and the final scene that was to be shot was the one where Tina sets Jason Voorhees on fire with her mind. Buechler was particularly bothered that morning. He told me over breakfast at Dupars at the Farmer's Market that not only was the production making the shooting experience a more and more unpleasant one, but he was growing increasingly nervous about Kane Hodder doing the full body burn in the scene that we were shooting that day. As I mentioned earlier, Kane had been horrifically burned in a stunt accident that nearly took his life years before, and despite there being no one more stable, knowledgeable, and well-adjusted on the subject of his accident than Kane himself, Buechler was still worried.

"Did he say he wants to do it?" I asked.

"He is *insisting* that he's doing it," Buechler replied. "I have complete faith in the guy. I just want him to be safe."

"Well, considering the hell he's been through, I don't think he'd be doing the stunt himself if he didn't think he could pull it off. Has he done other body burn stunts since then?"

"A few others, but none as big as this," Buechler said, downing his coffee.

"I wouldn't worry. Kane can put his head through a concrete wall if he wants to. He's a total pro; he is going to be fine."

Buechler looked at me in agreement. "And nobody knows that more than Kane himself. I just want him to be safe," he reiterated.

"Besides," I added. "What could possibly go wrong?" I was going for the laugh that didn't come as our eyes went wide in mock terror. We finished breakfast and headed to set.

The energy that morning was high and everyone was in a great mood. We shot all of the action in the basement between Jason and the character Tina leading up to the body burn. I was really impressed to see how many of the stunts that Lar Park Lincoln was willing to do on her own. Very seldom did we ever have to have the stunt person come in, as she was a complete team player. Even more impressive was her ability to sell the telekinesis part of her acting job. She really seemed to have it all down.

Finally, we had shot everything leading up to the body burn and everyone shifted gears into safety mode. Kane and his assistants prepped the fire stunt by dressing him in his thick fireproof suit and coating it with the cooling fireproofing gel. His Jason costume was placed on top of that. You would think that the set would be very serious while setting up such a huge stunt, but nobody seemed to be more excited than Kane Hodder himself. His excited and positive disposition alleviated any worry everyone had about all of us pulling the massively dangerous stunt off.

Three cameras were placed in various positions, then the set was cleared and lit. Kane's Jason mask and hockey mask were put on last. Every single step of the shot was carefully mapped out as he mimed reacting to the fire igniting and traveling up his body and stumbling around. The basement set was built with a furnace that had a false fireproof wall behind it. The physical special effects team set up a flame thrower-type device behind the furnace and wall and a monitor was set up so they could all see at the precise time to blast fireballs as Jason stumbled back into the gasoline that Tina had sprayed all over the floor. After several rehearsals where he showed everyone exactly where he was going to walk in his "fire dance," everyone gave the thumbs up that they were on the same page and we prepared to roll.

Kane stood with his arms held out wide as the flammable gel was slathered onto strategic places on his Jason costume. The room fell silent as the effects guy poured flammable liquid on the soundstage floor. Everything was buttoned up and John Buechler called action. The effects guys ignited the flamethrower and shot a huge ball of fire over the concrete which flawlessly set the flammable fluid on the floor into a growing trail of fire. Flames raced around Kane as he took his position.

On their second cue, the effects department blasted Kane again; this time, with a massive ball of fire that slammed into his backside and set the gel covering his body ablaze. In an instant, Kane's entire body was completely engulfed in fire as he turned away from the camera. Everyone on set held their breath as he rotated over and over, far more than we had rehearsed. Kane Hodder was really going for it, just like the boss that he truly is. After being on fire for a full forty-five seconds, twenty seconds longer than we expected him to be, Kane finally fell to the ground, which was the signal for the fire squad to come in and spray him down with extinguishers.

The crew burst into applause. It was a flawless stunt executed by a complete pro. Kane Hodder had just finished his biggest stunt of his life and right in front of our very eyes. We all congratulated him. He seemed completely relaxed as he smiled and peeled off his gooey costume. The only thing he said was, "Did it look cool?"

Yes, Kane: it in fact looked really, really cool.

The Monday after we wrapped in Los Angeles, the entire cast and crew flew out to Point Clear, Alabama. Everybody was taken to the Marriott Grand Hotel, a beautiful, sprawling property with a mile of hotel rooms and golf courses. Lining the edge of the property were several fishing docks and sandy beaches that ran along Mobile Bay. The rooms themselves were beyond plush and very spread out. You had to be driven to your room with a golf cart after checking in if you had a lot of luggage, and because we were going to be there for a while, we all had loads of bags. The first thing I noticed about Alabama was the small contingency of people that seemed to still be living in the past. Having lived in the diversity of Los Angeles for so long had made me forget that not all parts of the United States were as evolved at that time. I was mortified as more than one African American hotel employee scrambled to help me with my bags and open my door with a "right away, sir!" Call it white guilt, call it what you will, but I loathed the vibe and found myself constantly running ahead of them to get my own bags and open my own doors just to play it cool.

Equally different was the amount of rough, Southern white people that didn't take kindly to new strangers in town, especially scrubbed clean boys in their early twenties with hair highlights and cherry-colored Chapstick who sat reading *Vanity Fair* at the local greasy spoon. More than once, I nearly got my ass kicked just for being an outsider as I walked into the place.

Larry Cox and I were neighbors on the top floor of the hotel and I couldn't be happier to have him next door. I got settled into my room and was told to meet the cast in the bar. Around five that evening, I walked with Larry Cox over to the hotel's main lobby where we were all presented with our latest version of the script, again with many changes, along with our per diem. John Buechler gave everyone a little speech, telling us how happy he was with all of the work we had done thus far and after a group toast (where, of course, he drank nothing), he headed back to his room to get ready for the next day. We were told that a call sheet telling which of us were working and what time we should be on set would be slipped under our door after nine that night. Most of the cast was really starting to get to know each other and we further bonded as we all spent our per diem buying each other drinks and eating dinner. It was a fun scene. Being an actor can be a terrific life, particularly if you happen to be booking jobs.

By then, I was also a professional party animal and being young (and frankly completely stupid), I took no consideration that I very well may be called in early that next morning to shoot. Most of my scenes shot in the evenings, so I was under the misinformed opinion that I could party all night and still look terrific in the morning. I sat with Lar Park Lincoln, Larry Cox, and Jerrie Werkman as someone sent me a double Bloody Mary. There had been the slightest whispers that Lar and Kevin Blair were not getting along, but her beautiful face and Southern charm easily masked any clues I tried to get out of her.

I slammed my drink down within a matter of minutes and was instantly back at the bar ordering another one. Ten minutes later, I was right back up, ordering yet another double. Though my exact memory of the rest of the night in the bar itself is understandably hazy, I do remember ending up around the corner near the bathroom with one of the grips as we did coke and drank. Afterwards, I went back into the bar and ordered another double; by then, I had drunk six double Bloody Marys and done about a gram and a half of coke, and all within three hours. Well, ladies and gentlemen, I was about to learn one of life's very, *very* valuable lessons.

I went back into the bar area and sat back down at the table next to my new friends. I was there for a few minutes chatting with Lar, having a perfectly grand time, when all of the sudden, my eyes rolled back into my head and I passed out, face planting hard down onto the rug below. The next thing I (barely) remember is Larry Cox and Kenny Meriedeth dragging me from under the arms through the lobby as I vomited an unsavory tomato juice trail behind us. I was completely incapacitated. I couldn't walk or form a sentence. Hotel staffers buzzed around us, moving plants and furniture, opening doors and mopping up as my two new friends dragged my heavy carcass across the room.

Larry Cox backed one of the hotel's golf carts up as Kenny and one of the stunt men lifted me onto its mini-flatbed. Just as soon as my drunken body dropped down, Larry floored it, taking off in the direction of my room. I remember looking back and seeing most of the drunken cast standing at the hotel's entrance, watching me and waving as I sped away. Despite the entire situation being a complete shitshow, I do recall a massive amount of laughing, mostly by Kenny and Larry.

They made their way across the hotel parking lot and over to the wing of the hotel where my room was. Kenny told Larry to wait with me at the golf-cart as he slipped inside and instantly reappeared with a rolling room service cart. According to the boys, they rolled my unconscious body off the golf cart and up the walkway, passing several shocked tourists and hotel guests. My head was hanging down on the front of the cart and my legs were hanging over the rear. The boys wheeled me down the hall and into the elevator. Larry pushed the button for the top floor and the elevator ascended, and halfway up, it stopped. The doors opened to a stunned family standing there in shock.

"We'll catch the next one," said the concerned English father as he gawked at the unconscious body lying in front of his family. The doors closed and we finally made it to the top floor. The guys wheeled me down the hall and to my room, stripped me of all of my clothes, hoisted me into the tub, and turned on the cold water. It was obvious that Kenny, having had his own traveling rock band for years, had accumulated the perfect amount of experience for those who over-imbibed as he dumped a huge bucket of ice over me. After a few moments, I came to, hammered, but conscious. They helped me out of the tub, dressed me in my pajamas, and aimed me towards the bed. I lay down and closed my eyes, instantly falling asleep. The boys later told me that they waited for an hour, keeping an eye on me, and then quietly slipped out of my room. Now, for most sane people, this is where the story ends. However, this is me you are reading about.

My eyes opened as the door clicked shut.

The room was spinning and my head was suddenly pounding. I staggered up out of bed and went to my suitcase for aspirin. Finding nothing, I was dying of thirst and was determined to get ahold of something for my head, but unfortunately, the only aspirin around was at the hotel gift shop all the way back in the lobby. I pulled up my jeans, put on my boots, tucked my pajama shirt in, and drunkenly made my way back down the hall.

In a matter of moments, I was down the elevator and back on the golf cart. After ten minutes of trying to get it started, I finally fired it up and was off to the races. I careened through the parking lot, rolling over the pavement at an astonishing ten miles an hour, grazing bushes and trash cans like a blithering idiot. Just as I started to swerve my way towards the hotel valet area, a security guard called out to me. I slowed, turning back as he started running towards me. Being a young moron and frankly, drunk, I floored the golf cart, which isn't saying much being that it barely moved. I pulled ahead of my pursuer down the driveway and along the short pier that ran along the golf course next to Mobile Bay. The security guard was easily catching up with me so I had the terrific idea to take a shortcut along the pier. I swerved across the putting green and skid around the corner, losing him. But my victory was short-lived as I turned to head back towards the main lobby just as I lost control and drove the golf cart off the pier and flipped it over, down into the knee-deep water below.

Thinking quickly but not intelligently, I got out of the cart and somehow managed to stagger my way back to the room with no aspirin in hand but thankfully, my head still attached. I thought to myself, after everything I have been through in life, I am thankful that my demise wouldn't involve me being decapitated in a drunken golf cart hijacking. I got into bed at about midnight, closed my eyes, and went to sleep.

Later, I was awoken from the deepest sleep I ever had experienced by the phone ringing in my room. I looked at the clock; it was eight but somehow, still dark outside.

"Hello?" I could barely get the word out.

"Hello, this is your agent," the voice said in an unentertained manner.

"Oh hi! How are you?" I said, sitting up and slamming the glass of water Kenny had left for me on the nightstand.

"Well, I'm not too good actually," she said.

"Why is that?" I asked, despite already knowing the answer.

"Well, I just wrote a twelve-hundred-dollar check to the hotel to fix the golf cart that you drove into Mobile Bay." She said this with zero amusement.

"Oh?" I said in terror.

"Twelve-hundred-dollars that is going to be deducted from your first paycheck. And if anything else like this happens ever again, you will no longer have an agent. Good luck dealing with the production: they are not happy with you."

"Yes. I can imagine that they aren't thrilled. That is very understandable. It's a funny story really: I just was going to get some aspirin and—"

CLICK. The phone hung up.

I got out of bed and walked to the window, opening the drapes. It was dark outside. I crossed to the phone and called the front desk. "This is kind of a weird question, but what day is it?" I asked.

"It's Tuesday, sir," the hotel operator answered, a little shocked that I didn't already know the answer. I had slept for nearly twenty-four hours. I spotted the call sheet on the floor in front of my room and crossed to it, terrified. Holding my breath, I read it; somehow, I had dodged a bullet and had been off on Monday. No one knew that I slept through an entire workday. I went to the bathroom, brushed my teeth, and went right back to sleep.

What a professional actor I was turning out to be.

The next morning my phone rang. It was John Buechler. I held my breath as he greeted me with a good morning; somehow, he didn't know about my little low-speed pursuit. He told me I was off again that day but was hoping I would come and help dress Kane on set. The crew was heading to a local school campus where they were shooting all of the underwater shots in an indoor, Olympic-sized swimming pool. I agreed and headed to the lobby, where I was shocked at the amount of people who had no idea what had occurred Sunday evening (other than my throwing up in the lobby, but who's counting?). Like I said, those actors were cool peeps.

Word was, there was very little room around the swimming pool, so Buechler suggested that we dress Kane in his Jason suit before we left the hotel. As usual, Kane was in a perfect mood that morning. In all of the time that I have known him, I don't think I have ever seen him angry or grumpy. We dressed him up in his padding and shirt and brought his pants, cowl, and hockey mask along with us in the rental car. The area that we were shooting in was a very rural town called Bay Minette, right outside the area where our hotel was, but that morning, we headed into town to shoot at the school.

I rode with Kane in the back seat as we made our way through town. Somewhere along the way, we decided it would be funny for Kane to put both the Jason and hockey mask on and stare cars down as they passed us. It was awesome watching people go from smile-faced to sheer terror as they spotted the rotting corpse glaring from the car next to them. We were just about to turn off for the school when we happened to pass a police car and Kane made the very big mistake of looking over at the cop, who abruptly pulled us over. The redneck officer, right out of movie central casting, got out of his police rig with eyes widening as he slowly approached our car, relieved when Kane nervously pulled off his mask and pasted on a smile. I was half expecting the cop to laugh and just let us off the hook, but alas, there was no laugh.

"You folks workin' on that movie?" the cop said with zero expression.

"Yes, sir," the production assistant driving us answered.

"License and registration," he said, shooting me a cold look that screamed of a good ol' fashioned faggot lynching.

"Well, ya'll might think doing that kind of *thang* is funny in Los Angeles, but you're in the country now, boys, and you look at the wrong person with that mask on and you're gonna get more than you bargained for," he replied, staring us down.

We reassured the cop that we would never ever do it again and he let us off with a stern warning and a *Deliverance*-style lecture on driver safety. We drove away, all free men.

We pulled the same stunt just five minutes later.

The set was already a buzz at the school where we were shooting the underwater segments. The art department had taken black plastic sheeting and coated the inside of the pool's walls and lined fabric and sand along the bottom.

In the start of the film, Jason Voorhees lies dead and rotting at the bottom of Crystal Lake as the character Tina accidentally brings him back to life. All of the exteriors were shot at the real lake but everything below the water's surface was to be shot in the pool. Kane finished getting into his costume and climbed into the water. At the bottom of the pool was a huge boulder with a chain wrapped around it. The chain was locked around his neck as he made his way to the middle of the pool. Two scuba divers had been hired to work for the day and when Kane gave a hand signal, they swam up to him and let him take a breath of air from an air tube that they kept hidden off camera. The stunt was very dangerous, and everyone was on their toes to keep both Kane and the crew safe. I wasn't thrilled to be standing in the water that covered the concrete sidewalks surrounding the pool as dozens of high voltage cables were laid on top of them. It was constantly repeated to us that everyone needed to mind their footing.

One by one, we began to pick off the shots that were storyboarded by John Buechler himself. Kane put the chain on then floated up to the middle of the pool; they filmed the shot, then we cut and repeated the sequence. It was astounding to see how resilient Kane was and how long he was willing to hold his breath to get the perfect shot. He waited as long as he could before he asked to take another breath. Up top, there were some very tense moments watching him work beneath the water's surface and never coming up for air. His passion for giving the ultimate performance was becoming obvious to everyone involved. There was no stunt that he was not willing to try and execute.

Still, Kane nearly didn't make it through the entire shoot: a deadly accident unfolded without him even knowing about it. We were somewhere toward one of the last shots of the day when a grip carrying a piece of equipment accidently hit one of the lights, sending it toppling over. The big 10k light came crashing down onto the concrete, shorting out just inches from the edge of the pool. Somehow, the light had miraculously not fallen into the water and electrocuted everyone. Thinking fast, the crew quickly unplugged the light and swept it away before anyone even had time to react or be hurt.

No one said a word as Kane finally executed the last shot and emerged from the water, none the wiser that he had nearly met his maker.

The shoot continued and the hours were long. The longer the hours, the more blow the folks that functioned on it were doing, myself included. By then, a few members of the physical production team were having coke delivered by Fed Ex to the production office. This is long before 9/11 and sending drugs through the mail was not as risky of an activity yet. In hindsight, it was a stupid move as the recipient's name would have to be written on the package. Small bags of coke were taped into magazines and birthday cards and then sent overnight from Los Angeles to Point Clear on a daily basis. One of the production staff's boyfriends was a dealer, so we paid her part of our per diem and she placed the order. It was humorous to go to the office when the mail arrived every morning and see half the crew lined up to pick up their birthday Fed Ex packages. I grabbed my mail and went back to my room.

I was filming all night on that particular day and planned on staying awake the easy way. I was sitting on the couch in my room, drawing lines of blow on the glass coffee table when there was suddenly a knock at the door. Terrified it was one of my co-stars, none of whom partook, I quickly swept the drugs off of the table and into the open magazine that the stuff had been mailed to me in. I put the magazine in the dresser drawer and answered the door.

"You want your room cleaned?" said the beyond-bored, 400 pound-plus African American housekeeper.

"Uh, yeah, can you come back in an hour" I replied, wanting her out of there so I could finish what I had started.

"I finish in thirty minute," she said, staring me down.

"Well, then, no, I guess my room is fine," I said, starting to close the door.

"You want clean towels and glasses?" she asked, again clearly unimpressed with me.

"Uh, yeah, sure, come on in," I said to her. I opened the door and the rotund woman sauntered into the room. She put fresh towels in the bathroom and then went to put clean glasses on the glass table in the center of my hotel room. Before she set them down, she wiped it down. "Ya'll havin' a good time stayin' here in Point Clear?" she asked.

"Oh, yeah, we're having a great time."

"Mmm-huh," she said, looking up at me. "I can see that." She did not blink as she continued wiping the table.

Is she saying what I think she's saying? I thought to myself.

"Looks like somebody's doin' some cocaine up in here," she said, jaded.

I stared back at her, not knowing what to say. Busted. After a pregnant pause that went for what felt like forever, I pasted on a toothy smile and replied. "Want some?" I asked her.

The maid stopped wiping the table, plopped her big ass down on the couch, and looked over to me. "Don't hide it, divide it, baby," she said, clapping her hands and rubbing them together as I bolted for the door, locked it, then pulled the magazine of the dresser.

For the next three hours, that housekeeper and I sat in my room, doing drugs, smoking cigarettes, and chatting incessantly about our dreams and goals. Her name was Twanda and she said it was her ultimate dream to one day dance with the Harlem Ballet Company. Even in the height of my chemically-induced enthusiasm, I remember thinking that forty-five years old was going to be a late start for a four-hundred-pound ballerina. Still, I eagerly invited her and her entire family to visit the set, then gnashed my teeth as I helped her fold sheets and towels until the very moment when the van arrived to take me to set.

Susan Blu gets taken out by Jason on set in Point Clear

That night, just Kane, Staci Greason, and I were shooting a scene where I stumble upon Jason Voorhees. He chases me through the woods and ultimately shish-kebabs me with a large camping tent spike. Since our location was set right on the water, there were alligators everywhere. A regular member of our crew was a man known only as "Gator Man," a toothless old fellow who chewed tobacco and stood right by camera, shotgun in hand. Early on in the production, it was explained to us that there would positively be alligators showing up on set and that we should avoid them at all costs. They didn't have to tell me this fact twice, and I sure listened when the assistant director told us to be sure to run in a zig-zag pattern if we found ourselves being chased by one.

The other menacing thing about filming in the woods was that the place was crawling with deer ticks that carried the Lyme disease virus. Apparently, their ticks' chosen mode of transportation was to drop from the trees and onto a head or body. There was so much more to consider beyond the fact that Kane would positively kick your ass if he caught you in a chase scene (or try to make you believe that he was going to, anyway).

Getting the point from Kane Hodder aka Jason

The shot came up where Jason Voorhees was to run me down through the woods and knock me down in some brush. I took my mark, but not before scanning the area for any waiting toothy reptiles. I nervously looked over at Gator Man who just shrugged at me. Take after take, I sprinted through the woods and hit my end mark, falling on my face in the dirt, terrified that my head would end up in the mouth of an alligator or I would rise up covered in ticks. *Is this what my acting teacher meant when she told me I had a great career ahead of me?* I thought to myself. I really didn't think avoiding Lyme ticks and alligators were ever a part of the equation.

After trying to get the shot perfect take after take, I was relieved to hear John Buechler finally yell "cut" as someone helped me up and brushed me off. We were finally moving on. I walked up to John as I exhaled, so relieved that I wasn't crawling around near the water's edge anymore. I asked him what was next.

"You see that tree right there?" he said with a smile.

"Yeah?" I said, eyeballing the big, overgrown—and most likely, tick-covered—red maple.

"I need to film a shot where you're hanging upside down dead in it," he said.

I stared him down as Jerrie Werkman stepped up and rubbed dirt all over my face while her assistant simultaneously sprayed me in a cloud of anti-tick spray. What a life I was living. If you look close at the shot where I am lying dead in that tree, the horror in my eyes is not from the terror that Jason Voorhees had just put me through, but rather, the wonder if I was going to spend a lifetime with a rashy fever and swollen lymph nodes. Lucky, I think all the drugs in my system killed off any tick or other living organism, for that matter.

Kane later told me a great story about that very night. After we wrapped at about two in the morning, Kane, still in his Jason costume and hockey mask, decided to walk back along the trail to his trailer instead of riding in the van with Staci Greason and me. Along the way, he crossed paths with a local guy who was walking on the trail. When he came into Kane's eye line, Kane, still in character, stopped in his tracks and turned towards him with a jolt. The two men just stood there staring at one another for a moment.

"Are you with that bunch of folks out here filming a movie?" the guy nervously asked.

Kane said he just stood there, tilting his head from side to side in Jason's signature move.

Growing nervous, the guy asked again. "You're with the movie, right?"

At that moment, Kane lunged at him as the man took off, staggering backward and tripping onto his ass after falling over a log. Kane moved towards him as the man got back up and ran off into the night. The next day, he ran into Buechler, who said he was disappointed because a guy from the police department was supposed to come by the previous night but never showed up.

"Oh, really? That's too bad. I wonder why he didn't show up??" Kane exclaimed innocently.

As the shoot progressed, most of my acting scenes had already been shot, but since I still had to be there for the handful of shots I had left, I offered to help the guys in Buechler's effects team a hand on my off days. Buechler assigned me to help dress Kane. By now, we had suiting him up down to a science, but since the suit had pretty much been beat to hell and in and out of the murky lake, it began to stink to high heaven. It also never ever seemed to dry out, so every time the guy put the thing on, it was, for the most part, soaking wet.

"Stinky Voorhees" quickly became my nickname for him every time we got him zipped up and the entire room filled will the smell of wet moss and algae. The name stuck and pretty much everyone on set began to call him by that handle, as you could smell him coming from a mile away. Still, Kane, being the consummate professional, never said a word. He told me that the mossy stench helped him get into character.

Every day we dressed him; our routine was the same. Body suit, followed by damp Jason wardrobe over that, then pull over his faceless rubber cowl; his Jason prosthetic make-up was applied over that by artist Greg Johnson, followed by the legendary hockey mask.

"Put on your little hatty," I said as I finally finished up by putting his hockey mask on. As usual, the moment Kane was completely suited up, he was one hundred percent in character.

We were starting to wind down on our schedule; every scene that we shot was quickly developed and cut into the rough cut. The studio had set up a makeshift editing bay for the editor in one of the hotel rooms and he and his assistant feverishly edited each of the previous day's work. This would be the first and only time I ever worked on a film that was delivered just a couple of months after it was shot.

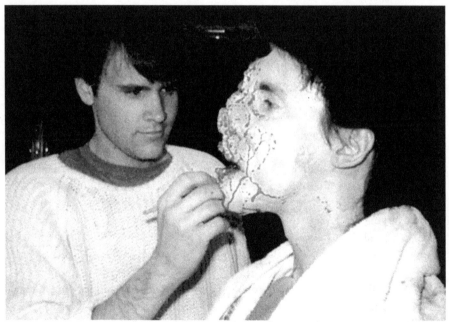

Painting "Gash Man" on Friday the 13th Part 7

Larry Cox and his stunt double on set of Friday the 13th Part 7

The rest of the shoot went well, minus the night actress Heidi Kozak catching hypothermia from the scene that called for her to dive into the freezing lake. I was more concerned about her becoming gator bait as she padded into the water, but her overwhelming shivering and blue face when she emerged out of the water was enough that the production had the set medic sweep her away to a hot bath and warmer temperature. She was a lot braver than I ever could be.

We wound down to the finale when Jason and Tina go toe to toe to try to finish each other off. Each shot was more interesting than the next as Kane put himself through a dozen dangerous stunts, from being wired from head to toe with hot sparks to hurling himself face down into a puddle of mud, holding his breath for what felt like a full minute before springing back up.

At one point during the night, Buechler and Kane came up to me with a weed wacker. Kane had seen it in the art department and wanted to use it as the weapon Jason uses to kill Terry Kiser's character, Dr. Crews. Originally, he was supposed to kill Terry off with a machete but a weed wacker seemed far more creative and was a weapon Jason hadn't yet used. The guys wanted me to quickly figure a way to replace the blade on the wacker so he could safely chase Terry down. Thinking quickly, I took a pizza box from the craft services area and traced the blade onto the oily, cheese-covered cardboard. I cut out the round shape with an Exacto blade and spray painted it silver. Ten minutes later, they were shooting and it looked amazing, proving once again that pizza truly does make things better.

The last night was finally upon us, the night that we were scheduled to blow up the entire cabin. In the story, Tina sets Jason on fire in the basement and of course, he springs back to life, and after he does, he chases both Tina and her love interest Nick out of the cabin. She sends the porch awning crashing down on him. Always the team player, Kane had no problem with the special effects guys dropping a real wooden awning on his head; if you look closely you can see him slammed to the porch. The thing easily weighed a thousand pounds. Normally, a stunt like that would be achieved with a lightweight balsa wood, Kane Hodder had no problem with them dropping a truck load of lumber onto his head to make it look right.

After Buechler called cut, the crew scrambled to dig Kane out of the rubble as he flashed them the "all clear" sign. It was really a wonder that he wasn't crushed.

After that, everyone who hadn't already flown back to Los Angeles came to set to see the house explode for one of the last shots. The idea was to detonate an explosion that blew the windows out of the cabin with fireballs that shot out across the front of the building. It took hours for the effects team to rig the house with explosives well into the night, and working well into the night meant that the bag of coke was once again being handed around by some of the members of the crew. Since we were on the last night of shooting and the following day was the wrap party, the bag of blow was larger than usual. They call it an eight-ball, which is about three grams. Imagine three packets of Splenda and you'll get the visual.

My turn to take a bump came around and the baggie was handed off to me. I palmed it and put it into my pocket without looking at it. I made my way to the porta potty behind the cabin set near the make-up trailers. It was incredibly dark out that night as I made my way inside the plastic latrine where it was even darker. I fished around in my pockets and found the little plastic bag. I couldn't see at all as I tried to get it open, ready to do my thing and get back to set. No matter how I tried, I couldn't seem to get the seal open. Frustrated, I put the baggie in between my two thumbs and rubbed them together until I heard it finally snap open. I grabbed my key and dipped the end of it into the little sack, pulling it out and putting it under my nose. But as I inhaled, I realized there was nothing there. I felt around, feeling the bag. It felt like it was empty.

I stepped back out into the woods and over to a portable light that had been set up. Sure enough, there was nothing in the little sack.

"You good?" one of the crew members asked as he approached me for the hand off.

"Uh, no, actually. I think you handed me the wrong one. There is nothing in this." I showed him the empty baggy.

"What are you talking about? It was full!" he said, bolting for the porta potty.

I followed him, looking over his shoulder as he pulled out his mag flashlight and shined it on the floor. It was covered in spilled cocaine. In the darkness, I had accidentally opened the baggie upside down and pour the contents all over the floor.

"My bad?" I said in meek terror. Needless to say, I was shunned by the rest of the crew that night as word got out. Thank God it was the last night of shooting.

It was about four-thirty in the morning when the riggers finally had all the explosives in place on the house set. Three cameras were set up and the entire cast and crew lined up behind what was designated as the safety line at the water's edge. On Buechler's call, all three cameras powered up, everyone ducked down low, and the effects guys started the countdown from five. On the last beat, the detonator was ignited.

Everyone was expecting several impressive fireballs that exploded out the windows, but what they got instead was one massive explosion that vaporized the entire house. Fire and burning, flying debris hurled through the air towards us; one piece of lumber knocked an entire camera out of its position and sent it rolling to the ground. The detonation was ten times bigger than anyone expected it to be. How no one was hurt and we didn't set off a huge forest fire I will never know.

John called cut and the local fire department rushed in quickly to put out the flames. There was nothing left of the cabin. After a beat of complete disbelief, there was a huge cheer from everyone involved. It was fitting end to an amazing experience. After shooting a handful of loose end shots, final wrap was called and we all headed back to the hotel for one last time.

The next night, we all went into Mobile and went out for one of the best wrap parties I've ever been to. We sang and danced and drank. I woke up a complete mess on Sunday morning, hanging on by a thread rather than hungover. In just a couple of years, I had redefined the art of show business misbehaving in a huge way.

On the plane ride home, I thought about how very lucky I had been to be a part of the project. I had gone to see the first *Friday the 13th* at the drive-in, and here I was, appearing in one seven years later. It was such an honor for a kid who lived for the horror genre. Filming the picture was everything I had hoped it would be. I exhaled, thinking that I had just tackled my first big goal and in a big way. I was a long way from sleeping in my car in a pizza parlor alley. I also realized that I was going to have to severely dial down my wildness if I was going to try and sustain a serious acting career. I told myself that this was going to be the last time I hit it so hard in my down time. It was my first time on location for the specific reason of performing, and I had dove into the deep end of filmmaking's debaucheries headfirst. I decided to say goodbye to the chemically induced fun for the time being and focus more on why I moved to Los Angeles in the first place.

Only two weeks after I was back home, I was invited to screen the rough cut of *Friday the 13th Part VII* with Buechler and a few other members of the cast and crew. Though the special make-up effects were cut in as John had originally envisioned them, the first cut was less than spectacular. It didn't help that there was no music. The film was overly long and several of the scenes simply didn't work, particularly the one when Elizabeth Kaitan's character Robin was killed. Jason exploded into the room and stabbed her in the gut with his machete, but the foam rubber breasts and torso looked laughable. The gag looked completely thrown together as she lay in bed with this hunk of foam clearly duct taped to her body, making her look six months pregnant. Another kill that happened too fast was when Diana Barrow's character Maddy was killed. There was no build up to her demise: she simply wandered outside after her *Friday the 13th* glam makeover and was offed by the big man in the mask.

We all left the screening feeling completely deflated, but not John Buechler. Despite being beaten down by the studio, he still had a vision on how he was going to tweak his movie for the better. A week later, we were all in Topanga, shooting at the same cabin where they shot *Friday the 13th: The Final Chapter.* John completely reshot Elizabeth's death scene, changing it from her getting a machete to the gut into her being thrown out of the upstairs window. Though her double looked nothing like her and her wig was akimbo, the scene worked much better after it was cut in. To tweak Maddie's death, John shot more of a lead in and had her take shelter from Jason in a tool shed until she is ultimately offed.

After the new scenes were cut in, the film was shortened and the traditional *Friday the 13th* music was laid in, and the movie really started to work. John's next obstacle would be the MPAA who gave the film an astounding X rating eight times after it was re-edited and resubmitted. An X rating on film would kill the film's chances of playing in theaters, so John was forced to go back in and shave frame after frame until there was hardly any of the original effects and gore still in the movie. Hugely disappointed but never discouraged, John finally cut the film down enough where we could get the rating that would make the film be released nationwide. Finally, we had reached the journey's end and a premiere was scheduled.

Friday, May 13, 1988, only five months after we started shooting *Friday the 13th Part VII*, the cast and crew, along with our director John Buechler, all walked the red carpet at Mann's Chinese Theater for the premiere. My mother and father came for the big night and I was able to invite all of my friends to the event.

A local urban radio station had sponsored the premiere and had given away two hundred tickets, so the theater was a bizarre combination of legitimate filmmakers and rowdy teenagers, some of which were there to raise hell. Still, it was fun to hear young people scream things like "Don't go in there!" at the movie screen. When it came to my onscreen death, a young girl sitting in the seats right behind me and my parents yelled.

"Fuck him: he was a nerd anyway!" she snapped.

My mother turned around and said very firmly, "That is my son you're talking about!" My dear mother, always looking out for me. *Friday the 13th Part VII: The New Blood* grossed twenty million dollars that week. Not bad for a film that was made for less than three million dollars. It was official: I loved acting and I wanted more, and more was just what I got. More of everything, some of which I didn't want.

21

PUT OUT OR GET OUT

One thing about being a newbie male actor in Los Angeles in the 80s that was starting to grate on my nerves was the number of male producers and directors that were suddenly hitting on me for sex in exchange for acting jobs. I was never Brad Pitt, mind you, but trust me: it happened more than I would ever care to acknowledge. I am, however, not claiming to be a victim in this scenario: not in any way. I was a very smart young man and could spot a letch from a mile away. I attended many a steak dinner and audition appointments in homes and or in hotel rooms knowing full well what was expected of me in some of them. Many were disappointed when there was no payoff at the end of the night. Mostly.

Sometimes, my chance for booking the job went away after I smiled and nodded at their compliments as I ordered everything on the menu, thinking, *Boy, are you gonna be pissed when I ghost on you after dessert.* There are many great things about being raised around the fair and carnival, but being able to spot someone that's up to no good has been one of its most valuable assets while living in Los Angeles. I learned at a very young age to always stay one step ahead of anyone who tried to manipulate or use me. I ate a two-hundred-dollar dinner, listening to my potential predator try and crack my combination, knowing full well that the martinis they were piling on me would not have the payoff they were hoping for at the end of the night. I don't feel bad for using them; they all had it coming. I will say this, however: whenever I was invited to a hotel room for a meeting, I positively knew that there was a chance that it was not just for business. I certainly cannot be the only actor in town to have figured that out.

The most notable of these disgusting beasts were some of the guys who ran DEN, the Digital Entertainment Network. DEN was a brand-new production company that boasted a seventy-five-million-dollar credit line made available to them to create several movies and television series broadcast on their own new platform. It was a very clever idea, and DEN was the precursor to platforms like Netflix, but the technology wasn't there yet to pull it off properly. Worst of all were some of the chicken hawks that were eventually revealed to be running the place.

I was called in several times as both an actor and spokesperson by a few execs who seemed to be very interested in me. Like, really interested. My agent Flo Joseph called me excitedly after my appointments, telling me that they really liked me and were determined to find the perfect show for me. I got called in time and time again with no booking as I began to know the guys running the place by name. They were very nice and extremely complimentary; each time, treating me like the reading I had just done was nothing short of Oscar-worthy, and even though I did smell a rat early on, they made me feel like I was someone special. I later learned that this was a usual part of their routine.

My enthusiasm for DEN and a few of the producers involved deflated after I was invited to a big party at one of their houses one Saturday afternoon. It was held at one of the lead producer's beautiful homes, and I was told to bring a bathing suit as it was a pool party, but being a modest guy with a less than ripped body... okay flabby, I opted to ignore the request and show up in jeans and a t-shirt. It was very unusual for me to be invited to a party before booking a job that I was close on and I began to become sure that all of the kindness they were laying on me had motivations beyond my getting an acting job. As I suspected, the crowded party was mostly packed with young, scrubbed males: very young, in fact. There were boys from the ages of what appeared to be 12 to 20 running amok around the lavish backyard and I was instantly uncomfortable. Pinocchio's Pleasure Island came to mind as I came upon tables of junk food and open bars everywhere I looked.

I met guy after guy my own age and younger, all of whom had the exact same story that I had with the company. They all seemed to be "very close to booking a leading role" on the network. When I was offered a drink, I was handed what must have been a triple vodka cranberry, and never one to turn down booze no matter how strong, I accepted it and sat down to people watch. It was then that I spotted a kid no more than fourteen sitting in the jacuzzi with the friendly producer that had been calling me. The sickening feeling that I once felt from my own awful molestation started to once again come over me and I knew it was time to bail, booking or not.

A pudgy and pink older guy sat down in the chair next to mine and tried to make chit-chat, giving me his card and asking me if I was an actor. He asked me if I had ever done any modeling, a question that got a huge laugh from me as I messed with him, telling him I had once been a foot model for Buster Brown shoes. The guy didn't get it, proceeding to tell me I had a "great look," one I could only guess must have been of the "shaken up" variety at that moment. I decided I wanted out of there. I was disturbed to see that the rumors of parties like this were true.

"Want some X?" the creepy guy asked me.

I accepted, then pocketed the pill, nervously getting up and going inside the house. As I headed to the bathroom, I spotted a beautiful blonde kid who couldn't have been much older than 16, lying passed out on the couch as a thirty-something creeper gave him a foot rub.

"Want to be next?" the guy asked me. I didn't answer, but headed straight for the door and bolted, completely freaked out.

I'm not sure exactly what unfolded the rest of the night. But rest assured, the rumors that you hear about pedophiles in Hollywood are true because I saw it for myself firsthand. The next week after I ghosted the party, my agent Flo Joseph called me to let me know that I had been released from my upcoming callback, and we never heard from or about DEN ever again; that is, until the media reported that charges had been filed against one of the execs for molesting a thirteen-year-old boy, and the company ultimately folded. One of the men has since fled the country and has been gone ever since.

Years later, as I became a director, I heard many stories from young actors that the exact same sort of parties were still being thrown by some of Hollywood's biggest producers and directors. These stories are in no way exaggerated. It's not hard to figure out who it is if you do a little digging on the internet, but you didn't hear it from me.

Headshot from 1986

22

A FACE YOU WANT TO HIT WITH AN AXE

By that time, my face was starting to become synonymous with horror films. I was in no way famous or revered on a grand scale, but little by little, I was gaining friends and fans as I appeared in many films where I would meet an untimely demise and I was loving every minute of it. I started appearing in genre magazines and was invited to many conventions and that's mostly thanks to one person.

Former *Fangoria Magazine* editor Tony Timpone was instrumental in helping put my face and name out there and was truly the guy responsible for me becoming a "name" of sorts. He always treated me with a tremendous amount of kindness, total respect, and consideration, running articles that featured me whenever it made sense and always putting a positive spin on it. He often referred to me as a "horror staple" and eventually, the idea that I was somebody to look out for started to stick with the public. I made appearances at almost every Fangoria convention for many years on both coasts, becoming acquainted with the likes of other personalities like Dario Argento, Clive Barker, Tobe Hooper, and so many others as a result. This was back in the day when conventions were full-on spectacles, with sets, music, and lighting, and I always looked forward to the sense of community felt when that huge group of similarly-minded horror geeks were all gathered into one room. I will never be able to thank Tony enough for always associating me with the Fangoria brand, an institute that I had loved and cherished since I was a kid. It was thanks to him that my name became synonymous with horror.

"Do you have a problem with working in South Africa?" my agent asked one day.
"What do you mean?" I asked.
"Harry Allen Towers wants you to act in a film for him out there."
"But we're in the middle of apartheid. I'm not doing that!" I snapped.
"He says he'll give you eight grand a week for five weeks," she whispered.
"Let me check my passport," I told her, digging through my dresser drawer.
Harry Allen Towers was a prosperous filmmaker who was responsible for producing many films and television programs as far back as 1955. He was mostly known by the public for his successful series of old "Fu Manchu" films starring Christopher Lee among others. Of course, he was also known by some for the white slavery charges that were filed against him back in 1960, but who's counting.

Back when he was younger, Towers used to split his time between London and Canada, and one night, at a party held by American millionaire Huntington Hartford, he was introduced to a beautiful young woman by the name of Mariella Novotny. According to the charges, Harry told the girl that he could make her into a star if she followed his specific direction and advice. In December 1960, Mariella Novotny arrived in New York City from London to connect with him. She later told a friend that "I would have done anything to be famous."

Harry moved her into a hotel and (according to Novotny), instead of putting her in acting classes and grooming her career, he immediately began pimping her out to powerful, high profile male customers. A few months later, she was arrested by the FBI, charged for soliciting. Three days later, Harry himself was charged with violation of the White-Slave Traffic Act, alleging that he had transported Novotny from England to New York for the sole purpose of prostitution.

According to her, Harry was bringing her to men who paid her $40 per sexual acts to "subsidize the money it took to house and feed her while they were establishing her career." Foolishly thinking this was the way a girl worked her way into the business, she continued entertaining prostitution dates regularly, earning about four hundred dollars a week. Miss Novotny later claimed that Harry kept three hundred of the four hundred dollars.

Harry, however, told the Feds a completely different story, telling them that he'd had an affair with her in England and had no idea that she was a hooker. He eventually jumped bail and fled the country, not to return to the U.S. until ultimately, the charges were dropped but not without many unanswered questions.

I had known of Harry's film work since I was a young kid and was star struck when I first met him. I'd also worked with him briefly doing an effects gag on Golan-Globus' film *American Ninja 3* a couple of years prior and we got along well. Having been raised around the carnival, it was easy for me to spot a grifter, and boy, did Harry fit the bill. He had a reputation in the movie business as being somewhat of a swindler, but truthfully, a lot of the executive producers I was coming across were shady, so I just measured his words carefully. He was extremely charming and jolly and always in a suit, tie, and hat. My main goal was to do my job as best I could with him and cozy up to him in the hopes of booking future acting gigs. Back then, I would literally hand my picture and resume to your grandmother if I thought it would get me an audition, so a potentially crooked filmmaker was not much of a threat.

While I was on set for *American Ninja,* I slipped Harry my reel and information after we hit it off hanging out on set. He seemed to have a soft spot for me after I gushed, telling him what a fan I was of all of his old films. I suppose that's what got me in the door with acting for him. He knew I didn't judge him for his indiscretions and more so, that I was interested in his filmmaking history. When I found out that the film he was shooting in South Africa was inspired by Edgar Allen Poe's *Buried Alive,* I didn't hesitate in agreeing to take a meeting for the job.

I got called to casting directors Bob MacDonald and Perry Bullington's office at the Cannon Film Group building. Cannon was a company owned by Menahem Golan and Yoram Globus, successful filmmakers responsible for producing hundreds of movies including the highly popular *Death Wish* sequels starring Charles Bronson and the *American Ninja* film series. Their office building was huge, located in Beverly Hills, and was the very first building I had ever been to where you were asked to empty your pockets and walk through a metal detector before entering.

Of course, the more I got to know Menahem, the more I understood why he needed to beef up his security. He was a cantankerously cheap old fellow with a knack for raising funds and putting a film into profit before it was even shot. This was back in the day when a beautiful movie poster alone was enough to raise cash to produce a movie. It's some of the sources of that cash that were questionable, thus, the metal detectors. I am sure some of the films were paid for in cash.

I made my way to the floor where the casting offices were located. The door to Bob and Perry's office was open and I could see a dark-haired, handsome young man lying on the couch as the three of them chatted and laughed as if they were good friends. Bob stuck his head out into his lobby and said hello as the dark-haired kid looked at me with a smile.

"Hey, what's up?" he said.

Bob handed me some audition material, telling me to come in. "This is Keanu."

I didn't realize at the time that this young, ratty-looking skateboard rat would ultimately end up a huge movie star. It was Keanu Reeves.

They finished their conversation and I sat down. My audition went quickly; at the end, they told me that Harry said I had the job if I was willing to do it. The guys were hilarious. Bob and Perry were a longtime gay couple who had been together for many years. They had cast many films for Cannon and were filled with stories. They had just finished casting the film *Barfly* starring Mickey Rourke and Faye Dunaway who they described as a "insanely venomous" woman. They told me that Robert Vaughn from the old *Man From Uncle* TV series was also starring in *Buried Alive,* along with renowned film and stage actor Donald Pleasence from the *Halloween* franchise as well as John Carradine himself. Carradine was a prolific actor who was born in 1906 and had been an actor since the 30s. He was one of the most famous performers in movie history. Still, I was shocked to hear he was still around.

"John Carradine is still alive?" I asked, completely astonished to hear the guy was still kicking.

"Just barely. He's 82," Bob replied.

"Well, I guess 82 isn't too terribly old," I said, hoping for the best.

"He looks 102," Bob quipped. "He's in a wheelchair these days and can barely hold his head up. He's known Harry for years and wants to do the role, so Harry is flying him out."

I was really excited to be performing with so many legends. Along with the heavy hitters was a beautiful young actress and former Playboy bunny model, Karen Witter, and a young newcomer, a seventeen-year-old girl by the name of Nia Long. Nia would later go on to star in many films and TV shows including *The Fresh Prince of Bel Air, Are We There Yet?* and *Big Momma's House.* She is now considered a movie star and is still a wonderful lady.

Co-starring in *Buried Alive* was an actress named Verda Bridges—Todd Bridges' older sister—and porn star Ginger Lynn, who was playing my girlfriend. I was excited to meet Ginger; at the time, she had begun to do legit acting roles. Word was, Ginger could act and was giving it her best shot. I was happy to be a fully clothed scene partner for her. Besides, I had thoroughly enjoyed working with the porn star Jamie Summers (aka Denise Stafford) back on *Terror Night,* and I was ready to grill Ginger for information on the subject of her former employment. It was a request that I later found out Ginger happily obliged. She is one of the coolest chicks on the planet and someone I still know and love.

I talked to Bob and Perry on the subject of working in South Africa and they assured me they had done several other productions there and hadn't heard any bad reports, safety-wise. They basically told me I would be going from the hotel to the studio and back, so I had little to worry about as the studio was a very secure space. I wasn't really aware of what apartheid was and the impact it had on the people of color in South Africa. These days, I don't think I would have gone, but back then, I was young, dumb, and really wanted to do the movie, so I agreed.

I honestly didn't put much thought into where I was potentially headed. All I heard was that I was going to Africa. I half-expected chimps to be running the airport and zebras to be running down the freeway, alongside the cars. The bamboo car from *Gilligan's Island* came to mind when I pictured who would pick me up at the airport: I was *that* uneducated on what South Africa was all about. Did they, in fact, bowl with coconuts? This was way before computers, so the idea of sitting down and googling the country wasn't an option. I threw caution to the wind, called my agent, and told her I would take the job.

A couple of days later, I was sent to Steve Johnson's special make-up effects lab and had my head cast done so they could create the make-up effects the role required. By then, I was used to having the cold goopy alginate all over my head as my face had been casted many times. Some people panic, but I always manage to use the experience as a tool for meditating.

When I arrived at my appointment, the guys told me that Steve Johnson wasn't around so they had to work fast, as the movie I was in was a side gig for all of them. Sitting on large tables around the room were big sculptures of these angel-like pollywog-looking creatures. The artists explained to me that they were the creatures for the new James Cameron movie entitled *The Abyss.*

"We have to work fast, because if Steve Johnson or James Cameron comes in here, they'll be furious if they find out that you've seen the creature designs," said the guy molding my head.

"Would it matter to them if they knew that I could care less about the project?" I asked. By that point in my career, I had seen one of everything and leaking information about a movie I knew nothing about was not high on my list. Still, in the world of movie making, everything is typically a secret, and I am sure that they had all signed non-disclosures.

The guys covered my head in the minty alginate molding material, followed by a layer of plaster bandages. During this process, the entire head ends up encased, so I could see and hear very little. The only place I could breathe through was my nostrils, which they kept clear while I was under. I must have been sealed up for about five minutes when I suddenly heard a man screaming and yelling. I didn't know what was going on. Was there a fight? Was the place on fire? I wondered if I should rip the plaster off of my head and run out of the place. After what sounded like a heated confrontation, the room suddenly fell silent. Not long after that, they guys asked me to lean forward as they pulled me out of the mold.

"What was all that noise?" I asked.

"Uh, well, James Cameron stopped by the shop and was furious that you were here," one of them told me. They were both stone faced.

Assuming that they were just busting my chops, I pushed them to tell me what really had unfolded. They stuck to the story. Still to this day, I never really know what truly happened. Maybe they *were* busting my chops. Everyone has stuck to the story until this day. Hearing that James Cameron blew his stack is certainly feasible considering everything I have heard about him throughout the years.

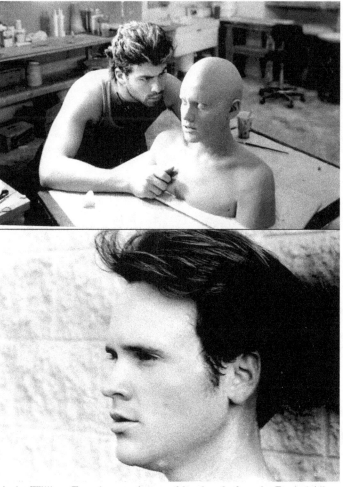

Artist William Forsche creating a rubber head of me for Buried Alive

A few days later, I was packed and on a plane to South Africa. I was picked up at the airport, not by chimps driving a bamboo car but by a town car that raced me through a bustling city. I was completely surprised at how beautiful Johannesburg was. There was no jungle, no zebras, just beautiful tall skyscrapers and lovely two-story houses. Even more surprising was how kind the people were. On the off chance that one of my American friends gave me an earful when I returned, pounding into my head how racist and wicked the people of South Africa were, I made it a point to see for myself, and I never saw any of it while I was there.

Johannesburg Sun Hotel

I was taken to the Johannesburg Sun Hotel. It was a beautiful, luxury skyscraper that had recently been refurbished with a full restaurant and bar. Despite the neighborhood seeming completely safe, the driver told me a few basic rules that I should firmly follow during my stay there. First of all, and most importantly, I was told that Johannesburg was a police free state.

"If you are robbed in the street and run after the person robbing you, the police can shoot you both dead if they believe that you are a threat to the safety of others," he said. "So, if you are robbed, whatever you do, don't chase the person."

"Copy that," I replied, looking out to the people filing down the busy sidewalks.

"People selling things on the street are usually out to rob you and driving on surface streets can get you kidnapped," he added.

I am never leaving my room, I thought to myself. I was also warned to not go sightseeing or walk around town without a local with me. The driver told me that there were slum neighborhoods where a white face could mean certain death, but again, I never saw it. One of the more popular ways to kill a person was to give them what hoodlums called a "necklace," which was filling a tire with gasoline, running up behind your victim and slamming the tire around his shoulders, pinning his arms down, and then setting the tire on fire. I was terrified of the place before I had even checked in. I wondered if the money I was making on this show was worth risking my life over.

The truth is, for the most part, I never saw any of that firsthand. The people of Johannesburg were very nice and the talent pool was huge. I met many terrific actors and crew people while I was there both from the stage and screen. Johannesburg certainly had its problem just like any big city, but the people I came across seemed to be very forward thinkers. I thankfully didn't see any racism or burning tires, just mostly funny, kind people who I quickly grew to love as friends.

The studio where we shot at was a large compound surrounded by a high wall. The story of *Buried Alive* took place at an all-girls' school where one by one' the students were taken by a mysterious killer. The interior of the school had been built in a huge soundstage, and we shot many of the other scenes in an actual school that was on holiday break.

I went through make-up and hair and asked the first assistant director to introduce me to Ginger Lynn. She had just started dating Charlie Sheen who at the time was a huge star, and she didn't hesitate to share many stories about her life and former career. As I had learned from Jamie Summers, the first porn performer I worked with, making porn films is not that far off from making mainstream films: the process is nearly the same...except in porn, you're undressed and having sex.

"I mean, I'm not gonna lie, you have to love having sex or being a porn star is not the career for you," Ginger said to me at lunch one day as she entertained me with stories that had me rolling on the floor with laughter.

I sat on the edge of my seat as she regaled me with hilarious tales of her favorite and not so favorite experiences and of the many on-set mishaps that unfolded, including the results of a poorly timed pre-shoot enema and a camera man accidentally getting an eyeful of ejaculate. The more sickening the story, the more entertaining it was to me.

Ginger Lynn and I in front of the now abandoned Johanasberg Sun Hotel

We started shooting and it was a total blast. By then, I was completely comfortable on set as a performer and I loved every minute that I got to film. Newbie Nia Long and I also became pals: she was an absolute doll, a beautiful girl and terrific actress even at the young age of seventeen. Nia and I broke the company's, and frankly, the country's rules for that matter, and grabbed a taxi every night to go out and eat dinner together. Since most countries had placed an embargo on South Africa for their racist actions, there weren't a lot of American-owned business franchises around. There was, however, a slew of knock-off look-alike businesses including a fake Hard Rock Café restaurant that Nia and I frequented. It was oddly decorated with dusty guitars and music posters, serving the same basic menu as the place it was trying to duplicate but never quite hitting the mark. We tasted cheeseburgers served with a side of deviled eggs and onion rings served with what can only be described as watery tomato sauce and not ketchup. Every eye in the restaurant was on the two of us as Nia, a stunning young African American girl, and I had dinner there without a care in the world.

It was so strange that people of different colors eating together in public was something to be gawked at. However, no one ever said anything or bothered us. Everyone was perfectly polite, just staring a lot. In our youthful minds, I think we somehow thought we were teaching them a lesson by going against the grain and being seen out and eating together, though these days, I'm not so sure I would be so bold. You would think by now the idea of segregation in South Africa would be over, but despite apartheid concluding in 1994, the separatist mentality certainly remains.

Nia Long and I on set of Buried Alive

Me, Verda Bridges and Ginger Lynn in South Africa

Filming continued and my first day to work with actor Robert Vaughn was upon me. We were shooting a scene in the basement of the old girls' school where Headmaster Robert (who had been revealed as the killer) buried Ginger Lynn up to her shoulders as I was tasked with trying to save her from being buried alive. In the action, I sprang out of nowhere to push Robert away from the open grave, ultimately ending up in a fist fight with him until we fell to the ground. Finally, he buried a cement trowel into my skull.

Robert, who little by little revealed himself as a humorless, sourpuss of a man, sat in a chair scowling as the stunt man walked me through the paces of the action. Robert refused to get up and walk through the scene with me. When the stuntman was done, Vaughn stood up in his chair and pointed at me. "You," he said, looking in my direction. "Follow me."

I realized he was speaking to me and I followed as he led me outside the stage and around the corner. He stared me down for a beat. I thought maybe he had come up with an order of business to do in the scene, but that wasn't the case.

"I want to make something very clear to you, buddy," Robert said, staring me down with daggers in his eyes. "You hurt me in any way in there, and your career is over."

I laughed, thinking he was joking.

Robert grabbed me by the shoulders, abruptly shutting me up. "Do you hear me? You hurt me and I will make sure that you never work again," he reiterated.

"You're not serious?" I asked.

He shot me the side-eye, then turned on his heel, heading back into the sound stage. I felt flattered that he even thought I had the capability of hurting him. He was a big guy and I'm sure he could have easily kicked my ass. I went back to where the scene was about to unfold as Robert stood holding a shovel, glaring over at me.

The cameras were set in place and the camera assistant took his position with the clapper. I looked over at Vaughn and winked at him as the kid clapped the board. "Never *ever* again?" I called out from across the room as he scowled at me, gritting his teeth, staring me down as the director called action.

Always one to question authority and certainly the idle threats of a grouchy old former TV stars, I took a breath and charged that motherfucker as hard as I could, slamming into him and knocking him several feet back until we both stumbled to the ground. He looked up at me in total shock, furious as I extended my hand to help him up.

"I don't really have much of a career for you to end," I said to him as he stood up, saving face as he dusted himself off and reset. From that moment on, he never said another word to me; there were no more threats to end my barely-existent film career. He just grimaced every time I walked on set as if he were smelling something awful.

Robert soon enough got his revenge. The last scene of the day was one where he was to bury me alive. He smiled wickedly as he looked down and winked at me. Take after take, he threw shovels full of dirt directly in my face as I held my breath. I refused to flinch in fear or let him know he was getting to me, but man oh man, he was giving me mouthfuls of dirt. Payback was indeed a bitch.

I had to stay buried as I was visible in the next scene where John Carradine was due to come wheeling in and somehow kill off Vaughn. The script described this huge fight between Carradine and Vaughn, duking it out, but John could barely lift his hands, so I wondered if they were going to just have him back his wheelchair over Robert and run him over. Still, I was as mesmerized by Carradine's very presence as much as I was by the fact that he was somehow still living. He seemed completely out of it as he sat in his wheelchair, barely awake as director Gerard Kikoine spoke to him. I remember thinking it was cruel for his agent to allow him to be put through the rigors of a film shoot: it could not have been his idea to appear in the movie as he appeared to be mostly motionless in his chair.

"Bring Carradine in!" the first assistant director called out.

"Better do it quick," the second assistant mumbled under his breath.

They put John in place and the director introduced him to everyone. He just stared at me, not opening his eyes or responding as I smiled at him, only my head and shoulders sticking out from my premature grave.

"Big fan," I called out to him from down in the dirt below.

Carradine opened his eyes, seemingly surprised to see me buried there in front of him and just moaned in response. They put the camera on him and rolled. The director fed him his lines, one by one. He had no idea what he was saying or why he was saying it as they shot him out and replaced him with a stunt man and me with a rubber dummy. Days later, after John had flown out with a stop in Rome, he passed away. I guess the second assistant director wasn't kidding when he said to shoot him quick. I was fortunate to have been in the very last movie scene that John Carradine ever shot.

A few days later, we shot the exterior scenes that led up to my death. I was completely excited as it was the same day that Donald Pleasance was working. I found Donald to be a completely charming and kind fellow. He had gotten his start on the stage in London and moved on to appear in such classic movies as *The Great Escape* and the James Bond movie *You Only Live Twice*. But the biggest impact his work had on me was certainly his performance in the *Halloween* movies directed by John Carpenter. I was sitting outside next to the school, waiting to work, when Donald came outside and sat down next to me. He just smiled and patiently listened as I instantly transformed into an embarrassing fan boy, listing off a variety of movies and performances of his that I loved.

I sat on the edge of my seat as he told me about what it was like working on *Halloween*, arguably one of the greatest horror films ever made. As Irwin Yablans told me a year earlier, they didn't have any idea that the film was going to be the hit that it was.

"What drew you to the part?" I asked, completely nerding out.

"Truthfully?" he asked with a smile. "It was tax season."

He laughed. "I liked the script enough and you could certainly see that John knew what he was doing, but I had no idea that the film was going to turn out as well as it did. None of us knew. That's the testament to John's incredible ability to visualize." He continued, telling me that some of the scenes were shot on Orange Grove Street in Hollywood and the production had to pay off the noisy prostitutes walking Sunset Boulevard to go set up shop elsewhere while they were rolling. He told me that the white mask that Michael Myers wore was a complete afterthought. They had simply painted a William Shatner Star Trek mask white.

He told me that the budget was very tight; they had eaten a lot of pizza and Jamie Lee Curtis had brought sandwiches for everyone. I was so happy to have one on one time with him. Donald was one of those people that when he looked at you, you felt like you were the only person in the room, and you never met a more relaxed actor. I watched as he spoke to the director and added little details to his character, like his wearing a bad toupee and that his character couldn't stop eating Jolly Rancher candies, none of which were in the script.

"How is your acting career going?" he asked, handing me a Jolly Rancher.

"Good," I said. "I've been in a bunch of horror films so far, maybe too many at this point. I'm anxious to branch out and do other things as well. You don't suppose I'm pigeon-holing myself, do you?" I asked.

Donald looked at me over his reading glasses. "Well, what is it that you're trying to accomplish?" he asked, putting another candy in his mouth.

"Well, I want to be an actor," I said.

"From where I'm sitting, it looks like you're doing exactly that," he replied.

I smiled and sat back in my chair. Donald Pleasence had just spelled it out for me. I just nodded, point taken. He was called to set and we decided to have dinner that Saturday night at the hotel before we both flew out on Sunday.

The next two days I was off, and Karen Whitter and I went to the marketplace where a lot of the indigenes sold crafts and other handmade goods. I felt like an idiot as I, along with several other scrubbed, extremely white tourists, made our way through the rows of baskets and bracelets, buying everything up. There was even an area where one tribe was pulling in tourists, dressing them in grass skirts and headdresses and taught them to clumsily dance to native drums. It was mortifying. I cannot imagine what they were all saying to each other on their coffee breaks.

That Saturday, I shot my last scene, promised Nia Long that I would stay in touch, and headed back to the hotel for my anticipated and sacred dinner with Donald Pleasence. The phone rang in my hotel room as I got out of the shower.

"William, it's Donald."

Holy shit! Donald Pleasence is calling me and I am standing here—naked no less, I thought to myself, trying to play it cool but failing miserably.

"I'm afraid we'll have to cancel dinner tonight," he said.

My heart sank. "Oh. Well, okay. I understand." I pretended I wasn't about to burst into tears.

"It seems someone's been shot dead in the lobby just outside the elevator and the police have the area completely taped off," he said.

Could that possibly be true? I thought to myself. Most people just say they have a headache to get out of dinner. Confused by the excessive excuse to cancel (though, how could you blame him if there were indeed a body lying there at the entrance to the buffet), I told Donald that it was really nice meeting him, thanked him for the stories and advice, and hung up the phone.

I wondered if someone were really dead downstairs. I got dressed and took the elevator down and sure enough, there were two hotel maids on their hands and knees, scrubbing blood out of the pitted stone floor of the lobby surrounded by yellow crime scene tape. I pushed the button to my floor, the doors closed, and I went right back up. Someone had been shot in the hotel. The word was that a tourist had made the foolish mistake of trying to shortchange a local drug dealer and got more than they bargained for. The next morning, I was packed and on my way back to Los Angeles.

Not long after the cast and I stayed there, the Johannesburg hotel district continued to decay, and the hotel was eventually closed due to the rising crime and excessive violence in the area. Somewhere around 1998, Holiday Inn tried to reopen the place, but after another brutal murder happened during a botched robbery, the hotel was closed again and has been boarded up ever since.

Back in Los Angeles, everything was better than ever. I was auditioning regularly, about three times a week. I booked both a 7-Up and a Ralley's Hamburger commercial that were running at the same time.

One day, I got a call from Cannon that Harry Allen Towers had sent my paycheck to the office, and I headed over to get it. The check was for around forty thousand dollars. I was so happy to have a little breathing room to take my time and figure out what my next move was. I took the check to the bank and deposited it. The teller at the counter handed me my receipt, and it said that only twenty thousand had been deposited. Confused, I asked her why she only credited me with the twenty instead of forty.

"That check was issued in Canadian dollars," she said, looking at me like I was a dummy.

Turns out, dear old Harry had made a deal with me to work for eight thousand dollars a week, Canadian. Furious but helpless, I knew there was nothing I could do as he was by then, long gone. I took the twenty thousand and focused my energy on trying to find another acting job.

It was a beautiful spring that year. I stayed in touch with both Nia Long and Karen Witter. Karen was extremely kind and very encouraging when it came to me staying away from drinking and drugs, and Nia and I went in another direction entirely, spending our nights hanging out in clubs and having a blast. I'm happy to report that nothing too nefarious unfolded: she was always such a good girl. Eventually, Nia's career caught fire and she was off to the races, and I eventually lost track of her. She seems to have done just perfect for herself, just like I knew she would.

Actress Gail O'Grady and I also continued hanging out during that time. We were thick as thieves, as they say. Gail introduced me to the Firefly, a Chicago bar on Vineland and a place where they poured 151 on the counter every hour and lit it on fire; that is, until the place burned to the ground one day when they set the bar a blaze and couldn't put it out.

We went out to dinner at the nicest hotels in town and then dared each other to leap in the place's swimming pool, fully clothed. I loved Gail very much and still do; she is the only woman I have ever met that I would marry, minus the small detail that she isn't a man. Life can be so complicated. So many rules.

Gail O'Grady and I still friends after 30 years

Gail also had a new hangout she was frequenting, a 1950s throwback diner called Ed Debevic's that had just opened up on La Brea and Wilshire. The place was famous for its good food, table dancing, and over the top rude waiters and waitresses. There, I met a whole bevy of hilarious performers biding their time before their acting careers took off, including Ingrid Berg, Romy Rosemont, and a hilarious redheaded girl by the name of Rusty Schwimmer. Rusty was a Chicago transplant and Gail's good friend who ultimately went on to be a highly successful actress, appearing in films like *The Little Princess* and *The Perfect Storm*. The two of them, along with their good friend actress Virginia Madsen, arrived in Los Angeles around the same time to make careers for themselves.

I spent nearly every Friday night at Ed's after I got back from South Africa. Aside from the staff becoming hilarious new and cherished friends, Ingrid also kept me fed. When I wasn't working, I was broke. There was a period of about three months where I lived on nothing but chili cheese fries.

Rusty and I became close outside of Ed's and we got stoned and went on all kinds of insane excursions. One night, I picked her up in my rickety old gold Volkswagen Bug that had no brakes, and we drove downtown to watch Disney on Ice completely smoked out. Every time I came to a stop light, the brake pads sparked and smoked as it was pure metal on metal. Rusty, being a true Chicagoan, transposed what must have been sheer terror into laughter every time I slid to a grinding halt. Ah, the stupid bravery of youth.

Ingrid Berg, Me and Rusty Schwimmer at Ed Debevics

"So, there's something I've been meaning to talk to you about," I said to Vulich as we nursed our free drinks one night at the Ed Debevic's bar.

"Uh oh: now what?" John said, feigning mock fear.

"Well…I…wanted to…um…I wanted to talk to you about the conversation we didn't finish at Residuals a few years back," I said, terrified.

He looked over at me, raising his eyebrows, and finishing his drink.

"I…do prefer the company of guys in my private life. I didn't think it was gonna stick, but it did and I have been hooking up with dudes for some time now," I said with every ounce of air I had in my nervous lungs.

Vulich stared at me for a moment. "Duh," he finally said. "What took you so long?" He laughed and ordered a round of shots.

"I just love all of you assholes so much, I was afraid it would make you like me less. Maybe not at all," I confessed.

"Trust me, there are a lot of other things to not like about you, but that's not one of them," Vulich said, giving me his usual treatment that made me laugh at just the right time. "Just do your thing, no one cares, and just so you know, everyone has been waiting for you to open up."

I was so relieved, I thought I was going to burst into tears sitting in that gawdy bar. It was a very hard conversation for me, one that I had never had before and it was over. "Thanks for being my friend, John," I said as we hoisted shots of whiskey.

"No problem...faggot," John said as we shot 'em back with a laugh.

23

THE SAW IS FAMILY

I was at Bally's gym on Hollywood and Gower when I picked up my messages and heard I had been called by New Line Cinema to audition for the latest *Texas Chainsaw Massacre* sequel. By that point, auditioning for horror films was a solid part of my repertoire and stereotyped or not, I was stoked to be going in. New Line had been hitting them out of the park with their *Nightmare on Elm Street* sequels among many other successful films.

I drove to their offices and met with the casting director Annette Benson, who listened to me read some pages from the script then told me that she was calling me back to read for the director. I was happy to learn it was none other than Jeff Burr who had told me that he would call me in sometime and sure enough, he had done just that.

Back home, Viggo helped me study and get my head around the material for my callback. I was pretty much broke again, so we read the script together as we shared a single can of vegetarian chili while watching *Texas Chainsaw Massacre 2* on VHS to get an idea of the tone of the films. Viggo had only done a few movies at this point; the biggest project he had done was *Fresh Horses* with Molly Ringwald and Andrew McCarthy, but his knowledge on acting was always undeniable. Even way back before he'd made his mark, I always knew the guy was going to end up a huge star. Everyone did. Except for him, who would often say he just wanted to get a job in a hardware store.

The *Leatherface* script, written by David J. Schow, was really in the vein of true *Texas Chainsaw Massacre* style. It was very violent and terrifying; in fact, I wasn't sure if I had the stomach to participate, even if they did decide to hire me. There were scenes where the insane inbred family cut a hole in my character's stomach and pulled my intestines out. The fans loved it, but I ended up puking while we were shooting it. No matter how many times I worked with fake blood and guts, I still got queasy. Even more concerning to me was the level of acting that actress Caroline Williams gave in *Chainsaw 2*. She gave a spot on, top rate performance in that film, and I was worried that I would not be able to get anywhere near the level of acting that she'd served up on that project.

All that week before my callback, Viggo coached me on my scenes and I worked hard, keeping my stress level down with my usual amounts of excessive exercise and walks. Keeping myself in shape was routine and I continued to get thinner. I had finally reached my goal and I was never going back.

I went to my callback and it seemed to go very well. Each time I got called back in, my agent called afterwards to tell me that I was that much closer to the job. I'd learned not to get excited when they told me I was getting close to booking something. A great audition sometimes led to them ultimately passing and a terrible audition sometimes got me the job. There were always so many variables to booking an acting gig.

There was also my usual insecurity caused by seeing every handsome face in Hollywood sitting there in the lobby with me. I had to completely block out any of the good-looking guys sitting next me in the waiting room. I always figured if they were going to hire someone for their looks, it certainly would not be Billy Butler. Lucky for me, most of the time they looked for personality over beauty. By the way, I later learned that as a general rule of thumb, the prettier the actors are, the less they know how to act.

New Line Cinema had read me about twelve times until they finally got it down to two candidates to play the role of Ryan. I later learned that they had seen almost 500 guys for the role of the mildly annoying medical student who was ultimately going to be taken out by Leatherface. Little by little, they started pairing me up with girls to play the role of Michelle, the strong-willed young girl who ultimately survives as she fights for her life through several ultra-violent scenarios. Kate Hodge, Marcia Cross (soon to be from *Melrose Place* and *Desperate Housewives* fame), Willy Garson and I ended up being the final four potential choices. We all got called into New Line on the same day for the final callback. The four of us sat in the New Line lobby in silence. I remember being insanely nervous, but I played it cool as Marcia and Kate were called in one by one. Kate and I had previously been asked to read together for CEO Robert Shaye and had already gotten his stamp of approval, but we had still to read together one last time for Jeff Burr so he could make his final decision. I wanted the job so badly. It wasn't about just getting another acting gig. At that point, I was living the ultimate fan boy's dream.

I'd been in a *Friday the 13th* and several genre films for Charles Band. Being in a *Chainsaw Massacre* would be the ultimate get for me. Terrified to make chit-chat and shake myself up before going in, I pretty much ignored Willy, who at the time was not very known. Eventually, he made a massive mark when he ended up performing as a regular in *Sex in the City* among many other terrific works: by far, bypassing my career. Truthfully, he was ten times the actor I was, but I cared not. I wanted this.

They called Willy in as I sat there alone. Ready to puke from nerves, I went into the bathroom and sat on the toilet, meditating to calm myself. *Who the hell am I kidding?* I thought to myself. I wasn't good enough to pull this movie off. I went through my relaxation exercise that Viggo had taught me. Breathe, relax your head, then your neck, your chest…one by one, let your body parts go limp and sure enough, by the time you go through all of your various parts, you should find that you are, in fact, relaxed. I walked back into the lobby just as Willy was leaving the audition room.

"Have a great fucking time on the movie!" he said angrily, exiting.

Totally broadsided, I stood there in shock and confusion as Benson peered out of her office and motioned for me to come inside.

"We've decided that we'd like you to play the role of Ryan," Jeff Burr said to me.

"Really?" *Could I be dreaming this?* I thought to myself.

"Welcome to the cast. We're gonna have a great time," Jeff told me, shaking my hand.

I couldn't believe what I was hearing. I had just booked a huge acting gig and for once in my career, not for my willingness to also paint slime on hand puppets at the same time, not because I knew anyone in the production, but just because I was right for the job. It meant everything to me. Jeff Burr later told me that Bob Shaye liked me best because I sort of resembled Michael J. Fox at the time. I was never really sure if that was a plus. I never asked what happened when Willy went in for his callback to make him snap at me like that, but getting the news that I had booked the gig meant everything to me for so many reasons.

Jeff and Annette asked me who I felt more comfortable acting with. I told them Kate Hodge. Marcia was doing a soap opera at the time and was made up with full pageant hair and beauty make-up. I couldn't see her falling for a dorky guy like me even on her worst day. Kate was beautiful but far more accessible and we had undeniable chemistry, both on screen and off screen as immediate friends. Jeff agreed, saying that Kate was also his choice, and suddenly, it was done. Kate and I were cast as the two leads in *Leatherface: The Texas Chainsaw Massacre 3*. I made my way home and celebrated that night by heading out on the town with Kate.

The following Monday, I got called to go into the New Line offices to sign my finalized contract and to have my measurements taken for my costume. I went into the casting director's office who seemed frazzled and distracted as she talked on the phone, motioning her me to come over. She shuffled my finalized contract over for me to sign, hung up the phone, and was about to push me out the door when I asked her what was wrong. She explained to me that they had just lost the actor who was playing the role of the murderous Tex and she was scrambling to replace him. Normally, this wouldn't be an issue, being that we were in Hollywood where a million actors live, but since filming was starting the following Wednesday, she was in a panic.

"How about Viggo Mortensen?" I asked.

"He wouldn't touch this project," she snapped at me, opening the door to show me the way out.

"He might. I know him," I said.

"Sure you do. Then tell him to read it and get back to me," she said as she shooed me out into the hall. I don't think she believed me, but that night I spoke to Viggo and told him what I had heard about the guy dropping out. He took my script and read it, and the next morning, he told me he was interested in stepping in. I called Annette to give her the news and she in turn contacted his agent. About three days later, we found out that he, too, had booked the movie as Jeff Burr actually liked him and chose him as the Tex replacement.

Kate, Viggo, and I decided that we would carpool to work every day. The movie was shot in Valencia right behind the Magic Mountain theme park near the set for the television series *China Beach*. We were so close to the amusement park that sometimes we had to redo takes as you could hear people screaming as they rode the rollercoasters there.

Paranoid that I wouldn't have time to work out every day while we were shooting, I got up at four in the morning and headed to Universal Studios to jog the backlot. My friend was running the finance department at Spielberg's Amblin Studios at the time and she called in a walk-on pass for me every day so I could get into the studio backlot.

I changed my sunrise running path every morning, jogging down the Western street, sometimes through Rome, and sometimes through the town where villagers once charged to lynch Frankenstein's monster. These days, you can barely get on the lot even if you do have business there, let alone jog across it.

Kate and I met with the costume designer, who dressed us in what can only be described as "Garanimals." Garanimals were a clothing line for small children in the 70s with fashioned challenged parents who could easily create matching outfits by combining pants and shirts that sported the same animal character tag hanging from them. Our costumes were not unlike the garishly colored combinations. We were both in multiple layers of primary colors, purple and green, and because it was the late eighties, we both wore leg warmer socks with our pants tucked into our high-top white Reeboks. We looked like complete idiots but were wearing what everyone else was wearing in most movies at the time, so it was no reflection of the costumer's ability but more so of the times. Everything was big hair and brightly colored excessiveness back then.

Our rides to work were always awesome as we listened to music and talked about the work for the day. Viggo and I were stoked when we learned that we would once again be working with Kane Hodder. Kane had been hired to coordinate the stunts and to double Leatherface when there was dangerous action involving the working chainsaws in the film. Kane, as usual, was up to his usual antics, this time bring a little fart-making device to the set and keeping everyone laughing as he walked by them and let it rip.

This was also when I started to become good friends with effects master turned legendary *Walking Dead* producer Greg Nicotero. I had known Greg peripherally for years as my friends Robert Kurtzman and Howard Berger were his partners at KNB Effects group. Before we started shooting, Greg asked me to come into the shop so I could have my entire body molded so they could create a realistic dummy that they were going to use in the scene where the killers bash my head in with a sledgehammer. This was a true testament to my level of body comfort at this stage in my life, as Howard handed me a Speedo and had me put it on. I walked back into the shop half-naked as they led me to a piece of plywood and had me lie down on it. Four effects people surrounded me, each with a five-gallon bucket of mint-scented dental alginate and quickly covered my entire body up to neck.

After the gel began to set, they followed up with the usual round of plaster bandages and before I knew it, I couldn't move as the thing hardened. Eventually, the gang gathered around me and tried to collectively pull the mold off in one giant piece. This was 1990, long before body shaving and trimming came into fashion, and I was terrified to learn that the dental alginate had soaked down the sides of Speedo and into my pubic hair, locking my body firmly into the mold. Before I could launch into a full-blown panic attack, everyone in the shop gathered around the plaster mold of my body and got it off in one forceful yank, taking some of my body hair with it. The upside was that not only did I just have my body molded, but I had also received a fancy Brazilian wax job.

They helped up onto my feet as they whisked the mold away. You will never know the depths of your own humility until you walk around a cold make-up effects lab in a damp Speedo, the creases of your undercarriage speckled with the flaky remnants of a body casting.

Afterwards, the gang did my head separately and as always, I found the process to be completely relaxing and zen-like. The artists at KNB were top notch and the process went off without a hitch. When they were done working their magic, the dummy of me turned out beautifully and very realistic. It eventually became the set mascot when we were done with it as everyone took turns defiling it for Polaroid pictures. Greg later told me years later that my naked body appeared in many other films whenever a stiff was needed.

Every day for six weeks, Viggo, Kate, and I rode together to set in her little car. My beat-up Volkswagen was towed away after I didn't pay a stack of parking tickets and when I did the math for how much it would cost to get it out of impound, I discovered I could buy a new car for that. Many times, after we got off work at six in the morning after shooting all night, we opted to just drive home covered in fake blood, dirt, and bruises instead of showering on set, and sometimes, we very nearly caused a multi-car pile-up on the five freeway.

Little by little, the shoot became a tough one as the production began to hassle our director Jeff Burr. It wouldn't be until later in my career, when I myself was on the director's whipping post, that I realized that bad behavior on a studio's behalf was pretty much just another day at the office, but it was really hard to not say anything as they berated and questioned Jeff's decisions in front of everyone.

Jeff was a terrific director and I was so proud to be working with him and blessed to have his input on my performance. He seemed to really like me. Other members of the production, not so much. About two weeks into shooting, I was called into the office to be interviewed by the Unit Publicist for the publicity that they would be releasing on the film. The woman had me sit in her office and when she stepped out to get us some water, one of the film's producers walked in. I could hear them talking outside and he didn't realize I was already there. He told the publicist that she was doing a great job.

"Thank you," she said. "I'm about to interview the two leads."

"Good, I would focus more on Kate Hodge than I would William Butler," he said. "He dies about three quarters of the way through the movie, and from what I can see in the dailies so far, it's a blessing."

"I heard that," I chimed in from the other room.

I got up and stuck my head out the door to find the producer standing there, white as a ghost. "Oh, I was just kidding," he smiled with a pasted-on smile.

"Uh-huh. Well, we're two weeks into shooting. We both know New Line is too tight to replace me. So, I'd suggest you find something about what I'm doing that you like, because we both know I'm not going anywhere."

He came into the office and sat down across from me, trying to convince me that he had only said it because he knew I was sitting there, but he and I knew otherwise. I didn't really care as I was as unimpressed with him as he was me.

Back on set, shooting continued along and the more we shot, the more the production hassled Jeff Burr. There were many days when things got downright uncomfortable as Jeff sat quietly with the brass standing right next to him, monitoring his every move.

This was also around the time that I started having a sharp pain in my lower back. I had a history of bad kidney stones triggered by rapid weight loss and I knew the signs that another one was coming on. For those of you who have never suffered from this awful condition, the best I can describe it is that you feel like two twirling, serrated steak knives are sticking in your backside. Determined to not be the actor who was complaining or high maintenance, I tried to play it down until eventually it got so bad that I went back to my trailer in between shots to lie on the floor, doubled over in pain.

One of the times that I was lying on the floor, I started to smell the undeniable scent of urine. I reached over and felt the floor and realized it was indeed wet. Thinking there was a problem with the bathroom, I got up and checked the toilet, but it seemed to be functioning fine. I went to the head of transportation and told him that something was going on in there, but he couldn't figure out where it was coming from. They checked the bathroom and the sink; they double-checked the trailer's sewer line and could never figure out what was going on. Some days it was fine and other days, I walked in there and was hit by a huge hot wave of pee smell. I finally started spending as little time in there as possible, but no one could figure out what was happening.

It wasn't until years later when Kane Hodder's memoir, *Unmasked*, was released that he admitted that it was him that was going in there and peeing on my rug. Only he would find humor in something so gross. In hindsight, the idea of me lying there in that fresh puddle, trying to figure out what was going on, is kind of funny. Eventually, the pain subsided as I passed the stone at my house one morning. Hilariously enough, it was in the perfect shape of a heart and I disgustingly kept it in an old pill jar for years until it eventually turned to mush and I chucked it.

Aside from the rampant unpleasant on set politics, most of the scenes in the movie were terrifically fun to shoot. There was a lot of driving in the film. I was surprised to see that the car was put on a flatbed trailer for all of the driving sequences. The entire crew pile on as I pretended to drive that ugly teal blue Mercedes back and forth over the same half mile of street that doubled as the old Texas highway leading up to the Leatherface house.

In one scene, we were to have accidentally hit a little armadillo that runs out in front of us. They had a stuffed armadillo that we were ran over and a real one that was used for the close-up where I decide to put it out of its misery and crush it with a rock. This was during a time when the ASPCA was very getting very strict about making movies with live animals, so every precaution to keep him safe and happy was taken. Two years earlier, while filming the movie *Project X*, in which Matthew Broderick played a young man determined to save a chimp from being recruited by the military for nefarious means, it was reported that the chimps were regularly beaten into submission with lengths of garden hose. The animal rights people were suddenly all over any production that involved animals of any kind and our production was no exception. This little armadillo made three times the amount of money that Kate and I did and had a beautiful air-conditioned trailer that had us all beat. As you can see in the movie, it was a terrific actor. My only regret about the scene where I supposedly crush the little guy is that it is clear I am clearly squeezing the foam rubber rock that the prop department gave me.

The heat out in the desert was unbearable and the cast and crew kept wet towels on their necks in between shots to try and keep from fainting in the 116-degree heat, but shooting was an absolute blast as Kate, Viggo and I kept each other laughing while we weren't sweating profusely.

One particularly hot day, we were filming at the gas station set where Viggo's character is introduced, and I lost it with him on camera. Hot and exhausted, I wasn't understanding the huge pauses Viggo was taking in between each of his lines, and I stopped and glared at him on one take. That's the take that's in the movie. Watch closely when he's showing me on the map that he thinks I am going the wrong direction. I have a line and then Viggo is supposed to come right in with his, but he doesn't in this particular take; instead, he just stands there, staring at me. You can see me standing there, waiting for him to say what's next, and when he doesn't, I finally drop character and look up at him like I am ready to punch him. For whatever reason, it works in the context of the scene: another testament to his ability as a performer. His character was trying to irritate me, so therefore, he was irritating me. I mean really irritating me.

Viggo Mortensen and I on set in Valencia

One of my other favorite moments in the movie is the scene when he gets a blowout and I have to change the tire. We begin to hear the squeak of Leatherface's brace as he approaches. I must have changed that tire forty times as we shot the scene over and over. I got so good that I could get the old wheel off and the new one on in less than a minute. If you ever have a flat, don't hesitate to drop me a line. That night was also the first night where we started performing with both Leatherface and a live chainsaw.

R.A. Mihailoff was cast in the role of Leatherface. The chainsaw was huge and loud and many times they would have to use the one with the actual blade on it, especially if it were close to camera. This was long before computer graphics could easily replace the saw and there were many times that it came very close to both Kate and me. There is a scene where I jump into the backseat as Kate struggles to get the car in gear to escape the killer, and I remember being completely scared that I was going to get my head cut off when the real chainsaw got too close for comfort. I remember looking over at Jeff after each take and seeing him sitting there, happy at how cool it all looked, so my shattered nerves were worth it. As each night of chainsaw action unfolded, I started to go home completely shaken up from tensing up and cringing from exposure to that thunderous blade every night.

After a few days of going home shaking, I called my old acting teacher and asked her if she had any advice on how to better navigate the scenes that involved wall to wall chainsaw torment.

"Your scene partner is a live chainsaw, darling. I don't have any worldly advice that'll make your performance any easier," she purred with her usual dry and biting wit. "Just go with it."

Kate Hodge and I in Leatherface

Finally, the scene where I was to meet my maker was upon me. We shot an amazing stunt where our car drives off a ravine, plunging thirty feet below. After the car was mangled and in place, Kate and I were supposed to come climbing out of the wreckage, dazed. The trouble was, we were filming in the foothills of Valencia and the place was crawling with rattlesnakes. The studio had hired a man in snakeskin boots who walked all around the car, poking around with a stick to see if any of the critters had slithered into the area we were filming in. First, it was alligators and Lyme ticks, now it was snakes. Nothing about making a movie is glamorous.

Viggo and I in Leatherface

The scene after that was one where Kate and I are given sedatives by actor Ken Foree. He played the role of Benny, the ex-marine who tries to help our characters and ultimately meets his own fate by taking a chainsaw to the skull, or so it was originally written. I was such a huge fan of Ken's work. Not only is he a funny, kind, and wise man, he is also a terrific actor. Once again, as with other people I admire, I was star struck as I played opposite him. Here I was, working with one of the very actors that I idolized as a kid. Ken and I talked about our crazy times back when we worked in Italy on *From Beyond,* and his wonderful acting skill elevated my own performance in the scenes I was in with him with only a couple of exceptions, one of them being when I scream "I'm about to lose my mind!" at the scene of our flat tire. I very am proud of my work in that movie. I finally knew what I was doing.

We spent our final nights filming with Leatherface hunting us down through the woods. Kate and I shot several scenes and angles where we walked faster and faster as we were being stalked, and finally, the shot came where I get my foot caught in a bear trap that the family set to catch us. I assumed that it would be a rubber prop trap that was painted to look real, but when I walked on set to work I was surprised to find that they planned to put an actual steel trap on my ankle. Jim Landis, the prop man, opened the trap and offered it up for my foot to step in. I watched him with eyes peeled as he slowly let it clamp down on the meat of my leg.

"Is that okay?" he asked.

"Oh, yeah, not bad at all." I was lying. It hurt like hell, but once again, never one to complain, I kept my mouth shut and told him it was fine. I decide to just use it to communicate the pain in the scene. When you see me wincing in the shot as I try to pry it off my leg, I am not faking it in the least.

Finally came the shot where Leatherface grazes my chest with the chainsaw. R.A. was suited up and given the saw with no blade. Again, there was no acting required as I looked up at his hulking figure running that roaring saw blade over my body. After that, we headed back to the farmhouse where they hung me by my ankles and finished me off. It was completely gruesome, but I was never happier. Booking that movie was still one of my proudest moments and provided me with so many great memories. I had once again somehow gotten myself cast in another one of my favorite horror franchises. I was the luckiest movie nerd on the planet, and one week later, I was done shooting and off to go find other work.

I later heard that New Line had decided to go back and reshoot the ending of the film, making Ken Foree's character now somehow alive with a bandage on his head after test screenings showed that audiences were sad to see him go. It was a ridiculous idea and between that and the massive amounts of cuts the MCAA was requiring before they would remove the X-rating they were trying to give the film, the enthusiasm for the project began to fade for everyone involved. It's always so entertaining when movie execs hire someone that they seem to trust to create a project for them and then all they do is turn around and question everyone's decisions and contributions. It wasn't the first or the last time that I would experience people meddling and insisting on giving input that did not make the project better. I went out to set to visit the gang as they shot the very last re-shoot scene. We all hugged it out and said our final goodbyes. Kate and I drove home together that day; despite all of the turmoil and drama, we were happy to be a part of the *Texas Chainsaw Massacre* legacy. The movie later premiered at Mann's Chinese Theater to a sold-out crowd.

Never a fan of impending poverty, I immediately went out and got myself a job waiting on tables at the Gingham Garden restaurant on Larchmont Street; the place was a beautiful garden restaurant that was within walking distance of my house. I got the word that the place was hiring from Kate Hodge who had also gotten herself hired. But she wasn't there for long as fate soon smiled upon her and she only had the chance to come in for one lunch shift as days later, she booked the lead in her own television series, *She Wolf of London*. Nicotero and I took her out for breakfast the morning before she flew out to London to begin principal photography.

Greg himself was leaving to go on location for a few months, so he offered me use of his beautiful 1976 baby blue Cadillac convertible while he was away. His offer was a godsend as I hadn't yet saved up enough money to buy a new car yet. It's virtually impossible to survive in L.A. without a ride. I whole-heartedly agreed to take him up on his offer and promised I would take really good care of his baby while he was gone. The guy loved that beast of a car. I bid them both farewell and faced the hard fact that I was going back to the grindstone until I found myself another acting gig.

A couple of weeks later, I was working the breakfast shift at Gingham Garden. Other than the cook and the eighty-year-old owner, a hardcore East Coaster with a thick Brooklyn accent, I was there waiting on the tables all by myself. The place was jumping that morning, but since I had been slinging food since I was old enough to get a job, I was keeping up and hustling tips. As I was running food to one of my tables, I saw the actress Elizabeth Perkins come in and sit down at a booth in the front of the place. She was a big star at this point, having starred in *About Last Night* and *Big*, directed by Penny Marshall. She made direct eye contact with me as she smiled and nodded for me to come to her table.

I was used to waiting on famous people and always remembered the number one rule to never gush or be overly chatty when serving them, so I was polite but acted like I didn't know who she was when I took her order. She asked me for a toasted bagel, lox, and cream cheese with a side of capers. I apologized and told her that we didn't serve capers, to which she said:

"Oh. Can you ask the owner if you can run to the store and go get some?"

I looked around the room at the other tables full of people as an old lady raised her empty coffee cup, motioning for me to warm her up. "But I'm the only one here," I told her.

She calmly smiled and said, "Oh, it won't take long. Thank you so much."

Slack-jawed, I went to the back patio where the owner looked up at me from her *New York Times*. "Get ready for this," I said. "The actress Elizabeth Perkins is up front and wants me to go to the store and get her a bottle of capers for her friggin' bagel. Can you believe that?"

The old lady glared at me and said, "So? What are you waiting for? Go get 'em."

"Seriously? There are thirty people in there and no other waiter," I told her as she stared me down without responding.

I shook my head in frustration and headed out as she yelled, "And charge her ten bucks!"

I got into Nicotero's whale of a Caddy and screeched out of my parking spot. The store wasn't far down the street, but being that I had eight tables of customers I thought I'd better drive as opposed to run in order to get back in time to keep everyone happy. I figured I had about ten minutes before people would start noticing that I was gone. If only it were just ten minutes.

I put on my sunglasses, cranked on Van Halen, and was turning right on Melrose Avenue towards the Pavilions' grocery store when suddenly, there was a loud crack followed by a loud metallic grinding. The car began to slow and lose power as the noise grew louder. I gripped the steering wheel, afraid to breathe; something heavy was dragging underneath the car. Suddenly, Greg's ride rolled to a stop and right in the middle of Melrose. Cars behind me began to honk as a long line formed instantly from the morning commute. I got out of the car in a complete panic and lay down on the pavement, looking beneath the car as my heart sunk. The car's axel was broken in two and was lying on the street as a huge puddle of fluid poured out.

Car horns continued to blow as I got back into the car and started it. "Please God, let this car move," I said as I put it into gear and depressed the gas, but the car lunged and then stopped as there was another loud crack. I closed my eyes and put my head on the steering wheel; the honking built to a cacophony.

Three guys walking down the street saw me helplessly sitting there, got behind the car, and pushed me to the side of the road as the rear two tires buckled inward. I thanked them, panicking as I remembered my tables back at Gingham Garden. I ran down the street to a payphone. I dug into my pockets but found no change. I ran back to Greg's car and dug around, looking for some coins, but found nothing. I immediately broke out into a sweat, running back to the payphone. I looked up the restaurant's number in the phonebook and called collect. I held my breath as the frazzled old owner answered the phone in a complete panic and angrily accepted the charges.

"Fran, I have a real problem on my hands," I said, completely defeated.

"I'll say you do! Where the fuck are Elizabeth Perkin's capers?!" the old woman squawked.

"Fuck her capers, Fran! Fuck her fucking capers to hell!" I yelled. "My car is broken down in the middle of fucking Melrose!"

"I don't care if you're broke down on the goddamn planet Mars; if you're not back here in five minutes and with capers, don't bother coming back at all!"

I hit my head against the phone booth window and looked over at Greg's broken car. "It was nice meeting you, Fran." I started to hang up, then hesitated. "By the way, I've been giving away free pie!" I screamed and slammed the phone receiver down.

I sat on the sidewalk next to the payphone, staring at Greg's ride. As much as I just wanted to disappear and walk away from the whole scene, I knew I had to call him. He'd been so nice to loan me the car and now it was inoperable. What's worse was, I didn't have any money to have the thing towed away. I felt awful.

After fifteen minutes of procrastinating, I bit the bullet and finally called his hotel. He was on set at the time, so I left a message at his hotel for him to call me at home. I put the top up, locked the car and started the long walk back home to Handcock Park. It was a true testament of our friendship when Greg called me back later. I ashamedly explained what happened as he quietly listened. After I apologized profusely, he paused for an incredulous beat then calmly told me to not worry about it and sent one of his assistants to pick up the key so they could have the car towed away. Greg has always been a wonderful friend and huge support system for me, but that day I never appreciated him more. As for Elizabeth Perkin's capers, I hope she managed to make it through her morning without them.

The next thing I knew, it was Christmas, 1990, and Ken Hall was having a huge holiday party. By then, my effects artist friends and I were one big family as we had known each other for nearly ten years. That particular year, somehow, some of us had been wrangled into singing Christmas carols at an old folks' home with our dear friend

Lynette Johnson who was coordinating the charitable venture. At that point in our lives, we were all pretty wild. I think that we thought that agreeing to do something nice for the elderly would somehow offset the bad behavior we exhibited for the rest of the year. The only problem was that we were scheduled to sing on Saturday morning at eleven and Ken's fiesta started at nine o'clock. We were all seasoned party animals and a gathering meant that most of us were going to be blithering well into the night, so singing Christmas carols in the morning was most certainly going to be a task.

In no time, the rec room of Ken's apartment building was packed with drunken people, many friends I recognized and a few that I had never met before. One guy in particular was holding court in the corner: a chatty, extremely smart and friendly fellow who seemed to be a walking encyclopedia on movie knowledge. I walked over, joined the circle, but quickly zoned out as the guy didn't ever seem to take a breath in between sentences. There was no movie that he didn't have boatloads of knowledge on.

"Is he a producer?" I asked.

"No, that's Quentin Tarantino. He's a writer/director. He just did his first movie," my friend answered.

"Does he ever stop to take a breath?" I asked.

"Only to come up for air so he can keep talking," he smiled.

Quentin was really funny and animated and I did my best to keep up with him. I had no idea that years later, I would be such a fan of his. After a few moments, I split away from the circle and headed over to the bar. I was refilling my drink, feeling pretty buzzed, when one of my wilder pals nudged me and held up a little plastic bag full of white powder.

"You want?" he asked.

"No, I'm not doing that crap anymore," I said, slamming my double shot of tequila like any other health-conscientious person would.

"Come on, man up: it's Christmas. Don't you know you're allowed to do drugs two times a year?"

I shrugged, not following. "Huh?"

"Halloween and Christmas. You can do drugs on those two days and it doesn't count. Now come on."

I followed him outside, somehow taking his made-up point as a good enough excuse. We walked out around the corner of the building as my friend checked to see if the coast was clear, pulled out the baggy, and dipped a big bump of the powder on the edge of a car key. He held it under my nose as I took a huge whiff. Instead of the usual rush and burn that I felt from coke, I started violently gagging and staggered back. I ran over to the garbage dumpster and threw up on the ground, then turned to him in anger. "What the hell was that!!??" I said in between gags and coughs.

"Heroin. I thought you knew that was my new thing?" he said.

"Heroin?!" I screamed, ready to strangle him. "Are you fucking kidding me? You never said you had a new thing!"

"Calm down. You'll be okay, you pussy," he laughed. "Just don't do anymore, and you'll be just fine."

He was right. I was more than fine. Moments later, every muscle in my body began to completely relax as I felt like I was being swaddled in a giant, warm flour tortilla. I drifted through the room in slow-motion, happily smiling at everyone. I was suddenly the most beautiful, loving person at the party and I couldn't even begin to summon an ounce of worry for what I had just done. The song "Everything's Gonna Be Alright" echoed through the room and boy, was that an understatement.

I found myself back in the chatty circle, and everything Quentin Tarantino said became beautiful and made perfect sense. I wanted to give him a hug and lay my head on his shoulder as he and my pals discussed the very best of Roger Corman.

The next thing I knew, it was two in the morning and we were all sitting in a big booth at Denny's on Sherman Way. Truthfully, I was lying down in the booth, only rising up to grab a handful of the fries that I had ordered.

My friends propped me up and I sat perfectly still with drool on my chin. I gazed across the booth at Tarantino, positive that I could walk across the table and climb inside the pupil of his eye if I chose to do so. I was that comfortable.

"Rise and shine," Ken said to me the next morning as I stirred on his couch. I tried to pry my eyes open, but they weren't cooperating. I felt like my head had been slammed by a metal baseball bat as it pounded uncontrollably. I slowly came to, running to Ken's bathroom and becoming violently ill as I did.

"You gotta get dressed; we're going to be late for Christmas caroling," Ken said.

"Are you fucking kidding me? I can't go Christmas caroling while coming down off heroin!" I cried.

"Well, you can stay here if you want, but I'm telling you right now, I've known Lynette Johnson for years and if you don't show up because you're too out of it, she will never forgive you."

I stared him down, taking a sip from a room temperature Big Gulp that had been left on the coffee table.

"Ever," he said to me as he threw me my pants that were, for some reason, lying on the floor across the room.

The next thing I knew, I was bundled up in a Christmas scarf and Santa hat, profusely sweating drugs and alcohol out of every pore in my body, singing Christmas songs to elderly people, some of whom seemed completely startled when they opened their doors and we burst into song. After each apartment, I ran around the corner and threw up into the nearest garbage can or laundry bag.

'Twas truly the season.

24

THEY'RE DEAD, THEY'RE ALL MESSED UP

As usual in my insanely lucky and yet unpredictable life, right around the new year, opportunity once again knocked just when I really needed it to. Viggo gave me great news that he'd booked an acting gig on *Young Guns 2* and needed someone to come with him to watch his little son Henry while he worked. His wife, rock musician Exene Cervenka, was about to go on tour and the baby needed to go with him to the New Mexico location. He offered to hire me to help take care of the baby and I excitedly accepted. The next thing I knew, we were in New Mexico. During the morning, I took little Henry on walks and then hung out in the hotel, trying to teach him his numbers and alphabet. He was a really funny, good little kid and I grew to love him. He's now a grown man who runs his own publishing company. My, how time flies!

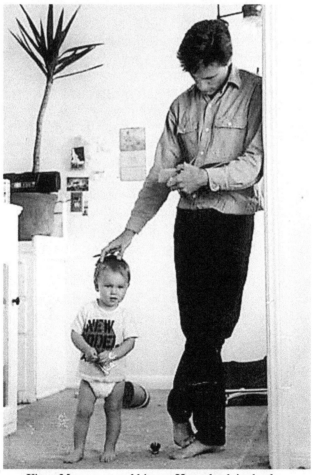

Viggo Mortensen and his son Henry back in the day.

"George Romero is gonna remake *Night of the Living Dead*," John Vulich said, calling our hotel room from his newly anointed make-up effects lab company, Optic Nerve. "Tom Savini is directing. I just read the script and there's a part in there that's perfect for you. 'Remember the guy who shoots the gas pump at the end of the movie?'" The original *Night of a Living Dead* was a black and white independent film made in 1968, written by John Russo and George Romero. The film, produced by Russ Streiner and Karl Hardman, was created with the camera equipment that Romero used to shoot television commercials and had a budget of about a hundred thousand dollars.

Vulich explained to me that George had lost a lot of money on the first film due to a copyright error that made the project public domain. Anyone could show or sell the movie and profit off of it and they did. George's idea was to remake his original work and beat everyone to the punch before anyone made an unauthorized version. John and his partner Everett Burrell had been hired to create the zombies and were actively in pre-production. He told me he would mail me the script and asked me to have my agent send my demo reel to him so he could forward it to Savini to look at.

A couple of days later, Viggo brought a thick envelope from the front desk. Sure enough, John had mailed me the script. That day, I took little Henry out to lunch and read it. The script was fantastic, very close to the original classic film. Seeing "written by George Romero" on the cover was so exciting to me, but his writing was so perfect that just having the opportunity to hold it and read it was almost enough. I thought, at the very least, I had been gifted by John with an amazing piece of movie memorabilia.

I called my agent and told her that I loved the script and that I would kill for a chance to work with both Savini and Romero. I even offered to fly myself to Pittsburg and audition for them both in person. A couple of weeks passed, and I didn't hear anything back from my agent or John about the movie, so I sort of started to forget about the project. You learn fast to not stress about appointments in the world of acting as the odds are so very stacked against you most of the time. Johnny also could be pretty headstrong once he set his mind to something, so I figured that he was too pushy with Savini and turned him off to the idea of me being put on tape. I was more preoccupied with staying warm, as it had been freezing in New Mexico while *Young Guns 2* was shooting.

Every morning, I bundled little Henry up and put him in his backpack; first, I took him on a walk to get some fresh air, then, we visited the set. One exceptionally frosty morning, I loaded Henry onto my back and stepped out onto the third-story landing of the hotel, ready to hit the trail and make it to set in time for breakfast. I walked to the top of the frozen metal stairs, stepped onto some unseen ice, slipped, and fell forward. I didn't even have time to react or try to catch myself as the next thing I knew, I had crashed down onto the steps and was sliding all the way down three flights of stairs on my chest. My entire body was scraped up from head to toe by the time I finally slammed to the bottom landing. I would have sworn my nipples were gone as every rigid steel step had cut into my chest as I had plunged forward. I lay there for a beat, praying that Henry, still strapped behind me, was okay. I really expected him to be banged up or hurt. I had fallen hard and was in quite a bit of pain. The silence was deafening as I finally took a breath and cautiously rolled to my side, turning back to face him. My view was anything but grim. There Henry was, looking down at me, beaming with a single toothed grin as he broke out into huge belly laughter. He smiled at me with his big bright eyes and wiggled in the backpack as if he were encouraging me to climb back up and do it again.

I picked myself up, limped up the stairs, and went back into our hotel room just as the phone rang. "Savini loves your demo tape! He wants you to do a video of yourself reading some pages from the script!" John said. "I think you have a really good shot at this: he seems really interested."

I tried to not get excited. The news alone that Tom Savini liked my tape was a huge honor for me. Could it be that I was finally figuring out how to be a decent actor and people were starting to notice? I called my agent and gave her the news. She called the casting director and got the page numbers for me to read. Right after I finished *Leatherface*, I purchased a camcorder so that my friend Patti Lesser from the *Theatersports* show I was in could make comedy videos. At that point in my life, I was filming pretty much anyone who would let me, so I had my camera and plenty of blank tapes with me.

Later that night, after Viggo wrapped shooting, he videotaped me reading the eight-page monologue scene from right after the character Tom comes up out of the basement. Since I had so much down time at the hotel, I had memorized the scene and was feeling good about it. Viggo had me do it over and over, directing me until we got it the best that I could. The next day, I Fed Ex'd the tape to Savini's production office and hoped for the best. I felt really good about the performance I gave, but time quickly passed and I never heard anything back. *Young Guns 2* finished shooting and the three of us headed back to Los Angeles.

In a matter of days, my audition for *Night of the Living Dead* was just a memory, but my acting bookings began to pick up. I did an episode of the television series *Freddy's Nightmares*, a movie with Kris Kristofferson called *Perfume of the Cyclone* (in which I ended up on the cutting room floor), a murder-mystery entitled *Innersanctum* with Joseph Bottoms, Margaux Hemmingway, and very boozy Tanya Roberts, who made daily rounds around set, offering people shots from her very own bottle from which I gladly partook. I shot a Dr. Pepper commercial and even a *CBS Schoolbreak Special* with *Hellraiser* actress Ashley Lawrence, who played my pregnant teenage girlfriend. I also went to the network to screen test for *The Outsiders* television series. I was up for the role of Two-Bit, which ultimately went to David Arquette. In fact, most of the time if I showed up at an audition and I saw David sitting there, I typically could count on him booking it before I did. He was and still is such a terrific actor. You couldn't lose a job to a better guy.

It was around this time that my love of writing and filmmaking began to grow as my friends and I started using my camcorder to create comedy shorts and live sketch comedy for local theater groups during my downtime. I found myself writing a good portion of most days and I was really loving it. I read the book *How to Write a Movie in 21 Days* and fell in love with the process of screenwriting. Just so we are clear, you positively cannot write a screenplay in twenty-one days—or a good one anyway—but the exercises and structure the writer teaches in the book sent me on a path that made me rethink my love of acting. I spent every free moment trying to figure out how to write a decent screenplay.

In the evenings, I spent my time at John and Everett's make-up effects shop. I lay around John's office, listening to music as he sat at his desk playing on his computer. John and Everett were the first two make-up artists to use a computer to design special effects make-up and as with anything that interested John, he was instantly obsessed with computers when they made the scene. Since I had known him, Johnny Vulich had always kept the strangest hours. He slept all day and stayed awake all night, rarely going out into the sunlight. I often accused him of being a vampire as he never seemed to be able to get his head around waking up and working during the day. For many of his co-workers, this made him incredibly difficult to collaborate with as he often arrived at the lab at six in the evening, right around the time everyone was about to leave for home, yet he'd expect them to stay so he could get caught up on all the happenings.

For me, his crazy schedule worked just fine and there was never a day when anyone ever doubted his genius. I loved him like a brother and any time I could spend with him, I did. I tried to hustle acting gigs and work out by day and then head to Sun Valley to hang out with him by night; there, we created art and talked about our mutual love of movies, how we wanted to grow, and what we wanted to do in the future. We often talked about learning as much as we could, then ultimately producing and directing our own projects.

Sun Valley is a mostly run-down and secluded area of North Hollywood, home of a huge dump landfill, many run-down bars, countless meth heads, and dirty donut shops. It's also the home of many big, affordable, and non-descript industrial warehouses that effects artists can better afford to do their work in. The anonymity of these non-descript buildings also makes it the perfect place for artists to create expensive effects for film in seclusion as there are very few ways to get a look at the work that is taking place inside. I often stayed there at the shop until three or four in the morning, and you can't even imagine the craziness that unfolded almost nightly.

One night, at four in the morning, John and I were sitting in his shop as he worked on a sculpture. When he looked up from his work, he froze and his eyes bulged in shock. Terrified at what could possibly be standing behind me, I turned around slowly to find a four-hundred-pound, completely naked man with a raging hard-on standing at the entrance to the open cargo door. As I spotted him, the man turned and bolted through the parking lot. Laughing hysterically and not considering the danger that a large naked man with a boner might bring, John and I ran out into the parking lot after him as the man climbed into a beat-up old van, started it up, and sped off. For some, this would be a completely shocking scenario. For us, it was just another night in the valley.

A few days later, I was at my house in Handcock Park, cooking dinner, when the phone rang. It was my agent. "Are you sitting down?" she asked.

"Should I be?" I responded, stirring my penne and sauce.

"You booked *Night of the Living Dead*!" In the background, she and the gang in the office cheered.

"What?! I thought they forgot about me!" I said.

She quickly explained that I was indeed booked, how much money they offered me, and that I would be leaving for Washington, Pennsylvania in just a few weeks. I was so floored: not only had I just booked an acting job on a remake of one of the most influential horror films of all time, I was going to be directed by none other than my childhood idol, Tom Savini, in a film produced by the granddaddy of horror, George Romero, and it was all from one single audition that I taped myself. I called John to say thank you. Without him, I never would have been considered.

The next day, Savini called me on the phone to welcome me to the project. I was so nervous, I could barely speak, as Tom thanked me for reading for him and told me that the reason that he had cast me was because he looked at Katie Finneran's Judy Rose and my character as angels trapped in hell. I liked that a lot. By then, he'd cast about half the actors for the film; I didn't know of any of them except for Bill Moseley who was going to be playing Johnny.

Moseley was not only Viggo's and my neighbor, but also my savior. At a convention once, back before I realized that you can't sit at the bar drinking every single cocktail the fans offer to buy you, I had just done an appearance in Cherry Hill, New Jersey and stumbled out of the bar after drinking six martinis. I took a nose-dive in the lobby near the elevators. Thinking quickly and being the sober angel that he was (and still is), Moseley scooped me up, helped me into the elevator, and aimed me towards my hotel room door after we got to my floor. I will be forever grateful for his kindness and am so happy that we remain friends to this day. Once again, duty was calling, and once again, drinking, drugging, and staying out all night was put back on hold as I put my nose to the grindstone and tried to figure out just how the hell I was going to pull this off.

During pre-production in Los Angeles, Vulich, Everett, and their top rate team of effects artists worked closely with Savini to ensure that the zombies in the film were exactly in line with his vision. Despite his reputation as the wild "King of Splatter," Savini wanted to be respectful of the first picture, keeping the make-ups very subtle and realistic. John and Everett used forensic pathology books and pictures of real corpses as resource material. Ultimately, their efforts paid off because the dozens of beautifully hideous make-ups that ended up in the final film set a precedence for many movies and television shows after that. The guys truly nailed it and with a very small team.

We all flew into Pittsburgh as our shoot date was finally upon us. The night I arrived, Vulich took me on a whirlwind tour of the city, including a trip to Savini's museum-like home, a beautiful old structure filled with hundreds of original props, masks, and other horror memorabilia. From the basement to his workshop in back, there were movie memories around every corner. I was so nervous to meet Tom at first. He'd only ever seen me work as a performer and had never met me as just my boring self. I was nothing like the character I was playing: a gun-sporting, mildly-dim redneck, and as he put it, "angel in hell," and I was scared to death that I would be fired before I even got started.

Immediately, I felt awkward around Savini, terrified that he was thinking he was going to meet the guy he'd seen in the video tape and then be disappointed when I showed up. It's weird when you go from extreme fan to an actor in the remake of a classic movie. I had such a hard time playing it cool. I wanted so desperately for him to like both me and my work and I longed to have my own crazy stories of him suddenly sucker-punching me or throwing bowie knives at my head from across the room. For the most part, our first meeting was quiet at best. No flying bowie knives in sight.

Later that night, John and I ended up at the legendary Dirty O in the Oakland area of Pittsburgh. The Dirty O, an old hot dog shop that despite being filthy and unkempt, served the best hot dogs in town and with piles of French fries as big as your head. The whole pushy "what do you want?!" vibe of the place is truly what makes it the number one must-see restaurant in the area. John said I would never forget the place and he was right: I never have.

The next morning, I was taken to wardrobe and hair where the designer had me try on several different outfits for my character. I was so happy when she came into the room with an "Iron City Beer" sweatshirt that really suited the character. I had been working hard on my Pittsburgh accent and wanted my character to be as authentic as I possibly could and Iron City Beer was a Pennsylvania staple. Jeans and a hunting vest seemed appropriate and the deal was sealed when she handed me a weathered Pittsburgh Steelers baseball cap.

I was then taken to hair and make-up where the ladies talked me into darkening my hair. One of the earlier projects that I had done before *Night of the Living Dead* had me putting highlights in my hair and it looked a little light for a kid whose idea of fun was shooting squirrels. I was shocked at how dark it was when they were done with me, but I went with it. I figured I resembled the guy from the original film even more, so it worked. After they were done, I was driven out to set for Savini's approval. At the time, I used to wear a small elk skin Gris-Gris pouch necklace that Viggo's wife made for me. Tom liked it and asked if I wanted to wear it in the film, and I did.

I stayed and watched as he went back to shooting the scene in progress. It was the "they're coming to get you, Barbara" scene between Moseley and Patty Tallman in the graveyard as they are attacked by the undead. Many of the zombies that appeared in the film were highly trained acting students and teachers from Carnegie Mellon University so their performances were spot on. After they were cast, they were all sent to "zombie lessons" where a movement specialist taught each of them how to walk and growl per Savini's direction. There were zombies of all shapes and sizes, including an extraordinarily thin African American man who was recruited after he drove Tom to the set in a taxicab.

We also had a whole herd of friends and genre personalities who came to make cameos as zombies; most notably, Gahan Wilson, the brilliant comic writer and illustrator known for his macabre entries in *Playboy* and *National Lampoon Magazine*. *Film Threat* magazine creator/editor Chris Gore appeared in the film as one of the undead along with novelist/screenwriters John Skipp and Craig Spector. Every single day there was at least one zombie *du jour* as everyone from a correspondent from *Inside Edition* to members of the production staff made a cameo. It would be hilarious seeing them all sitting around smoking on their breaks or huddled together eating lunch. We actors had a very firm unwritten rule that we were to eat away from all the carnage, especially on BBQ day.

The beautiful farm location in Washington, PA.

The crew getting ready for a massive zombie scene. I should have bouoght that house.

I immediately found Patty Tallman to be extremely friendly and welcoming as she came over and gave me a hug to welcome me. Vulich told me in advance that I was really going to like her and that she had already appeared in several films for George Romero including *Knightriders* and *Monkey's Paw*. I watched as she and Moseley perfectly executed both their scenes and stunts like total pros. Vulich and Everett had created a lifelike silicone dummy of Bill that made for a cringe-worthy effect as his character eventually falls and breaks his neck on one of the tombstones. The scene ends as Patty climbs back into their car and is forced to pull the emergency brake to try and get away just as a zombie bursts through the car window in his attempt to devour her. The script called for the car to whiz past a big oak tree and coast down a hill towards the farm where the bulk of the story takes place. However, when the emergency brake was pulled and the car was sent rolling, it raced down the hill, veered to the left, and slammed directly into the tree, demolishing the rear end of a car that was, in fact, the Line Producer's actual ride. After reassuring the producer that he was due for a restored bumper and some quick thinking, Savini had Patty just scramble out of the wreckage and race to the house on foot. In the end, it all cut together perfectly.

Night of the Living Dead - Patty Tallman as the heroine, Barbara

The farmhouse itself was a beautiful three-story home that the production had obtained for an astonishingly low amount of money. The place had about eight acres of land, a grain silo, and two huge barns, one of which we turned into the special make-up effects lab and grip and electric storage.

Our art department was a funny, top-notch group that did a spot-on job, not only by paying homage to the first film by following the precedent it set, but by elevating the look of the place by dirtying it up in all the right places. It was really hard to tell where the art direction began and the old rotting house ended. On the front porch beneath the house's address, George and Tom had the art department put the name M. Celeste, an homage to the mysterious real-world ship that was discovered drifting at sea with no captain or crew on it. There was even food still cooking on the galley stove that had just been left there cooking with no sign of anyone on board. That allusion was continued when Patty walks into the house for the first time and finds eggs burning in a frying pan in the house's kitchen. Most of the big farmhouse was tented in black material for all of the interior night shots with few exceptions. It wasn't until later that our characters went outside, and that we filmed in the evenings.

My character Tom was no stranger to guns. I pretty much had to carry one in every scene, so it was really important that I looked like I knew what I was doing. In real life, I'd never even seen a real gun in person and had only ever fired a BB gun.

Savini made an appointment with me at lunchtime on one of my first few days and showed me how to hold, carry, and load a weapon. I could see him tensing up as I clumsily tried to duplicate all of the awesome gun tricks and moves that came to him so easily. After many failed attempts, I eventually learned to at least look like I knew how to hold and fire the thing but I was never any Wild Bill Hickcok. Still, I could tell I had lost street cred with Tom as he slowly started to realize that I was nothing like my character in real life. I would have to say that our working relationship was hopeful but increasingly awkward in the beginning of the movie. I was crushed to think that I was letting down someone who I so looked up to.

My nostril acting was in full effect.

The day came when all of the leads in the film were finally scheduled to work together. I first met Tony Todd in the make-up chair. Tony turned out to not only be a brilliant performer but a very kind fellow with a strong and commanding presence both on and off camera. Tony played the role of Ben, the wise and brave leader of the group of unfortunates who find themselves stuck in the abandoned old farmhouse, forced to work together as they fight to survive against a massive zombie apocalypse. Tony had serious chops, having originally trained with the Trinity Square Repertory Theatre Conservatory, and had done mostly television guest star spots before booking the lead in *Night*. His unbelievable level of acting skill combined with the fact that he was tall and not unlike the actor from the original film made him an easy choice for Tom and George. It later came as no surprise to me that he went on to have a huge career where he continued working non-stop, including being cast in the revered horror film series *Candyman*. His role there was so iconic that he is rumored to be returning to it in Jordan Peele's reboot of the film.

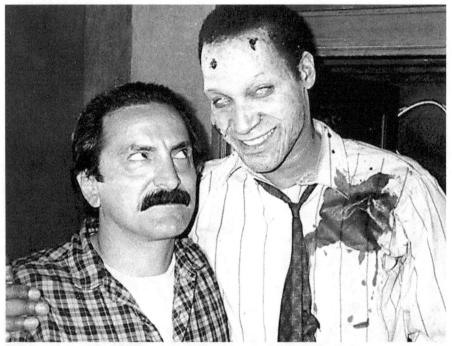

Night of the Living Dead - Tom Savini and Tony Todd

Mckee Anderson, who played the role of Helen in the film, was a military kid who had originally traveled the world doing theater ever since she was a child. She was a great lady with a tremendous sense of humor. She never had a bad thing to say about any of the crazy situations we were all put through and I looked forward to the days we worked together. Playing my girlfriend Judy Rose Larsen was a beautiful young girl and terrific actress by the name of Katie Finneran. It was Katie's first movie and it was funny to watch her figure out all the ins and outs of navigating her way through scenes and learn how to work the camera. She was originally from Florida, and it has been a pleasure to see her continue working and blossom into the revered thespian she is today, but hands down, my favorite person on set was actor Tommy Towles.

I knew of Tommy from his Oscar worthy portrayal of Otis in *Henry, Portrait of a Serial Killer*. Vulich and I had seen the film at the Egyptian Theater in Hollywood when it first came out. Early on, before Tommy was cast, I remember John telling me that he was trying to convince Savini into casting Michael Ironside in the role of Harry Cooper, which made a lot of sense in the beginning. There were also rumors that Ed Harris had originally accepted the role but later dropped out due to a scheduling conflict. After seeing the phenomenal performance that Tommy gave on *Night* from the very first day, you could instantly see that Savini made the right decision.

Tommy was a gregarious guy with a hugely funny sense of humor. He and I were friends from the moment we met; I adored him. He sat with me every day and told me great stories about how he had been in the Marines and eventually drifted into the Chicago theater scene working with the likes of my dear friend director Stuart Gordon and the Organic Theater Company. After booking a small part in *Dog Day Afternoon* with Al Pacino, Tommy found himself drawn to performing in film and television where he began a long and busy acting career.

Despite my and his character always being at odds in the story, we got along better than anyone. Tommy was my kind of guy. He drank, cursed, smoked, and tremendously loved talking about his absolute favorite subject, pussy. Tommy Towles could sit and talk about his female conquests longer than anyone I had ever met. He'd bedded dozens of women and had a hilarious story for each and every one of them. He once told me he had been dating a woman who had a boyfriend and when the man surprised them one night by coming home from work early, Tommy was forced to hide naked in an antique packing trunk at the foot of the bed. He was a hilarious human being, a shameless flirt who was charming with women off camera as well as on, and he could portray a prick or a crazy person while in front of the lens. Tommy pulled up to set in his big, beat-up old car that he decided to drive to the location so he would have wheels. Often times after we wrapped, he offered to take me back to the hotel in his car. I always took him up on his offer, as many times, we grabbed dinner or breakfast depending on what time we were off work. Days passed and little by little, I started to realize that the car had a strange smell to it. Tommy smoked like a chimney, so I just assumed the musky smell I was catching was old cigar or nicotine. Most of the time he kept all of the windows rolled down, so the stench wasn't too overwhelming, but one particularly cold day, Tommy was forced to roll up all of the car windows as we made our way back to the hotel. As the inside of the car warmed up, it started to smell like hell on earth.

"Tommy, I've been meaning to ask you."

"Yeah?" he said, taking a drag of his cigarette.

"What the hell is that smell?" I blurted out as I did my best to hold my breath.

"This is my father's car and he is elderly," he said.

"Are you saying that smell I'm smelling is old man smell?" I asked.

"No, I'm saying it's full diaper smell. He's incontinent." He turned to me and smiled, looking down at the seat I was sitting in. "And I do all the driving in the family." From that moment on, no matter how much I loved the guy, I always found my own ride home. Tommy was one of the coolest people I have ever known. I was crushed when I heard he had passed on so early in life in 2015.

Shooting the shit with McKee Anderson

Waiting to shoot on a very late night with Katie Finneran

Just within a couple of days of shooting, we were already upon the scene where I finally come up out of the basement. The scene required me to perform several pages of dialogue all at once and I had studied for weeks. By then, I was finally comfortable in my own skin and with my acting ability, so I was more than ready to rip the scene out by its throat; that is, until I heard that George Romero was going to be visiting set that day. I instantly broke into serious head sweats as the crew started to set up the scene.

I made my way to my dressing room and stood there staring into the mirror, petrified. *Don't screw it up. You can do this, Billy,* I said to myself, over and over. I read and re-read my script until the assistant director finally came around and called me to the set. Would George hate what I was doing and think I was a fraud? There was definitely a different vibe going on when I got there as everyone was on their toes.

There, sitting in a chair next to Tom Savini, was none other than George Romero. I walked over and shook his hand and thanked him for agreeing to put me in the movie, and he thanked me for agreeing to do it. *You say that now, until you see me completely screw it up,* I thought to myself.

George Romero was an immensely kind guy with bright, smiling eyes. He also had a very good sense of humor and you could tell he knew what he was doing and exactly what he wanted within just a few moments of meeting him. Every moment I spent with him was insanely cool. I also wanted so badly to please Savini. I had been such a rabid fan of his for my entire life that it was a little jarring to suddenly be directed by him.

Everyone in the cast was so polished and their level of ability elevated my own work. But within just a few days of shooting, Savini seemed like he was becoming bothered. By then, it was becoming obvious that production was hounding him into doing the film the way they wanted him to do it. Tom was a creative idea machine with a very clear vision, but not all of that vision was in line with the rest of the production's idea of how the movie should turn out. There were many times where he would get vetoed and sometimes right in front of the cast. It was very uncomfortable at times. I can't imagine how Tom must have felt, but it clearly affected him, as he became quiet and distant during part of the shoot. Later, when I became a director myself, I better understood how that kind of treatment can affect you.

I can remember that he was in a particularly bad mood the morning I shot my first big scene. He didn't say much to me before I started shooting, other than "don't be afraid to be vulnerable," like he originally told me. I took my seat in front of the basement door and was stunned to see that George Romero had a monitor of his own just a couple of feet away from me. His wife, Chris, sat right next to him. They both looked over and smiled as I thought to myself, *Well, it was nice knowing everyone.* I was positive that I wouldn't get past one take before George pulled me aside and fired me. I remembered back to all of the times that Vulich and I lay in front of the VHS player watching movies like *Dawn of the Dead*, *Martin*, and *The Crazies*, and here I was, somehow in one of his movies myself. The odds of me making it and acting in one of the films I loved must have been astronomical, and it was time to sink or swim.

The camera rolled; I sucked it up and somehow, was able to block out everyone in the room. Miraculously, I managed to pull it together and deliver. Take after take, I remembered all of my lines and pulled it off. After shooting the scene a few times, I glanced over at both Chris and George, who both gave me the thumbs up.

"Was that okay?" I whispered to George.

"It's more than okay, kid: just keep it up," he said to me, laughing. I looked over at Savini, who gave me the kindest smile. It looked like I hadn't screwed up after all, and I had made it through my hardest material. The rest of the film was mostly me shooting guns and nailing windows shut. Again, the happiest horror fan on the planet was living the life.

That night when I got back to the hotel from work there was a big gift basket in my room from George and his wife. I exhaled as I read the card out loud. *Keep up the good work. George Romero.* Still, to this day, I kick myself for not keeping the card. Thank you, George and Chris, for your support and belief in me. Mostly, thank you to my now friend and forever idol Tom Savini for hiring me and making me not only a part of your tremendous vision, but a part of cinema history.

Tom Savini remains a dear friend

One Friday night, the cast and crew decided to head out on the town to some of the local bars. Our crew was a tight group of mostly Pennsylvania locals who'd worked together on a lot of Romero's movies and other local Pittsburgh productions, including *Mr. Roger's Neighborhood.* Word was that our key grip Bomba Tallo was legendary for the time he had hidden naked in Mr. Roger's closet one day, terrifying Fred Rogers as he opened the door to grab his beloved sweater.

The *Night* crew would do so many things to make the shooting days more fun. They'd hold "Dollar Day" where everyone would sign a dollar and put it into a hat, then later, whoever's name was drawn would get all the money collected. Every other day, the denomination would climb from "Dollar Day" to "Five Dollar Day" all the way up to "Hundred Dollar Day" when someone won two thousand dollars. They'd also have special crew dress-up days like "Skirt Day," "Hawaiian Shirt Day," and "Wig Day." It would be hilarious to see some grouchy grip talking serious movie business with an electrician while they were both wearing long, flowing wigs.

Hanging out in the grip truck between shots

The night Film Threat magazine's Chris Gore came to visit and be a zombie.

We all ended up at a local bar that one of the zombie extras had recommended. Vulich and Everett stayed behind this time around as they prepared for a huge zombie scene that we were shooting the following Monday. The bar was as to be expected in the Washington area: small, run-down, and completely packed with locals. We were all having a rowdy great time until word got out that a bunch of movie people had crashed the locals' regular haunt and all hell started to break loose. In a matter of moments, we were all warned by the staff to leave as a bunch of bruisers who claimed the bar for themselves planned on punching their way through the place. We all piled in our cars and headed back to the hotel.

Buzzed, I went back to my room and lay down in my bed and crashed. Saturday morning, I woke up at about eleven and got up to go to the bathroom. Groggy and half-asleep, I walked across the room and nearly jumped out of my skin when I found the Bill Moseley rubber dummy sitting naked in my tub with a towel on his head, sunglasses on, and fake blood all over him and the tiled walls of the bathroom. Johnny had somehow charmed his way into my room and snuck the Moseley dummy into my tub.

Hours later, when Vulich finally woke up, I called him and gave him an earful, telling him to come get his naked bloody friend out of there. Well, of course, in true John Vulich style, he was in no hurry to come pick up the rubber corpse, so it sat there through the weekend and to be honest, I kinda got used to him just sitting there. After the initial shock, which was huge, I really didn't think much about the bloody scene beyond that. I saw John later on that Sunday and he said his guys were going to come load the dummy into the transpo van and take him back to the shop on Monday. What we didn't take into consideration was that we would all be called into shoot at 7 a.m. on Monday.

I got up that next morning and headed to set, forgetting about the dummy as I was busy right away. One of my least favorite things about the movie was the amount of times we had to rip apart furniture and carry old doors up and down stairways, nailing them over various windows and doors. Originally, I assumed that they would create lightweight doors, considering that we would have to reshoot shots ten to fifteen times, but the heavy doors and furniture were all real. What's worse was that my character was hammering the nails with a large monkey wrench throughout the film, so nine times out of ten it came apart in two pieces as I clumsily tried to pound a nail through solid wood with it. Katie Finneran was a newbie back then and unaware of how to consistently hit her mark, so there were many times when I carried lumber up from the basement and ran across the room only to find that she was out of focus because she was standing in the wrong place. There was more than one time when I was very rude to her out of sheer exhaustion as I snapped and told her to please hit her mark. Sorry, Katie. I was quite full of myself back then. I should have been more patient.

I had a break in shooting and walked out of the house to find two of the producers looking at me as they chatted with each other. They were not pleased.

"What's up, fellas?" I asked.

"The hotel called," the line producer said.

"Yeah?"

"Uh, yeah. I guess you have…a dead body in your bathtub?"

"Oh my God! Vulich didn't take the Moseley dummy out of my bathroom?" I said, completely embarrassed.

"I'm not even going to ask you clowns why it's in there, but your housekeeper went in to make up your room this morning and was last seen running down Highland Meadow Drive, crying and clinging to her rosary beads."

"I'm really sorry," I said. "Those guys got into my room on Friday night and put it in there to scare me. They were supposed to get it out of there."

"Well, I hope that they had a fun time and that *you* know how to make your own bed, because she's not coming back," he growled.

I can still hear Vulich's jackal-like cackle as I told him how much trouble he caused. "It was a joke. They all need to calm down. The housekeeper didn't really quit, did she?" he said, defiant as ever, calling one of his guys over to go get dead Moseley and clean the place up.

The shoot progressed and we continued on what was turning out to be the toughest movie I had ever worked on. In addition to the constant stress from acting like I was worried I was going to be eaten by zombies, Tom purposefully got inside our heads in between shots. He'd pointedly warn us about the zombies, telling us to think of the living dead as an analogy for AIDS or other deadly diseases. It was perfect direction as we all lost our shit right as he called action.

I got so stressed out between shots that I wanted to slug the zombie extras away. If you watch the film and see the scene where Judy Rose and I are nailing a big table to a window, you'll see a zombie arm burst through the glass behind me and grab my face. I panicked so much that I threw all of my weight into the table and very nearly broke the guy's arm. Later, when we ran outside to put gas in the truck, I full on kicked a zombie in the chin that was told to scramble up to the tailgate. Still, to this day, I run into that extra at conventions and he introduces himself as the "guy you kicked in the face." My only argument is that there was no doubt that it looked real. There are also many people who ask me about the zombie at the tailgate whose head I shoot off in the film, or as it was shot, anyway.

The zombie in question was performed by make-up artist Earl Ellis and the make-up appliances were made of silicone which was a very new medium at the time. The reason they used silicone for this particular zombie, "the burn zombie," was because they wanted it to match the gelatin head they made for me to shoot off. The gelatin head consisted of a white plastic skull and red bits of rubber surrounded by flesh and red colored gelatin that was airbrushed to match the make-up. I assumed that they would be exploding the head with pyrotechnics, but when it came time to shoot it, the physical effects guy simply came to set with a real shotgun. Everyone gathered behind the camera as they propped the head up on a C-stand, weighting the bottom so the powerful blast didn't knock it over. The effects guy climbed into the back of the truck and took aim. The hope was that he blew away part of its face, revealing some of the skull and brain, but when the guy finally pulled the trigger on Tom's action, the entire head simply vanished in a bloody red mist. Later thanks to the MPAA, the shot was removed, but if you dig on YouTube, you can see the end result for yourself.

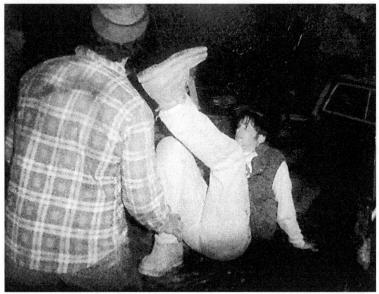

The shot where I nearly broke an extras jaw kicking him out of the way.

The head from the Earl Ellis zombie evaporated when they shot the gelatin head with a real shot gun.

One of my last nights of work came and I finally got to do my shots outside where I drive up to the barn and get blown up. In the story, my character believes he has found the keys to the gas pump, so he and his girlfriend take the truck up the hill to gas it up.

When the zombies start to converge on him, my character realizes in his panic that he, in fact, has the wrong keys and tries to shoot the lock off of the gas pump, blowing both of them to smithereens.

The truck the production bought for me to drive was an old rusty pick-up that they had painted to look a lot newer than it really was. The bed of the thing was rusting so badly that anywhere you stepped, your foot broke right through. In the scene, I was to make a run for the truck as my girlfriend pulls away. I was supposed to leap up onto the tailgate and scramble backward into the bed, but every time I did it, my hands and feet broke through the rusty metal. As always, not wanting to complain, I said nothing but was genuinely worried for my safety.

To make matters worse, Ben, played by Tony Todd, tossed a burning torch into the back of the truck with me. Because the stunt man was driving so fast, the torch kept falling out, so the effects guys came up with the idea of wiring it into the brittle rusty bed. In order to keep the thing burning, the table leg was wrapped in gauze and heavily coated with a flammable gel. As the camera rolled and the torch was lit, I could see the burning gel dripping down through holes in the bed of the truck and onto the gas tank that was equally as rusty. I was positive that the thing was going to blow up. I can assure you that the panic you see on my face during that scene is far from acting. Luckily, the truck somehow managed to hold together all night—that is, until the effects guys blew it up later. The rig nearly flipped over, the explosion was so massive. It was spectacular to see in person.

I was so afraid the truck was really going to blow up.

I stayed on set until late that night to watch them shoot the zombies dragging my dummy body out of the flaming wreckage and eat me. I must say I looked delicious. It was hilarious to watch them dig what was essentially sliced roast beef covered in BBQ sauce out of a hollow area in my torso and gobble it down. It's so funny what some people are paid to do in this line of work. Some of the extras were getting grossed out and gagging, it was so realistic. After their feast was done, I was finally wrapped and the crew applauded. I hugged everyone goodbye, shook Tom's hand and thanked him for the job of a lifetime, and headed back to my hotel room. I was thrilled to find a note from George Romero waiting for me, inviting me to breakfast before I flew out.

The next morning, George picked me up and took me to Elby's Big Boy for breakfast. I was so happy to have gotten to know him during the shoot; having his approval and friendship meant everything to me. George thanked me for the hard work and told me how happy he was with the cast and the film in general. I seized the moment alone with him to tell him how inspired I had been by him for so long. I thanked him for all of the hours of joy he had given me and Johnny Vulich throughout the years and told him that I was hoping to continue writing and start directing myself, mostly because of how much he had inspired me. George encouraged me to follow my bliss and give it a shot, offering to be there for me if I needed advice along the way. I later took him up on this offer many times.

For many years afterwards, it was always a pleasure to run into George Romero at conventions and signings; his gregarious, kind nature was not one you come across often in the world of film production. I loved the guy very much and was truly saddened the day that I heard that he had passed. George was a brilliant man, responsible for creating an entire genre and influencing hundreds of future projects from films and television to comic books and pop art, generating billions of dollars.

Getting Ready for a Zombie Bonfire

Still to this day, I am proud to have been in the company of everyone involved with the *Night of the Living Dead* remake, especially Tom Savini, who took a chance on me and gave me the opportunity to experience his wonderful ability to tell stories. No matter how slighted that he may have felt while we were in production, I had and still have so much respect for the man who truly help shape the horror genre.

Many years later, Tom contacted me and apologized for being distracted and cool while he was directing the movie. He didn't need to. It was my complete pleasure to have been included. Tom will remain someone that I love and respect for as long as I'm around. As for the film itself, the shooting of *Night of the Living Dead* had been a very tough but very satisfying one. and the film remains one of my most favorite projects I was ever blessed to be involved in.

Greg Funk getting the last few touches before the camera rolls.

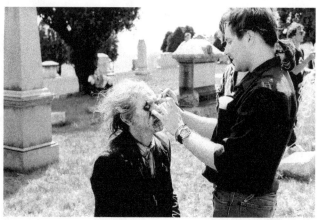

John Vulich and his ponytail on set of Night of the Living Dead

John Vulich working on Uncle Rege

John Vulich Ready to Dispatch the Dead

Some of the zombies really opened up on set.

Tom Savini Directs the Dead

25

BACK TO THE GRINDSTONE

Back home in Los Angeles, I was immediately in full swing, auditioning and doing stage work right away. I joined a couple of theater companies, including The Bubalaires, a gibberish show starring impeccable improvisors Helen Slater, Alice Vaughn, and Laurie Kilpatrick, among others. I also caught up with my friend Larry Cox from *Friday the 13th VII* who had turned me onto the Theatersports improv classes where I worked my way into performing at the rookie shows on the weekends with my newfound best pal Patti Lesser. Finally, Kate Hodge, fresh off of her latest TV series and winning streak at booking acting jobs, gave me a small budget to create a short film entitled *Black Velvet Pantsuit*. It starred Penny Hamilton, the original Snow White from the legendary *Beach Blanket Babylon* show in San Francisco, along with Viggo and a brilliant stage actor by the name of Mark Nassar from the hit play *Tony and Tina's Wedding*. The story revolved around a self-doubting, under-achieving ordinary woman who buys a black velvet pantsuit at a garage sale that turns out to be magic. Her life is instantly changed as she goes from beat down employee at Dog on a Stick to a superstar recording artist.

It was during the filming of this little project that I quickly learned my true love for writing and directing far outweighed my love of on camera performing. Plus, I could start eating more than two hundred calories a day as a writer and director. On my thirteen-year journey of my acting career, I had gone to bed hungry every single night in my effort to stay thin. The idea of just following my bliss and not focusing the majority of my day exercising and grooming myself was a most appealing thought.

Penny Hamilton in the first short film I directed, Black Velvet Pantsuit

About halfway through my short, Penny called me to tell me she was in the hospital for a few days with some issue with her liver. I put the short on hold, hoping that we would be able to keep shooting in a couple of weeks. I was shocked days later when my friend Laurie McIntosh called me to tell me that Penny had died of liver cancer. I was heartbroken at both the loss of my dear friend as well as at the fact that there was no way I was going to be able to finish my film. I took the footage that I had managed to shoot and was able to cut a trailer, and that was the end of that. For years after, despite the movie not being finished, I was able to use the footage in my very first directing reel and eventually got jobs from it.

Mike Deak on Black Velvet Pantsuit

Black Velvet Pantsuit - On set with Patti Lesser

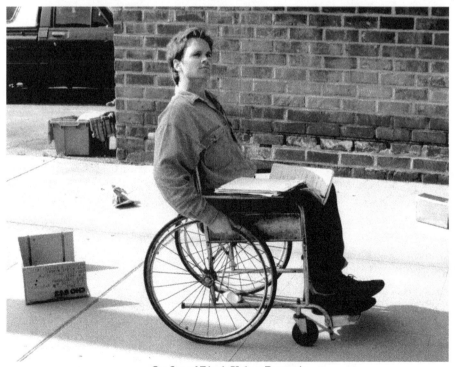

On Set of Black Velvet Pantsuit

One day, I got a call from my pals at KNB Effects Group; they asked if I would be the test subject for a make-up that they were working on for a film called *Johnny Zombie*. The movie was about a young guy who's murdered in a botched robbery and later comes back to life to try and win the hand of a young girl that he is smitten with. Being that I adored Greg Nicotero, one of the owners, combined with the fact that I loved the idea of being made-up into a zombie by his legendary effects shop, I agreed to be the subject without hesitation. For once, I could be the bad guy. I asked if I could read the script beforehand to see if there were anything that I might potentially be right for and they agreed to let me take a peek. I got ahold of the screenplay and there was indeed a bunch of parts in there for generic young dudes-next-door like me, so I planned to be on my very best behavior in the hope of possibly being noticed, but certainly with no plans to be too pushy or hungry (which never ever works).

I arrived at the effects shop early in the morning and the guys put me in the chair right away. I was surprised to see that the producer of *Johnny Zombie* was none other than Sean Cunningham, who was there for the test by himself. Cunningham was and remains a filmmaker of huge acclaim, mostly for his work producing and directing the very first *Friday the 13th* film among many other films, including *House* and *DeepStar Six*. His projects have had a huge impact on the genre and I was both a huge fan of his legacy and genuinely happy to meet him. I introduced myself and told him that I had been in a *Friday the 13th* film and that I was a big fan. It was entirely laughable that I received next to zero response. He just stared at me with a pasted-on smile. "Oh, yeah?" he said. I wanted to hit my head against the wall, having put my foot in my mouth once again. At that point, what actor *hadn't* been in a Friday the 13th?

My friends, who were about to make me up, softly tried to build me up by telling him about the other projects I had been acting in and how I was evolving into horror's boy-next-door. He just looked at me, comically unimpressed. I clammed up and sat quietly as the boys got to work. After all, Cunningham wasn't there to meet an actor; he was trying to figure out the look of his undead character, and I shouldn't have presumed he would fall for my charm and ultimately hire me in any capacity, but God damn, I tried. We narcissists are funny that way, always assuming people know who we are and that we are in demand, absolutely crushed if others don't become immediately obsessed.

The make-up process took about two hours as the artists tried several different looks for the undead character. I joked with the guys and held still while sitting across from Cunningham who looked on. The subject of the script came up and I mentioned that I had read it and that I really liked it.

"It's really good," I said. "But—"

He looked up at me with a *Now what?* look on his face.

"I don't think the movie is called *Johnny Zombie*," I audaciously blurted out.

"Oh, you don't?" Cunningham said, chuckling at my nerve.

"Nope. I think it should it should be called *My Boyfriend's Back*."

He just stared at me and once again, I got the message to shut up and make like a zombie, which I did. Finally, the work was finished and they put me in front of the camera, filming me in a variety of lighting schemes and scenarios. In the end, the test was a success: it really looked terrific, which came as no surprise, considering KNB's insane level of skill. I'm not sure if they ultimately did the job but I sure looked like an awesome zombie. Another dream checked off the Butler bucket list.

The boys took me out of the zombie make-up and I went out into the shop to say goodbye to everyone. "It was nice meeting you, Mr. Cunningham," I said to Sean.

"Yeah, thanks and oh, kid: if I decide to hire a thirty-year-old to play a high school student, you'll be the first person I call," he said, slam-dunking me and shattering my backboard. Feeling like a total idiot, I forced a smile, thanked my friends, and slumped out of the effects lab.

Time passed and I eventually forgot all about the embarrassing scene and took it as another showbiz lesson for me to keep my mouth shut. I should have just clammed up and not thought that I was so valuable that I could hustle an acting gig while helping a friend. As a grizzled old timer, I now know better, but back then, I was a shameless self-promoter.

One day, I was at Dupar's, reading the morning paper at breakfast. I turned to the movie section to check out the new releases for the week. In the middle of the page was a big ad for an upcoming movie: *My Boyfriend's Back*, produced by Sean Cunningham and starring my friend Traci Lind (who, for the record, was the exact same age as me).

Ah, the life of a thespian and hustler. You're welcome, Sean.

Back at home, Viggo's career really started to take off. He booked the movies *The Indian Runner, Crimson Tide*, and a bunch of other high-end projects. While his acting work was increasing, his love of Los Angeles seemed to be fading. He often spoke about packing his family up and leaving town for greener pastures. I had hoped he was just thinking out loud. Little did I know, the friend I had grown to love and rely on would be packing up his car, wife, and son and moving to Idaho in just a few months. I was crushed to see them go, but it was obvious that huge things were ahead for him.

Up until then, I hadn't realized how completely codependent and unpleasantly possessive I had grown of my friend. Of many of my friends, in fact. I know firsthand that you can love your friends too much and drive them away if you don't give them enough space. It took me many months to get used to him not being around, though being the mensch that he always was, I often heard from him until we both got so busy that we eventually lost touch. It wasn't until years later, after he became a huge star, that we somehow reconnected and stayed in contact. I appreciate and respect his friendship now more than ever.

By that point, I had done so much horror work, I was considered a full-on genre personality, a "Scream King" of sorts. "The Mickey Rooney of Horror," I once heard. I was making monthly appearances at horror conventions all around the world, and most of the appointments I was getting called in on were for horror films. I was up for Wes Craven's *Shocker, Leprechaun 2*, and *The Blob*, and I screen tested for the role of Willie Loomis in the *Dark Shadows* TV series reboot. It was also around this time that I got a call from my friend Robert Kurtzman about a film he was putting together that he wanted me to be in. It was something that I remembered he had been working on for years, a vampire movie that he had created entitled *From Dusk Till Dawn*.

Bob was in the middle of putting a pitch package together that included a bunch of genre personalities like me and film footage he shot of the late actor Joe Pallotta in the leading role. I read the story that he had worked on with Quentin Tarantino. I loved the project and agreed to play the role of a guy who ends up getting taken hostage by Pallotta and his crazy brother. Together, the family and the murderous thieves find themselves holing up in a strip joint as they are forced to fight off an army of blood-thirsty vampires. This was also around the time that Quentin Tarantino's career had really taken off. He had done *Reservoir Dogs*, a small movie that was a huge hit, as well as *True Romance*. Suddenly, the *Dusk Till Dawn* screenplay and anything else Quentin touched had massive buzz. Everyone in town wanted to check out *Dusk*, and the project quickly became bigger than it was ever originally intended to be.

Out of nowhere, all discussion with me on the *From Dusk Till Dawn* front suddenly got very quiet. In a matter of days, I wasn't hearing anything further about the movie. I figured that maybe, as with many other projects I had come across throughout the years, this one had also maybe stalled or been delayed; that is, until the morning that I got up and read in the trades that not only was Quentin now producing and starring in the film, but Robert Rodriguez was attached to direct it. I got dressed and made up an excuse to go visit Bob Kurtzman at the make-up shop.

"You've been replaced by a young Chinese boy," Kurtzman said, laughing as I walked into his shop.

"That's showbiz," I said, waiting for him to shout, *Just kidding!*

"Seriously, Quentin's rewriting the screenplay and you're out," he laughed, half-squirming.

"Damn, I knew I should have been nicer to him at that fucking Christmas party!" I said jokingly.

Just another day of life in Hollywood, really. I wasn't offended at all and was instead thrilled for Bob's movie blowing up. George Clooney and some Chinese kid were in and I was back to looking for another acting gig. Even more ironic was that KNB Effects Group later offered me a fun side job helping them make the goopy puddles that the vampires erupted into when they were staked. Never one to ever say "no" to any work, I whole-heartedly took the gig with a smile, but I cannot begin to describe the depth of the awkwardness I felt when Robert Rodriguez came in to see the shop's creature progress.

I had gone from shop monkey to genre personality to shop monkey once again. It was all a part the ever-fluctuating, completely blessed, and surprising career of William Butler.

26

SHIFTING GEARS

Around 1998, going to acting auditions was starting to bore me. I was getting really worn down on the auditioning front. I hated the dumb sitcoms I was auditioning for, I wasn't getting called in on enough mainstream film projects, and the idea that I would have to come in and read for another horror film after having starred in so many of them was laughable to me. Many casting directors were beginning to see me as a performer who only flourished when I was working in genre films. I was not getting considered for any drama or comedy, and it was beginning to really bother me.

All of the insane fun I had appearing in horror franchises ultimately painted me into a corner. It got to the point where I was only getting called in for the exact same part: the guy next door who is ultimately taken out by some kind of garden implement. I wanted to do something new and different. By now, it was also very clear to me that I was never going to be Tom Cruise—not that I ever wanted to be—and my boy-next-door shtick was getting harder and harder to pull off with each passing year.

Little by little, my interest in writing and creating began to flourish. I finished my first screenplay, found an agent, and started circulating it around town. I wrote and sold the pitch *The Gingerdead Man* for Charlie Band at Full Moon, and my love of sketch comedy continued to grow. I auditioned for and was cast in *The National Lampoon Live* show in Santa Monica. I spent nearly every night in the Lampoon offices, writing and workshopping sketches. I became friends with a brilliant young actress/writer named Jessica Hughes, who I still know to this day and with whom I have maintained a loving, professional working relationship with. Jessica has helped produce several of my TV and film projects.

Mac Ahlberg shot the proof of concept for the Gingerdead Man franchise that I created

Gingerdead Man

NATIONAL LAMPOON PLAYERS

It was clear at the time that my passion for performing was waning as I slowly realized my love for writing. I was also getting older and I wasn't self-aware enough to just cross over and evolve into a character actor. I had spent so much energy focusing on trying to be a young male ingénue that I hadn't put any thought into how to age gracefully and just transition, so I became completely lost.

I began to write every single day. I feverishly continued writing in my journals and helped my friend Ken Hall write the story for a horror film entitled *The Clown at Midnight*. I loved acting, but the kind of material I wanted to do wasn't coming around and I was no longer willing to audition to play parts where I ran from cutlery. I grew to live for my time spent writing and I slowly realized I was good at it. The truth is, I am a much better writer than I ever was an actor. The day finally came when I decided it was time for a major gear shift and to make the jump.

I can remember the very last audition that I went to like it was just yesterday. I was called in to read another young student role for the casting director on the old *Murphy Brown* television series on the Warner Bros. lot. The short scene I was auditioning for was only a few lines. I was trying to do more mainstream work, so I'd told my agent I would audition for what the industry refers to as "under-fives," roles that have five lines and under. I did several of those parts, including appearances on *Melrose Place* and *Beverly Hills 90210*. As long as the show was big, I was willing to take a smaller part for the chance to get my face in front of television execs and hopefully work my way up the network TV food chain.

I arrived at Warner Bros. with plenty of time before my appointment, but when I pulled up, I was told that guest parking was full and that I would have to go find street parking, a next to impossible task in Burbank at that time of day. It wasn't an unusual circumstance for an actor in the least, but no less a pain in the ass as I desperately searched for a spot. After frustratingly circling the studio several times, I managed to finally find parking six blocks away. I ran down the street and got myself through security and onto the lot with five minutes to spare. I walked up to the office, now a complete sweaty mess, only to find no one sitting at the sign-in desk. Again, not unusual, but there was no sign-in sheet and the place was packed with several guys that looked just like me, only nineteen years old, and with no chairs left to sit down on. I asked the others how long they had been waiting.

"An hour," one of them said to me, looking like he was about to fall asleep.

I stood in the corner until I got bored from standing there and sat on the carpet with a couple of the other fellows. There I was, sitting on the floor for a job interview at 35 years old.

After a few moments, a frazzled casting assistant came into the room to call the next person in and after a debate over just exactly who that was, I asked her if there was a bathroom I could use.

"No," she said, about to close the door behind her as she went back in the office.

"No?" I repeated. "There's no bathroom on the entire Warner Bros. lot?"

"Ours is out of service, and by the time you get back from the next closest one, you'll have missed your appointment."

"I'm willing to take that chance," I said.

"You'll be done in a few moments, we're going to speed through everyone from now on," she said as she went back inside, closing the door behind her.

I turned to the guy next to me. "Thank God the material isn't that funny," I said. "Who knows what would happen if I got in there and laughed so hard, I lost control of my bladder." The guy just stared me down as I turned away in shame.

I could hear her laughing and making small talk with the new actor who had just gone into her office, obviously someone she knew. I was positive I was going to piss my pants. Fifteen minutes went by and eventually I was able to get up off of the ground and sit in a chair. I could barely sit still, but finally, the assistant came back in and called my name. I stepped inside the casting director's office just as she took a bite of an awful smelling deli sandwich that permeated the room. It was obviously an insanely busy day for her as she quickly tried to choke the food down. She had no interaction with me other than motioning for me to sit down.

"Go ahead," she said, taking another bite.

I did my best to forget how much I needed to use the bathroom and started the first sentence of the material just as her phone rang. She snapped her fingers and pointed for me to stop reading. I sat there quietly, trying not to blow a gasket as she proceeded to dress down an agent for five minutes. I sat there listening to her go on about some actor who had been sent in earlier in the day and how she wouldn't use any more of his clients if he ever sent someone in that was so bad ever again. I sat there, zoned out and losing interest in the gig more and more by the minute as I waited for her to finish her call.

Finally, her tirade ended as she hung the phone up and looked back at me. "Keep going," she said.

I sat for a beat staring at her, not continuing. I was seething.

"What are you waiting for? Go!" she snapped.

Something clicked in my head. I no longer cared about anything that was unfolding in the room. "Nah, I think I'm done," I said.

"What?" she said, bristling. She looked at me, like how dare I be put off with her wasting my time and giving me half her attention during my meeting.

"I think I'm done…with all of this." I calmly smiled, set the material on her desk, stood up, and left her sitting there as she shrugged, not caring that I was leaving as she called the frazzled assistant and told her to bring in the next victim.

The absolute truth is, there was nothing that this lady had done to me that was any different than any other actor has endured on a daily basis, really. Not one thing. We actors are expected to study for the appointment, get dressed, drive all the way across town, find parking, and smile as we sometimes sit on the floor in the lobby or watch complete strangers gobble pastrami as we try our best to perform and book work. The fact that I considered her behavior to be unacceptable was a very clear sign that it was time for me to find something else to do. Because that is how it is. Sean Cunningham was right: I could no longer pull off the young loveable boy next door, mostly because I was growing into a grouchy, impatient adult. At that moment, I did not get the idea that I was growing up and the roles I was going in on needed to grow with that. My frustration was outweighing my love of a craft that I had longed to work in my entire life.

I had finally gotten to the point where I had enough of the acting rat race for a while. It was time for a big break. I'd had enough starving myself to be thin, enough being broke during the times when I wasn't working. I desperately needed a major reboot. It had become very clear to me that I was no longer totally loving what I was doing and that is so important for an actor's sanity. I called my mother when I got home, asking her if she would be disappointed if I started focusing more so on writing, directing, and producing.

"I've been waiting for you to say that for years," she said. "You no longer have anything to prove to anyone. You did what you said you were going to do. Now go and do what makes *you* happy for the next chapter of your life." My mother: always there for me when I need her the most.

Immediately after that call I went out to lunch and ate the biggest meal I had eaten in close to fourteen years. And that was it, the start of a seventeen-year break from performing on camera and I didn't lose a single night's sleep over it.

It was only just recently when I became comfortable with who I am and how old I am that ever even considered starting acting again, but what happened next in my life was even more spectacular than any acting job I could book.

At first, I kept my self-imposed hiatus to myself, my agent, my family, John Vulich, and my friend Greg Nicotero. I asked Greg and John to please hire me here and there so I could pay the rent while I figured out what I was going to do next. I also took a job with a company called Precision Effects, owned by effects artist Michael Hood, where I designed face masks for Madonna's *Girly Show* tour.

Throughout the show, Madonna wanted to wear these creepy white masks as she portrayed a Pierrot-like clown as a transition in between songs. At first, she wanted to just wear a plain white expressionless face, but since she was adamant about not wearing off the rack, an original one had to be designed. I started out with sketches of generic white ones, but soon, the idea of it being a plain white mask evolved into one with a mustache and many, many other versions. I ended up doing about seventy-five different designs as ideas flooded into the office. It was really fun coming up with all of the variations, and the fact that we were working with such a huge icon made it all very exciting. I was really looking forward to meeting her and hoped she'd be happy with what I came up with. The day came when we had to meet up to show her the designs and do a fitting for the strap that held the mask on.

We gathered the drawings and brought a cheap white plastic Halloween mask from Party City to use as a temporary stand-in along with some black elastic to adjust on her head so the actual mask would fit snuggly while she was moving around. We were told the fitting was going to be at the biggest soundstage at Fox studio where she was rehearsing the show and were warned to not be a minute late.

That day, we arrived at Fox twenty minutes early just to be safe and patiently stood on the sidelines waiting for her, watching as the dancers went through their music numbers, all of their numbers, to be exact. Twice. We waited and waited, standing there for nearly five hours without her showing up. At six o'clock in the evening, we were finally ready to throw in the towel and wrap it up. It was obvious she wasn't going to show. We gathered our stuff and walked outside as we noticed the staff suddenly started scrambling and the two huge soundstage doors began to slowly creak open. A line of smiling assistants lined up at the doors as a beautiful white convertible Bentley sped down the backlot street and drove directly inside the stage.

There she was, Madonna herself, who pulled the car to a stop and climbed out like a boss as she was instantly surrounded by her team. She was quiet and much smaller than I had imagined. In my crazy mind, I believed she was going to somehow realize how awesome I was and bond with me during our meeting. We'd of course end up lifelong friends. In my hilarious delirium, I imagined us laughing it up at a barbecue thrown at her beautiful house in the Hollywood Hills or that she would invite me backstage later to see my design work in action. But of course, that couldn't have been any further than what really happened.

By then, I had learned to expect the unexpected from the famous, and Madonna was no exception as she made her way from person to person, quietly giving cold one-word answers and signing paperwork from behind sunglasses that never came off. She truly was the epitome of a rock star: beautiful, pale, and exuding humorless confidence. I mean, who else whizzes past VIP parking spots at one of show business' biggest backlots and drives a two hundred-thousand-dollar car directly into a soundstage? Her assistant eventually got her attention and steered her in our direction as we nervously spread my mask designs out onto a folding table. We introduced ourselves to her with no reply as she began taking my designs and one by one and tossing each one as she briefly thumbed through them. My heart sunk and I was quick to realize that not only was I not going to end up at a barbecue at Madonna's house, I very well might be fired.

As the last drawing flew, she turned without saying thank you, and walked away. Her assistant followed her. We all looked at each other in puzzled defeat as he came back.

"She wants this one," he said, holding up the crappy mask from Party City.

"But that's the generic one that we just used for fitting the strap. It's off the rack," Michael said.

"Then make a mold of it and recast it, so it isn't off the rack."

We stood there stunned for a moment. "Okay, but should we at least make it, so that it fits the size of her face. This one is too big."

"She wants this one," he interrupted, glazed over as if he had heard it all before.

We got the message and agreed to just do what she asked. I picked my designs and went home, disappointed but certainly not surprised. The whole scene once again reinforced the cold hard fact that bad behavior in show business is not only tolerated, it's often rewarded.

The next day, we took that generic Pierrot mask and made a mold of it, pouring up an exact copy. When we were done, the three-dollar mask that we bought from Party

City ended up costing her six thousand dollars just so she could wear something that was created just for her. That summer, the only barbecues I attended were the ones I threw, and I can assure you: there was no Madonna on the party's playlist.

It was around this time that I was ready to try my hand at writing my second screenplay. The first one I had written, a superhero movie about kids who get super powers, had made the rounds and eventually flatlined, but I really felt in my gut that this was something I could really excel at.

To make extra cash, Nicotero offered me a little gig helping him in Bodega Bay on John Carpenter's remake of *Village of the Damned* and I jumped at the chance. Not only was I a huge John Carpenter fan from way back, but the town that we were shooting in was the same coastal town where scenes from his movie *The Fog* were shot, as well as Alfred Hitchcock's *The Birds*. It was a beautiful, quaint town just north of San Francisco and I had always wanted to check it out. The movie starred Christopher Reeves, Kirstie Alley, Mark Hamill, Linda Kozlowski, and Michael Pare. Greg and I arrived on location and cruised the area before checking in with the production office.

One of the first places Greg and I visited was the old Lypnoski house at Inverness. The Lypnoski home was an onion-domed, Russian-style house that was featured as the babysitter's home in Carpenter's film *The Fog*. In the movie, Adrienne Barbeau plays Stevie Wayne, a local jazz D.J. who leaves her son with her friend Mrs. Kobritz while she broadcasts her radio show from a lighthouse station nearby.

Ultimately, Mrs. Kobritz meets her maker at the hands and hooks of the pirate ghosts that emerge from a mysterious fog that shrouds the tiny coastal town on the anniversary of their murder. The home where they shot, The Lypnoski house, was built on stilts above the bay and sat resting above a sandy shore while the tide was out but became completely surrounded by water as the tide rolled in. The only way to get into the house while the tide was up was to walk on a small rickety bridge-like dock that connected to shore. Greg and I were surprised to find a "For Rent" sign on the front door as we drove past it, and we instantly made it our mission to check out the inside. We wrote down the phone number and headed to the production office.

Greg, being the completely charming fellow that he is, goaded the production into helping us get a look inside; he also talked them into letting us stay there instead of in our hotel rooms. They thought we were crazy to want to stay in the old salty house, but staying in a location that we had loved since we were kids instead of a boxy hotel room was, to us, a much better plan. There were even rumors about the place being haunted, which only made it more exciting to both of us.

We booked the house and headed to the grocery store to stock up on food for the next few days. Greg and I bought loaves of bread, cookies, chips, fruit, boxes of cereal, meat, booze, you name it. We got to the house and unloaded everything. We were totally stocked up and so happy for the chance to be staying at that creepy place…or so we thought.

House from The Fog

After Greg and I got off work that day, we came back to the house as the tide began to come in. We made dinner and then watched *The Fog* on the VHS player at the house later that night. As we were kicking back, watching the movie, we started hearing weird sounds. They were just scratching at first and then they graduated to occasional thumps. We thought maybe it was just the house expanding as the place was entirely built of wood and the tide was now fully in. Greg got up to check to see if the door was locked and looked around the house. We both started to get creeped out.

As the night progressed, the noises continued happening all around us more and more frequently, but we couldn't figure out what we were hearing. We laughed to ourselves, thinking that the place might really be haunted and rethinking our decision to give up perfectly good suites to stay there. After one exceptionally big thump, we put the movie on pause and went outside. After walking the perimeter deck that surrounded the place, we didn't find anything. Completely creeped out at this point but figuring we were overreacting at the sounds of the bay, Greg finally went to his room and I to mine. The rest of the night was very quiet and I fell into a deep sleep.

"I think I found our ghost," Greg said as he pushed my bedroom door open the next morning.

"What is it?" I asked as he motioned for me to follow him to the kitchen. I got up and followed him then froze in my tracks. I couldn't believe my eyes as I walked towards the kitchen counter. There was virtually nothing left of the groceries we'd bought the night before. The Lypnoski house was haunted all right, haunted by hordes of rats.

The loaves of bread we bought had been ripped open and were all but gone; the fruit had been carried off the counter and was lying half eaten on the kitchen floor; the cookie containers, cereal, and anything else in a paper box had been ripped open and was all over the place. I walked over to the window and found a piece of pizza crust in the front entry way.

Greg and I stood there stunned for a moment, then quickly packed our bags and bid the Lypnoski house a not so fond farewell forever. We checked back into the motel and the rest of the shoot went smoothly. The cast was really friendly, particularly Mark Hamill, who was very funny and approachable, as well as Christopher Reeves, with whom I briefly spoke and really liked a lot. None of us had any idea that this would be his very last movie before his tragic horse-riding accident left him a paraplegic for the rest of his life.

Before I knew it, the shoot was over, and I was set to take a little time off and continue writing but not before I took one last effects job with Ken Hall on *I Got the Hook-Up*. I did a special make-up effect that made actor Jeffery Combs from *Re-Animator* look like his dick had been shot off. I had worked with Jeff so many times at that point that it was just another day at the office when I grabbed his bits and pieces and yanked them back up through his legs, duct taping them to his backside. It's always nice to know you have a skill to fall back on, I guess.

27

THE FRACTURED FAN

I moved to a small studio apartment on Harper Avenue to try and save cash. It was very weird going from being a working actor with money back to struggling, but I was really ready to go for it and continue writing and filmmaking. The building was filled with artists and actors who were all friends who looked out for one another and I was very happy there. In a matter of weeks, writing slowly became my main focus and I began holing myself up at home and writing everything from short stories to screenplays.

However, as a result of this massive shift, I was no longer booking work, and after a couple of months, my money was gone. It was suddenly as if I'd just moved to Los Angeles and started all over again. I was so poor, trying to live on the small residual checks I got from my past movies and my three hundred dollar a week unemployment check, but truthfully, I was never happier. I cooked Top Ramen noodles or white rice and salsa for myself every night and designated my futon on the floor as my official office. The place was crawling with cockroaches; many times, I felt them climbing through my sheets at night.

Still, I lay in bed, staring up at the beautiful houses in the Hollywood Hills, positive that I would turn things around and end up there some day. Every single day, I got up and made myself coffee and sat and wrote on yellow pads for hours. The days of me going to the gym twice a day and never eating a single carb were also behind me, but staying thin now wasn't a problem because I had no money to buy food.

Not far down the street from me was a bar where you could eat all the peanuts you wanted if you bought a drink. Sometimes, when I was particularly broke, I went down to the bar and sat watching their TV, eating piles of peanuts until I was full. One night, when I was walking home from the bar, I heard someone call my name.

"William Butler?" the voice called out to me. I turned around and spotted a wall-eyed young man with long brown hair, dressed in jeans and a t-shirt, standing not far behind me. "You're the guy from *Chainsaw Massacre*, right?" he asked.

Flattered that he knew who I was, I told him I was. He sped up to walk beside me as I continued home. He introduced himself as Brad Cherry and told me he was a big fan. He seemed to know a lot about my work, so I figured he must be the real thing. Either you have never heard of me at all or know everything about me, and there is very little in between. Not only did he know the more popular projects I had been in, but he also knew dialogue from some of the very obscure stuff.

I asked him if he lived around the area and he told me no. He said he was homeless and was panhandling his way through town on the way to San Francisco. Feeling bad for the guy, I gave him all the money that I had on me, which was only about seven dollars. We chatted about movies, and he told me a hard luck story of being abandoned by his parents and struggling with addiction as he walked with me all the way to my apartment building.

I was about to tell him goodbye when he asked me if he could have an autograph. Once again, flattered that he knew who I was, I walked to the curb where my car was parked, grabbed a pen, and signed my name on the back of a slip of paper that I dug up. Brad thanked me, and I shook his hand and wished him luck as he continued down the street. I have to say, as I went up the stairs, I was a little puzzled over what the chances were of me running into a homeless person that knew I was in *Ghoulies 2*, but I do get recognized in the strangest places every now and then so I shrugged it off.

I headed upstairs and went inside my building. Plenty full from my peanut eating haul, I took a shower and started getting ready for bed. I put my robe on and was just about to lie down when there was a knock on my door. I went and looked in the peephole. Standing outside was this Brad Cherry guy. I left the chain locked as I opened just enough to speak to him.

"Hey, William, I'm sorry to bother you again, but I was wondering if maybe you had a picture you could sign for me. My mom'd be so stoked to see that I met you in person," he said with a smile. I was really surprised and a little shaken that he had somehow gotten into my secure building and what's worse, figured out where my apartment was. Why was he wanting a picture to show his mother when ten minutes ago he was telling me she had abandoned him?

I started to suspect that maybe this guy knew where I lived all along. A few months back, I had gotten mail from this horror fan site where they had figured out my home address and posted it as a place where you could get me to sign stuff. I was only marginally known by most of the public, but the people who knew and liked my work were a dedicated bunch who I loved. I'd never had any issue with stalkers, but I was weirded out that this guy had just shown up out of nowhere. Years before, just a couple of blocks from where I lived, a relatively new TV actress by the name of Rebecca Schaeffer had been shot in the face by a fanatic who had just shown up at her door.

Brad explained that he'd told the landlord, a friend of mine, that he knew me and the guy had stupidly buzzed him in. "Your apartment number is on your mailbox. You should take your name off of it so people can't find you so easily," He said to me. *People like you?* I thought to myself.

By then, I had already dealt with a couple of crazies at conventions, so I knew better than to curse him out, which was my first notion. I asked him to wait for a moment as I scrounged up an 8x10 of myself and signed it. I opened the door up again, slid the photo out with the chain still locked, and told him it was nice meeting him. He thanked me and smiled as I closed the door on him, locking the bolt. I immediately went to the phone and called my landlord to give him an earful, but he didn't pick up. Figuring I was getting worked up over what was probably nothing, I shook it off and pulled my blankets down and started to get in bed. Just as I was about to lie down, there was another knock on my door. Without hesitation, I went back to the door, opening it to—of course—find Brad Cherry still standing there. This time, he didn't get a warm reception.

"Yes?!" I snapped.

"Sorry, I just realized the next bus isn't until eleven-thirty, I have forty-five minutes to kill, and I was wondering if you wanted some company until I have to walk back down to Santa Monica," he said.

"No, thank you, I'm good. And you really shouldn't be showing up at people's apartments like this. You never know what you'll get in L.A.; it was nice meeting you, but I have to go now. Goodnight," I said, closing the door on him once again as he started to speak.

I went back to my phone and called my landlord one more time, and again, the call went right to his answering machine. I was leaving the guy a heated message when the knocking on my door started again. I turned the TV off and ignored it, getting into bed as the knocking went on for the better part of thirty minutes. Frustrated and growing increasingly worried, I got up and walked lightly to my door, slowly moving to the peephole to get a look at him. I don't know if my head blocked what little light I had on in the room, but he seemed to know when I moved my face close to the door because when I did, he pounded it so hard that I jumped back from the jolt. He looked pissed off as he continued to knock.

I backed away from the door and after trying my landlord one last time, I decided to call 9-1-1. The operator listened in complete boredom as I explained that a homeless guy had followed me home and wouldn't stop knocking on my door. The operator asked me if he had threatened me or hurt me in any way. I told her no, but that I was feeling trapped in my own place because he wouldn't leave and I was starting to think that he was mentally unstable. She said she would send a cop car out to my building, but unless he had made any attempt to hurt me or made any threats, there would be nothing that they could do other than tell him to go away. I told her that was better than nothing as I turned the television on and sat on my bed, trying to call the landlord over and over, until the knocking finally stopped about thirty minutes later. After waiting a good long hour on my bed, I eventually got up and quietly looked out the peep hole, relieved to find that he was no longer standing there. I took a sleeping pill and lay down to go to sleep, eventually drifting off.

It was about three in the morning when the fire alarm went off in my building. My eyes bolted open and I dove out of bed and put on my robe. I opened my door as other tenants walked out into the hallway looking around for smoke, but it was clear. Outside, I could hear a fire truck's engine rumbling and saw red flickering lights in the window at the end of the hall. As I turned to go back inside to get my key so I could go downstairs…I realized that my entire door had been smeared with what looked like dog shit. I ran inside, grabbed my keys, and headed downstairs to find the fire department hosing the row of mailboxes on my building's front porch. Someone had dropped lit matches into my mailbox and set the junk mail that was inside it on fire. I instantly knew that this lunatic Brad Cherry—if that was even his name—had set it. I told the Fire Marshal that I thought I knew who might have done it, gave him my name and number, and went back inside to scrub my door.

I was really shaken up afterwards. I didn't sleep a wink the entire night and after all of that, the police never even bothered showing up. The next morning, when I went out to my car to go to the gym, I found that he had also smashed my car window. Like my door, every inch of the inside of my car had been smeared with dog feces. I luckily never saw the guy ever again, but considering everything that had gone down, I decided that maybe it was time to move.

28

LIFE WITH LESLIE

A couple of months after the harrowing dog-poop and burning mailbox incident, my friend, brilliant character actor Leslie Jordan, started asking me if I wanted to move in with him. Leslie was an amazingly entertaining soul that I met many years earlier through friends, and we bonded over a catalog of nefarious reasons. He was and remains a wonderfully kind, hilarious, and generous human being that I love having in my life. Like I wrote earlier, he's mostly known for his Emmy Award winning portrayal of Beverly Leslie on *Will and Grace* and for his work on his new hit series, *Call Me Kat*, and he is currently the darling of Instagram with over five million followers. He has been a very busy working actor for many years and has just about as many insane stories as I do. Dare I say more than I do? Most likely. Just don't believe any indiscretions he might say about me.

Standing at a little over four-foot tall, Leslie is a modern-day Truman Capote of sorts, a man who has self-deprecatingly referred to himself as a "walking sight-gag" in some of the acting roles he's been cast in, but he is in fact, a very brilliant writer and performer with impeccable timing and skills. To know him is to love him even on his worst day, and trust me: I have seen all shades of those days.

Leslie saw firsthand that I had been struggling since my career shift, once he came over and realized that I had no power in my apartment as I waited for a residual check to come in and I could pay my electric bill. For a week solid, I read by candlelight and used the oven to heat my apartment, learning many years later how incredibly dangerous the practice is. In hindsight, I don't know why I didn't just keep acting while I was trying to start writing. I could have easily done a horror film or two to stay afloat, but I just know at the time, I was really ready for a change. Trying to stay thin every day of my life had become a complete bore to me and I wasn't going back. One thing was for certain: it was clear I had put myself back at square one by altering my course.

After one particularly depressing day, I called Leslie back and asked him if he were still interested in taking me in as a roommate. Living with him would cut my bills by half and it would be good for me to be around other people rather than just sitting around my apartment alone. Les lived in a beautiful house in Van Nuys with a big swimming pool. There was a big room for me and I pretty much could have run of the entire house, so there was very little downside to living with him, not to mention the small detail that he also had a constant steady flow of electricity.

Also living with Leslie was his longtime roommate, a gentle and kind woman by the name of Miss Carla, a former Southern debutant turned Lawry's steak-house waitress, a gal who was gentle, generous, and endowed with an unquenchable thirst for Coors beer after her late-night shifts at the restaurant. The three of us met and agreed that it seemed like we were a good fit. Leslie and I had a lot in common. We were both actors with similar schedules, we loved keeping to ourselves, we were tidy, but most of all, we both had growing penchants for finding trouble in our downtime and the downtime was in abundance.

Leslie's longtime boyfriend, Bobby the drug dealer, had moved out, and by "moved out," I mean he'd been sent to prison for trying to rob a Taco Bell drive-thru. That marked Bobby's third strike which sent him to the big house for a long time. His first strike was for dealing drugs (to me and Leslie mostly) and the second strike was for the time that he was arrested for trying to shoot Leslie with a crossbow. Yes, you read that right.

Leslie pulled up to my apartment in his beat-up old blue pick-up truck with a faded camper shell and helped me move to his place and what would prove to be an insanely wild adventure for the next few years. The laughs were plenty. Our audacity was immeasurable. We were a shameless duo who completely fed off of and encouraged each other's bad behavior.

Leslie Jordan and I

Before I go into all of the lurid details of our pretty entertaining, mildly-unsavory, and positively illegal activities during our time spent as roommates, I want to remind you that my friend Leslie Jordan has been sober for over twenty years now. He is a shining example of how one can completely turn their life around and make the very most of it. He not only lives a better life these days but has been a beacon of sobriety, encouraging many others into living a good clean life. My drug days are also now a very long distant memory. I am now somehow hilariously, staunchly against using drugs of any kind in what I know in hindsight is the ultimate hypocrisy, but back then, we were both the wildest drunks and committed piggish druggies you'd ever meet. There wasn't a synthetic challenge that we both weren't willing to try and tackle. Yes, dear reader, the boy who once used to drunkenly crawl out of bars on his hands and knees with peed pants while coming down off of ecstasy is now kissing Pomeranians, planting tulip bulbs, and in bed by nine o'clock every night. I'm happy to report I am a clean teen, but boy, are there a lot of miles on my odometer. I can only pray that I will live to see the day where I write the final page of this book. Back then, oh lord, Leslie and I were insanely unbridled: a gruesome twosome who had no off-switch when it came to having a good time.

We looked out for each other like brothers, sometimes fighting like brothers as well. But one thing was for sure: we went after anyone who caused either one of us grief. I remember one night, we were out drinking in a bar, and Leslie was out dancing on the dance floor as some mean-spirited queens started making fun of him for his size. I dove into the crowd, slugging my way through his mockers until a huge brawl broke out. We were insanely protective of each other; plus, if anyone was going to make fun of that little imp, it was going to be me.

His truck, our only mode of transportation, was held together with duct tape and barely running. We smashed every fender on that blue truck of his in a variety of distracted parking lot incidents. We hopped into that thing, threw it into reverse without batting an eye, banging into bumpers or flooring it as we scraped out of tight parking spots like we were breaking through the wall of Jericho. We were sloppy, careless, and forever on a search of the next good time, and we found it in abundance.

One of our favorite haunts was a rundown and mildly dangerous bar on Santa Monica boulevard near Vista street called Hunter's. Hunter's was a grimy old watering hole that had been around forever. They served cheap drinks, had a scuffed-up pool table that sometimes doubled as a place to sit and eat a greasy Astro's hamburger, and the nicest streetwise bartenders you'd ever meet. The cliental was a colorful and admittedly dangerous collection of all sorts of unsavory characters, including Leslie and me. Bearded transgender hookers, hustlers, drug dealers, parolees and flat out thieves on the lamb could be found there on a daily basis. Most people would do anything they could to avoid a bar like this, but Leslie and I took great joy in hanging out there. It was hilarious that two guys who had been raised to be such good boys reveled in surrounding themselves with such a motley crew.

Every single one of the patrons had a fascinating story or background, made-up or otherwise. If you'd just gotten out of jail, you positively claimed you were framed. If you desperately needed to borrow money to eat, it was really because you needed cash to score drugs or to pay off a loan shark who was about to break your leg. There was "Pete," the clean-cut UCLA chemistry major who'd graduated with a doctoral degree and had figured out how to cook meth out in the desert. Pete had made himself twenty pounds of the strong amphetamine and sold it all at once for an astounding amount of money, then quickly got out of the business and retired at thirty-four. There was a wheelchair-bound little person/drag-queen named "The Goddess Bunny," a chatty, overly made-up street urchin whose claim to fame was that she once was in a Marilyn Manson music video. Her breath could stop a freight train. Once, Leslie and I were in the bar and witnessed Goddess Bunny and a trans hooker get into an argument that ended with the kid putting her foot up on Bunny's wheelchair arm and shoving it, sending her rolling fifteen feet back across the bar and slamming into the jukebox, her tiny legs flying up as she hurled towards the men's room.

Other regulars included gruff tattooed bad boys who came to Hollywood seeking fame, but instead ended up walking the boulevard turning tricks, preying on rich married businessmen who were there looking to hire them. There were sailors and thugs, all of whom somehow knew to get off the Greyhound bus, fresh off of shore-leave or getting out of jail, and head right for that seedy bar and we'd be right there waiting for them. They were all rough around the edges but also a never-ending source of laughs and stories. The truth is, we genuinely liked most everyone that hung out there; we just always knew never to leave our wallets lying about or to follow any of them down a dark alley. Even the dangerous ones had a lot of heart once you got to know them.

Hanging out with the underbelly of life was a terrific distraction to the struggle of living in L.A., especially when you knew at the end of the day, you could leave it all behind at that bar. It was there that I first realized how much your childhood truly shapes you into who you are as an adult, much like writing this book has done for me. So many of those lost souls had the saddest childhoods that you could ever imagine but somehow had adapted skills to survive on the streets. Leslie had such a kind, gentle way with all of them, always willing to try and help them out whenever they came up with a story or ploy to get money out of him. His generosity was endless.

One day, he and I had stopped by Hunter's for an afternoon drink and didn't end up leaving until around seven in the evening. We piled into his truck and made the forty-five-minute drive back home to our house in Van Nuys, singing along to Tammy Wynette on the way. As we pulled into the driveway, we were shocked to find a homeless man emerging out of the back hatch of Leslie's camper shell. Apparently, the man, a total stranger, had climbed into the truck while we were in the bar and had fallen asleep there. We had unwittingly driven him all the way to the valley, not realizing that he was back there rolling around untethered as we sped down the highway.

"Well, welcome to Van Nuys," Leslie said without batting an eye. "Enjoy your new home. Now, go on …git!" He opened the gate and sent the guy wandering down Baltar Street. Events like this were a weekly occurrence.

Though we were as thick as thieves and forever friends, Leslie and I really encouraged the very worst of each other's behavioral flaws. We both loved to drink, we were both fascinated by dangerous and unsavory characters in life, and we eventually became dedicated drug buddies together. Thankfully, our living together eventually marked the end of the run of partying and just in the nick of time.

However, not two weeks after I moved in with him, I started in with any drug I could get my hands on. We headed to that bar and got buzzed until we found ourselves heading off to some dark and dangerous corner of L.A., usually with a total stranger in the truck, as we looked to score. This was back in the day when prostitutes used to walk up and down the streets of Hollywood. Sunset Boulevard was populated with dozens of garish female hookers in pink fun fur and hip boots, while Santa Monica Boulevard was bustling with rough male trade on every corner, all of them willing to lie down for cash. These guys often frequented Hunter's and we befriended many of them, always keeping in the back of our minds that despite being pals, they might, in an off night, murder you. We quickly learned that most of them knew how to find pretty much anything we wanted.

One day, Les and I took one of our hustler friends to go score at a seedy hotel that he said he was living in. We yanked a hundred dollars out of the ATM and went driving down Santa Monica towards his place, pulling up as he jumped out. He leaned inside the car and told us to wait there and that he'd be right back. A likely story. Well, as you probably can imagine, we must have sat there for forty-five minutes before we started to suspect the strong possibility that he was not going to be coming back. After another five minutes, I got out of the car and walked into the hotel's main front door only to realize that there was another exit at the very end of the hall that opened to the next street over. He had taken our money and run through the hotel and out the back door.

Most people would have chalked-up being ripped off by a street hustler as predicable happenstance, but not Leslie and I. We angrily drove up and down every single street in Hollywood until we eventually tracked that guy down. Since Leslie is so small and cute and was famous to many even back then, he knew most of those guys by name and they certainly knew of him and his unbridled generosity and wouldn't hurt him. In fact, there was an old saying among many in Los Angeles back then that went, "You can always tell when Leslie Jordan is booking work. Every street hustler on Santa Monica Boulevard has a new pair of tennis shoes."

Leslie stormed out of his truck and charged up to the guy, demanding our drugs or money back. The guy apologized with some crazy made-up excuse about waiting for someone to bring it to him and he promised to catch up with us later at the bar. We went back to Hunter's and continued our debauchery, not expecting him to show up in the least, but sure enough, he surfaced just as we were leaving, handing us what we later realized was a small plastic bag of drywall chunks. Another lesson learned. We were ripped off tons of times, but that never stopped us. We used to refer to incidents like that as "the luck of the draw." It served us right. Neither one of us had any business dabbling in such affairs.

There was another time at Hunter's that I nearly got my neck wrung as Leslie and I were sitting at the bar and I made the huge mistake of busting the chops of a rough street transvestite named "Kelly." Kelly was a big, black, bearded football linebacker/street-walker in an akimbo wig, spandex mini-dress, and poorly applied lipstick. Kelly had clearly been over-imbibing in something chemical that day and was dividing her time in the bar between twitching, ticking, and being overly disruptive in an argument with herself. She must have played the TLC song "Waterfalls" ten times in a row that afternoon as she gleefully shadow-danced with the "people" she appeared to be seeing.

Thinking that I was being funny and trying to make Leslie laugh, I leaned over to Kelly, whose acrid armpits reeked of drugs, rubber cement, and pickle juice and said, "Would it be possible for the next show to be downwind a little?"

Kelly's eyes bugged as she dove for me, furious. She fought to get at me, her mini-skirt hiking up around her waist as she was pulled back by four of her friends. Leslie and I ran out of the bar as Kelly vowed to take me out for insulting her. After Kelly's meltdown, Leslie and I hid out back home and didn't go to the bar for a few weeks as word on the street was that Kelly had branded me dead meat for my poorly-crafted and disrespectful joke.

"When Kelly full, Kelly dangerous," Our friend Angel, the transgender dental hygienist and most likely part-time prostitute said to us from her beat-up barstool at The Rainbow, another seedy bar we used to frequent.

"Full?" I asked.

She took a drag of her cigarette and looked at me with streetwise, heavily mascara-encrusted eyes. "Too high, drunk, whatever the fuck she on. When she full, she dangerous. Lay low for a while, Billy. You on Kelly's list," she said with a deadpan gaze. "I seen her beat a motherfucker's head in with a parking meter once. You don't want that: take it from a girl who's seen it firsthand."

I swallowed in fear. "Kelly dangerous?" I said.

Angel nodded. "Uh-uh. Kelly got nothing to lose, she been cutting throats her whole life."

For a brief moment, I felt like I was a character in one of those "woman behind bars" movies: an innocent suddenly thrust into danger as I am thrown into the clink. As much as I was genuinely scared, I was also getting such a rush from it all. I took Angel's advice to heart, as not only did Leslie and I not go back to the bar, we didn't go to Hollywood *at all* for months until word started to circulate that Kelly had been incarcerated after being arrested for stealing an ice cream truck and trying to drive it to Atlanta.

I got settled in at Leslie's and during one of my periodic moments of sobriety and clarity, I took a job helping my friend Ken Hall at his foam fabrication shop, brilliantly named Total Fabrication. Ken's shop wasn't far from the house Leslie and I lived in and I loved and appreciated working with him. I helped organize and paint foam fabricated props and costumes like the monsters and robots we built for *Power Rangers* and several other big walk-around characters used in theme parks and at conventions. One day, I learned that Ken had been hired to create several puppets for a new kids' interstitial series on the Fox Family Network called *The Basement*. He took creative meetings with the producers of the show and little by little, I started to get to know them.

Atul Rao, Kim Saltarski, and Greg Van Riel were this tremendously creative group known as The Membrains. They had a long run producing several very successful interstitial series in Canada and came to Hollywood to make their mark in television with Saban Entertainment. Saban had bought the Fox Family Network and was going to launch in a matter of months. The Membrains were to help shape the kids' block with their insanely clever interstitials.

Seeing this as a potential opportunity to break into TV and possibly start writing, directing, and producing professionally, I brazenly asked the guys if I could audition to puppeteer one of the characters in the show, telling them that I would happily do double-duty writing and producing digital shorts as well as puppeteer and do fabrication maintenance for them, all for the same price. They graciously gave me the chance to be put on tape puppeteering, and after a couple of auditions and meetings, they watched my very slim directing reel and offered me a job.

The opportunity was life-changing, as they pretty much gave me the chance to try and prove myself in any creative department that I wanted, in conjunction with my puppeteering duties. My main gig was operating a huge slave-unit puppet built by the Chiodo Brothers Effects Group named "Ab Motad" or "All Being Master of Time and Dimension." Ab Motad was a wise-cracking giant wad of pink bubblegum with one big eye that wandered the room and another that peered out from an old TV set embedded in his head. The radio-controlled puppet was the best-case scenario for a puppeteer, as all I had to do was sit on the side of the set in a director's chair and open and close my hands while I improvised with the other cast members. Ab often joined the cast of teen hosts of the show and we did comedy sketches and interviewed young stars in between the afternoon programs that played in Fox Family Channel's afternoon block. We interviewed everyone from 98 Degrees and a very young and polished Mandy Moore to Aaron Carter and even Destiny's Child back when they were still in cornrows and Adidas jogging suits.

Not long after I started, The Membrains allowed me to write and produce digital shorts for the show. In a matter of weeks, I realized that was right where I belonged. I loved what I was doing and worked three times harder than was expected of me in my attempt to be noticed as a director. The newfound responsibility forced me to live a cleaner and more responsible life and I grew to love it. I worked really hard to become a team player, taking any assignment that they gave me with a huge smile on my face. With each passing spot I produced, I started to get better as I learned what I was doing.

My work got enough notice with the execs upstairs at Fox Family Channel that when *The Basement* was eventually cancelled, I was offered a contract with Fox Family in the special projects department. My supervising producer, Mark Pinsker, was a gruff but extremely lovable and wise creative that took a huge chance on me, giving me my own office and a never-ending stream of assignments that ranged from animated pilot demos to commercials and music videos. I was learning so much on a weekly basis as my assignments were vastly different from project to project. Mark's belief in me only encouraged me to work harder. Eventually, I started becoming known as a writer-director. Honestly, I was never happier. I finally found the thing in life that brought me absolute bliss. I took every single assignment and worked as many hours as they asked me to.

It was right around this time that Leslie Jordan and I finally made the well-overdue solid decision to pass the baton when it came to the subject of partying. Our "awakening," as we refer to it, came during the summer when both of us had eye-opening experiences that made us finally somehow see the light. Leslie already had two DUIs within a year. One would think that would be a sign to us to clean up our act, but for a while, it didn't soak in for either one of us. One late night at about two-thirty in the morning, Miss Carla and I woke up to the sound of the phone ringing. We staggered out of bed, listening to the answering machine as it picked up. It was a very drunk Leslie Jordan.

"Hey, ya'll it's me. Well, I did it again. I got my third DUI. I'm in the pokey. I don't expect ya'll to come get me. I just wanted to tell you guys, I won't be coming home until morning."

Carla and I looked at each other. "I'm not going downtown again," she said as I shook my head and went back to bed.

Five minutes later, the phone rang again.

"Hey, ya'll, it's me again. Listen, on second thought, there's no place to lie down in here and I am exhausted. Will one of you come and pick me up, real quick?"

Again, Miss Carla and I looked at one another and shrugged as we went back to bed.

"Nope," I said, lying back down. That's right around the time that the phone rang once again.

"Now, you two, listen to me! I know you're standing there just listening to this. Someone has got to come pick me up! Do not leave me in here! It's dangerous!" And with that, he slammed the phone down.

The phone rang a fourth time. Miss Carla and I didn't even walk out of our rooms as we stared at one another from our bedroom doorways. We both shook our heads "no" as the phone hung up without the caller leaving a message. It was only moments later that there was another ring. I just stayed in bed.

"Someone, get me the fuck out of here! I am going to be murdered!" Leslie's voice screamed at us from the machine. "Now you get your fat asses up out of bed and get down here!" The phone hung up one last time and thankfully, he didn't call back.

The next morning, he showed up at the house totally raggedy but all smiles and apologies. He sat Carla and I down and told us that he was sorry and that he was never drinking again. Sure enough, somehow, he didn't. He kept that promise to himself, starting with the solid month that he ended up serving time for getting his third DUI. He was released only after Robert Downey, Jr. was convicted and checked into the same cell: the county needed space for Downey in the celebrity ward.

Somehow, Leslie's decision to clean up his act really stuck. Once he got out of jail, he did indeed stay sober and has been for years. In fact, he went on to become a revered speaker on the subject. Inspired by his new lease on life and the fact that I had finally found my true calling as a writer-director, I realized that my ride on the party train needed to come to an end. It did, but only with the help of a very unlikely savior.

Leslie is hands down one of my most cherished trusted friends 30 years strong.

I was still working at Fox Family Channel at the time and it had been a very long weekend. It was Sunday night and the second night of an unbridled stretch of hard partying. Muffy Bolding and John Vulich joined me on a field trip to the Seventh Veil strip club in Hollywood and we were on a tear. All night long, the three of us were drinking, shamelessly doing coke right out in the open, and laughing it up as we tossed dollar bills onto the stage for our naked new friends. There I was in all my glory, a shining example of a producer from the Family Channel. Muffy, typically a completely sober church mouse, nudged me for the handoff and did a covert bump in the shadows of our booth. Of course, no one noticed as all eyes were on the thick Ukrainian girl writhing around on John Vulich's lap.

Muffy allowed herself one single night to run with the pack, and boy, was this going to be one to remember. As it sometimes happens, she did the hit of coke and instantly broke into a sweat, suddenly motivated to use the bathroom. For those of you uneducated in the art of self-medication, there is sometimes the unpleasant effect of your bowels rushing when you do that crap, especially if it's been cut with powdered baby laxative, which is most of the time. Muffy dove out of the booth and scrambled across the strip club trying to locate the ladies' room in a big hurry, only to realize in sheer horror that the place didn't have one. Her search became more frantic as she considered ducking into the men's room, but one of the strippers spotted her and waved her behind the curtain. Sure enough, the only bathroom for women was backstage in the strippers dressing room, and it had no door, just a toilet sitting in the middle of an empty room.

Later, Vulich and I howled with laughter as Muffy told us that she had run straight back through the dressing room, past complete strangers dressed in g-strings, putting make-up on. She sat on the toilet not three feet away from them. Muffy unleashed her churning bowels from beginning to end and in plain sight of six other woman who did their best to ignore her while she did her business. She was mortified. We were completely entertained by the anecdote and the three of us exploded into laughter.

The night progressed and we continued to brazenly party. Soon enough, I zoned out and lost track of time. In my boozy, stupid mind, it was only about ten o'clock. I thought I could easily be home by midnight, catch some sleep, and be ready for a Fox Family Channel shoot I was doing the next morning at Universal Studios. I was directing the twelve-year-old sisters known as Mary-Kate and Ashley, the Olsen twins. I had become the guy who did all of the girls' promotional stuff and had a very good working relationship with both them and their team.

The night crept by and I eventually started to tire. I leaned over and asked John and Muffy if they thought we should head home. Just as I did, something strange caught my eye. I looked up at the ceiling and spotted a thin, bright glowing white line that ran along the black cottage cheese stucco above.

"Hey, you guys: what's that?" I said to Muffy, pointing up.

She looked up and suddenly froze. "Uh, Butch, that would be daylight."

"Daylight?! What time is it?!"

Vulich cackled and looked at his watch. "It's eight-thirty," he said.

"Eight-thirty? In the morning?!" I was supposed to be at Universal Studios at eight. "What the hell am I gonna do?! I'm not even showered or dressed for work, let alone sober enough to be in front of people from the fucking Family Channel!"

"Man up," Vulich said. "I show up on *Buffy* hungover all the time."

"The woman who plays Buffy is not twelve and being hungover is the least of my problems!" I yelled at Vulich as I threw on my coat, and, never one to waste, slammed what was left of my drink. I walked outside with Muffy and John and couldn't believe my bleary eyes. We had indeed been there all night. The people waiting in traffic at the stoplight gawked at the three of us and I fell into a deep shame.

"Now what? I'm completely exhausted." I asked my cackling Jackal friends.

"Well, I don't know a lot about that crap, but it seems to me the very best you can do is just cannonball it," Muffy said.

"Cannonball it?" I said.

John nodded, "Get in the car. I can fix this," he said. The next thing I knew, I was doing a giant rail of blow off of a Paula Abdul *Forever Your Girl* CD box. In a matter of moments, I was wide awake again. Muffy gave me baby wipes from her purse, a commodity she always carries without fail. I washed my face and quickly tried to pull it together as we raced to the valley.

John spit in his hand and slicked my hair back, then slapped me in the face a couple times and gave me his sunglasses. "Put these on and do not take them off," he said.

"You can do this, Butch." Muffy told me, lovingly caressing my sweaty face.

"Really?" I said.

They both burst into laughter. "Fuck no! You're totally fucked!" they laughed, peeling out as they left me standing at the gate.

I stood there for a moment, taking a shaky breath. How in the world had I gotten myself to this point? This was not why I moved to Los Angeles. High as a kite and about to direct the fucking Olsen twins? Are you kidding me? I was positive that I was going to be fired. I deserved to be fired. I somehow made my way through security and over to the soundstage, trying to hide the fact that I was completely afraid of my own shadow. I honestly did not know if I could make it through the morning. I promised God that if he somehow got me through the day, I would make some big changes. It was a promise I had made and broken a million times before, but this time, I genuinely meant it.

Every minute that passed as I approached the soundstage felt like an hour. I was exhausted, time was crawling, and I wasn't even in the building yet. I finally walked in as everyone greeted me. Following John's instructions, I didn't take his sunglasses off as I set up my stuff. Mary Kate and Ashley gave me a hug. I remember Mary Kate looking at me as if she noticed something was different. It may have been my yellow face from lack of sleep and the fact that I was wearing sunglasses inside a dark stage, but I'm just guessing.

I did my best to keep it together as one by one, we started picking off the shots we needed for the spot. I sucked it up and did my best, but I was obviously out of form. I am normally very chatty and friendly, but this morning, it was all I could do to remain upright. Luckily, no one really seemed to notice as I pretended to be working on my laptop in between shots to send people the signal to stay away. I was pretending to be answering my fiftieth email of the morning when I felt a little hand rubbing my upper arm. I looked over in terror with a jolt, finding Mary Kate Olsen's angel face beaming as she looked up at me with a smile.

"Just breathe in the good and breathe out the bad," she said, patting my arm. "We'll be done soon, and then you can go home and get some sleep."

I stared at her for a moment, lost in thought. Does she somehow know I was up all night? Does she just think I'm tired? Did I just get an intervention from one of the Olsen twins? I thanked her and apologized, telling that sweet little girl that it was just that I wasn't feeling well.

The rest of the day went as well as it could as I continued to whisper direction from behind sunglasses with my coat collar turned up. I honestly had never felt such shame before. When we wrapped, I went home and took a well-needed nap that lasted all the way through to the next day. When I woke up, I flushed everything that should not be in my house or system down the toilet. And that was it. The baton had officially—and finally—been passed and I was on the road to living a much cleaner life. I started going to NA, CA, and AA meetings, said goodbye to other friends that I knew would tempt me into going back, and finally started focusing on growing up. As a result of my newfound clarity, I began to climb in the company at Fox and was renewed under contract as a writer-producer.

I had finally, finally seen the light. God bless the child, the Olsen child. Not only am I terrified at the thought of ever doing a single drug ever again, I am completely preachy to my young friends who choose to partake. I have no idea how someone as scared of that lifestyle as a child somehow found himself fully committed to the wicked fun of it all and for so long, but I am sure happy that it's now the furthest thing from my mind and that I'm somehow still alive to write about it. These days, it's two drinks once a week and I am ready for bed by nine o'clock. I don't even smoke weed. The glorious day finally came when I grew up, if even just a little bit.

From that moment on, I never ever showed up to work hungover or with anything in my system that should not be there. I lived a much easier life in a house I'd bought and had the distinct pleasure of shacking up with my two adorable dogs and best friends, Gibby and Henry, and from that moment, we lived in absolute peace and clarity. I began quietly dating a beautiful and kind gentleman who made me feel happy and loved. It was a banner moment for Billy…well until we broke up, but the business of show is and always has been my one true love anyway.

Thank you, Mary Kate Olsen. I really do appreciate you helping me through the worst day of my life. Give me a call if you ever need a pep talk yourself.

29

WRONG ZOMBIES, RIGHT TIME

One day I was sitting in my office making notes on a cut, when my boss, Mark Pinsker, stuck his head in. "Hey, get to my office. I have a friend of yours on the phone," he said.

Puzzled as to who the hell he could be referring to, as we knew no one in common, I ran down and took a seat in front of his desk. Mark took the person off of hold.

"Tom? I have William Butler sitting here," he said. "Tom produced *Night of the Living Dead*. Do you remember him?"

"Mark, I produced *Return of the Living Dead*. It's a different franchise," said the voice from the speaker.

Return of the Living Dead was an insanely popular comedy-horror film that follows a group of edgy teenagers as they head out to party the night that the contents of a mysterious military canister are released, somehow bringing the dead back to life. Tom Fox said that he was about to produce *Return of the Living Dead 4,* and he was calling Mark to see if he had any leads on writers who might be willing to help him develop a story for the latest sequel in his film series.

Pinsker nodded at me and raised his eyebrows, pushing the mute button. "Tell him you'll help him," he said to me.

"He's not gonna want me!" I said, waving him away as Mark took the call off mute.

"Billy is a really good writer with a long history in horror films," Pinsker said. "I'd bet you two could come up with something really terrific. I highly recommend him."

I closed my eyes, waiting for the rejection in the short silence. Then, "Would you be willing to have lunch with me to discuss that idea?" Tom asked.

I could not believe my ears. "Yes!" I exclaimed, looking at Pinsker in disbelief.

Like so many others along my journey, Mark Pinkser had just changed the course of my life and put me one step closer to a lifelong goal. In fact, Mark changed my life in so many ways that I will never forget, like by having me work for him, for starters.

A few days later, I met with Tom Fox at Jerry's Famous Deli in Westwood and it was love at first sight. Tom was an extremely eloquent, charming, and well-dressed man with bullfrog like features. His laugh filled the room and he was far more interested in those around him than he ever was in himself. We quickly became friends and knowing him was my absolute pleasure.

Tom explained the history and backstory of the *Return of the Living Dead* franchise, how he had produced the original films and that the rights had recently reverted back to him. It was his turn to do another sequel. He explained that originally, way back when John Russo and George Romero had parted ways after *Dawn of the Dead*, Russo had retained the right to do his own projects with the *Living Dead* stamp in their titles as he had long ago written a novel called *Return of the Living Dead*. He and Tom decided to create a film based loosely on Russo's book that was to be directed by Tobe Hooper. The original *Return* script was written by Dan O'Bannon with Hooper directing, but O'Bannon stepped in to direct at the last minute after Tobe bailed on the project to direct a "vampires in outer space" epic called *Lifeforce*.

The original *Return of the Living Dead* film, considered by many to be a comedy, originally started out as a serious horror film, but O'Bannon brilliantly shaped the project into the funny, punk-rock inspired movie that it turned out to be out of respect for George Romero's previous *Living Dead* works. The result was a cult film with a unique and humorous tone that is loved by millions. Tom told me that he himself had no idea that the movie was going to end up funny. He went to the premiere expecting a horror film and from the minute that the first reel started rolling, the audience was laughing. He was equally shocked the next morning when Roger Ebert gave the project a rave review for being so hilariously innovative. *Return of the Living Dead* had turned out to be nothing like the film that Tom had set out to produce, but a terrific one nonetheless. Fox told me many hilarious tales of his non-stop battles with writer-director Dan O'Bannon, who according to him, constantly threw tantrums, inappropriately hit on the actresses in the film, and eventually moved on to write several other huge hit screenplays including *Alien*, a script written by the light of a never-ending stream of porn films that permanently played on his office television set.

After a few meetings and a decent grain of an idea, I was locked into the team and headed to helping Tom Fox create the latest chapter of the film. At the time, I was so grateful for the opportunity to try and help continue the film's legacy. I wish I had known that the end result would leave me sticking my head in the sand for the better part of two years.

During our meeting at Jerry's Famous Deli, the first thing I told Tom Fox was that we had a huge task on our hands. The *Return* fans were a very hardcore dedicated bunch and would be quick to turn on a bad sequel and everyone involved if it didn't specifically fit in with the other previous films. The story's rules had to be strictly followed; it was imperative that we create the project in the same tone and with a few of the actors or characters from the first two films. Tom whole-heartedly agreed with me that the rules had to be followed and was very open to us developing something spectacular, but he also had a very specific guideline: we couldn't use any material or characters from any of the previous works due to copyright issues. I would have to come up with all new scenarios and characters.

My first pitch was a story called *Return of the Living Dead 4: Necropolis*. In my sequel, humans now lived in a world that had grown accustomed to the zombie apocalypse that unfolded many years ago, so much so that people no longer feared zombies as pretty much everyone was armed, their houses and cars all armored and zombie-proofed. Running a zombie over on the way to work or taking one out in a grocery store parking lot were just everyday occurrences in the small city where my story took place.

On the edge of town was a highly popular attraction called *Necropolis*. The massive place was an extremely high-tech theme park of sorts where zombies were the main source of entertainment. Sort of the Knott's Berry Farm of flesh eaters. There were dark rides and rollercoasters where chained zombies came dangerously close to you; there were shooting galleries where the undead staggered around a 2-D city set as you shot them and even a cage match where you could place bets on how soon a human opponent dressed in safety gear could dismember an attacking zombie until he no longer was mobile.

Behind the scenes there was much more going on at *Necropolis* than met the eye, as the corporation that was running the park was also up to no good. They were also quietly working with the military, sharing their advanced technology to help try and create the ultimate solider, eventually building an army of the dead that could be parachuted into other countries should another world war break out. Their zombies were cool, big hulking beasts armed with lethal weapons that were grafted to their bodies and limbs.

In the story, a group of teenagers wander out of the amusement area and lose track of their little brother. As they search for the little boy, they stumble upon the park's dirty secret and end up fighting for their lives, battling hordes of zombies that the park officials release to try and extinguish them in order to keep a lid on their operation.

It was a simple, fun pitch that Tom Fox bit on right away, and within a couple of days, I was contracted to officially come on board and fully flesh out the story. I was working on the project for a couple of weeks when Tom told me he wanted me to meet with Tobe Hooper of *Texas Chainsaw Massacre* and *Poltergeist* fame as he was considering coming on board to direct the film. After a couple of pitch meetings at Jerry's Famous Deli with both Tobe and Tom Fox, the story was finally approved and locked. Tobe was attached as director and I continued fleshing the story out with his input.

Tobe Hooper was a true anomaly. I must say, I have never met, known, or worked with anyone like him, ever. Brilliant? Positively. Crazy adjacent? That, too. I myself get crazy-adjacent on a semi-weekly basis so I was in good company. Tobe was funny, smart, and very Southern, a true redneck genius and a rebel who was not easily impressed by others, particularly film producers. He was a guy who'd be in the middle of explaining a plot point he wanted added into the script and would suddenly go off the rails with creative ideas that were way outside the box. Way, way outside. Like the box would be nowhere in sight. Sometimes these ideas were brilliant and sometimes they were extremely hard to follow. I can remember one meeting where he told me that he wanted one of the zombie attacks to feature the main characters crying long red ribbons that came unfurled from beneath their eyes at the sight of their friend being ripped to shreds. I smiled and took the note but later had to re-read it three times to try to figure out what he was talking about. Regardless, no matter how out-there his ideas were, there was no doubt he was a true artist. I loved working with him and my face hurt from smiling every time I was around him. What an honor it was to know him.

Vulich had worked with Tobe on *Texas Chainsaw Massacre 2* and warned me that he was very eccentric, which of course meant they got along well: John was a far bigger oddball than Hooper ever was. Johnny told me that he and Tobe spent many nights sipping amphetamine-laced cans of Dr. Pepper while enduring the long night shoots on *Chainsaw*.

The *Return* project was gaining quick momentum; we were all very excited at how the film was shaping up, and we'd made sure to adhere to the rules of the franchise, keeping steadfast to the fact that the *Return* zombies cannot be stopped with bullets. For those of you unaware, the zombies in Dan O'Bannon's story will not die unless they are completely incinerated or blown into a million pieces. George Romero's zombies are the only ones that can be killed with a shot to the brain. It's all in the details when it comes to killing the undead. There were also plenty of moments in our film for cool rock music to be placed in the project. Most of all, Tobe Hooper's insanely creative ideas on how to execute the film was what would have really made it shine. He knew exactly what he wanted, even if sometimes some of us had no idea what he was talking about. Never question a genius. I do dare to say that between the three of us, we nailed it. It really felt like we had created the ultimate *Return of the Living Dead* sequel.

Days later, Tom Fox called me at my house in Silverlake and told me that Screen Gems loved the pitch and wanted us to come in for a meeting about the next potential steps. They were very interested in doing the film, provided that Tobe Hooper was indeed attached as director. Tom pushed me to try and crank out the first draft of the screenplay in just a few weeks as everyone that was reading the twenty-page story outline was asking for it, but I was still working at Fox Family during the day, so I would have to work all through the night in order to pull it off, and I wasn't sure I could do it.

The movie was continuing to get traction around town as other companies were also reading it and liking it, so even though I was not getting paid at the time, I agreed to try and do double duty and crank out a script as fast as I could. I figured it any draft would be a good starting point and that we could shape it the same way we collectively did the story.

Tobe Hooper and I

It was at that point that I began to look at Tom as a father figure. I quickly became attached to him and his loving family. He began to call me every morning and ask me to tell him of one thing that I was going to do to propel myself closer to my goals. He reminded me time and time again that he truly thought of me as a talent who was going places and it meant everything to me. He and his wife often invited me up to his house in the hills and we sipped wine and ate the most awesome spread while talking about our day. They became as important to me as my own family.

Tom used to look at me incredulously and say, "I cannot for the life of me imagine why your father doesn't fight to have a relationship with you. He's really missing out on a marvelously spectacular person." Little did he know, it had been my call to stand clear. Still, his sentiment shook me to my core. I didn't even know what having a real father was like.

After one meeting at Tom's house, I stopped at Mexicali Cantina restaurant in the valley for dinner by myself. I sat there for a couple of hours re-reading the pitch, trying to figure out how the hell I was going to flesh it out a tangible screenplay by myself in three weeks. My waiter was a friendly young guy who I assumed was an actor as he was a handsome lad. He told me his name was Aaron and he seemed to be very interested in what I was doing. I told him about the cool assignment I had that was unfolding quickly and how I was stressing over how I was going to get it written.

I finished dinner and headed home. That night, I pecked at the computer, trying to get started, but because I was so exhausted from writing at work at Fox all day, I crashed after only two pages. I honestly didn't know how I was going to be able to pull off working all day and writing all night.

I talked to John Vulich the following night. He was neck-deep in the effects for a brand new and yet unknown television series called *Buffy the Vampire Slayer*. John told me to come over to his shop and he would act as a sounding board while I wrote, but I declined. I had to leave for Fox at seven the next morning and I knew that going to his place would only encourage me to stay up all night and that wasn't the answer. I went to bed, got through my next day at Fox Family Channel, and stopped off at Mexicali again on the way home. As I sat at the booth, I saw that I had the same friendly waiter that I had from the last time I was there. This time, the guy introduced himself as Aaron Strongoni; he explained that he was working on becoming a screenwriter. We chatted as I ate dinner and he divided his time between his tables and myself.

As I finally finished and was about to leave, Aaron handed me a package. It was a screenplay that he had written and was hoping I would look at it and tell him what I thought. I took the package, but honestly didn't think I would really read it. He was a nice enough guy, but I barely ever want to read my own writing, let alone someone else's. So, I took the package with no plans of opening it. But while I was at work the next day, I took the script to lunch with me and really liked it. It turned out, the kid was a really decent writer.

That afternoon, after I was off work, I headed back to Mexicali once again in the hopes of running into him once more. Sure enough, he was there. I told him that I really liked his writing and encouraged him to keep at it. We talked about our love of the craft and our strengths, weaknesses, and ultimate goals. In many ways, we both had the same hope of where we would land in show business and that was to just get to a place where we were working consistently: not a lofty goal but certainly a good one. We both didn't need to run a studio to be happy; just being working writers was good enough for us. He was driven and hungry, and he was exactly what was missing from what I had going on. Before I was even done with my guacamole, I realized that fate had probably put him in my lane for a reason.

I asked him if he would be interested in helping me write the first draft of *Return of the Living Dead: Necropolis* and he agreed. He was thrilled for the chance and I was relieved that maybe somehow the script would get done.

Two days later, Aaron and I were pounding out pages and bonding in a new friendship that ultimately lasted for years. He was focused, much more than I was, and a very good sounding board, even when he didn't agree with me. Aaron was the perfect writing partner as I can be a complete steamroller when it comes to writing a script. He sat patiently listening to me belabor my point and whenever he finally could get a word in edgewise, which wasn't often, he made a valid and wise comment and I shut up and took the note (sometimes). I knew that I had found someone I would grow to depend on, not only because he was a diligent writer, but he was also far more focused than I could ever be.

Before I knew it, we had the first draft pounded out and met with Tobe for feedback. We sat with him at Tom Fox's house and got the good news that he loved the script. This time, he had far fewer ideas that were hard for us to follow. We grew to love the guy and were mesmerized by his stories and insanely cool history. It was really hard to not gush whenever Tobe was around. His street cred came from a very real place and he was by far his own person with a very opinionated view of the world, but nothing he ever said, no matter how politically incorrect it might have been, ever offended us.

For example, one time at Tom Fox's house, we were all sitting around, sipping wine and working on the script with Tobe, and I brought up the correlation between a zombie outbreak and a pandemic disease like AIDS.

He just stared at me for a deep-thinking beat, then said, "They should put every last queer on an island and just fucking nuke the fuck out of it."

Aaron cringed as I laughed out loud. I didn't have the heart to tell Tobe that if that happened, he would have no further polishes. I could care less about what he said. Part of what made Tobe Hooper cool was the amount of fucks he had to give, which were none. Finally, the script got in terrific shape and we were ready to start going out, and that's when things started to get complicated.

Tom arranged for our first pitch meeting with Lakeshore Entertainment. Lakeshore was a well-known boutique production company that had many movies under its belt, including *Runaway Bride* and *200 Cigarettes*. Tobe, Tom, Aaron, and I arrived at Paramount in the afternoon, parking on the lot. I couldn't believe I finally had worked my way onto a movie lot. All of the other times I had been there, I had just bluffed my way in. We walked across the lot and over a small grassy area in front of a building that used to act as the high school *The Brady Bunch* kids attended.

After being watered and coffeed properly, we were then taken to the Lakeshore conference table as several executives and development people filtered in. Aaron and I pitched our movie and they seemed to be visibly pleased, responding positively as they looked to Tobe for comments that didn't come. It was quickly clear that pitching was not Tobe Hooper's forte as he mostly sat silently listening. If I pitched a plot point and turned to Tobe to try and hand it off to him, he just looked back at me and nodded for me to continue. Never to be one to pass up on the prospect of work, I turned on the Butler steamroller and barreled through. After all, I figured that Tobe was a complete icon and if he felt like talking, he certainly would.

The executives turned to him smiling, waiting for him to speak up, but it didn't happen. There sitting in front of all these people was the director of *Poltergeist* and *The Texas Chainsaw Massacre* and up until that moment, no one had gotten him to speak or even asked him a single question, and frankly, it would have been better had they not, as one naïve executive made the mistake of finally asking a very stupid one.

"Well, I can see that there is the story there. But what kind of movie am I going to get out of this?" the exec said, staring Tobe down.

Tobe sat up in his chair, bristling.

"Exactly what is your vision?" another continued, brandishing the trademarked show business robot face.

Tobe reached up and twisted his beard with his hand, staring the guy down. "What's my vision of the movie?" Tobe pasted on a half-smile as he looked around the table, the gears clearly spinning. I was about to burst out laughing, because I knew him well enough by now to know that his reply was going to be good. "What's my vision of the movie?" he repeated, then chuckled, shaking his head in absolute disgust. "My vision of the movie…is for you to pull a dump truck full of cash up to your fuckin' bank when I'm done. That'd be my vision."

Aaron and I burst out laughing as everyone else in the room sat with blank looks. They clearly didn't see the humor. The president of sales, a very pretty, tattoo-sporting woman named Stephanie Denton who was also at the meeting burst out laughing with us. Even though she and I never spoke to each other during the pitch, our eyes kept locking every time something stupid was said, which was most often.

After the meeting, Stephanie invited Aaron and I into her office. We talked about the film and how much she was behind it and quickly bonded over many things, the largest being our mutual hatred of the many stupidities that exist in Hollywood. They were too numerous to mention. The funniest thing about stupid people in Hollywood and in general is that they don't know that they're stupid. The stupider you are, the more you are adamant that your voice be heard. That's just how it works.

I instantly knew that Stephanie was one of the coolest people I had met in a very long time, and the fact that she was the lead salesperson on the movie *Frankenhooker* only elevated her from potential friend to total rock star. Almost twenty years later, I am still friends with her. Back then, Aaron and I could truly feel that good things were going to unfold there and we were right, sort of. A couple of days after our *Return of the Living Dead* pitch, we were asked to get on a call with Tom Fox and the executives at Lakeshore.

"We love the project and want to move forward with just a couple of caveats," one of the upper execs said. We were happy that the very first place we had taken the movie had bitten, but the next comment threw us for a curve. "For starters, after meeting with him, we think a talent of Tobe's magnitude would be wasted on a film like this. This is out of his wheelhouse."

A film like *Return of the Living Dead 4* was out of Tobe Hooper's wheelhouse? I was pretty sure the director of the original *Texas Chainsaw Massacre* could handle the undertaking.

"We are willing to fast track this project," the exec continued, "if Tobe is released and we can find a new director." *He must have really pissed them off*, I thought to myself.

Always the businessman looking for a fast deal, Tom Fox was very quick to say that he would be willing to discuss a new director coming in, which was jaw-dropping but not surprising, considering how hard we were working on trying to get the movie made. The *Return* films were a big part of Tom's livelihood so it was understandable that he would do anything to get the project going.

The executive continued. "We want to find someone young with a fresh new perspective, one who understands the genre with a new set of eyes and—" *And is fucking cheaper and doesn't curse at you*, I guessed.

"The second note we have is bit of a broad one," the exec said. "We love that your movie takes place in a zombie amusement park, but we have just two small changes."

"Okay," Aaron and I eagerly said, sitting poised with pens in hand.

"Take out the zombies and take out the amusement park."

"Say, what?" I blurted out.

The executive went on to explain that they really loved the idea of teens finding themselves lost and searching for someone in a secret government facility, but in his mind, zombies were "over." Still to this day, it's the most laughable note I think have ever received in my history of corporate entertainment and that is certainly saying something. As I write this over twenty years later, zombies are anything but over.

It was true, Lakeshore wanted us to turn the attacking creatures in the *Return of the Living Dead: Necropolis* script into mutants not unlike the monsters in *Hellboy*. They planned on turning the project into its very own franchise. Being team players and not to mention complete whores, Aaron and I agreed to take the notes. Truthfully, we loved the idea of making it into a monster movie. As outrageous as the request was, we really wanted to work with their team and figured we could later just come up with another pitch for *Return* and get Tobe back on the project as it was set up somewhere else.

The new plan stuck and with that, Tobe Hooper was out of *Necropolis* and the story evolved into a movie about mutants that run amok at a military facility. Tobe, as you can imagine, was less than thrilled, but he just shrugged and shook his head in disgust as Tom broke the news to him. He'd seen scenarios like this unfold time and time again.

We were told to not hold back when it came to the creatures. A budget of ten to fifteen million dollars was discussed and Aaron and I started to write. Writing with him was fun and came very easily as always. In about a month, we had finished the polish and to our surprise, Lakeshore loved our first whack at it. The next thing we knew, they wanted to start talking about papering the deal and to start looking for a director right away. At the same time this was happening, Aaron and I began working on a story for Tobe's version of *Return of the Living Dead*.

Since going to rave parties and taking party drugs were all the rage during that time period, we came up with a story we entitled *Return of the Living Dead 4: Rave to the Grave*. The story was—what we considered anyway—a comedic tale about a group of funny college kids who find one of the Trioxcin 5 cannisters and discover that the fluid inside has hallucinogenic qualities if you ingest micro-doses of it. Even just a small dot on your tongue would send you into a psychedelic life after death experience that everyone on campus suddenly wanted to experience. Unfortunately, the mild side-effect was that after you trip your brains out, you also end up transforming into a violent, flesh-eating zombie, which completely ruins your high, obviously. We had a blast writing the story. All of the bloody, gooey, synthetic drug fun unfolds at the biggest Halloween rave ever held. What better person to shape a movie about drug-idled twenty-somethings than me?

The movie was basically *Animal House* meets *Return of the Living Dead* filled with guns, large-breasted girls, and boatloads of over the top gore. In other words, yes, a film for the entire family: families who like watching people being eaten alive, anyway. Tom Fox and especially Tobe Hooper loved the pitch and signed off right away.

Suddenly, both projects were back on target and in full swing. We fleshed it out the *Rave* story with Tobe as we wrote on *Necropolis* for Lakeshore at the same time. One of the development people at Lakeshore introduced us to a manager, a hilarious and very matter-a-fact guy by the name of Jonathan Hung. Hung, as he was known by most, put our deal discussion in motion. He was and I assume remains a very funny guy who Aaron and I both loved so much. Word on the street was that the character Lloyd, the sassy agent assistant from *Entourage*, was inspired by him. I never knew it as a fact but whenever we asked, Hung just smiled and blushed. Hung was a very to the point and no-nonsense manager famous for his unimpressed quips, especially when it came to our writing.

"I've sold worse" was one of my favorite emails we got from him after he read a horror screenplay that we had just finished writing. He was also famous for his two-word emails when sending out the news that a studio passed. "Universal passed" and "Lion's Gate passed" were just a couple of the beyond brief emails that we got from him when studios passed on our work.

When we fished with him to see if they gave us any feedback at all, he said things like "Yes, I forgot to tell you: they loved the script and think you're both brilliant writers, but they still don't want the project. Is that what you need to hear?"

We learned very quickly to man-up and not fish for compliments with this show business wildcat. The truth was, his job was to sell scripts and not tiptoe around fragile egos, especially mine. I learned fast that rejection came frequently as a writer, even more so than what I was getting back when I was an actor, but things were never better and I was honestly never happier. Tom Fox was attached to the all-new and improved *Necropolis* as producer and just as soon as our deal was signed, we started looking for a director.

The new pitch for *Rave to the Grave* also started circulating around town, now with a much happier Tobe back involved. The project quickly started gaining traction again and everything was on target exactly how we hoped it would be just about the time that the rains came.

It started pouring rain. Pouring. For a month. El Nino hit L.A. hard and the entire city flooded. It rained every day for a month solid. Houses were flooding and sinking into the ground; driving was sometimes impossible. I was tarping off my porch when I got an abrupt and devastatingly unfortunate call.

"They're pulling the plug on *Necropolis*," Stephanie Denton said to me, drained.

"Say what?" It was my go-to response for all things that floored or horrified me.

I stood motionless in the pouring rain as she went onto explain that they were starting the *Necropolis* deal with Tom Fox when their legal department got a call from an angry stranger. The man, who was an acquaintance of Fox's and claimed to be a producer, said he had previously met with Tom for a lunch meeting on the film and was attached to the project. During this lunch, Tom had apparently, in a friendly gesture, half-invited the guy to potentially come on board as part of the team. Of course, this was way back before the movie was even written or set up anywhere, especially at a production company with its own in-house producers. An outside producer was not needed as Lakeshore was crawling with them.

Nonetheless, the guy threatened to dig his heels in deep and sue Lakeshore if they moved ahead with a deal without him and with one phone call, our fifteen-million-dollar movie went away. A person, I remind you, who was in no way shape or form involved with the creation of any part of the project, had just shut down a hundred-thousand-dollar script sale for my writing partner and me. The film was instantly buried, all because some stranger felt he was entitled to a paycheck after having lunch with Tom Fox. I was devastated. This would have marked our first big sale and for an A-list company with a massive pedigree. It also marked the first of many times as a filmmaker that I was dragged into or threatened to be pulled into a frivolous lawsuit. Those who can't, sue.

Aaron, Tom and I were crushed. We had worked so hard to turn the movie around and shape it into the film that Lakeshore wanted it to be, but it was true, it had indeed completely flat-lined. Little did I know, this sort of activity was just another day at the office for filmmakers. These days, when a project falls apart, I simply smile and focus on something else. Back then, though, I was floored by what had unfolded. Writing and making movies was certainly not going to be any easier than booking jobs acting in them.

30

IT'S A MADHOUSE

I lay in bed for two days solid, listening to El Nino's pouring rain continue to pound my house as I kept the sheet pulled up over my head. All that work seemed to be for nothing. After weeks of taking direction from the Lakeshore development department, shaping the project into something cool, the project was suddenly dead. Leslie Jordan, who in a reversal of fortune was now renting the guest house at the house I had bought, came upstairs and calmly knocked on my door.

"There's some water on the floor of my place," he calmly said in his thick Tennessee accent.

Shaking it off and figured the ceiling had sprung a small leak, I grabbed a roll of paper towels and went downstairs, stunned to find the entire floor completely flooded with two inches of flowing water. His big black Labrador retriever Samson sat on a footstool, whimpering as he looked at the water as it raced past him and out the open door. The place was completely flooded.

Leslie took his dogs and headed to Big Bear Lake while I was left with the arduous task of figuring out where the leak came from. Three days and a hundred plastic tarps later, I figured out the flower beds on the upper levels of the house were filling up gopher holes and sending a flood into Leslie's place. My life had gone from awesome to irritating in a matter of days. That is, until the rains finally stopped.

My phone rang as I was playing with my growing herd of lap dogs. It was Stephanie Denton from Lakeshore. She told me that that she had just gotten out of a meeting and that the company was still really interested in our writing and were wondering if Aaron and I had anything else we wanted to pitch. They might even be willing to discuss me directing something. Thrilled at the idea of getting another chance but exhausted at our newfound knowledge of how the business works, Aaron and I thought on it and then decided to step up and scramble. We poured through everything we had to see if anything fit the sort of projects that they were looking for.

In one weekend, we came up with a short story for a murder-mystery/horror film entitled *Madhouse*, a story of a young man who goes to audit the medical practices of a rundown asylum and eventually finds the place to be haunted *(spoiler alert)* ultimately, by himself. It was just the kind of slow burn horror that we loved to watch and an homage to many of the asylum movies that we were fans of.

Aaron and I went in and pitched the story to the Lakeshore brass, this time with no Tom Fox or Tobe Hooper in tow. Our meeting went great. We were shocked to see them eat up our story, half of which we had made up in the car on the way. (It was a practice that we continued as long as we were writing together.) It went well and the team said they would discuss the project and get back to us. I figured we should chalk it up as a terrific meeting and move onto something else, but Aaron, always the more positive of the two of us, felt like something really great was about to unfold.

Back on the *Return* front, little by little, *Rave to the Grave* began to cool as we started to get fewer meetings on the project. I forgot about the movie as I continued working at Fox Family Channel and got back into the groove of kids' programming and writing other spec screenplays. Aaron and I continued to write pretty much on a daily basis, developing other projects and polishing the old ones we had already written. Always one to stay in touch, Tom Fox invited Aaron and I to lunch at Chin-Chin in Studio City, a Chinese food joint that he referred to as "our favorite place" despite us not really liking the food there at all, but whatever Tom wanted, we were ready to do. We loved him and his unflinching positivity. I really looked forward to every moment I could be around him. Tom gave us daily pep talks, told us to keep the faith, and assured us that he was going to eventually get the movie going. After all, it had taken him five years to try and get the original *Return* movie going.

It was around this time that Tom started to not feel well. The number of meetings we took with him began to dwindle as he suddenly fell quiet. My daily phone calls from him slowed to once a week and when he did call, he seemed very tight-lipped about what was going on. One day after some prodding on my behalf, he finally admitted that he wasn't sure what was happening, but that he was having trouble keeping his appetite up and his weight was starting to drop. Concerned but hopeful, I assumed his situation was manageable. Despite his lack of appearances, he was still the funny jovial self that he always was when I finally got him on the phone.

The days in between calls continued to decrease, and I assumed it was probably because of bad news on his health front. One day, he finally called me and this time, his tone was different. He wasn't laughing and joking but spoke in serious, measured tones, apologizing for not being around or telling me what was going on with him. After weeks of not feeling himself, he had gone to the doctor and they had discovered a small cancerous mass in his stomach. Though it didn't look like it was going to be a fatal situation, he explained that he was going to have surgery to remove it. He asked that I keep the news to myself around town and assured me that he was going to be fine. Hoping that it truly wasn't life threatening, I agreed to adhere to his wishes and focused solely on our work and not his condition. Sadly, it wasn't long before I realized that things were not as manageable as he'd hope they would be.

I met with Tom at Jerry's Famous Deli in Westwood and was shocked at the amount of weight he had lost. In a matter of a couple of months, he had clearly lost around forty pounds. He told me not to be alarmed and once again assured me that he was going to be fine, but truthfully, I was very concerned. He looked drawn and tired. At the end of our lunch, he stood up to leave and his pants fell down around his ankles in the middle of the restaurant. Tom, ever the conservative and utmost gentleman, was mortified. I helped him pull his pants up and we hugged it out in the parking lot. I could see in his eyes that he himself knew things would not end well for him. He had his surgery and rested for only a month, quickly wanting to get back to work.

"What did you do to propel your career forward today?" Tom Fox said to me over the phone line.

I was overjoyed at the sound of his voice. He sounded completely back to normal and I was hugely relived to be hearing from him. Tom excitedly explained that all of his cancer had been removed and he was on the mend. I sat on my kitchen counter eating out of a Nutri-System's ravioli pouch as we laughed and talked for three hours. He was indeed back to normal.

Tom was such an unstoppable, positive, and authentic force, and I was so grateful to be back in his company. He told me he was finally off of bed rest and was ready to go back to pitching the *Return* project like gangbusters. Thrilled that he was back and ready for action, I offered to do everything I could to help him. We decided to meet for lunch—at Chin Chin, of course—so we could make a plan.

It was around this time that Fox Family Channel was sold to Disney. I was so happy and grateful to be one of the few people who got grandfathered into ABC's cable network as part of the deal. The trouble was that the Fox Family special projects department that I had worked in for so many years no longer existed. For the last seven years, my main responsibilities had been producing commercials, pilots, music videos, and narrative content, and since that department no longer existed, I was sent to work in the ABC promo department.

Promos are the simple thirty-second-long shorts they play in between television shows to remind you when you can tune in upcoming productions. Producing these shorts is by far a very important and equally specific skill, but not in any way the job I was used to doing. I had never produced a promo in my life. Word got back to me that the promo department was just as shocked as I was that I was being moved there and less than thrilled that I was going to be joining the long-established team. While I still needed a job and was under contract, I had no interest in becoming a promo producer and my attitude clearly reflected it. What's worse, my contract had recently been extended for three years. When I asked to meet with Human Resources to see where else I could be placed, it was explained to me that I had my choice of working in the promo department or accepting nine cents on every dollar as a buyout of my contract. Figuring that I should stay there until I found something better and not lose thousands of dollars, I took the job and immediately regretted it.

The work was no longer challenging to me and my new immediate supervisor, a diminutive banty rooster of a man in a perpetual Lynyrd Skynyrd t-shirt, clearly loathed me for being dropped into a department that I obviously had no interest in. You can't blame them all for hating me as they all loved what they did and here came this guy who genuinely did not want to do the work.

Working there was hell for me. No one talked to me. My half-assed attempts at promo spots were met with dead silence upon viewing. I was never invited to lunch or included in conversations around the water tank and "chicken little" went as far as to call me into his office to tell me that my saying "hello" to people in the company halls in hopes of getting to know them was making everyone uncomfortable. My assignments were annoying bits of meaningless fluff that no one else wanted, spots like helping push the new, extremely short-lived Joy Behar talk show. Joy was a woman whose grating, humorless personality on the phone in no way mirrored the hilarious old Italian aunt that I had seen on *The View* for so many years. It seemed very clear to me that the plan was to make me feel as unneeded and unwelcome as possible until they were able to eventually stake me through the heart and get me to quit, which eventually happened. But, boy, I rode it out as long as I could. At the time, Billy Butler positively did not turn down high paying work.

After one particularly awful day in the promo-pit, I was notified that I was the only producer not being invited on the company trip to Promax, the Oscars of promos, if you will. I sat in my office, listening to the other producers excitedly making plans of the drunken activities they were all going to do while out of town, going quiet only as they hushed themselves and peeked into my office to see if I was overhearing them. I sat for a few moments with my head on the desk. I hated it there. I hated most of the people I worked with. They hated me more. Something had to change and I realized that I finally had enough.

I picked up the phone, took a breath, and called Human Resources to tell them that I would take the offer of nine cents on the dollar to pay off my contract. I packed my backpack, nabbed some of the primo office supplies in my desk, walked down the hall, and told the banty rooster that I was giving my notice. I remember seeing a look of disappointment on his face when I gave him the word that he would have to find a new dead mouse to bat around the office.

I left a Post-It on my computer. It read: *Billy Butler will NOT be back after these messages.*

It was around six in the evening. I was sitting in my car, weeping and stuffing my face in the Carl's Jr parking lot when my phone rang. It had been ringing all day, but since I was such a wreck, I hadn't been answering it. After it rang three times in a row, I finally picked it up.

"What?!" I yelled, taking a huge bite out of a six-dollar burger in a binge right out of my old ways of life. It was Stephanie Denton from Lakeshore.

"Where have you been? I've been looking for you all day," she said.

"I just quit my job. I'm on a huge burger-binge. I gotta call you back," I told her.

"No! Don't hang up! It's good you quit your job," she said.

"Why?" I asked, ready to throw the phone out the window.

"Are you ready for this? They greenlit *Madhouse* this morning!" As I choked on the huge bite I was about to swallow, she continued. "They want to talk to you about directing it."

I had quit my shitty job on the very day that I had got a movie greenlit. There is most certainly a God.

The next thing I knew, I was in meetings with the execs at Lakeshore. It was true: they liked what we had come up with and were willing to discuss me directing the project. I was invited to several meetings where they grilled me and I endured it all with a smile. Some seemed convinced I couldn't pull it off, while others, like Stephanie, were excited to give me a chance and encouraged me to suck it up and keep coming back.

The first thing I had to do was explain to them that you can indeed make a film for under a million dollars. Most of the naysayers sat there in disbelief as I showed them my past work, much of which was made on a shoestring budget.

"It is impossible to make a film for less than five-hundred thousand dollars," one executive said to me with a laugh. I didn't have the heart to tell them that many of the low budget films that were being made at that time were in fact for two-hundred thousand dollars and below.

After many meetings where I sported my patented expressionless "robot-face" while having my ass roasted over an open fire by the execs, I finally, kinda, sorta convinced most of them that I knew what I was doing and found myself approved to direct my first movie. And that was it. After years of hoping I would become a writer-director, I was indeed just that and never prouder or more pleased.

The next goal was to make the company that had hired me as happy as I was able so I could start building on the relationship. A lifelong dream had come true and I promised myself that I would show gratitude and do my absolute best to make everyone around me happy. I was so grateful for them to be taking a chance on me. Once again in my career, all I wanted to do was please them and make them money so they would let me keep doing what I loved so much. I am, by nature, a decent person who thrives when the room is filled with kindness and gratitude, and I was so honored to be working with such a cool company that I immediately wanted to hug them all.

I had only asked for five hundred thousand to do the project, but they generously and most surprisingly gave me a million. My plan was to take the cash overseas where the dollar was strong and create an epic horror film that we would all benefit from. I was so thankful to them all, especially to Stephanie who really helped make it happen. Lakeshore had given me a shot at just the right time in my life.

It wasn't long after that I noticed that my good nature was one that wasn't well received by some of the production team. "You cannot possibly be this nice." One of my film's producers said to me, and he was serious. I honestly didn't even know how to respond to him, feeling guilty that my graciousness was being perceived as false. One of the weird things about being positive and friendly at work is that it's sometimes mistaken as ass-kissing, mostly by people that are unable to be positive or happy themselves. Still, I slugged my way through with a smile as I honestly was so happy that I often felt like I could fly through the hallways. Making film is my entire life.

It was just a few weeks after my film was in production that Stephanie Denton was suddenly offered the job of a lifetime and left the company for another gig. I was going to be on my own there, but the Lakeshore group still moved forward with my film. It was a little nerve wracking, thinking of what production was going to be without my number one supporter in my corner, but I was so excited and felt so positive that I carried on, trying to make sure everyone was happy at the company. I guess I should have known that my million-dollar budget and lack of experience came with the even bigger price.

From the moment the ink was dry on my contract and Stephanie was gone, I was hit with a hundred rapid-fire questions about how I intended to execute my film. There were some who never seemed convinced that I could deliver, and I realized that I was going to be fighting an uphill battle. Still, hugely eager to please, I kept my cool and sense of humor as I answered their questions with as little snark as possible, which for a smart-ass like me, can be very difficult. I gave casting suggestions and talked them into shooting in Romania where the dollar was strong and the production values bigger, and to their credit, they listened.

My dear friend, director David DeCoteau, had pioneered shooting in Romania and recommended a beautiful hotel structure to double as the insane asylum where my story took place. The Hotel Lebeda was located just outside Bucharest. Once a palace many years ago, the massive building later became a tuberculosis hospital and had recently been turned into a luxury hotel. Word was, the place was struggling because many locals believed that the tuberculosis once rampant there in the building was still festering within the structure's walls. Never one to be intimidated by tuberculosis, I pushed hard with the Lakeshore staff and somehow convinced them. It was no surprise that we were able to buy the entire hotel out for two months at the mere price of twenty thousand dollars.

The Hotel Lebada sat alone on a rose garden covered island on the middle of a murky pond just outside of Bucharest. It was the absolute perfect setting for a ghost story. Every night, along the shore on the other side of the water, several gypsy camps became illuminated by campfires. Some nights after we wrapped, we sat on the hotel's steps and listened to them play music and dance around their campfires. I remember how disappointed I was when I looked into a pair of binoculars and saw that gypsies did not, in fact, wear garish colors, kerchiefs on their heads, and big hoop earrings.

Wild and sometimes dangerous dogs ran freely over the property and in big numbers, an effect of "systemization," a communist regime-enforced law that forced many people to give up their homes and live in apartments. Many were forced to simply let their dogs run away. We were warned right away not to approach the dogs as most of them were quick to bite.

Making movies is so weird. Sometimes you pitch them for five years before you get them made, while other projects get a greenlight two weeks after you think of the idea while driving to the meeting in your car. We quickly moved into casting *Madhouse*, and because of Lakeshore's sterling reputation for quality movies, every cool young actor in town came in to meet with me. I met with everyone from Lake Bell to Laura Prepon for the female lead, both of whom were complete rock stars and nice ladies. I eventually chose the beautiful and talented Jordan Ladd, who was getting a lot of heat from her appearance in Eli Roth's *Cabin Fever*.

The male actors who came in to read varied from TV stars to then still unknown upcoming movie stars like Paul Dano, an actor who later appeared in the Oscar winning movie *Little Miss Sunshine* and portrayed *The Riddler* in *The Batman* starring Robert Pattinson. I ultimately cast the terrific actor Joshua Leonard, who was still huge off of his appearance in the highly popular *Blair Witch Project*. Other performers who ended up in the film were my good friend and cohort in crime, Leslie Jordan, as well as Patrika Darbo, Denrie Taylor from *The Fighter*, and Natasha Lyonne, a hugely-talented, but (back then, anyway) bucking bronco of an actress that I cast despite the multiple warnings that she was not in any state or mood to be working.

Natasha Lyonne has since completely turned her life around in a hugely positive way and become a show business powerhouse. She is a woman of tremendous talent and I was so saddened when I heard she was hospitalized with an infection in her heart. I always made sure to let her know that I was rooting for her, no matter what her circumstance was. After all, she didn't invent bad behavior like that; I did. Natasha and I got along well in our meeting in L.A. and I had no doubt she would help elevate my material. It's no wonder that she is a star, as you could sit and talk to her for hours; her interest in film and the latest good book made me truly fall in love with her. I asked for the team to book her and we moved forward to paper her deal.

By far, the best casting get of the film was the casting of legendary actor Lance Henricksen in the role of the Hospital Administrator. Amazingly, one of the producers was friends with Lance and talked him into reading my script and considering taking a shot with a first-time director. I will be forever grateful for both of them taking a gamble on me. I was so nervous at the idea of meeting Lance; to me, the guy was a legend. I had been a huge fan of his ever since he appeared in *Close Encounters of the Third Kind* way back when. Lance was not only the most professional person I ever have worked with, he was also the only actor in my history of directing who gave me a present upon his arrival on set. My film was set in a mental institute and Lance gave me a beautifully bound book on mental studies.

For the most part, Lakeshore agreed with all of my minor role casting choices and I was so happy to be allowed to include everyone that I loved. Even my mother and new stepfather Roy Nakamura planned to travel to Romania to see the production being shot. It was as if we were all heading out on a big working vacation. A vacation on the Romanian countryside. It was an amazing time.

Joining the cast at the last minute was my writing partner Aaron, who asked if he could try his hand at acting in the film. He wanted to play the role of Carl, a gentle patient who is convinced that he is in fact sane and doesn't belong in a mental hospital. I had originally booked my dear friend, actor Todd Stites, to play the part, but after learning Aaron's yearning to break into the acting craft and how hard he had worked to help me get everything going, I thoughtlessly bumped Todd out and over to the part of an insane transsexual who lives in the basement of the hospital. Saying it was a difficult conversation is an understatement as I gave him the news that I was switching him from a well-written patient role to one that dressed him in ladies' panties, a bra, and a garter belt. In hindsight, I should have spent a little more time on making that decision.

Even better was when I got to cast my longtime friend Muffy Bolding as Polly, the hospital wet nurse. The part of Polly was small, but she really made the most of it. I loved having Muffy on set so much. Giving people their SAG cards is one of a producer-director's great joys in life. To think, when I first met her, still living at home as kids living in Fresno and there we were in friggin' Romania. I put her in as many scenes as possible, even had her walking through the background of shots she wasn't in so she would for one, pick up another day of pay, and two, I had her good vibes, tremendously funny company, and support.

Muffy and I had the production assistants running in a constant wild goose chase as they fetched us non-stop platters of candy bars and caprese salads. I put Muffy in so many scenes in the background that we later noticed that her character sometimes broke the space-time continuum by appearing in the cafeteria in one scene and seconds later, be walking through a hallway on the completely other side of the building. I figured that if I was ever asked about her character's ability to leap from room to room and in time, I could simply tell them that she was actually a set of triplets. True film artistry at its finest.

Me and one of the most hilarious, creative people I ever met. I wish her every happiness.

Romania is a very beautiful and unique country. Nowhere else in the world can you get into a traffic jam in your car side by side with a horse and carriage or visit grocery stores that have four full isles of pork products. There are also hundreds of potholes in most of the city's poorly paved streets. You never realize how much body fat you truly have until you ride in the back of a Romanian taxicab as every excess bit of flab violently jiggles in every direction as the driver tries to navigate the wear and tear on the road.

Vulich and his team joined us to provide all of the special make-up effects as pre-production quickly progressed. It was hard to believe that after growing up dreaming about working together on movies, Muffy, John, and I had finally done it. Working with John was amazing and giving Muffy her break into film acting was one of my greatest pleasures. I couldn't wait to see what came up for her next as she continued to flourish on her own.

Muffy, Johnny and I right where we thought we would be.

Romania was beautiful, a very old country that was making huge strides from some pretty archaic laws and customs, including the recent decriminalization of homosexuality in the year 2000. Despite positive changes, the country was still very conservative in many ways, and I warned Leslie Jordan to keep to himself when it came to be partaking in temporary male companions. I warned him time and time again that many of the rough trade males that hang out in bars in Romania had horrible reputations for drugging and robbing people, and he should by all means steer clear of any of them. Vulich, however, wasted no time making new "friends" as the hotel arranged for a line-up of eight beautiful working-women, all of whom wanted to meet a couple of Hollywood make-up artists and come to the hotel for a night of fun and makeover glamor. Not that the girls needed a lot of help: Romanian women are beautiful. A line-up showed up in the lobby, and the boys selected two out of the eight. They then took them into the make-up room, did full makeovers on them, then partied well into the night.

I will never forget Leslie Jordan going to the concierge in frustration.

"It's not fair that you keep getting Johnny and Mike girls," he said. "When are you gonna find me a boy?!" he moaned in mock complaint. The concierge laughed and told Leslie that he would try to find him one.

A couple of days later, the concierge flagged Leslie down as he passed through the lobby. "Mr. Jordan, I found you a boy, but I am very sorry to say, a date will be very expensive."

"What's expensive?" Leslie said.

"Three hundred dollars, sir."

"Three hundred dollars?!" Leslie yelled. "The make-up team have been paying twenty-eight dollars for those broads that have been coming through here!" he ranted.

"Yes, I understand, but this boy has never done anything like this before," he said, holding his hand at waist level. "He is, after all very young."

It was at the moment that Leslie realized that the concierge had mistaken what he meant by asking for a "boy." He thought that Leslie meant a child. "Are you crazy?! I don't want a little kid! What on earth is wrong with you?!" Leslie gasped. "I meant a fully-grown man!"

I remember sitting in the hotel bar when Leslie walked in white as a ghost. "Oh, my God: they thought I wanted a child!" he said, mortified. As shocking as it was, it was also my biggest laugh of the week.

You would think that would have been the end of Leslie's search. But it wasn't. The industrious Leslie Jordan did eventually find himself a fully-grown man: a quite handsome one, in fact. One night, during our first week, we all headed to town to a secret underground club in Bucharest. As usual, Les managed to somehow quickly sniff a guy out. He was a big, blonde Romanesque dude who was dressed very nicely and had zeroed in on Leslie from the moment he set foot inside. The next thing I knew, the guy was climbing into the van on the way back to the hotel with us.

I pulled Leslie aside as we disembarked in front of the hotel. "What are you thinking?!" I whispered in anger. "Don't you remember what you were told about these guys?"

He glared at me. "You're not my mama, Billy Butler!" he said. "You just worry about yourself!"

I warned him that he was on his own if anything bad happened, but he shot me a look and motioned for the handsome kid to follow him inside. Leave it to Leslie Jordan to find rough trade in Romania.

The next morning, Leslie was called to the front desk where they quietly warned him that he was keeping the company of a gypsy, but Leslie, always willing to give someone a chance, told them that he was safe and assured them that the guy was a decent person. As decent as a Romanian gypsy you meet in an underground bar can be, anyway.

Later that afternoon, I was high up on a camera crane as we prepared for a big shot that virtually everyone in the cast was in. There were twenty people standing on various levels of a huge staircase that led up to the building. I was ready to call action as I noticed one of the actors was missing: Leslie Jordan.

"Where is Leslie?!" I called down to the assistant director, just as Leslie came exploding out of the hotel doors, dramatically falling to his knees like Scarlett O'Hara.

"That gypsy stole my pocket-book!" he called out in a whirl of loud drama. Furious, I asked the grip to lower the crane to the ground. I marched over as everyone gathered around him. "He took my passport, my credit cards, he even stole my brand-new tennis shoes!" he sniveled.

Everyone, spotting my glare, stepped back as I moved in close. "You listen to me, itty-bitty," I said. "I worked really hard to get here and you are not going to fuck this up for me. Do you understand?"

Leslie glared back. "Back off, bitch, or I'll take you down, just like I did that night at La Poubelle." He was, of course, referring to the drunken fistfight that he and I had gotten into many years before and in the middle of a high-end French restaurant, no less. As I recall, we both may or may not been having dinner with someone with whom each of us were under the impression we were on a date. When each of us realized that the other had big plans for our guest at the end of the night, we broke into a furious fisticuff and ended up getting thrown out onto the street by the management. Of course, he remembers the battle ending differently than I do, though I can assure you: I curb bounced that little imp's face into his crepe suzette.

La Poubelle - Los Angeles, CA

"I warned you about those gypsy hustlers, now get on your mark and do the scene, please!"

"Glass houses, Billy Butler!" he yelled as he took his place. I started to go back to the camera crane as he called out to me a little more sweetly. "Billy?"

I turned towards him, ready to murder. "Yes?"

"Why am I saying all of this?" he asked.

"What?" I replied incredulously.

"I'm asking you, why I am saying what I am saying in this scene," he explained begrudgingly.

My face turned red. "They think you're the murderer, Leslie. Didn't you read the script?" I snapped.

"I just tore *my* pages out." He said this with such a lack of shame that I started laughing. "Face it: I'm a walking sight-gag! I don't need to know what the rest of the story is!" he snapped. "I'm preoccupied! In case you've forgotten, my room has just been ransacked by a gypsy!"

With that, I turned and walked back over to the crane. Of course, when the cameras finally rolled and I called action, Leslie knocked it out of the friggin' ballpark as usual. Maybe reading the entire script *is* overrated. Everyone has their process.

And for the record, that gypsy hustler eventually showed back up at the hotel, apologizing profusely to Les and returning all of his things.

The shoot progressed and I grew to love the Romanian people. They were all so welcoming. It was also very clear that their level of artistic skill was off the charts in all departments. Still, it was a very poor country and many of the local crew members were not used to the amenities that Americans had grown to expect on a movie set. I remember Muffy Bolding bursting into tears as one of our poor production assistants said that our set lunches were the first time he'd ever been served bread rolls and butter at a meal.

The film crew was marvelous, and things were going really well. Sort of. Everything was going just as we had planned; that is, until my friend, make-up artist Jerrie Werkman, told me that trying to get Natasha Lyonne made up was turning out to be more difficult than anticipated. "I'm not making her up," she said, laughing.

"Why?" I asked.

"For one, she can barely hold her head up and she keeps slapping my hand away every time I try to put the sponge to her face."

"Nah, she's cool, she'll let you do it," I said. Surely, she didn't plan on coming to set with no make-up on.

"Even if she did allow me to make her up, she is sweating so profusely that the make-up won't stick to her face," she said, shaking her head.

"Sweating profusely? It's fifteen degrees outside," I said. "Why is she sweating so bad?"

"Don't know, don't care. She's on her own." Jerrie went back to her room to make up the others.

I went to Natasha's room to talk to her, but she wasn't there. In fact, no one could find her anywhere. A couple of hours passed and the search went on. I scrambled to move the shooting schedule around while the crew tried to find her, eventually locating her in her friend's hotel room. They finally talked her into coming to set as I quickly tried to do her scene and get caught up. I was so disappointed. I had admired her for so long and she was completely distracted and uninterested in what I was trying to do.

I could see that Jerrie was right: Natasha walked into the freezing room soaking wet, smoking a cigarette and texting on her cellphone and without a bit of make-up on. As a person with past substance abuse issues myself, I could see that something was probably going on. I asked to speak to her in my room and she agreed. We went and sat on my bed and I told her that I could see she wasn't feeling well and that I had been in the same state many times in my life. Many, many times. I told her that I wasn't judging her and that I honestly did not care what she was doing in her downtime but that I would go down in flames if I didn't get all of her stuff shot correctly.

She was very nice and said she would pull it together, which wasn't the reaction I expected but certainly appreciated. I think that perhaps she realized that she was with one of her own in regard to self-medicating. From that moment on, she was really cool to me and completely professional. She turned out to be a really nice and down to earth girl who I grew to genuinely like.

Sadly, as many know, her health situation got a lot worse before it got better, but eventually, she pulled herself together in a miraculous turn-around that has made her a more successful actress than ever. Still to this day, she is one of my favorite people to run into and one of the coolest actresses I have ever had the good fortune of working with. I am completely inspired by her sobriety. There has not been one time when I text her out of the blue that she doesn't write me back, no matter how much time we have spent apart. I am so proud of the woman that she is and am glad I got to know and work with her.

Natasha Lyonne and I getting to know each other

I got a call from Lakeshore back in the U.S. "I don't want to put the cart before the horse, but these dailies are incredible," my executive said. "This could be the start of a long-running franchise."

I was so happy that they were pleased. It was such a huge relief, especially since when I first met with them, none of them believed that a movie could even be made for a million dollars. My movie was the smallest budget that they had ever approved. I was used to having to try and finish a project in two weeks, so the idea of having an entire month with top shelf actors was incredible and made a world of difference. I was finally able to shine.

The praise continued and before I had even finished shooting, the company sent me another horror screenplay and said they would like to talk to me about doing a three-picture deal. I felt like I had truly arrived and broken my way into the system. Another week passed and I finished principal photography. I said goodbye to the crew that I had grown to love and a country that I had a newfound understanding and respect for.

Quite possibly the most insane set photo I have ever seen.
This was the night of the launch party in Romania.

Leslie Jordan, Patrika Darbo, Jerrie Werkman, Aaron Strongoni,
Muffy Bolding and myself after a very long day of shooting.

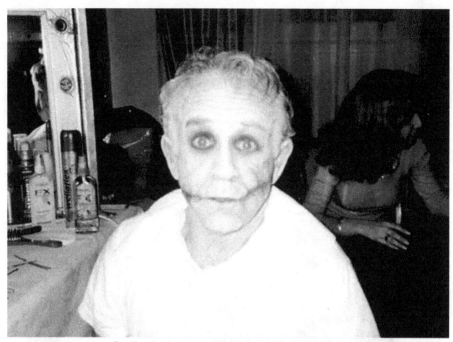

Leslie playing one of the ghosts in the hospital

Taking a break with the little boy who played the hospital ghost

Madhouse - On set with the beautiful Jordan Ladd

My writing partner Aaron Strongoni playing a ghost in one of the flashbacks

Good Times in Romania

After a quick vacation in Paris with John Vulich, I headed back home as the editing on *Madhouse* began. I was sitting in the edit bay, showing Tom Fox the rough cut of the film when his phone rang and he answered, lighting up in joy as he hung up and said he had great news. There was a producer in L.A. that was interested in buying both *Return* screenplays and filming them back to back.

This was the absolute best-case scenario. Not only were we in post-production on a film that really seemed to be really coming together, days later we got a terrific money offer for both zombie scripts. The trouble was, we now had to return the *Necropolis* script, which had been turned into a mutant movie, back into a zombie film. We were told to hold off from starting the polish until a deal was completely done and that the new producer wanted us to work with their "development" people to expand on our original idea.

We should have seen it coming, but we were so thrilled at how well things were going that we agreed to meet with whoever they wanted us to. In a matter of weeks, we were about to close the deal on the scripts and were signed at ICM talent agency as a result of our newfound thunder. It seemed that we were well on our way to having lucrative careers.

Just when I didn't think things could get any better, Tom Fox called me and asked me to have lunch with him at the Formosa Café, which was right outside the gates to the studio where I was editing my film. He told me that he loved what I had done with *Madhouse* and was wondering what I would think about being attached as director of both of the *Return* films. I couldn't believe my ears. I told him of course I would do it and that I would work my absolute hardest at delivering films that both he and the fans would love. We sealed the deal with a handshake and he said he would commit it to paper.

Tom had a conversation with Hung, our manager, and told him to make the call to our new executive producer to feel him out on the subject of me coming aboard as director. We sent several clips from *Madhouse* along with a bunch of scenes I had directed for Fox Family Channel over to the execs along with my bio and resume. While we waited for a reply from the new exec, I introduced John Vulich to Tom in the hopes that John could get the make-up effects job on both projects.

At first, Tom wasn't sure about John's matter-of-fact, sometimes curt in-your-face style. I pleaded with him to give John a second chance by taking a tour of his shop and when he did, he saw the light. John's past work was brilliant. Vulich was also a great businessman who excelled in executing zombie make-ups and Tom decided he wanted him on the project. I guess all that study of rotting chicken skin as a kid had really paid off. John and his team were cleared through the new exec's team and he was officially brought on board. I was so happy to have connected him. After John had so graciously introduced me to Savini, I was thrilled at the opportunity to pay it forward.

"The *Return* e.p. doesn't want you," Hung said to me in his usual unimpressed tone.

"But Tom said that I was attached," I said as my stomach dropped.

"He doesn't want you," he said again.

"Then I'm not selling the scripts to them. Forget it," I said, bristling.

"Listen to me, Billy. If I tell them you will not sell them the scripts unless you direct the movies, this deal is going to go away. He does not want you to direct the movies," he knowingly said. "This is a huge amount of money to be turning down just because you won't be able to say that you directed a *Return of the Living Dead* sequel. No one is going to even watch these movies. My advice to you is to take the cash and move on."

I could tell he was serious and he certainly knew better than me. Plus, what the hell was I going to do? Turn down hundreds of thousands of dollars because the new producer didn't pick me to do double duty? I also had my writing partner to consider. Furthermore, I had no proven track record yet to argue; I was not special. Fearful that the deal would indeed go away, I swallowed my pride and took the money, but man, what a stash. We accepted the offer and Aaron and I were both paid a large sum of cash for both screenplays.

I went back to focusing all of my energy on finishing *Madhouse* and started having meetings at Lakeshore on the new film they wanted me to do. The next project was a horror film about the ghost of a murderous old librarian who starts killing the teens in a small town. It was a female Freddy Krueger story of sorts and I was really excited about it. I knew it was going to be a big franchise and my greatest work yet. At the same time, Aaron and I started going out on a lot of introductory meetings and things continued to heat up. It was the greatest time. We both could feel terrific things unfolding.

The day finally came when I locked picture on *Madhouse* and everyone seemed pleased and ready to begin the post-production process. A couple of days later, I was called into one of the top executive's offices at Lakeshore. He told me I was doing a great job on both projects and wondered how sick my mind must be to think up such horrific imagery. I took that as a compliment. He went on to say how everyone had really enjoyed working with me thus far. After I was appropriately buttered up, he finally got down to business, telling me that the reason he was calling me in was because he wanted to talk to me about the musical score for my film.

When I originally pitched the movie, I had presented my composer friend Kenny Meriedeth to do the music and they had approved him, but the company suddenly had a different plan of attack. The exec unconvincingly explained to me that a friend of one of the executive producers had a son who was a terrific music composer and they wanted me to consider using him instead Kenny.

I hated the idea. I had already promised my friend the job, and after they had given the thumbs up, we had been letting him watch parts of the movie so he could start composing. I politely told him I would listen to the kid's samples, but that I was pretty set on my own guy, a response that was met with a cold stare. This was way back when I was constantly worried what my employers thought of me, so despite being really pissed at their random request, I agreed to at least listen.

"Who knows, maybe he's better than Kenny," Vulich told me that night at his place. "Don't listen to his work with your ego. Listen for what's best for the movie." Once again, he was right, but later that night, I put the guy's CD in my player and I could not believe my ears. The music was laughably awful: poorly composed and not scary in the least. I thought for sure that there was no way anyone in that office had listened to his work before they gave it to me. It was as if someone had created the cuts playing a Casio keyboard while sitting on the toilet. (I know this because I grew up listening to John Vulich playing a cheap Casio keyboard while sitting on the toilet.) There was none of the tone or dark moodiness I was trying to convey in my film and I adamantly resisted the company even considering the guy.

For some reason, they kept pushing. I stood firm for as long as I could, pointing out that his level of skill was in no way up to my own standards and certainly was nothing compared to what they themselves typically presented in their own movies. The kid's music was bad. Very, very bad. However, they kept pressuring me to just give in and hire him.

For a solid week, they asked me over and over again to use the new guy, growing agitated when I didn't buckle. They even contacted Todd Stites, who was running post-production on the film, and asked for him to nudge me into approving the guy, which only made me resist even more. I secretly knew they could do whatever they wanted and most certainly would, so I decided to refuse to participate in the bizarre tug-a-war that was unfolding and just flat out ignored them on the subject.

My response was clearly not what they were expecting as up until then, I had pretty much gone along with everything they'd asked of me in the hope of becoming someone they liked. I was nice to everyone and operated in a constant state of gratitude and good energy. Big mistake. Moments after I finally passed on hiring the music guy for the very last time, telling my execs to please to stop asking, I instantly went from being the director that everyone in the company liked to being treated like I was a selfish, difficult prick.

Directing movies is so goddamned weird. You get hired and think that your employers are going to love you because you're working hard to create something that hopefully makes them a lot of money when in fact, they spend the majority of the time telling you how you're doing things wrong. Up until then, I had taken their notes and direction with a smile on my face because I was happy to have had the opportunity. Finally, the day came when I walked into the edit bay and saw a stranger sitting on the couch, watching my movie.

"Who is this?" I rudely said in front of him.

"This is your music supervisor," Todd Stites said to me as he took cover behind his desk.

The brass had just gone and hired the guy anyway. I had been overruled and no one even bothered to tell me. I excused myself and made the call to my friend Kenny that the company had given him the sack without me knowing. It looked like all the times that he worked for me for free in the hope of one day booking one of my real paying gigs didn't quite have the pay-off we had both hoped for after all. That is indeed showbiz.

It was official: the new music guy was in and my guy was out. My standing my ground had not gone over well as I also started to notice that, little by little, I was being left out of the loop on much of the post-production communication.

"You fucked up," Vulich said to me as I lay on his office couch in a mock therapy session.

"How?" I asked, ready to scream.

"You were too nice from the start," he said.

"But I am nice. And I'm grateful to be doing a job I love," I said incredulously.

"People who work at your level don't need to be nice. You're making them money. If you're too nice, they look at it as fear. They think you're being nice because you have to be. Talented people, or people who think they are talented anyway, don't kiss ass ever."

"I *do not* kiss ass," I said, completely offended.

"Maybe not, but you were too nice and they looked at it as fear," he said, all-knowing as usual. I wanted to tell him to fuck off, but as I looked over at him I saw he was sitting next to three Emmy awards. "I got these and I haven't been nice once in my twenty-year career," he said.

I really hoped he was wrong. It wouldn't be until later that I realized that he was one-hundred percent right. Regardless of whether I agreed with him or not, I followed his direction. I stopped being overly nice to everyone in the office and started showing up to the edit bay unannounced to see what was going on when I wasn't there. I started questioning every unauthorized decision that was being made on my movie without me. It was an unexpected action that was met with stunned reaction by everyone in the office.

They were so used to me skipping through the place with a big smile on my face and a "we can do anything" attitude, and my quick shift in attitude only made matters worse.

Not long after that, a little bird whispered in my ear that people in the office were starting to screen my film by themselves and give the editor notes. Having worked on the front lines of corporate television, I expected there were going to be comments and changes, but what I didn't think would happen was that everyone in the office would be privately watching the movie and making changes without talking to me about it. Despite getting good feedback and being hired to do another project with them, I was told to not come in some days, while everyone from the Head of Production to the development girl locked the editing room door and took a turn making changes on my movie. Suddenly, everyone was contributing but doing it in a covert way and I suppose it was mostly because of my sudden shift in attitude. Later, I realized that this was just another day at the office in the world of film production, particularly on low budget films, but without knowing this, I couldn't help but to feel slighted. Maybe they were right: maybe my being overly kind was to mask that I was secretly an artistic prima donna. When I no longer let people walk all over me, I was suddenly branded an uncooperative asshole.

This was the very first of many very important lessons that I learned while working in film and television production. If you're a young filmmaker and want to gain anything from reading this book, let it be this: people in Hollywood film production indeed look at overt kindness as a weakness. Do not ever forget that. Keep to yourself from day one. Do not let them get into your head. Do not let them get to know you. Do not friend them on social media. If you always play nice and don't stand your ground on points that you are truly passionate about from day one, they will override you without even asking. Never forget that everyone in show business is also making it up as they go along, just like you are. No one truly knows any better than the next person when it comes to creative choices. It's all a matter of taste. Okay, so maybe you have really bad taste, but it worked for John Waters, didn't it? He stuck to his guns and it ultimately paid off.

You cannot worry if there are a few people in the office that hate you because you hold tight on decisions that are different than theirs. Never be afraid to tell someone you disagree with them as long as you do it politely and with respect. Choose your battles wisely and remember there will always be a certain an amount of give and take when it comes to corporate storytelling, but make sure your voice is at least heard and fully understood before you give in and go their way. Always be polite, explain your position, and make damn sure that you remember this: if someone else's bad idea is forced upon you and it fails, they will be the first person to blame *you*.

This is why for years after this occurrence; I always utilized what I call my "secret-weapon" when it comes to pushy movie creatives who get out of line. It's one thing if you are working on a commercial with a twenty-person protocol and you are all collectively working at a common goal, but if you've been hired to tell a story in a film it's because you know what you're doing. Tell the story you would want to hear or die trying. When someone from above is aggressively forcing an idea on me that I know in my heart is a bad one, I quietly give in, but always make sure I say—and in front of other people— *Okay, no problem, we'll do it your way, but we're gonna make that one your idea.* It cracks faces every time and make no mistake, they will hate you for doing this as no one in show business likes being held accountable for choices that are eventually considered bad ones. Bad choices, particularly ones that lead to financial loss, often lead to being dismissed in the world of entertainment, but playing this card most certainly takes you out of the line of fire when a clunker causes the shit to hit the fan. And boy, have I seen shit fly in my day. Back then, when I was creating *Madhouse*, I sadly wasn't there yet.

Worried that I was rubbing them the wrong way too aggressively and uncomfortable with the immediate shift of their treatment of me, I backpedaled and played nice. I started interacting with the music guy that they hired, and that's when things got even more complicated, because, of course, he turned out to be as tremendously kind and accommodating as he was missing the mark creatively. He was a good composer, just not a horror film composer. The least he could have done was be a prick so that it would be easier for me to hate his work as much as I did. But alas, despite his musical shortcomings, I grew to love the guy. He was really nice and very eager to please, so I vowed to try and make it work. I did everything I could to help nudge the music cues more to my liking, including flat-out handing him movie soundtrack albums from other movies and simply saying "just do this." But every time I showed up at his bedroom studio, he smiled, sat back in his chair and played cuts of music that were not elevating the project.

To make matters even more awkward, his lovely mother had flown in from Italy and sat in on most of our sessions. She was a beautiful and well-dressed Italian lady who'd serve Todd Stites and I appetizers then sit down directly across from us, waiting for a positive reaction to her son's latest work. I guess it should come as no surprise that it was right around this time that my food binges returned. I nervously pasted on a smile and stuff my face with antipasto, cheese, and crackers and on the chocolates she brought in from the Italian airport as she eagerly looked at me for acknowledgement. I never had it in me to tell him his work was anything but terrific. I practiced gratitude as best I could and tried to be the company bitch to keep the peace.

"It's very good, yes?" his mother asked me with a prideful grin on her face.

I nodded, holding up the Waverly cracker and slice of buffalo mozzarella that she had offered me. "Yes, it is! It's really hard to find fresh real Italian mozzarella in the states," I said as I swallowed, instantly reaching for another.

"She's talking about his music," Todd replied with a deadpan gaze.

I smiled and nodded to her, then ripped open a box of Toblerone she had handed me and emptied it into my mouth. "Uh-uh, just terrific," I lied. I was so frustrated. Up until then, every part of my movie had been micro-managed and now suddenly everyone at the company was looking in the other direction as the musical aspect of the project was being phoned in and from the foot of someone's foldout bed, no less.

I emailed some of the music cuts to one of my execs and got him on the phone.

"Are you going to tell me that you think this is good?" I calmly asked as he played a cut that sounded like it belonged in an old video game.

"It's terrific, what are you talking about?" he raved unconvincingly.

I was starting to feel like I was a character in that old movie *Invasion of the Body Snatchers*. Everyone seemed to be covertly conspiring against me, trying to gaslight me into believing that the music I was hearing was good.

After I realized that the musical situation simply wasn't going to get any better, I came up with the diabolical plan to have the sound effects designer lay down wall to wall scary ambient noises throughout the entire film. I can still remember sitting in the film's final sound mix after I told the mixer to just turn the music all the way down and crank up the sound effects.

"Billy, I can't hear my music," the composer said to me as we sat in the darkened mix stage.

"No, it's in there! It sounds great!" I said to him, which garnered hushed snickers from the other staff in the recording studio. What was good for the goose was most certainly good for the gander, I thought. *Now, who's gaslighting who?* I thought to myself. "Beautiful work, this music is really terrifying." I added, feigning a terrified shiver that wasn't really coming over my body.

After two full days of mixing and a lot of back and forth on whether or not the film's soundtrack was in any way audible, the movie was mixed and completely finished. The movie wasn't perfect, but it worked. I was so happy that my team and I had somehow pulled it off. Even better was the day when I got the news that Lion's Gate had bought the picture and that it was already in profit. *Madhouse* was to be released theatrically in the spring, Despite the harrowing post-production process, I was never prouder.

The day finally came when it was time for the final approval of the film with the in-house staff. Everyone gathered in a screening room at a studio called The Lot in Hollywood. This would be the first time that one of the high-level executives would see my finished movie and I was nervous as I could be. The main producer was a well-off guy with a very commanding presence and a cut-to-the-chase attitude that always kept any dialogue with him very short. Appearing to not know what you were talking about or not having a quick, direct answer was an invitation for a potential tongue lashing, so I tried to stay on my toes and was very inspired by him. I wanted nothing more than to make this person happy.

My writing partner Aaron sat beside me as the producer shook our hands and sat beside us. The movie started playing and he immediately began reacting to some of the horrific imagery I had put in the film. Flashes of preschoolers having brain surgery conducted on them while they're still awake, snakes swimming around inside a man's head, and an insane transsexual (thanks to Todd Stites) licking a pane of glass flashed in bright bursts of light. You know, the usual family fare.

"You have a very sick mind," he said.

"Thank you," I gushed. I looked around the room as everyone smiled at me, acknowledging the good feedback.

"Where the hell do you get all of this from?" he continued, grossed out. I was feeling so good, positive he was really liking the movie. At that moment, I truly believed

I had finally arrived. My decision to turn my back on acting and become a director was the right one. This guy was clearly eating this shit up.

And then, the end of the movie came and everything took an unpleasant turn.

In my story, a young man goes to investigate the outdated procedures of a dilapidated old mental hospital where the patients that cannot be cured seem to be dying or disappearing. While you are watching the movie—and here's your spoiler alert, so turn the page if you don't want to know what happens—you start to figure out that either the place is haunted by a murderous ghost or there is a maniac killer on the loose. Ultraviolent scenes begin to unfold as patients and staff are killed off. The viewers are led through a trail of clues where it's revealed that no one is who they seem to be and characters who are likely guilty are revealed to be innocent or eventually murdered. All of this leads up to a surprise twist at the very end of the film where the investigator eventually realizes that he himself is the killer, a mental patient who escaped the place as a child and is now back to murder everyone who did him wrong. Yes, it's been done a lot since then, but not back when I did it. This was ten years before the horror film *Shutter Island*, mind you, which is virtually the same movie, only with a fifty-million-dollar budget. It's pure coincidence: I wouldn't dare suggest that Martin Scorsese ever needed to borrow material from Billy Butler, just that the two movies are pretty damn close to one another. The only difference between a million-dollar movie and a fifty-million-dollar movie is on the bigger budgeted film you get more time, bigger stars, and a better grade of guacamole at the snack table. Other than that, there isn't a whole lot of difference.

The movie unspooled and the executive seemed to be eating it up as he sat through the entire film, looking like he was loving every minute of it. "Good job," he whispered to me. I looked over at Aaron and smiled. It seemed it was really the best-case scenario.

After all of the production battles and hard work, after all of the debates and creative differences, coping with the music missing the mark, being locked out of my own edit bay and being told that my kindness was disingenuous, none of it mattered, because the boss was clearly loving what he was seeing. But just as the final moments of the film unwound and the big reveal was about to happen, the producer slowly began to sit up in his chair. I looked over at him, anticipating another positive reaction as the twist was slowly revealed.

Up on the screen, the camera began to push into Joshua Leonard's face as his character begins to realize he himself is insane and is the killer.

"What?" The producer said, looking over at me as his expression changed from elation to anger. The picture dissolved as Josh's character is suddenly locked up in the very cell of a patient who'd helped him solve the mystery. Himself. He'd been talking to himself the entire time. "No!" the producer snapped as he furiously looked over at me. "That's not how this movie ends!" he said in sudden anger.

Everyone in the room went silent; suddenly, all of the big smiles and thumbs-up gestures I was getting when they thought he liked the movie came to an abrupt halt as everyone began to look at me as if I had farted.

"That's a great ending. It has irony," I said.

He looked at me like I was out of my mind. "If you honestly believe that's how you end a movie, you should get out of the fucking business!"

Remember how I told you earlier that I learned many valuable lessons along my journey in tinsel town? I was about to learn the biggest lesson of them all, the biggest mistake I ever made in my entire career.

"What?!" I yelled back at him as jaws dropped. "This ending has been in the script the entire time! It doesn't say MAYBE he ends up locked up in an asylum, it says he ends up in a mother-fucking asylum!" I barked. "Don't you read the scripts before you write million-dollar checks to have them produced into films?"

The producer's face cracked.

"I have done every single thing that you asked me to do on this movie. I kept every promise I made to you. I stayed on budget, I got good performances, I asked for nothing but to be left alone to get this done right, and I delivered every bit of what I promised you. I included that awful music on my project for God only knows what nefarious reason, not to mention the fact that I never said a peep as the entire fucking staff made changes on my movie while I was locked out of the edit bay."

The producer just looked at me and smirked. "You outta pack your bags and move back to Fresno," he said, reading me to filth.

And with that, my friends, I pushed the granddaddy of all buttons on the heated conversation. "And YOU can shove this fucking movie up your ass!" I stormed out of the screening room, angrier than I have ever been. You could hear a pin drop.

Moments later, I barreled through the backlot at Paramount towards our car with my writing partner Aaron hanging his head as he brought up the rear. "I would never direct another fucking movie for these people if they offered me a million dollars!" I fumed. "Not for a million dollars!"

"Uh…I don't think you have that problem anymore," Aaron said.

I stopped and looked at him, taking a breath as I started to realize that I had perhaps just made a huge misstep. Like diving head first into a vat of career solvent misstep.

My phone rang as I climbed into my car. Before we had even pulled out of the parking lot, I had lost my upcoming movie deal with the company and any others that were being discussed, and to make matters worse, they were going to make me direct new scenes that they were going to come up with to "fix" the ending of the movie. My exploding had destroyed my future at Lakeshore Entertainment.

And that, my friends, is how you implode the momentum of a successful and blossoming new career in film. In one short afternoon, I had gone from a completely booked movie director with an awesome future to an unemployed scourge of the Paramount lot.

For the week that I conducted my reshoots, most of the people that worked at the company barely spoke to me. The head production guy questioned and overrode my every move including overriding my direction in front of the crew. The A.D. they hired to run the show was obviously told to ignore my input and to not take any lip off of me as he rolled his eyes at any direction or request I made. They made me reshoot a perfectly good love scene that took place in the middle of the busy asylum's main living room, telling me to try and talk Jordan Ladd into getting naked in it to make it sexier. Horribly written flirtatious dialogue straight out of the Playboy channel was given to me as the veins in my head protruded from the stress of it all. It was completely laughable that they would believe two medical professionals would fuck in the middle of a heavily populated insane asylum's main common area, but I shot it.

The ending of the film was changed so that Joshua Leonard's character was somehow still alive and walking away from the asylum after having a huge rusty axe sever most of his major neck arteries in the previous scene. The whole effort was an unnecessary waste of time and money, but I shut up and did as they asked like a good little bitch. This time, my decency didn't matter. Most of the production ignored me as I followed orders and hoped I wouldn't get hit on the head with a rolled-up newspaper like a bad dog. The new footage was cut in and the film re-delivered. It was official: my absolute dream, my very first movie, had already sent me down the road to total anger and complete bitterness.

I was devastated. For weeks after, I stayed locked up in my house not speaking to anyone. No one at the company ever spoke to me ever again. They didn't even have a screening of the film for the cast and crew; I paid for one out of my own pocket, because I wanted the movie to be shown on the big screen in America if even for just one time. I was so proud of the work I had done and all that I had accomplished. Everyone I knew showed up that night to an amazing response, everyone except the staff at Lakeshore. Not one of the execs or a single staff member came to the screening. I had gone from the nice guy that they considered "impossibly friendly" and who should have a three-picture deal with them to just "impossible." *Note to self: don't ever tell the owner of a long-established production company to shove film cans up his ass.*

Years passed, and I was eventually slipped the overwhelmingly positive financial figures that my movie *Madhouse* had generated. After all of the ruckus and drama, the project had turned out to be highly profitable. I was told that percentage-wise, it was one of the company's biggest profit margins, considering its tiny budget. I later contacted them to see if they would let me get the rights to do a sequel or work with them on a sequel, but they squashed it. Later on, I learned to just shut up and keep my cool when it came to my employers, no matter how out of line they may be.

As you'll read in the following pages, I got much worse before I got better.

31

KILLING THE LIVING DEAD

Not long after, Aaron and I got the word that we were going to start getting notes on the *Return of the Living Dead* films. After the terrible experience I had with the post-production on *Madhouse,* I was not only ready to start on something new, but I wanted to make sure that we got the work perfectly right. This would turn out to be a terribly misguided notion. From the start, I planned on doing my very best not to blow my stack and implode the production this time around. It was a new group with new personalities, and I was looking forward to working with an all-new team.

It was clear that keeping my cool was going to be a challenge once again when Tom Fox gave us our first set of script changes. The first of many jaw-dropping notes and occurrences on the *Return of the Living Dead* films we got was that *Necropolis* and *Rave to the Grave* were now going to be shot back to back and needed to be connected as the producers had decided to use the exact same cast for both movies. To make matters even more confusing, after reading the amusement-park-free version of *Necropolis*, the new producers had also decided that they wanted that script instead of the original one and they wanted us to change the mutants back into zombies. Both screenplays instantly became huge, confusing messes. What's worse was they wanted the polishes in a couple of days.

"But everyone dies at the end of the first movie," I said in confusion.

"Not anymore," said Fox. "All of the characters have to live through the first film, so they can be alive for the second one."

"Well, who the hell is going to die if it's not any of the main characters?" I asked incredulously. "Some of the leads have to die: it's a zombie movie. That's how horror movies work: putting the characters you care about in peril. We have to kill some of them."

"Security guards? Cab drivers? The pizza delivery guy? I don't know; you'll figure it out," Tom said.

I held my breath and counted to ten, then told him that it wouldn't cost the production any more money actor-wise to just use a second cast because they could just use new people in the next film and we could kill folks off in the first one. He explained that they had recently decided to follow in my footsteps and shoot both films in Romania, and they wanted to save money on air fare by just keeping the actors there for both projects

"This also means that for all the characters to be alive at the end of the movie, *Necropolis* has to be completely rewritten again from page one for the eighth time," I said, trying so hard to not pass out in anger. It seemed like all of the drama I had gone through at Lakeshore was about to pale in comparison to what was about to unfold. I was right. I also reminded Fox that both films took place on an American college campus and there were dozens of parts that required young American actors. Having just done a film in Romania, I warned him that they would not find a single performer in that area who could pull off an American accent or even look American for that matter. Not one. We had to fly Americans out for the smallest of parts on *Madhouse.*

Tom reminded me that it wasn't our problem and the decision was already made. He asked me to shut up and be a team player and because I loved him so very much, I did my best to try and just do it their way. I gritted my teeth as the next set of notes came, asking us to change the comical roles of two bumbling FBI agents to KGB agents to try and justify the local actors' Romanian accents. They also wanted several scenes that originally took place in a Pittsburg salt mine moved to Chernobyl, a location where they had decided to shoot.

"Is shooting in Chernobyl even possible or legal for that matter?" I asked.

"Apparently he knows people," Tom said with a smile. "You don't have to worry, you won't be there," he said, laughing.

"Thanks for reminding me," I sighed.

The scenario continued getting weirder by the moment as both films were clearly beginning to unravel before they even started shooting. Every week it seemed like we were being introduced to a new "creative executive" who gave us the absolute worst notes I have ever received. My poor writing partner squirmed as my eyes bulged at the innumerable dumb ideas that were thrown at us. One guy who gave us notes told us he was a seasoned producer but we later learned was a bouncer in a nightclub; another guy claimed to be a development executive from Morgan Creek, but we later discovered that he hadn't worked there in years. We re-wrote page after incredulous page, scene after scene, as both scripts continued to get progressively worse with every passing day.

I remember the day we were sitting on some guy's patio in the Valley as he gave us notes that completely disregarded the franchise's own rules. In fact, I realized he had watched the wrong *Living Dead* movies and was making comments based on George Romero's universe. Time and time again, we got notes that the zombies needed to die with a bullet to the head.

"That's the wrong movie," I must have said a hundred times, grinding my teeth. "*Return of the Living Dead* zombies can only die if they are completely incinerated. It may seem silly to you, but the fans are very aware of this cardinal rule and ignoring it will be the death of the project." My comment was consistently met with a blank stare. It was as if he'd never even seen any of the *Return* films.

"The fans are going to hate these movies," I said to Aaron, who stared at me blankly as the guy giving us the notes went inside to go to the bathroom.

"I hear you. Just please be nicer to him. You are being really condescending," he said, encouraging me to just shut up and write.

"He doesn't know or care about the rules of this franchise and the fans and more importantly, the critics are all going to turn on *us* if we polish this the way he is asking us to," I said.

"Please be nicer," Aaron pleaded. In hindsight, it makes me laugh at what a cunt I must have seemed. Cunt or fortune teller, as it turned out.

Aaron was a truly great writer and an all-around terrific person, but we were two completely different personalities when it came to taking notes on writing screenplays.

He was the handsome, professional guy who smiled, nodded, and wrote down the notes in a positive manner. I was the guy next to him who was fantasizing that the person giving the notes would suddenly burst into flames, stagger back, and fall out a high-rise window to their death. After about a month of meetings with several different people, all of whom had different ideas and none of whom knew what they were doing, we had somehow massaged the two scripts into one long storyline. I continued to stew, knowing that none of these idiots were going to have their names on the film they had just ultimately and collectively ruined.

The story now ponderously followed a group of American college kids and their—for whatever reason—countless Romanian-accented classmates as they try to avoid the KGB while battling an unleashed horde of zombies from a completely different franchise. And they all somehow managed miraculously to stay alive for the next sequel. The story made zero sense. The jokes were totally dead. The Romanian locations looked like something out of a war-torn third world. I honestly did my best to do what Aaron asked me to do and kept my mouth shut unless I was speaking to Tom Fox or him, but when I did speak to them, I made it very clear that I could foresee a huge misfire coming. Again, I was branded a hothead because I wasn't afraid to say out loud that I could smell a huge blunder coming on that we were ultimately going to be held accountable for. No matter how much everyone thought I was a pain in the ass, I stuck to my guns and continually voiced my opinion that I was very worried.

It was also around this time that my best friend John Vulich and I started seriously butting heads. After I pleaded with Tom Fox into taking a second meeting with led to his hiring, John really hit it off with the new executive producer and had clearly seen the opportunity for advancement. Only a few weeks after he was hired, he was promoted to Associate Producer on the film. Suddenly, I found myself completely shut out of a production that I had helped create from the ground up, and by my best friend, no less.

Tom Fox informed me that he had gotten the word that I was now to run all script updates through John first. Being close with John, I didn't hold back when I told him that these projects were unraveling and needed major tweaking before they were shot. Our conversations quickly became heated when he suddenly started carrying himself as if he were my boss.

"Making changes in the script is a part of the business of writing. It's your job. You need to just shut up and implement the notes," John snubbed, suddenly large and in charge and speaking to me like I was a rookie.

"Not if the changes are from people that are unqualified to be requesting them. They are breaking the rules of the franchise and the only people that are going to take shit for these massive missteps are Aaron and I because our names are appearing full screen in the first five minutes of the movie as the writers," I said.

"I don't know what to tell you, Billy. It's how the movie business works, and if you don't like it, you should just get out of it," he said to me one day in a huff and hung up.

It felt weird to be so berated by a person who had spent a lifetime reminding me to stand my ground and believe in myself. I was crushed. It was the first time in my thirty-year friendship with John that he had turned on me. It was clear that Johnny had taken a big drink from the cup of show businesses upper management and he was ready to evolve into a producer with or without me. From that moment on, we didn't speak through the rest of the production. I was heartbroken.

It was around this time that I got word that my friend Tom Fox was sick again. I was told that he was back in the hospital and I dropped everything to be by his side. The news wasn't good this time. Tom was a very brave, strong, and gregarious guy, a true man's man, but both of us were reduced to tears as he struggled to tell me that his cancer was indeed back, and this time, it was spreading fast. His color was once again gone and he was much thinner than I had seen even just a few days earlier as he had lunch. His end was clearly coming. I tried my best to smile, but I was weeping so hard at the thought that he might not get better this time. Up until then, Tom was truly one of the only father-figures I had ever known. I was completely devastated and choked up that he was hurting. After all of our hard work trying to get his two films going for five years, after all of the time we spent encouraging each other and planning to build a movie company that we were proud of, fate had suddenly frowned upon us and was about to end a wonderful, sacred friendship as well as a trusted, strong business partnership.

A week later, he looked like a skeleton as I sat at the foot of his hospital bed, trying to hold back tears as he did his best to make light conversation about our plans for the future that I could not bring myself to participate in.

"I'm scared," I interrupted, mortified as tears exploded from my eyes.

After a long beat, Tom took a breath, wiped his eyes and said, "I am too."

I sat there for ten minutes in total silence as he and I didn't speak, but instead just smiled and looked at one another in exhaustion. Tom was a true friend, the kindest, most supportive person I have ever known. I went down to the lobby and bought him a candy bar and a *Playboy* magazine and brought it up, then hugged him, told him to get well soon, and left for home.

That night, I went to bed and fell asleep hugging my dogs, Gibby, Henry, and little Walter. At about three in the morning, I woke up and rolled over only to find Tom Fox somehow sitting in a chair beside my bed.

"Hello, William," he said with his usual beaming smile and sparkling eyes. It was as if he was back to his jolly healthy self and sitting right there in my room.

"Tom?" I said, completely confused as I tried to wake up.

"Yes, puss, I thought I'd come by and say hello," he said. "I just wanted to say thank you for being a true friend." My eyes started to well up as I could not believe what I was seeing and hearing. It was as real as anything.

"I also wanted to tell you something that I know that you will really appreciate," he continued. "I learned something very important this evening. Very, very important indeed and it's news that *you* really need to hear. From this moment on, I want you to live your life to the absolute fullest you possibly can. I don't want you to ever worry about your bills or bumpy relationships or dealing with people that are difficult. Because when all is said and done, nothing matters. You see, where I am, everyone finds worry, torment, and especially the fear of dying, rather humorous. Nothing troublesome that we humans concoct in our heads is real. A credit card bill is just a piece of paper with writing on it. Someone trying to manipulate or hurt you is really struggling with their own damaged ego, and death on earth is most certainly not the end."

He said all of this with complete relaxation and kindness in his eyes. "The only thing, the absolute *only* thing to consider in life, is to stay in a constant state of happiness and to get as much love as you can. Nothing matters but to love and pursue your own heartfelt bliss. Promise an old man that you will do that, always," he smiled.

"Sure. Okay, Tom—" I said to him, weeping.

Tom calmly watched me weeping for a moment, then looked back up over his shoulder. "Well, William, *she's* telling me that I've already said too much. I have to go. But don't ever forget what I told you, okay, friend? Everything is going to be alright, no matter how bad times ever seem to be." He smiled again.

I nodded and watched as Tom Fox looked back at me. "And oh, don't you stop doing that one single thing every day that gets you closer to *your* goals. Deal?"

"Deal," I said, completely wrecked.

"You'll get there. You don't need people around you to remind you that you are worthy. Just know it in your heart that it is so."

I nodded again. The conversation was a real as anyone I had ever had.

"And keeping reading the *L.A. Times*. It's a marvelous paper," he said.

I nodded one last time and closed my eyes in exhaustion as my room filled with the warmest bright light and Tom was suddenly gone. I really mean that. It was as if my dream had been produced by none other than the Industrial Light and Magic effects shop: it was exactly as you imagine it would be. I laid my head on my tear-soaked pillow and instantly drifted back into the deepest sleep I have ever experienced.

The next morning, I woke up and started my day, heavily affected by the crystal-clear dream that I experienced that night. I went through what Tom said to me over and over as I stayed shaken up through the entire morning. I was getting dressed to go see Tom in the hospital when his son T.J. called me at about three.

"Hey, I just wanted to make sure you knew that my father passed away last night," he said.

I was floored with sadness as I told him that I didn't know and thanked him for giving me the sad news. I sat on the foot of my bed and wept, positive that what I had experienced the night before was no dream. Still to this day, I whole-heartedly believe that Tom Fox came to say goodbye to me that night. Ever since hearing the deeply personal message he came to tell me, I try really hard to always remember his advice and will forever be thankful to him for including me not only in his life, but on the projects that he loved so dearly, no matter how the final outcome.

After Tom passed away, Aaron's and my connection to both *Return* projects completely ended as we no longer had anyone to go to bat for us and keep us involved. The production squashed our request to fly ourselves out to the set and visit and for Aaron to make a cameo as a zombie and after they were done shooting, they refused to let us stop by the office or edit bay to see how the film was shaping up or to show support, a process that my own best friend John Vulich was commandeering.

"*We* don't want any visitors in the edit bay," John coldly told me when I called to ask him if we come by and say hello.

Tom Fox was gone and clearly so was our connection to a project we had hustled for the better part of five years to get off the ground. We later found out that we also hadn't been invited to any of the screenings. I was really heartbroken to be completely cut out of a project that I cared so deeply about and had worked so hard to bring to life. Once Tom had passed, we heard nothing more about the films.

The first time that Aaron and I got to see the two movies was when we watched them from my couch during the Sci-Fi Channel premiere. The two of us sat there and watched in total shock as years of hard work had been turned into poorly executed, illogical pieces of cinematic horseshit. Most of the creative that we came up with on both films had been completely mishandled or ignored. Much of the script had been polished yet again and not in a good way; all of the franchise's rules were all broken, the homages to the first film misinterpreted or completely removed. They didn't even bother changing the voices of many of the Romanian actors playing American college students. There was no indication of the original film's punk rock esthetic or comedic timing. They were both huge disasters.

The movies were instantly raked over the coals by serious critics as well as by (even worse) the voracious internet reviewers who blamed Aaron and I for the shitty execution, just as I had predicted for months before the films even went into production. I'm sorry if anyone involved in the productions is hurt by this unfiltered raw truth, but if you had listened to people that know better, the projects would have been a success. Aaron and I certainly learned lessons and I hope we weren't the only ones.

People who worked at the horror zines and websites that had previously been my friends openly bad-mouthed us for supposedly ruining a beloved franchise. We were ripped to shreds for what viewers thought was our lack of respect and consideration of the perfectly unique films that came before them. I was so furious and affected by these scathing reviews that I clammed up and never said a word about how things had truly unfolded, until now. It was too late. Our insanely positive momentum as working writers temporarily came to a screeching halt. Serious damage had been done not only to both of our writing careers, but to the overall franchise itself.

It's been years since the two movies came out and no one has been interested in doing another one since. What's worse, not only were the films critical flops, they also flat-lined financially-speaking. They couldn't give these stinkers away with a hot meal. Nobody wanted to buy them for more than a few thousand dollars. It took years to finally get them distributed and both films were ultimately a loss. Years later, the film's negatives were placed on eBay in an attempt to recoup some of the money lost.

Despite my no nonsense and overly grating opinions, I had been right the entire time. I certainly didn't take any pleasure in the films being a total bust because the Fox family also took a huge blow as the value of their franchise went down the toilet. If the people in charge had listened, it would have made the difference in what amounted to possibly millions of dollars and continued success. I can only hope that one day, someone will reboot the film and rebirth it bigger and better. Whoever does, I sure hope they make Tom proud as that franchise was really his baby. He truly loved that original film. I carry around a huge amount of regret for not fighting harder to make things right for him. In Tom's case, it would have been worth having people hate me if the end result had been to his liking.

For months, a deep depression sent me on an eating binge that had me packing the pounds back on. I stopped walking or going to the gym and hid away in my house for the better part of a year, ordering pizza and indulgently feeding myself as I sulked in depression and anxiety. In a matter of months, I was back up to 270 pounds and counting. Bloated and feeling used up, I rarely even thought about the movie business, only occasionally showing up at conventions to stay in touch.

"Is that you?" a snarky kid asked as he approached my photo table at a horror convention and did a double take at my various acting photos from the 80s and 90s. I was clearly fatter and older, but yeah, it was me, alright.

"Yeah, but I was 19 in that picture," I said, knowing full well what he was getting at. The kid picked up the photo and held it up, shifting his gaze from me then back to the photo from *Friday the 13th VII*, then back over and over. "Wow, you really let yourself go," he said after a beat.

I held back from laughing. "How old are you?" I asked him, drained.

"I'm twenty," he said.

"I'm forty-two. Look me up in twenty-two years and we'll compare fat asses," I said. "Now, beat it."

Unbelievably rude, yet absolutely hilarious. I wouldn't have dreamed of mentioning his gingivitis or musky armpits when he had the audacity to hug me and ask to take a picture after completely dressing me down. But he was right, I was indeed eating and drinking a lot of how I was feeling and it was really showing. Something had to change.

A year after the avalanche dust from the *Return* debacle began to settle, my one-time close friend John Vulich started to come around, and he invited me out to dinner one night. Since my house of cards had crumbled and I had nothing more to lose, I took the opportunity to tell him that while I hated him turning on me for the sake of his own advancement, I understood him leaping at the chance. I also told him—with a laugh, mind you—not to expect any more job leads from me anytime soon.

John apologized to me and said that he didn't honestly feel like he was playing strategy at the time, but after seeing how bad the finished films were, he realized that he should have at least listened to what I was saying and fought harder to let us help guide the movies back to Tom's original vision.

He also apologized for betraying me in the worst way a best friend could. It was true that John had cut my throat in the hope of getting ahead. He promised me nothing like that would ever happen again. We both shook it off. I had known him forever and as far as I knew, I would continue to know him. The volatile playground that is the stage in which show business is set is no place to end lifelong friendships. We hoisted a whiskey like the true Jackals we really were, both said we were sorry for hurting one another and vowed to never turn on each other again. And we never did. In fact, the whole awful experience only brought us closer together.

Little by little, John began to share information with me about the *Return* movies and what a disaster filming was. He blamed the director, telling me that the guy seemed to be heavily medicated through most of the shoot, but I knew that the film's problems started well before the director came into the picture.

He also told me that there were many times when he tried to have me flown in to replace the director, a notion I never knew but sure was happy to hear. I liked the director very much and even if he could have convinced the executive producer to send me in, I wouldn't have taken the job anyway. The damage was done and our conversation further drove me to realize that I should just let it all go and move on.

The fact is, the entire *Return of the Living Dead* mess wasn't caused by any one person. The two films were *collectively* fucked up by a large group of misguided souls. There is no way either of the films could have ever been any good as the deck was stacked against both of them from the very start. There had been too many cooks in the kitchen with too little knowledge of how to make a horror film. Too many people that didn't understand the building blocks of telling a good story. I may not be Alfred Hitchcock, but after ingesting all things horror for so many years, I at the very least knew what route *not* to take.

From that moment on, John Vulich never questioned any of my creative decisions or insistence to stand my ground on work issues that I was passionate about. Our friendship was suddenly back on track, and he and I started treating each other better than ever. That's what true friends do. They grow and evolve, as nobody stays the same forever. One thing was for sure: my desire to work in film production was not going to come without its challenges. The question was, did I truly have the artistic temper to endure it? It was starting to feel like maybe I didn't.

It was around this time that I started producing digital shorts for television again. Digital shorts were beginning to dominate the advertising world and my contacts were suddenly throwing me more work than I could handle. I loved working with my favorite groups, especially Disney, as they had known me since I first began directing and producing. Because so much money is spent in advertising, I often made a better living in three days on a short than I would for working on a film for six months. Things were great: I upgraded, selling my house in Silverlake and moving up to swanky Mulholland Drive. *Casa De Mille Putas.*

Most importantly, I was finally back to working with people who I respected and who treated me with respect in return. I was lucky enough to bring my dear friend Peter Garcia on board as a producer and we started to produce multiple spots. I started breathing easier and worked harder than I ever had. Work was fun again.

32

FIRE AND ICE: FURNACE

That summer, I got called into a company that had watched *Madhouse* and wanted to talk to me about possibly directing a horror film for them. The movie was called *Furnace*. My manager sent me the script and I loved it. It reminded me so much of Courtney Joyner's script for the movie *Prison* that I had worked on way back in the 80s. I immediately agreed to take a meeting, and within just a couple of weeks, I was hired to both polish and direct the project. As with most films, everyone was kind and cooperative in the beginning, and Aaron and I started to polish what had started out as a very strong script to begin with.

The story revolved around a police officer who was investigating a series of murders that were taking place at the Nashville State Penitentiary that he ultimately learns are the evil shenanigans of a long dead little girl who was burned alive in the place's massive furnace. It was a great premise.

Once again, I asked Vulich to come on board, and artist Brad Hardin ultimately took the position as head effects make-up artist on the project. We started auditioning people and for once, it was looking like everything was going to be smooth sailing. That is, until the company's in-house lawyer, a friendly enough guy named Scott who had recently graduated to movie producer, called me into the office. As I knew by now, office visits on a film seldom ended well for me. I girded my loins, held my breath, and headed to Beverly Hills. This time around, the happy go lucky Billy Butler was now the serious and reserved Billy Butler. (Maybe there was an eyedropper of the cold and distrusting Billy Butler.) After my experience at Lakeshore, I had learned to not open myself up too soon.

"Billy, this is Matt," producer Scott said to me. "He's our office production assistant and a trusted filmmaker who we really admire."

I smiled and said hi, waiting for the kid to offer me a water or a cup of coffee, but it didn't happen. Matt was a smiling, handsome, young French-Canadian eager-beaver who instead sat down on the couch next to me. He was holding the film's script that had a bunch of Post-It notes stuck in it.

"Matt almost directed a film starring Cuba Gooding Jr," Scott said.

"Really? Why didn't he?" I asked.

"He didn't get the job," he replied.

"That'll do it," I quipped.

"But *we* think it would be really great if he helped you direct this film. He has a lot of really great ideas."

I looked over to Matt, pleading mercy. "Please no. Don't. Please, whatever you do, don't have ideas," I said to Matt who half-laughed, thinking I was joking with him.

"Matt also plays ice hockey with Jerry Bruckheimer," Scott added.

"I can relate. I slept with Steven Spielberg's gardener once," I joked. I wondered why this was information I needed to know. Why did they hire me if they thought I needed help? It was clearly official: my fresh new production hell had arrived. For the rest of the meeting, I was quiet and kept it all business.

"Is everyone in this fucking business a complete idiot?" I asked Aaron as we walked out to the car. By then, Aaron was *way* over me blowing my stack. He didn't even bother to answer.

I thought about the project for the rest of the afternoon. I had clearly made horrible choices trying to please everyone on the first movie. Was I seriously going to set myself up for another round by being a pushover from day one on the next? Later that night, I called producer Scott and told him that in all sincerity, if they thought production assistant Matt was the answer to making a good film, they should just have him direct the movie instead of me. By that time, I could earn more money walking across the room directing a commercial in three days than I could in a year's time directing a film that irritated me.

Still, I really did love Scott and the executive producer and was really in love with the project they had been grooming. Gaining a quick reputation for being a prick or not, I just needed to establish boundaries right away and the message seemed to soak in with the producers. They backed down and told me I was indeed in charge, a move I completely respected.

Matt, who clearly didn't get the message, continued to have "ideas" during meetings, despite my staring right through him and not reacting to his input. In hindsight, in my trying to stay in control, I overreacted. I shouldn't have blocked him out entirely.

I coined the phrase "The Helen Keller Treatment" on this movie. If someone irritated me in any way, I pretended I couldn't hear or see them.

Auditions continued and the coolest actors were starting to get booked. The local physical production guy for the film was a total pro by the name of Eric who was an expert at producing low budget films and had many connections to the rap world. He got us rappers Ja Rule and Paul Wall right away and I was tremendously thankful.

Before I booked Paul, Eric tried to present a chubby young new musician to me by the name of "Pitbull." I immediately shot him down. "That guy isn't going anywhere!" I said, not realizing that three years later, he would be topping the charts and leaving everyone in the dust, including me. Clearly, all of my decisions can't be gems, people.

Kane Hodder was booked as a murderous inmate who is killed by the ghost. Michael Pare was also attached to the film as the lead. I was not only a fan of his work but had worked with him briefly on *Village of the Damned* back when I helped Nicotero on set; I had also met him briefly in the hotel on my first film job in Spain. Another guy came in to read for the James Dean-type role in the film, a then unknown actor by the name of Taylor Kinney. Taylor was a beautiful male specimen whose only goal at that time was to act just enough to raise money to travel the world and surf. His lack of desperation for the job and natural acting skill pushed him to the front of the line. It never fails that the actor who comes in and clearly doesn't care somehow always ends up getting the job. We quickly hired him, gave him his screen actors' guild card, and welcomed him to the cast. Taylor, basically a surfing waiter at the time, graduated years later to booking the leading role in the television series *Chicago Fire*; he was also Lady Gaga's fiancé for a brief period of time. Face it, folks: I know how to pick 'em.

Taylor Kinney and Victoria Hester in the makeup wagon in Nashville

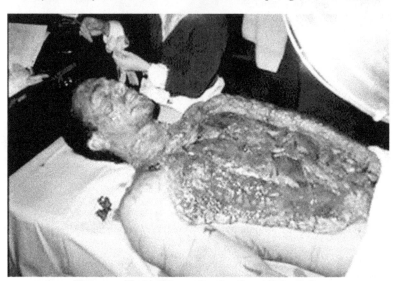

Furnace - Taylor Kinney Getting Some Rest on Set

Things seemed to be moving along just swell on the casting front, and on all fronts, frankly, as suddenly and without warning as I was hit with the biggest curveball ever, and it was all with the mention of the name Tom Sizemore. "No. No. No. No. and No.,"

I said when Sizemore's name was brought up in the casting room by the producer. They thought he would be perfect to play the crooked prison guard who ultimately meets his fate at the hands of the vengeful ghost.

"But he still has a lot of value overseas," Scott said.

"So does Charles Manson, but were not booking him either," I replied.

He laughed but continued to try to push me into meeting with him as I stood my ground.

"No. I'm not doing this. He is too much of a handful," I told them. I had heard horror stories about the guy from my producer and director friends for years and was in no way going to put myself in the line of fire. I explained to this Scott. "We can find someone else that'll get this movie sold in the foreign territories," I said.

Once again in my career, my response was not a popular one, but I will say, the team laughed and agreed to keep trying to find someone else. If only that sentiment had stuck. I hindsight, I suspect they planned on vetoing my decision from day one. I met with every bad boy actor in town in the hope that the production company would approve someone, but each time I put forth a name to play the role of Frank Miller, it ultimately got shot down and Tom's name was brought up.

"Ready for an interesting day?" my casting director Bob Macdonald asked as he placed a list of actors coming in for meetings in front of me. Written at the top of the list was none other than Tom Sizemore.

"What is this?" I asked Bob furiously.

"They told me to call him in," he said with a wicked smile. "Don't shoot the messenger."

"Who is they?" I snapped.

"Who do you think?" Bob grinned like a sassy Cheshire Cat.

"And you did?" I said, glaring.

"I didn't have a choice. Just tell them that you don't want him," he said.

"Yeah, that'll do it," I growled.

Bob turned to me like the wise old queen that he was. "Now, William. There are going to be times in your career when you have to direct people that you don't want in your movie," he said as he turned back to his computer. "You're trying to make the best movie possible, not throwing a dinner party. Who knows? You two might even turn out to be friends. Face it: you're both just about as fucked up. It might work." He snickered.

"Shut up." I snapped, knowing full well, he could be right.

I called Vulich and asked him to join me in the casting sessions for moral support. I had earlier brought him on as associate producer as part of his deal to provide the make-up effects, and he was getting very good at producing. The afternoon crept by as appointments unfolded, including one for a sort-of "scream-queen" personality (a term that is liberally thrown around these days), a girl who auditioned for the role of the hard-nosed prison psychiatrist. She came in wearing a short skirt and with no panties on, opening her legs in some sort of manipulative homage to *Basic Instinct* during her reading. I burst out laughing as she told me she needed a moment to prepare and took out a pair of reading glasses and put them on the end of her nose before she spread her legs.

"I'm ready," she said as Bob and I nearly cried we were laughing so hard. I didn't have the heart to tell her that minus Vulich, she was opening herself up for the wrong crowd.

"Who the hell called this girl in?" I asked in shock as she left.

"Who do you think?" Bob purred. I picked up the over-the-top, beyond sexy 8x10 photo of her in bra and panties, peering seductively over her shoulder as she lay on the hood of a corvette. I held it up for everyone in the office to see.

"Can you believe someone thought that this looks like a hardened prison psychiatrist?" I said in disbelief.

Vulich gazed at the photo with wide-eyed excitement. "She looks like a prison psychiatrist to me," he said. Thankfully, the next person who came in was a beautiful blonde woman that was also recommended by the production, one who easily pulled off the strength that a female working in the prison system would require and as an added bonus, she also had underwear on. This pretty, kind girl recommended by producer Scott was a terrific actress by the name of Jenny McShane. After only one meeting, I was sold on her and we immediately booked her for the film. She ended up being a terrific asset to the project.

The end of the casting day came and we were nearly done. Sizemore's appointment finally came and went without him showing up. I was starting to feel relieved, thinking that he was probably blowing the meeting off. It was a best-case scenario. I had reluctantly agreed to take a meeting with him and he didn't show up for it. It looked like I was off the hook. At seven o'clock, we started to pack up our stuff and hit the road, when all of the sudden, Sizemore strolled in the door. At this point in my career, pretty much nothing made me nervous, but him showing up unannounced, hours later than he was supposed to be there, shook me up a little as I took a seat and started our abrupt meeting.

Tom is a big guy and handsome, and he looked rested and was a lot calmer than I had been warned to expect. Even more impressive was he seemed to know a lot about the script and the character. He distractedly walked around the room checking out the knickknacks on Bob's shelves and thumbed through people's acting photos as he told me what he liked about the character and what he wanted to do with him. He made sense. Could it be that everything I had been told about him was exaggerated?

He was very professional and polite. Still, there is something about Tom, no matter what state he is in, that really strikes you when you are speaking to him in person. No matter what he is talking to you about, he always seems to have the look in his eye that he could snap and choke you out at any moment. I suppose it's why he is such a strong actor. His presence is undeniably huge, no matter how much of a loose cannon I heard he could be.

I decided to keep it real and flat out asked him if I could rely on him. "So, if I hire you, are things going to run smoothly for me? Am I going to regret it?" I asked.

"*So smoothly*," he said. "I'm all good and ready to go back to work. I need to do this right so that people know I can be relied on again. I'll give you a great performance. I really want to work with you on this, man." He finally turned around and sat in the chair across from me.

Tom had recently resurfaced after a series of arrests and horrendous reports on his behavior on some of the films that proceeded his run-ins with the law. He seemed perfectly fine in the meeting.

"By the way, I saw your movie *Madhouse*. Really good stuff," Sizemore said with an impish smile.

"No, you didn't," I said.

"You're right. But I watched the trailer," he said with a laugh.

"No, you didn't," I said.

"Nah, I didn't," he said, laughing again. His hideousness made me like him. Could my casting director Bob McDonald be right?

After some thought, I flipped back to my original notion. Though he was a lot calmer than I had been warned, I was in no way convinced that I should risk it and work with him. Tom had recently come off a variety of unsavory charges and unthinkable accusations including being accused of inappropriate behavior with an eleven-year-old actress while on the set of the movie *Piggy Banks*, a complaint that was confirmed by my friend and the film's producer James Rosenthal and *that have apparently* been *dismissed*. That, along with past charges of domestic violence against Hollywood Madame Heidi Fleiss and several various drug arrests and convictions, stuck in my head. Maybe he had, in fact, changed his wild ways, but I didn't want to be the guy to test the theory. Everyone warned me that he was famous for a terrific first meeting and later would go off the rails. It was told to me time and time again that we would end up killing each other. I thought about it, made a few calls asking about him and called the production company the next morning.

"I don't want to work with him," I said, sitting at my desk in the casting office, sorting through photos of other potential candidates for the role.

"You said he did really well at his meeting," Scott said as I shot my casting director Bob an evil look.

"He was okay. I've just heard so many bad things about him. I made a bunch of calls. Just doesn't seem like a good idea. Maybe he is good, but to be safe, let's reach higher and just find someone else of equal value," I said.

"We're pretty stuck on using him, Billy," he said. "Can you please just throw us a bone here and go with it? He is willing to cut us a deal and will be traveling with his sober coach. I think he will be fine."

I sat for a moment in impending defeat as I looked over at Vulich, who shrugged. "He's a phenomenal actor, dude," John said.

So, would I stand my ground and not be a pushover, once again be branded difficult by not playing along with the team? I took a breath and rolled my eyes, speaking into the phone. "Okay. I am going to agree to this. But I am not going to be held accountable if he dismantles the production in any way. I refuse to deal with him if he pulls anything that slows me down and if we go off schedule, it will be on you and the company. Not me. You guys will be solely responsible for managing him if he goes off the rails."

I could not believe that I had given in and just uttered the words, but I did. As much as I was trying to be strong, I also wanted to be a respected team member. My agreement was met with relief.

"Absolutely, we will take full responsibility for him," the producer said.

I hung up the phone and gave Bob the word to start the booking procedure. My gut told me I had just made a huge mistake.

Maybe he would surprise me.

Maybe it would work out.

Maybe all the trash-talking about Sizemore was just mean-spirited Hollywood gossip.

"You are so fucked," Jim Rosenthal, the producer of *Piggy Banks*, said to me with a laugh, throwing back a shot of tequila at the Mexicali Cantina on Ventura. "Sizemore will be a complete disaster to both the production and you."

"He was nice at his meeting," I said with stupid hope.

"He's going to eat you alive. Get out of the deal while you still can."

"Natasha Lyonne was a handful before she got sober. I handled her fine. How could he be any worse?" I said.

"He's a complete, dangerous lunatic, that's how," Jim laughed. "No comparison."

"He said he would be cool." Why in the world I felt compelled to defend the guy, I didn't know.

"Look Billy, you're too much of a cunt when you direct," he said. "You will not put up with his bullshit when he sabotages the film. It will not end well." he said.

"Well, it's too late now: he's hired, so let's hope you're wrong," I told him as he clinked my shot glass.

"Rest in peace, Butler," he said, which is now a very ironic statement as not long after that lunch, Jim himself passed away in his sleep. One of the funniest, hardest-working guys I ever knew was suddenly gone forever. His final words, though, were most certainly ones of wisdom, because as it turned out, he was right on the money. I was about to learn the hard way that I should have stood my ground.

It was sub-zero temperatures in Nashville that year. Despite the minus ten-degree weather, the local producers had gotten us a great deal for our prison location: twenty-five days at the old abandoned Nashville penitentiary at rock bottom prices. Built in 1898, the place was beautiful and crumbling in a gothic sort of way. The building was once a cotton plantation that operated at the same time that it was a prison so it was as beautiful as it was menacing.

Nashville State Penitentiary

Prison Exterior

On the day we got there, I checked into my hotel and we took a tour of the dilapidated facility. The place was entirely abandoned and there were certain hallways and rooms where you were not allowed to walk out of fear that you might fall right through the floor, but other than that, it was a stunning structure. I walked lightly as we checked out every room that we were able to visit. Some of the offices were still furnished with office furnishings and had prison paperwork scattered all over the floors.

One of the many places the property manager showed me was the main building's basement, a place where very few people were ever allowed. Hanging from thick wooden beams along the ceiling of the basement were these big sharp, rusty hooks. The caretaker explained that back in the early 1900s, when prisoners acted up or tried to escape the prison, they hanged them by the flesh of their backs on the hooks and beat them; sometimes, until they were dead. I immediately understood the uncomfortable vibe that I felt as we were descending the rickety old stairs that led downward, thanked them for the tour, and called it a day.

That night, when I got back to the hotel, I learned someone had been stabbed to death in the hall and the production was in the middle of relocating me. I should have taken it as a sign that more bad things lay in wait.

Muffy Bolding and I got set up in our room and braced ourselves for our latest adventure, which was looking like it was going to be unlike any of the rest. We were correct. Outside on the main strip, the town was amazing. It was my first time to travel to Nashville and I instantly loved the city; it was beautiful and vibrant and the people were very friendly. By far, my favorite thing that I counted on with everyone I met in Nashville was that each one of them eventually asked me the same question: "Are ya'll gonna go honky-tonkin' while you're here?" I didn't have the heart to tell them that I would not have the time to honkytonk, whatever that was, but I sure was excited at the anticipation of everyone asking me the question. They introduced themselves and started up a conversation and I patiently waited, thinking to myself, *uh-huh, just get to the part where you ask me if I am gonna go honky-tonking; you know you're dying to find out!* It sounded like a terrific time, honky-tonking. (I eventually did try it and learned what the big deal was all about.)

The Friday before we started shooting, I was once again walking the prison building, choosing rooms for each scene to be shot in, when I got an unexpected call from actor Kane Hodder. Apparently, his sister had fallen very ill and he wasn't going to be able to do the movie after all. After wishing him well, the production and I scrambled to try and find a new guy before we started shooting Monday morning. Somehow, producer Scott made magic happen and booked Danny Trejo as his replacement: a perfect exchange. I was really happy to be directing again, despite the plummeting temperatures and possible impending doom.

We had a very quick pre-production week as one by one, all of the actors began to arrive and we were all ready to go. All of the actors, that is, minus the man of the hour, Tom Sizemore, who was to arrive in the morning of the second day of shooting. Monday was there before we knew it and we started work.

Having not let up on the massive amounts of stress eating I had been doing for months, I had my assistant deliver a twelve-pack of White Castle burgers and I gobbled them up in my production RV with zero hesitation before I went out on set. Once again, I was so fat and uncomfortable, back to a whopping 300 pounds and I could not have cared less. Since my life no longer revolved around constant grooming for the camera, I had embraced being a fat boy once again and was eating out of control with my foot to the floorboard. I had gained back all the weight I had lost from my chubby childhood. I was physically miserable, looking like a trained bear as I wobbled around the frozen prison yard, bundled up in a ski outfit, a sweater, two coats, and two knit caps, along with ski gloves and boots. I could barely walk as I teetered over the thick ice-covered corridor floors, terrified I would be the fat guy to fall on his big ass in front of the entire crew.

Despite the cold and my precarious balancing act, the first day went without a hitch. I did my best to ignore production assistant Matt as he watched me work from the shadows, staring me down like some sort of character out of a Shakespearian play, ready for me to drop the ball so he could poison the king and dethrone him the moment he dropped his guard. Still, I was making another movie and thus far having the time of my life, believe it or not. Politics aside, the film nerd was back in action and as happy as a clam.

On day two, it continued to get even colder and began to snow. The setting was miserable and the work moved at a snail's pace because everything was so slippery and frozen. Temperatures dipped far below zero as all of us tried to work in the biting cold. Each day at lunch, they peeled the foil off the catering pans and the top of the food they brought in instantly froze over. The serving spoon hit the surface of lasagna with the sound of an unappetizing crunch as it cut through an immediate layer of forming ice. They were the absolute worst working conditions that I had ever endured, and it was only day two. Things couldn't possibly get any worse. Or could they?

How about comically worse?

Yeah, that about describes it. My fresh hell started with five little words: "Tom Sizemore's plane has landed." The first assistant director told me the news as I sat shivering in front of a space heater with my ever-present friend Muffy Bolding, once again appearing in my latest film and once again as a character named "Polly," a fast-growing tradition. I told the assistant to take him to his hotel and once he got settled in, to bring him by the set to say hello if he felt like it. He started at seven in the morning the following day and it was only ten in the morning, so I figured he might want to come by and at least try on his wardrobe.

We continued to film as I started my first scenes with Ja Rule. Back in Los Angeles, before I left for Nashville, I had received a call from one of the producers. He wanted to remind me that since this was my first time directing famous rappers, I should always keep in mind that some of them could be bit thuggish and dangerous at times.

"These are not guys that you want to give a hard time to," he said. "Make sure you treat them with total respect, or you might get more than you bargained for."

I thought to myself, they're acting in a movie, for heaven's sake. How tough can they be? Are they really going to shoot or beat me if I ask them to kick their performance up a notch or if we run out of cheese sticks at the craft services table? What's to worry about?

"We're very serious. Most of the guys are real-world gangsters," the crew at the production company warned. I have to admit I did start to think about their advice as they collectively warned me over and over again that smart asses like me, typically get smack downs from these types of performers.

I smiled but still used friendly caution when Ja Rule was finally due on set, and as I predicted, he was completely kind, cool and professional.

"Hello, I'm Jeff," he said as he pleasantly shook my hand. I smiled and chuckled to myself as he asked, "What?"

"They've been warning me that the rappers on set were going to be completely dangerous," I said.

"Don't let the image fool you," he said with a cool chuckle. "With that said, don't test me."

I agreed that I would not. From that moment on, the guy was a total pro. He hit all his marks, he knew his lines, he was never late, he had a really good sense of humor, and at no point did he use brass knuckles on me. It looked as if this shoot was going to be a lot easier than I had been warned it would be, yet again not taking into consideration Tom Sizemore.

"Tom says he's not coming to set today," the production assistant's voice squawked over the walkie-talkie.

"Okay, did he say why?" I asked.

"Nope, just went straight to his room."

I didn't think much of it. I myself hate leaving my hotel when I am on location. Plus, it was freezing. I figured he'd get some rest after traveling and I'd see him the next morning at work. Still he hadn't tried on any of his wardrobe. I told the production to try and call him and see if they could bring his wardrobe by. It was a request that went unfulfilled as he did not answer his phone.

At seven a.m. the next morning, the cast and crew gathered at the prison to kill it another day on *Furnace*. Everyone was there, except for Tom Sizemore, who wasn't on set and was nowhere to be found.

"Tom still isn't answering his hotel room phone or cellphone, and we knocked on the hotel room door numerous times," the second assistant's voice sheepishly called out through the assistant director's walkie.

The A.D. looked over at me. "Do we need to be concerned?" he said.

"Do you need to be concerned?" I said to producer Scott, who stood there like a deer in the headlights. I grabbed my assistant's walkie-talkie. "Pound on it," I said.

"Already tried that," she said.

"Then keep pounding until he opens up. Tell him he's in the next shot," I said.

"Copy that."

I was so busy that morning with other things to do that I didn't think too much of his absence. I figured they'd get him there one way or another.

Then ten o'clock rolled around. Then eleven, and he still wasn't budging.

"He's in there, but he won't come out of his room," the production assistant said.

"Send Strongoni over there: he's good with the fussy," I said. "He's been coping with working with me for years."

"Tom says he doesn't feel good and to come back in an hour."

I shot producer Scott a look.

"I'll handle it," he said, exiting, eager to give it the old college try. I was relieved to see that he was going to help wrangle the guy. After all, he was one of the team members who pushed the hardest for Sizemore. As long as they kept him in line and he acted as well as I knew he could, I really didn't care what shenanigans he pulled. If I had only known the depths of the impending shenanigans.

Another hour passed and Sizemore still hadn't shown up. I had filmed everything on the call sheet that didn't involve him, so suddenly, we were all at a standstill. Anyone who has ever worked on a low budget movie knows that there is no such thing as wasting time, so Michael Pare, always the consummate professional, agreed to do scenes that weren't on the schedule so we wouldn't fall behind. He went to his trailer and studied for ten minutes and somehow learned five new pages. Within two hours, we had shot all of the new material.

Still, there was no Sizemore.

"Scott's in his room and is trying to get him to the car," the second assistant director nervously relayed.

"What's his problem?" I snapped. Between the extreme cold and the unexpected curveballs of having to shoot scenes that weren't on the schedule, I was in no mood to entertain foolishness, and yet foolishness was raining down in abundance.

Damn you, Jim Rosenthal, for always being right, I thought to myself. Time passed and I focused on other things while Scott slugged away, trying to get Tom into the car.

"He'll be here in ten minutes!" the assistant's voice suddenly squawked in hopeful optimism.

I wasn't buying it. To be safe, I had the director of photography Viorel Segovichi shoot random establishing shots of the prison inside and out instead of just waiting for Sizemore to get there. The entire cast that was working that day was on set; by then, all of them were made up and killing time as they waited in their trailers. I was so lucky that they were all so patient as Tom held everyone hostage. Sure enough, thirty minutes came and went with still no sign of him. I grew more furious by the minute and Viorel eventually ran out of shots to shoot. It was around noon as we discussed finally giving up and just breaking for our frozen lunch when...

"He's here, he's here!" a young production assistant said as she ran up to me in glee. "Scott just pulled in and they're taking him straight to make-up and wardrobe. We'll bring him straight to set once he's dressed and made-up."

"How did you finally get him out of his hotel room?" I asked one of my friends who was sent to help coax the guy over.

"It wasn't easy. He was lying on his bed making chit-chat, rolling back and forth, and every time he rolled over, pills of all shapes and sizes came pouring out of his pockets. It seemed like maybe whatever he's been taking must have kicked in at a certain point, because he suddenly started acting super motivated. That's when we seized the moment and rushed him into the car before he changed his mind."

"Why do these druggies always come to work for me, but never offer to share the drugs?" I joked. It was only partially in jest. I honestly wasn't judging him in anyway. As long as he could do his job, I really didn't care what he was on.

The gang had pulled it off. Tom was finally on set, five hours late, but on set nonetheless. I breathed a slight sigh of relief as I called Jenny McShane and Michael Pare upstairs to the prison medical office so we could start blocking the shot until Sizemore got there.

The first scene we were shooting with Tom involved Jenny's character caring for a sick prisoner played brilliantly by actor Clay Steakley. I stood in for Tom as Jenny, Michael, and Clay ran through the scene several times, finally locking it.

As we finished, I asked the assistant director what Sizemore's status was.

"I think you might need to go down to make-up," he said, afraid to tell me why.

I didn't say anything but shot him an evil look and immediately headed downstairs, once again precariously slowly stepping my fat unstable body over that thick ice as I headed to the make-up trailer. I stepped up on to the trailer's icy platform, opened the door, and found Tom Sizemore sitting in a make-up chair, having his hair dyed.

"Oh, hi" he said. He looked over at me as if he barely remembered who I was.

"Oh, hi. What's going on?" I asked, my face turning red with fury.

"I'm having my hair dyed," he said with a defiant look in his eye.

"Hair-dying is for people who arrive at their call time," I coldly responded. "I am five hours behind schedule because you didn't show up."

He stood up defiantly and crossed over into my space, his barber bib flowing behind him. "What do you want me to do? Go to set like this?" he said, crossing up to me intrusively. His entire head was covered in black goop.

If he knew how crazy the film business was starting to make me, he wouldn't have asked that question, because frankly, I probably would have plopped a baseball hat on his head and filmed the scene at that point. Instead, I just glared, then turned and went back to set as we broke for lunch. It was at that moment that I was positive that this day—no, this *shoot*—was not going to end well, and I was right.

Not in the mood for our usual frozen "lunchsicle," Muffy and I bundled up and climbed onto the prison's golf cart and drove around the grounds, looking in buildings we had not yet seen. When I say looking in buildings, I mean just that: we floored the gas pedal and drove up the prison's hospital emergency ramp, through the swinging double doors, and up and down the dilapidated hallways full of rusting old hospital beds and examination rooms. We turned a corner and careened down a long moldy hallway, through the operating room, and into the old kitchen, complete with rotting food still sitting on the stainless-steel counters, not once considering that the golf cart very well might have fallen through the structure's rotten wood floors. It was the ultimate dark ride as we exploded through double door after double door, laughing like death-defying hyenas.

It was terrifying. It was brilliant. I have to say, it was truly one of the most exciting moments of my life, like riding through a real-world amusement park ride that very well could have ended in our own deaths. After our adventure, we floored it back through the old building and headed back to the catering area unscathed.

Lunch came and went and we were all back to set; all of us, except for—once again—Tom Sizemore.

"Where is he now?" I asked as everyone stared at me wide-eyed.

"He won't come out of his trailer," the assistant director said, now slightly delirious.

"Why is he even here? Why doesn't he just go home?" I asked, taking my headphones off, slamming them onto my chair, and walking back down the frozen stairs, once again waddling over the icy concrete and over to his trailer door to pound on it.

After several beats without any response, I jerked the door open and was met by a noxious cloud of chemical smoke with an odor I had never smelled in my life. Standing there in only his underpants was Tom Sizemore, smoking a cigarette and furiously playing the air guitar to music that was so loud, I couldn't hear myself as I tried to scream over the top of it. After he made no move to turn it down or try to listen to me, I walked over and yanked the cord out of the wall. The room fell silent.

"I'll be up in just a few minutes," he calmly said.

"We gotta talk," I said, sitting down at Sizemore's trailer dining room table. "Look, I don't care what you're up to. I really don't. Frankly, there is nothing that is most likely in your system right now that I haven't at least tried or been to counseling for, so I'm the last person to care or judge you."

He stared at me in red, sweaty-faced confusion. I could tell my response was not what he was expecting.

"So," I continued, "you can come to set and work, like you told me you would back in L.A., *or* you can stay in here and smoke, ingest, or cram up your ass whatever it is that you're doing. I really don't care. I just need to know what Tom Sizemore's plan is for the day? Do I have you all day? Do I have you for ten minutes? Because I'm more than willing to hang a black piece of fabric up in your trailer and just shoot every single one of your lines for today's scenes if that's what you want to do. I am also willing to stop shooting and replace you, if none of this sounds appealing to you."

He suddenly blew his stack. "Who the fuck do you think you are?!" he bellowed as he charged forward towards me, backing me out of his trailer and down the slippery metal steps and into the snow. "I have worked with some of the best directors in the world!" He barked. He got into my space, edging me back. "I worked with Oliver Stone!"

I manned up and stepped forward. "Well, you're working with Billy Butler now, pal. So what's that say about your career?" The next few seconds are a blur as I turned and started walking back towards the prison through the falling snow, followed by a galloping Tom Sizemore who called me every name in the book as he screamed at the top of his lungs. Finally, as we were about fifty-feet away from his trailer, I stopped and turned towards him.

"Tom!" I yelled. He stopped, his eyes wide. "You are outside in a minus-fifteen-degree snowstorm in your underpants!" I yelled, motioning to his pudgy, stench-filled nakedness. He looked down at his sweat-drenched person, shot me a look, and stormed back to his trailer, slamming the door and locking it.

"What are we going to do?" producer Scott later asked.

"What are *we* going to do?!" I barked. "I warned you that if this happened, you guys were going to have to figure it out. Get rid of him. He's going to end up costing us thousands of dollars in overtime and additional days. I was warned by everyone I know that this wasn't going to work. What's worse, I warned you."

"There is no way he's going home. The movie was greenlit based on him being in it," Scott replied.

"Then get rid of me, because I'm not catering to him," I threatened. "This guy has real problems that go way beyond my puzzle-solving skills."

"He'll only be here for five days. We can get through this," Scott said.

I thought for a minute as I decompressed. He was right. I suddenly remembered: Tom wasn't going to be there for the whole shoot. I realized that Scott was really the one running the show and he was right. Tom was only going to be there for a few days and as long as the company didn't mind that he was going to throw the schedule off and extend our days, why should I care? I was in no way, shape, or form afraid of Sizemore, so, all I had to do was get past working with the guy—when and if he showed up to work.

I agreed with Scott and told him I was going upstairs to try and figure a way to shoot the current scene without him in case he didn't show up and that's just what I did. Despite the constant turmoil that the production was clearly going to be in, I was really excited to be shooting what was turning out to be a good movie. When we got through the constant hoops that were set before us, the footage turned out great. "You're right," I said. "Let's just get through it. I will figure a way for him to not be in the next shot if he doesn't show up."

I told the assistant director to try one last time, then to tell Tom to just relax and that I was writing him out. I went into my RV and rethought the scene. It was an important one, but I didn't have any other choice. Little by little, I figured out how to reassign Sizemore's lines to the other actors.

Upstairs, we were about ten minutes into filming the scene without him when who came stomping into the office set in the middle of a take but none other than Tom Sizemore.

"Okay, I'm ready, let's do this," he said as I couldn't help but laugh.

I explained to him that we had figured a way to do the scene without him and that he could go rest, but he insisted on staying. He apologized to the other actors for his late start and we collectively decided to start filming the scene all over again from the top: this time, with him in it.

When I finally rolled and called action, however, Tom walked into the scene and started improvising lines that had nothing to do with the script. The other actors stood there, broadsided, looking to each other in total confusion.

"CUT!" I called. "Tom? What are you doing?" I asked in disbelief.

"I'm not doing those lines. I have better ones," he said.

"Okay, no problem, but would you mind telling us what lines you *do* plan on saying, so they'll know how to respond?"

He explained what he wanted to do, and frankly, I was so thrilled that he had made it to set, he could have been reading the phonebook for all I cared. Take after take, he changed the lines to completely new ones, but truthfully, his acting was really good when he was able to stay cognitive, so we somehow made it through the material with it looking decent. Despite whatever may have had going on personally, he was indeed a brilliant performer and I truly wanted him to do well.

After we were done with one angle and setting up for another, I stepped outside the room to speak to the lighting guy about what we needed for the next shot. I finished what I was doing and came back to the set only to find Sizemore, now sitting in my director's chair, which sat right next to five other empty chairs. He was having the video assist guy rewind the camera tape so he could watch his takes.

"What are you doing?" I asked.

"I'm watching my takes," he said, looking at me, getting the exact rise that he expected he would.

"Turn that off," I said to the video assist. "We don't play back takes on movies that have ninety pages to shoot in eighteen days and certainly not on ones where actors show up four hours late to set."

Tom stared at me as if he was going to punch me.

"And get out of my chair," I added.

Sizemore fumed as once again, he stormed off and went back down to his trailer. At that point, we were both in a contest to see who could piss the other off more, but I refused to be shaken by him. These days, I would have probably indulged him a little more. Had he even been trying to do a good job, I would have certainly indulged him back then. I have since learned to better manage my no-nonsense approach when it comes to directing unruly cast members.

The next scene involved all of the lead prisoners using sledgehammers on an old cinder block wall that sealed off a long-closed wing of the prison. As the prisoners knock the wall down, they are unaware that they are accidentally releasing the ghost of the murdered little girl who takes revenge on anyone who enters the furnace room. I loved this scene so much because it reminded of the setting in the script that Courtney Joyner had previously written for the movie *Prison*. I really wanted to make it an homage to Courtney's and Renny Harlin's style and show my true appreciation of the old Empire pictures vibe.

Ja Rule, Danny Trejo, Paul Wall, Taylor Kinney, and the rest of the cast came down to the wing where the scene was to be filmed. But instead of rehearsing and shooting, we once again waited an hour with no appearance by Tom Sizemore. At that point, I didn't care if he showed up as it wasn't pertinent to the story that he be there. I immediately started to reassign his lines and block the scene without him.

"He said he will be here in fifteen minutes," the second assistant said as she approached.

"Tell him I'm good without him," I said, going on with my work.

Five minutes later, we were shooting and once again, Tom showed up in the middle of a take. "Oh, Tom, we're good," I said in mock concern.

"Nah, I feel great, I'm here, I want to do it," he said like a scorned child who'd just had his bluff called for the 100th time. I was learning that aside from just ignoring him, cutting him out of scenes was enough to motivate him to show up, however late.

All of the actors were on one side of a huge cinder block wall. Because it eventually had to be knocked down and could not be rebuilt, the wall itself was very temporary with no inner-bindings to keep it permanently standing. It was about fifteen feet straight up and constructed of heavy scored cinderblocks and caulking that was barely holding it together. We worked our way through the scene and finally got to the point where Taylor Kinney was to break through to the other side. In order to get the shot, we had our camera and electricians go on the south side of the wall and aim the camera where a precut hole would be pounded open while the actors stood on the north. To save time and the wall itself, we also ran a second camera on the north side of the wall as Sizemore's character gave the final order to open it up.

Everyone took their places and both cameras rolled, but before I could call action, Tom, not realizing he was completely in view on my monitor, suddenly ran towards the wall and shoved it, trying to push it over. The wall started to tilt as cinderblocks rained down from above right in front of my cameraman Viorel and his crew. Everyone scrambled to try and keep from being hit by heavy bricks.

"It was starting to fall towards me. I had to try and stop it," Tom said, looking at me without a care in the world. We both knew he was lying. The truth was, he had tried to push a hundred cinder blocks over onto a bunch of unsuspecting crew people. Forget how insanely talented he clearly was; something was clearly not right in his head.

So much internalized anger was constantly brewing within Tom, and he seemed hell-bent on taking it out on everyone around him. We are so lucky that the crew thought quickly and dove out of the way.

"He's obviously in the middle of something personal," one of the more tender crew members on set said, asking me to try and show the guy some compassion.

"Horseshit," I said. "I've known a whole slew of party animals in my life. In fact, I've been a fucking person with substance abuse issues and not once did I ever think that pushing a cinderblock wall onto a group of unsuspecting people was a good idea. Tom Sizemore gets no pity from me. He cares about one person and one person only: himself. I will suck it up and get through this, but don't make the mistake of expecting me to do it with a smile or any empathy for him. He does not want to be here."

At that point, I was not afraid to appear as angry as I was becoming. I wondered if every directing job that I was ever going to book was going to involve me walking a precarious emotional tightrope or babysitting some lost soul? Did I truly love directing that much that I would accept carrying around so much anxiousness and worry that I or my co-workers might be hurt? When did I get to feel like I was creating film? When did I get to take a moment to think about the story I was trying to tell? Was every single movie going to somehow involve a caustic element? It was feeling that way. I still needed to learn to balance it all.

I pasted on a smile and crossed over to Tom, patting him on the back, mock-thanking him for his heroic (although completely made-up) effort to try and catch the wall and save everyone. He stared at me with a shit-eating grin, admiring my committed audacity. The truth is, we both knew that he tried to knock that wall over so we would have to stop shooting and he could go back to his trailer and lie around or play more air guitar in his underpants. One thing was for certain: Sizemore was starting to realize that he could not rattle me and it was clearly becoming a challenge.

I leaned in and whispered to him. "If you're trying to break me, you're gonna have to try harder than that."

Sizemore smiled at me as if he were about to slug me, but instead, he saluted and sauntered out of the cellblock. And with that, I knew that I could certainly count on him trying harder to break me, but at least at that point in the day, he would be pretty much asleep standing. We moved on to one short scene directly after the wall, and Tom literally fell asleep in the middle of the scene. If you look closely in the scene where Michael Pare and he are standing on the other side of the newly demolished wall, you will see Pare laughing during the scene because Tom falls asleep in midsentence. While standing up. The good news was, the scene was indeed short and our full day of hating one another had officially ended.

The Ghost from Furnace was not a happy fellow

Michael Pare remains one of my favorite actors

Step by step, Muffy and I carefully edged our way along the frozen sidewalks towards our rental car like Bambi trying to navigate himself across a frozen pond.

Producer Scott crossed our path as he suddenly slid into view. "Here are the new pages for tomorrow," he said, handing me a stack of blue pages.

"What new pages?" I asked.

"I did a polish for tomorrow's interrogation scene with Ja Rule."

"You did?" *Now, what?* I thought to myself.

"Yeah, I didn't feel like the dialogue was street-wise enough," he said. "I punched it up."

"Scott, no offense, but you're a movie-contract attorney on the wrong side of fifty. What could you possibly know about being streetwise?" I said, expecting him to burst into laughter, but he was serious. The three of us just stood there for an uncomfortable moment and I realized he wanted me to read what he had come up with.

I stood there and read his pages in the minus zero weather as Scott and Muffy waited for my response. In his defense, the pages weren't bad, but the excessive amounts of *'you know what I'm sayin?* and *don't get it twisted* type quips he added in made me laugh when I pictured the well-off, educated, old white guy sitting in his hotel room in his robe and fuzzy slippers trying to punch up the script's "gangsta credibility."

"Somebody rented *Boys in the Hood*," I said as I handed the pages back to him. "That's fine. I will say, though, if you choose to polish a writing duo's work without telling them, it should be astonishingly better when you're done polishing it."

Scott glared at me like I was a prick, which partially thanks to him and others like him, I had indeed become.

"You're no Shakespeare, stick to producing," I said with a head pop.

"William Butler, making film production friends, one person at a time," Muffy said as we continued to granny-walk our way over the ice.

The truth is, Scott was only trying to help. I was indeed being a cunt. I now know that my horrible and rude attitude was due to how incredibly exhausted and freezing I truly was. Sizemore's irritating contribution was driving me to the brink. It took every ounce of energy I had to manage dealing with him, but in doing so, I was taking how worn out I was feeling on everyone around me.

It was around this time that I was heading back to my car as I caught a glimpse of my assistant hustling up the prison stairs with a roll of tape.

"Where are you going?" I asked.

"Matt needs gaffer's tape," he said.

"Matt?" I asked in confusion. He couldn't be possibly talking about the French-Canadian production assistant.

"Oh—" Johnny said, his energy sinking. "I thought you knew that Matt was directing some second unit and insert stuff," he said in mortal fear.

I stood there for an incredulous beat, then snapped my fingers and pointed for him to lead the way. "Well, let's go," I said, grinding my teeth.

We headed to the top floor of the main building, where sure enough, I found young Cecil B. De'Matt running his own set as he shot a series of inserts for my movie, with Michael Pare acting in them, no less. Producer Scott had quietly approved a second unit without even bothering to mention it to me. Despite being completely insulted that no one asked if I felt I needed such inserts or if I had any shots for him to shoot, I acknowledged Matt's help instead of putting him into a verbal meat-grinder which was my first thought. I wasn't executive producing the film and really didn't have the control over whether or not they wanted him to shoot stuff. The guy clearly loved making movies and if I were smart, I would have cozied up to him a lot earlier and got some of the shots that I wanted while I was distracted, babysitting Tom Sizemore.

It was the fact that no one bothered to mention to me that this activity was taking place or if I had any direction that really put me over the edge. It was very clear that the monkeys were running the circus and all I could hope for was to get through the damn movie while somehow staying sane, alive, and sitting in front of a working heater.

Exhausted by the insane amount of tail chasing I had done throughout the day, I climbed into my freezing rental car and drove back to the hotel to drink copious amounts of Limoncello. Later that night, management and I reshuffled the following day's work, scheduling Sizemore to be in at seven in the morning, despite not really needing him until three. That way, when he decided to finally show up, he would, in fact, be to work early.

I went to my room with Muffy Bolding and we lay in bed, laughing at just how incredibly stupid my life truly had become. All I wanted to do was make movies. That's it. That's all I have ever wanted to do. I never thought that something that made me so happy would be a playground for so many others to irritate me so much. I just wanted to tell stories and have fun. Yet there I was in Nashville, sitting in the freezing cold every day, trying to pursue my absolute passion in life while enduring the irrational whims of others who would never be brave enough to try and direct themselves but who brazenly never hesitated to tell me how to do my job. It seemed like my dream career was going to come with some pretty big costs, starting with my sanity. All I could do was focus on the parts of the job that I did truly love and hope for a better day tomorrow.

I call this one FAT and FROZEN

Victoria Hester and I on set ready to put her in the prop furnace set

Just like in the movie *Groundhog Day*, the exact same fresh hell started all over again at eleven in the morning as I got my first Sizemore update.

"He doesn't want to come to work yet," the assistant director said.

"Keep pushing him. As long as he is here by three in the afternoon, he'll still be an hour early," I said, feeling like I might have figured out a way to saddle that thespian bronco.

"I'll get him here," Danny Trejo calmly offered. Aside from being a terrific actor and an all-around good guy, Danny had many years of sobriety under his belt and was well-versed when it came to dealing with people of Sizemore's ilk. I profusely thanked Danny as a production assistant offered him a ride and they headed toward Sizemore's hotel.

Good luck, I thought to myself.

My morning went marvelously that day. Michael Pare proved himself to once again be a dream of an actor who knew the script front ways and back, easily breezing through his scenes with actress Jenny McShane. Still to this day, he is the most cooperative and professional actor I have ever worked with and I truly appreciated working with him. Word got back to me that miraculously, Danny had quickly wrangled Tom to the set and talked him into going directly into make-up. Moments later, Sizemore walked onto the set, seemingly ready to work.

"How the fuck did Danny pull that off?" I asked, bewildered. "That was the fastest he's ever gotten here."

"He's Danny fucking Trejo," a crew guy quipped.

"He knows how to speak in Tom's vernacular," the assistant director said.

"Then hire him to do double time, moonlighting as one of the assistant directors," I said. As much as I was joking, Danny really did seem to know how to deal with Sizemore and I really appreciated his help. He was a tremendous help both on and off camera.

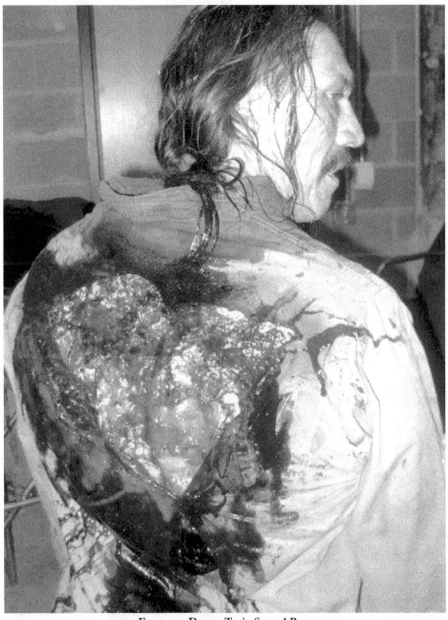

Furnace - Danny Trejo Served Rare

I went down to the old prison guards' security cage where Tom had a scene by himself where he watches Jenny McShane's character as she makes the rounds through the corridors. The camera and lights were set up as Tom, seemingly in a pretty good mood, came down and joined me. I walked him through the blocking and showed him where the monitor was and explained that what was playing on its screen was going to be added when the movie was finished. Tom, holding a hot cup of coffee, moved in close as he asked me why his character would be watching the girl. I explained that it was my belief that her character was condescending to him and not so secretly onto his character's bad boy antics and that maybe at one time, his character had been in love with her and she scorned him. Tom nodded as he stared me down. Even though he was listening, his eyes were sending me the clear message that he indeed did not like me. Slowly, his hand began to grasp tightly to the coffee cup handle and he began to make a fist. I could feel him studying my face as I continued and just as he started to slowly rotate the cup as if he were about to punch me in the face with it, I called out to him.

"Tom," I said.

"Yeah?" he replied, his hand gripping the cup.

"What are you doing?" I said, nervously looking down at the coffee mug. Sizemore looked down, loosened his grasp, and then turned away from me. I honestly believe that I was about to get punched in that face by that coffee mug. It was clear there was no love lost between us. At this point, I couldn't wait to get off the movie and that feeling was about to multiply.

Tom Sizemore on the rare occasion he showed up

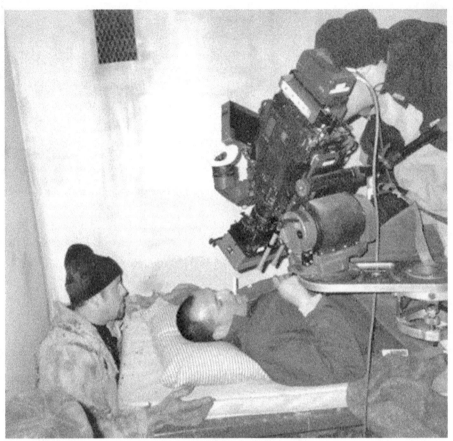

Tom Sizemore shooting his last shot

At four o'clock, we started setting up for some shots we were doing in Ja Rule's character's cell. In the scene, the cell bars were to start glowing red and catch fire so we spent a good amount of time lighting it and getting the bars rigged. After a couple of hours, we were finally ready to shoot, and I took my chair in front of the monitor and called action. Just as Ja Rule started doing his business, I heard the sound of a loud voice across the room. It was, of course, Sizemore, who was boisterously talking to one of the grips at the top of his voice.

"Cut!" I yelled. "Quiet!" I barked. The room fell silent.

We reset and started shooting again and sure enough, once again, Tom started talking at the top of his voice. "Cut!" I yelled as once again the room fell silent.

I told the assistant director to get him out of there before I rolled again. The crew and I waited as the assistant crossed the room and tried to get him to leave and the two of them nearly got into a scuffle. I got up out of my chair and walked across the room. Sizemore seemed to light up at the sight of me.

"You want a fucking reaction out of me?" I said as I closed in on him. "Well, here it is. Get the fuck out of here if you are going to be talking!" He looked me up and down, laughing. "I'm serious, Tom. If you have to talk, please get out."

He didn't move. "Fuck you," he said to me with a smirk.

"No, Tom, FUCK YOU!" I said. I turned on my heel and started back for the set as he jumped out of his chair and started barreling towards me. I stopped and turned back towards him. "I am not afraid of you," I said.

"I should have kicked your ass when I first had the chance, you fat cocksucker!" he screamed at me.

"FAT?!" I barked back as the entire crew exploded into laughter.

Leave it to me, a three-hundred-pound movie director to be more furious about being called fat than I was about being called a cocksucker.

Once again, that's when I snapped. I had had enough of that broken person. I moved in close to his face and instantly went Hannibal Lecter on him: calm and crazed. "Why don't you hurry up and hang yourself, Sizemore. You know as well as I do that the entire world is waiting for it to happen," I whispered to him.

Tom suddenly flew into a rage, grabbing one of the tall glowing red, lit, butane patio heaters we had on set and started to throw it at me.

Movie crews are an interesting bunch. We are, for the most part, a mismatched group of strangers that are suddenly thrown together, expected to instantly cohere as one big functional hive, all working together for the nearly impossible goal of creating a film. One thing's for certain: one of the results of this abrupt bonding is that the crew quickly becomes one big, dysfunctional family. I was both surprised and relieved when just as Tom lifted that heater up in the air, the entire crew ran in between us, creating a human barrier between him and me, and a grip stepped in and grabbed the heater away from him.

"That's not happening," the grip said as I caught my breath. At that moment, it wasn't me who was finally broken but Sizemore himself who ran off set. Producer Scott followed behind him as I did my best to pull it together, apologized to the crew, and continued shooting. An hour later, producer Scott reappeared on set with a smirk.

"Now what?" I asked.

"He wants me to fire you and he's offered to finish directing the movie."

"Scott, I am begging you to fire me," I countered. "Please do it."

"No way," He laughed.

"I'm serious. I would be good with that," I said to no reaction.

I excused myself for a break and took a walk, my adrenaline was still pumping as I honestly held back from bursting into tears. By then, it was about three in the morning and fifteen below zero. I walked around the prison yard and to the front of the beautiful building where a circle of concrete benches were. I sat there, bundled up and numb as I stared forward, feeling nothing, not from the cold but from the whole scene in general.

As had happened to me with acting, was I going to want to stop directing, too? I sat for a few moments, asking the universe for a sign, then pulled it together and finished my day. In a matter of weeks, I shot the entire film and was headed back to Los Angeles, never to run into Tom Sizemore ever again. Frankly, I couldn't be more thankful of such a blessing. In the end, the movie turned out good, so I guess the ultimate lesson learned is it doesn't matter how you get there as long as you get there.

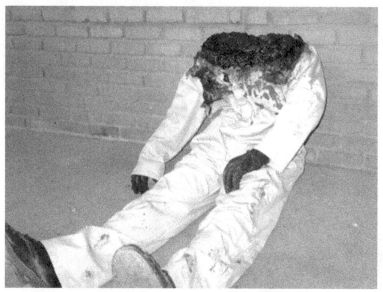

Furnace - Another day another beheaded body

About six months later after *Furnace* came out, I got an email from producer Scott.

Dear Billy,

I just wanted to drop you a note of apology. I just finished working with another producer-writer on another movie and went through the same experience with him as I did with you when it came to my desire to control things. Just wanted to say that I acknowledge that my actions didn't make things any easier for you on Furnace.

And you know what? That's all it took. From that moment on, I didn't have a single ounce of resentment towards him or the entire operation. Turns out, producer Scott was an awesome mensch. Being brave enough to admit when you are wrong is a tremendously attractive quality. I need to learn that one myself. His actions taught me that I, too, shouldn't be too proud to admit when I've made a hasty, ego-driven decision. It was the only time that had ever happened to me during my entire journey in the entertainment business. Producer Scott ended up with my complete respect. I never heard from him or worked with him ever again, but I sure did appreciate that note. It gave me hope that maybe there were decent people in the film business I could find to work with. As for production assistant Matt: I don't know what happened to him, but I sure hope he continued to follow his bliss. As show business goes, I am sure one day, I will read that he is the head of Universal Studios.

33

BREAKING BILLY

When I got back home, I took some time off. I was a huge ball of confusion. I had come to the conclusion that I still wasn't totally enjoying my work. I didn't understand how a career that I was so set on doing my entire life was little by little eating away at me, making me openly bitter, angry and resentful. Acting was no longer my focus and while I loved directing much more than acting, each project was raising my blood pressure and ultimately eating away at me. I couldn't figure out why I was so unhappy, but I knew something had to change.

I had hoped my entire life to work in film both in front and behind the camera but now the lifestyle seemed to be more bother than satisfying. To make matters worse, my writing partner Aaron Strongoni sat me down and told me he had decided that he wanted to go off and write on his own. He assured me that it was nothing personal, but after writing with him for years, I'm sure my obvious burnout and constant caustic attitude had become unbearable. It was a devastating hit, but I knew I would muddle through.

I decided to take a break and went to visit my parents. My mother, always my sound board and best advisor encouraged me to just stop everything and take a rest. She reminded me that I no longer had anything to prove as that I had pretty much tackled every goal I had ever set out to achieve, no matter the mid-level or minor notoriety I had ultimately attained. She encouraged me to consider all of my options, including just moving home and starting all over with something less stressful.

After a couple of weeks, I came back to L.A.. I sat down and made a list of everything in my life that made me happy and everything that disrupted my flow. The absolute first thing that had to happen was I needed to lose weight again and start taking care of my health. I knew I was never going to be the thin racehorse I used to be, but I had to trim down in order to clear my head in the self-loathing department. I started going back to the gym and started walking again. In a matter of weeks, I was casting a much smaller shadow, having lost forty pounds. This helped my self-esteem tremendously.

The next thing I did was contact my old digital short colleagues and told them I wanted to start producing for them again. Though my heart is in storytelling and filmmaking, I truly loved and still love working with the team of professionals there and the highest level of quality that the company expects. Working with them has always been very sacred to me. The fact that I was accepted and appreciated by so many top-level creatives had been a huge milestone in my life.

I took small gigs there and once again worked three times harder than anyone expected me to, and in a matter of months, I had graduated to creating a few short series for them to creating my own short series. In time, I branched out and very nearly climbed my way to the top of the heap in the digital-shorts world. In a matter of just two years, I went from being a one-man band to branching out and having my own on-going full-service production crew and a huge green screen soundstage in Burbank. My business expanded to other major studios as I briefly created trailers, programming, and digital shorts for everyone from Warner Bros. to Universal Studios.

My dear friend Dana Booton, head of production at Starz Film Roman, allowed me some office space, which helped me to expand my entire production operation even further. Things got so insanely busy that I quickly all but forgot my true love of filmmaking. Though I was no longer telling stories, I wasn't having to put up with the insane amount of misbehaving that producing film sometimes allowed.

Over the hump and back to beating the streets

I was able to not only live a life I had only dreamt of, but also to give many of my friends jobs. It didn't matter if you had ever produced or worked in the business, if you were a friend or family and needed work, I hired you and taught you the skills you needed to be a part of my team. Together, we all worked collectively as a growing squad and suddenly, I was making more money working seven days on a commercial or digital short than I ever would in eight months on a film. As a result of my newfound glut of income and sweet lifestyle, I also suddenly seemed to become more attractive to people who would not normally give me the time of day.

I started dating up: like, way up. I started helping people and new friends in need, particularly if I found out they were struggling. I spared no expense to make sure others were sheltered and safe. I think there was a part of me that felt guilty about all of the good things that were unfolding. Vehicles for those in need were purchased, vacations were often and endless. I bought a ninety-thousand-dollar Mercedes and moved into a nine-thousand-dollar a month house with a swimming pool way up on Beverly Ridge. I had everything that a person could ever dream of and there wasn't a single overly-medicated actor or wanna-be director there to ruin my day.

I was completely set up.

And yet, somehow, I still was not happy.

In fact, in a matter of four short years and tremendous success, I was unhappier than ever.

No matter the terrific lifestyle I had achieved, I still somehow had not found a happy balance in my life. I still wasn't getting it right. I had gone back to producing kids' programming, thinking that was the answer, but privately, I was completely lost. I had produced so many digital shorts that I could do them in my sleep, but the more I did them, the less I cared about what I was doing. My attitude gradually became awful as I totally checked out of life. I foolishly grew to resent a magnificent job that had provided me with a perfect life, yet it was a life that I felt completely trapped by. Since I had hired most of my closet friends, I felt deeply obligated to keep the machine going and growing to keep all of their heads above water as well. I got sloppy in my accounting and started paying my bills late; I completely stopped focusing on the creative aspect of my work and any idea of writing another screenplay. I had become a complete sellout.

As my attitude got worse, the people closest to me grew weary to be around me as I became more and more abrasive and beat down. Even Muffy Bolding, who I had loved with all my heart for a good portion of my life, was gone. My growing horrible attitude and the return of my extreme possessiveness was too much for even her. I sat every Friday, signing stacks of paychecks, going through thousands of dollars, sometimes getting to the last check and realizing there was barely enough money left for me. At a certain point, almost everyone around me was over dealing with me, but no one more than myself. I had honestly lost touch with how incredibly lucky I truly was and more importantly, just exactly who I was. Not thinking of the consequences, I desperately wanted to be free of the huge responsibility that I had grown to hate and I openly wished for it all to go away.

They say to be careful of what you wish for; sure enough, that wish eventually came true, suddenly and without warning. Things were about to get a lot simpler for me in a huge way. As my attitude got worse and my focus on my work faded, I thoughtlessly made enemies of people above me in what must have been an unconscious hope for it to all to go away. Little by little, I began to carelessly disregard any input or help the talented and respected creatives around me would offer. I would snap at people who tried to elevate the work, then rake them over the coals with attitude and sarcasm when they would try to discuss my bad attitude until one day, in one three-minute phone call, the biggest gig of my life abruptly went away.

It seemed, once again, Billy Butler was about to start all over. In twenty-five years, I had gone from sleeping in my car, to being a special effects slime jockey, to becoming a busy working actor, producer, and an even busier director…to having no job and with pretty much every bridge burned behind me. What's worse was that, in thinking that my work as a commercial director would never end, I had not saved a single penny. Not one penny. My sudden good fortune had crept up on me so fast I didn't even wise up and start saving before it was over.

Everything in my life suddenly came to a screeching halt. I had no idea where to turn or what was next. The complete reboot that I clearly needed once again was upon me. I started to think that maybe the universe was sending me the clear message that the entertainment business wasn't for me after all. I just didn't seem to be getting any of it a hundred percent right, no matter where I focused my attention. Despite being creative, I had zero direction. Completely distraught, I wondered if maybe my father was right back when I was a kid: maybe I would have been better off just getting a job at Montgomery Ward. One thing was very clear. Things were going to be changing once again in a huge way.

I packed up my beautiful house in the Hills with the help of my dear friends Mo Collins, Alex Skuby, Jerrie Werkman, and Kenny Meriedeth. I put everything I owned in storage, got rid of my car, closed my company, and laid off all of my employees. It was a hugely painful time.

It was during this period that I also witnessed unbelievable generosity as true friends old and new looked past my dumb mistakes and didn't flinch in their belief in me, many of them offering me money, work, and advice as I tried to see beyond the fog that I suddenly found myself surrounded by. My dear friend and show business powerhouse Dana Booton, who I had first met at Saban, offered me a job in development at Starz Film Roman to keep me afloat until I figured out what I was going to do. Her belief in me is truly a major part of what helped me pull through it all without doing anything foolish.

I will never forget my new friend Martha Brown from Starz coming to my office as I sat at my desk in shameful tears. She smiled, told me to pull it together and laid two thousand dollars out on my desk to help me survive. My post supervisor Jody Komai stayed with me at work to the bitter end as we both packed while hoping that things would somehow turn around. My wonderful friend Nick Byassee made up excuses to stop by, showing up with bags of groceries and the hilariously generous excuse that he "bought too many groceries and didn't have enough room in his fridge or cupboards." Longtime friend Jimmy James stayed in touch and gave me the kindest moral support a person could. Damn, people really step up sometimes. I will never ever forget the incredible kindness I witnessed. I love you all.

After all I had been through, after all I had earned, I was out of work, out of a home, and didn't have two dimes to rub together. It seemed I had ultimately failed across the board. It really felt like my entire career had ended. I'd spent so much time resting comfortably on Hollywood's middle shelf that I'd stopped pushing and aiming high, ending up in the ultimate crash and burn. People and hangers-on began to desert me left and right. It was during this time that I learned who my true friends were.

It seemed like maybe my journey in L.A. had come to an early end. After everything was packed and I said my goodbyes, I loaded up my dogs into a rental car and drove up north to stay with my parents for a while. By then, my mother had remarried after my stepfather Roy passed away. She and her new, very kind husband, a man I truly look up to and consider my father named Bob, both welcomed me into their home with open arms.

At first, I just sat quietly in their guest room, decompressing in my pajamas as I binged old movies for a month solid. Both of my parents were incredibly kind and generous, telling me to stay and clear my head for as long as I wanted. I had no idea of what was next in life, but one thing was for sure, I didn't feel much different than a penniless teenager, sleeping in his car behind that pizza place.

34

THE LAST CALL

I sat in that bed for days. I felt absolutely lost. Nothing was coming to me. I was in the middle of a complete disconnect and a total meltdown. Maybe I would just stay in town and direct the local news? Maybe I would end up working in a hardware store like Viggo always would say. I was clearly having a midlife crisis. Again.

Finally, after almost two months of my wallowing in complete self-pity and despair, John Vulich called, reaching out to see how I was doing and just in the nick of time. We sat talking on the phone for close to two hours as I caught him up on all the unsavory events that had unfolded and how I was feeling depressed about everything. I told him how I didn't think I had the patience or temperament to work in the entertainment business anymore and how it truly seemed everything was over before it really even got cooking. I fully expected him to tell me to take some time and not be too hard on myself, but like so many other times in my life, John didn't hesitate to spell it out for me with a valuable bit of eye-opening, shit-kicking, and totally unsolicited wisdom.

"Stop your fucking whining, you pussy," he droned in his usual bored tone. "Your career is only over if *you* say it is. Of course you're agitated when you're working the film business: it's an unpredictable piranha pit that employs and encourages sociopaths and stupid people." He laughed. "Never forget: stupid people don't know that they're stupid."

"Are you kidding me, John?" I said, sitting up in bed, furious. "Have you not been listening to me? I was just fired from a massive job. I have nothing saved. I don't know really anyone in the business that I can go to for another producing job. I've bitten the head off of every executive producer that I have worked with. I hate auditioning. I don't want to starve myself anymore. I can't get arrested, John. No, wait, arrested is probably all I will get when all of my unpaid bills eventually catch up with me. I'm an unemployed nobody," I said, finishing off the last bite from a carton of rocky road ice cream I had snuck out of my parents' garage freezer.

"You've been unemployed for less than a year. Stop being a drama-queen," John said. "You're not a nobody and you know it. Billy, everything you've experienced in your career has pushed you forward. Both good and bad. Up until a few months ago, you hadn't stopped working since you got into L.A., so how can you say you're a failure? You wanted to learn special effects, you did. Okay, so you were no Dick Smith, but you knew your way around the make-up room and were booking jobs that took you around the world three times. You wanted to be an actor, you became one. Again, you were no Robert DeNiro, but you had a successful career that made you happy and that *you* decided to walk away from."

"Is this pep talk supposed to be making me feel better?" I sneered.

"You wanted to write, you wrote; you wanted to direct, you directed," he said. "You're a good director and you're still learning. You're a really good producer. You've done every single thing you've set out to do. Why is your life suddenly over?" He paused. "You honestly think you're the only one in show business to burn through a pile of cash and be broke? You think you're the only one in show business that's had a show cancelled?"

"My life is at a complete standstill and I don't know how to fix things, John. I've been making every bit of this up as I go along," I said.

"We're all making it up as we go along, asshole. Look, you put your movie career on pause and turned your back on what makes you truly happy. And you did that because you were a whore for cash. We all are. No one blames you. Anyone would have taken that high paying job. But gigs like that don't last forever and you're frankly lucky that it didn't. Those digital shorts are great but you should never have made them your main focus. That's a side gig for someone like you. You've been making films since you were in sixth grade. You didn't break your talent bone. The current big gig ended. Not only is your movie career not over, you're just getting started. Snap out of it, pick yourself up, get back to L.A., and move on. You act like you're the only one in show business who's had a slow period," he said with zero hesitation or sympathy. "You're just pissed off you're not making boatloads of cash right now. Grow up. You'll be there again before you know it."

I lay there listening, wanting to murder him as I stared up, listening to the clank of the janky ceiling fan hanging above my mom's guest bed. I wanted to murder him…

…because he was one hundred percent right.

"I fucking hate when you do this," I said.

"Why?" he laughed.

"Because this means I have to pack it up and go back to that shithole town again," I moaned. Truthfully, I guess I was half-excited at everything he had just said to me. As upside down as everything was, the fact was, I was not ready for it to be over.

"Your life is whatever you decide it is, Billy," John said. "Find the one thing in everything that you can do that makes you the happiest and just focus on that. Just the *one* thing and stick with it."

"The film business turns me into a hateful prick," I said.

"No, you were already a hateful prick way before you started working in film and that's exactly why we're friends. Because I'm one too," he quipped. "Besides, the film business prides itself on turning people into pricks. If you aren't a prick you aren't doing it right. You think the successful guys I work with on *Buffy the Vampire Slayer* are a joy to be around?

"You're not hard to work with, you like things done right and you don't like answering to people that don't know what they are doing," he continued. "Stop working with people that don't know what they're doing. As long as I've known you, you have *never once* said *no* to a single job. You've never realized that you're above some of the work that's been offered to you. You'd be directing studio movies by now if you would've just said *no* a lot more often in the last few years. Stop sharing your talents on projects that are beneath you and start looking to work with people who deserve your attention, are at your same level, and recognize your worth."

I listened to his every word, quietly pulling air into my lungs as he drove his point home. "I have three Emmy Awards and I can see your worth, why can't you?" John said to me with genuine brotherly love. "You have never recovered from your old man raising you to believe that you are worthless, pal. It's time for you to man up and realize it for yourself. When you finally do, I promise you that things will get better. I promise."

Friends, as hard as it was to hear everything that he said to me in that call, that's all it took. My eyes were open wide. Suddenly, the chains of my own pathetic despair dropped from my wrists. Okay, so maybe Vulich yanked them away, but I had indeed seen the light. My beloved brother from another mother was right. Again. Not only did I like working in the entertainment business, I loved working in it. I just hated working with people I didn't respect or on projects my heart wasn't completely in. I had been spending years ricocheting from department to department, not choosing any one particular skill and just putting all of my attention on whatever was in front of me. For years, I had been ignoring my heartfelt urge to create what was my idea of art just for the chance at fast employment and a grab for easy money. All because inside, I didn't truly believe in myself. All the years that I was carrying myself like a boss, I was secretly going home and flogging myself, secretly thinking that I wasn't worthy enough to cut to the chase and just aim higher. That fucking parrot on my shoulder had never really left.

I hung up the phone and lay there for an hour, thinking about our conversation. I thought through every choice I had made throughout the years, good and bad. I thought about the tremendous amount of risks I took to make things happen and how I must have known what I was doing for any of them to unfold on any level. I emerged out of my parents' guest room, looking like ten miles of unwashed, unshaven bad road and told them that I had finally figured it out. I saw my mother smile in a way that told me she always knew I would come around.

This time, I was excited to go back and see what would unfold.

From that moment on, I made the unflinching decision to be a lot pickier about who I worked with, what jobs I took, who I hired, cared for, and loved. There were certainly going to be assholes to deal with in the future, but at least it would be on projects that I was proud to be a part of. I would no longer feel badly about standing my ground, no longer sign on to movies or projects that my heart wasn't completely in. From that moment on, I would appreciate the big paying jobs and the people involved with them just as much as the small ones because I was only going to do gigs that I had passion for. I would go out of my way to be far more positive and respectful of every single person who deserved it and that respecting included myself. I would better manage my time, money, creativity, and most of all, myself. It was honestly the biggest awakening of my life.

I know that despite John Vulich being as smart as he was, he never truly knew how much he had saved my life with that conversation. But he sure did. Within a couple of days, I was finally up out of bed, showered, dressed, and pecking out my first solo screenplay I had written in a very long time. I decided I was going to make a movie all on my own: no writing partner, no big team, and frankly, no money. I didn't know how I was going to do it, but I positively knew it was going to happen.

I called everyone I had been an asshole to and apologized for being a thoughtless beast, and if I didn't call them, I showed them with my actions. I sat in that room and put every ounce of energy I had into my writing. I wrote a kids' feature film *My Babysitter the Super Hero*, and it turned out to be some of the best writing I'd ever done. All by myself. My best friends, actress Mo Collins and Alex Skuby, a couple who continuously stayed by my side while I was both stinking rich and rock bottom poor, invited me to come stay with them while I decided what I was going to do for work, and it was right around the time that my friends from the digital shorts world came back around and started hiring me again. This time, I truly appreciated the work I was blessed with. This time, I was far more kind and respectful to the people I worked with and much wiser when it came to my financial and time responsibilities. I worked hard to make amends with everyone I had been caustic to and no longer allowed users into my life. I balanced my time between entertainment that made money and film that I had passion for.

I sent my script out to several of my established acting friends in L.A. and told them about my crazy idea to try and make a film with no money and somehow, not a single one of them passed. Maile Flanagan, Jim O'Heir, Mo Collins, Alex Skuby, Melissa Peterman, and Paul Vogt all stepped up and appeared in my project with zero begging on my behalf. In a matter of weeks, I was fully cast, crewed up, and shooting an entire film on just a few thousand dollars, much of which was given to me by my friends and family. I teamed up with several of my dear friends from the post-production world and we edited the film together with great success.

Table read of My Babysitter the Super-Hero

**Friend and brilliant actor Alex Skuby as Commander Kruel
in My Babysitter the Super-Hero**

Paul Vogt as the Bubinator in My Babysitter the Super Hero

Melissa Peterman was one of many actors who stepped up
and helped me get my juju back.

My mother making a cameo in My Babysitter the Super-Hero

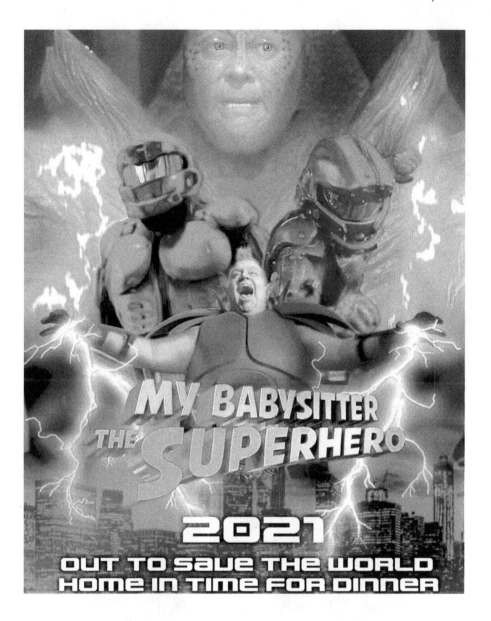

Before I knew it, I was back on my feet and working constantly. I was no longer making money hand over fist, but I was making money nonetheless and living in a much, much happier state of mind. Not long after that, I wrote a second kids' movie, one called *3 Bears Christmas*. Feeling confident once again, I went out and found my own financing. A year later, I finished the film and sold it worldwide to be seen by millions of people on virtually every digital platform, where it garnered five-star reviews and received the Dove Award's highest recommendation.

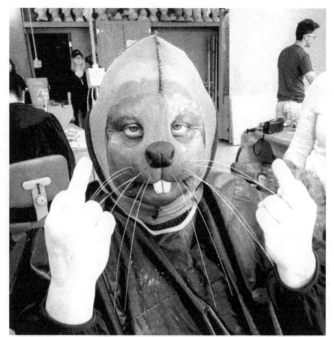

Maile Flanagan as Mrs Beaverton in 3 Bears Christmas

Elissa Dowling in 3 Bears Christmas

My insane journey of ups and downs finally led me to my absolute bliss and on my own terms. If I wasn't getting hired on the projects I wanted to work on, I created my own. Opportunity doesn't knock? Build a fucking door. No more big staff, no living above my means, no longer financially supporting people who didn't appreciate it, and never again would I work on a project just to be working. I finally figured it all out. Talk about your slow learners.

The best part of the story? The positive shift in my energy brought back nearly everyone in my life that I had once chased away. Anyone that mattered, anyway.

I was truly happy. I am still truly happy. I was finally in total control of my own bliss.

But just as I exhaled, my life was once again about to change in a way I could never have expected it to.

35

JOHN IS GONE

"John is gone," John Vulich's girlfriend's voice came over my cellphone as I answered it.

"Where?" I asked, not even close to understanding what she was saying.

"No," she whispered. There was another big pause. "John…is gone. He died," she said. I could tell she was crying.

I stood there for a shocked beat in complete disbelief. "Don't say that," I said, afraid to breathe and praying that she was joking.

"He's dead, Billy." I sat down in the chair behind me as every bit of energy drained from my body and she continued. "He woke up this morning to go to set and said he wanted to sleep another ten minutes. I went to the kitchen to cook him an egg and I heard him breathing funny, so I went into the bedroom and he was just lying there. He stopped breathing," she said.

"Did you call a fucking ambulance?!" I screamed at her.

"Yes! They came…he's gone," she said, crying.

I hung up without saying goodbye, dropped whatever I was doing, dove into my car, and raced towards Vulich's apartment. I was positive I had to be dreaming. John was still so young; a highly intelligent, indestructible cockroach of a man who would certainly figure a way to outlive us all. He barely drank, he no longer touched drugs of any kind. There was no way he could really be gone. There was no way.

On the way there, I called my mother, begging her to tell me that I was in the middle of a bad dream. She quietly assured me that I wasn't. I could not imagine or accept life without the brother who I deeply loved and who had changed my life in so many ways. I got to John's building and raced upstairs to his apartment. There, sitting at the kitchen table, was his girlfriend, weeping in total sadness. I remember seeing a single uneaten fried egg in a frying pan on the stove and not wanting to move beyond the kitchen to see any more than that.

After about thirty minutes, I got up the courage to go and see John. I can't even remember taking a breath as I crossed to his room. Sure enough, there he was, lying there in his bed, completely lifeless. My best friend and brother of forty years was indeed gone forever. I went into his bathroom, put the lid down on the toilet seat and sat there looking at his body as it lay in his bed, covered with a blanket. I sat weeping for what felt like three hours, but in hindsight, it must have only been a short while. As I sat there completely broken-hearted, I thought way back to when I first met John in my filmmaking class, through all the days when we used to race around Fresno in his Mustang, raising hell as teenagers, our all-night horror movie marathons, the countless times when he told me to be brave and have self-worth back when I felt like I was invisible. I remembered how much we wanted to meet special effects wizard Tom Savini and how we had somehow both ended up working with him. Our lifelong storyline together had come to an abrupt end. A fucking horribly unfair ending. Never again would I get to hear his insane jackal-like cackle laughter or get irritated with him when he obsessed over his latest conspiracy theory or wage war on people he considered competition for no real reason. Never again would he help guide me through a life where I truly needed guidance.

I walked to the foot of his bed and stood there for a few moments in complete sadness. I reached down and tugged on one of his ugly monkey toes and said goodbye for the last time. "Goodbye, Jackal," I said as I held back an insane amount of grief.

My eyes were so flooded, I could barely make my way to the living room as I sat on the couch in complete sadness, petrified as I found his shoes sitting on the floor next to me. His reading glasses were resting beside his beloved computer that he spent every waking moment on, and a half drank glass of water was sitting on the coffee table beside that.

I went out onto his tiny balcony and cried my eyes out, not looking back once as the coroner finally arrived and took his body away. The devastating day had come when my very best friend was gone and entirely too soon. I took out my phone, tried my best to pull it together, and then made the hardest phone call I ever have had to make in my entire life as I struggled to tell John's parents that their son was dead.

I cannot begin to put into words the overwhelming sadness that his mother's horrified grief brought me. She screamed in agony as I told her the news. Like me, she thought all of this was a cruel joke that couldn't possibly be true. But it was. I sat quietly and patiently as she cursed me out for the cruel joke that she thought I was pulling on her. I didn't say a word as, little by little, she slowly realized what I was telling her was true.

After I was finally able to get off the phone, I pulled together any ounce of energy I had left and called a few more of his friends, all of whom were totally shocked and brokenhearted.

After just a few short hours, his parents arrived. His friend Rob Lucas and I carried John's invalid father up several flights so that he and his mother could see his apartment, only to watch them leave after a few minutes when they saw for themselves that John was really gone. They were completely destroyed. I went home and lay in bed for the better part of three days. A few days later, I held John's funeral at my house. It was graciously paid for by Rob Lucas and so many of his other friends who all stepped up, including my friend Mo, who made the most beautiful flower arrangements. I was so happy to see so many of the people and colleagues from our long journey in Los Angeles as they came to pay tribute to him.

John Buechler, Ronny Pipes, Greg Cannom, and Michael Burnett were there; even our childhood idol and inspiration, Tom Savini himself, graciously came all the way from Pittsburgh to say goodbye to the grand poobah of all Jackals. I could barely get through the memorial as I got everyone situated and went upstairs to bed.

John would have been so flattered and happy to see how many people cared about him enough to show up. Effects wizard, producer, and dear friend Greg Nicotero even showed up to say goodbye, despite Johnny not being very kind to him in the last few years of his life. It was a wonderful reflection of Greg's character for him to be there. In fact, it was beyond moving to see that so many of the people that we started out with were there to say a final goodbye.

For one day, there was no hard feelings about past disagreements or competition with one another, only the loving memory of a guy who'd started out just like the rest of us in the pursuit of his own bliss. The day was harrowing; the love and connection, hugely obvious. We all said goodbye to a friend and character that had affected so many of us in so many ways, but no one more than me.

John Vulich's Memorial Service

Three weeks later, a cardboard box arrived at my house. Inside the box were all three of John's Emmy Awards: one for *Buffy the Vampire Slayer,* another for *Babylon 5,* and a third for *The X-Files.* I set them up on my fireplace mantle, remembering the time that John took Sarah Michelle Gellar to the Emmys and won the award for best special effects make-up on *Buffy.* He told me that right after he received the award, he was so excited that he thrust the trophy up and stabbed himself in the chin with Emmy's wing, cutting his face open and spending the rest of the night with blood all over the front of his shirt. It was a fitting anecdote for a man who had dedicated most of his life to horror.

Sometimes, I look at the trophy and think maybe someday someone can clone him from the tiny bit of blood that is still caked on the tip of that wing. It's my belief that the world needs much more of John Vulich's very matter of fact, Yugoslavian potato-dick energy.

After a year of grieving, I was finally able to get on with my life, but there sure isn't a day that goes by when I don't think about my friend John. I cannot express to you, dear reader, how much he influenced me and impacted my life for the better. I will continue to think of him every single day that I am lucky enough to be around.

John Vulich on his last trip overseas

John, his girlfriend Celeste and myself on set of Night of the Living Dead

John Vulich on the set of Night of the Living Dead

Less than two years later, our tight group was sadly brought back together as our dear friend and the man who gave so many of us our start, make-up effects artist and director John Buechler also passed away after a tough run with cancer. Kane Hodder, *Sharknado* director Anthony Ferrante, and I sat at the foot of John's bed, talking to him, the very morning of the day that he died. We were so grateful to have the chance to tell him how much he meant to us all before he passed. The last thing he said to me was that he loved me. Once again, the entire MMI gang converged at my house and held each other tightly, reminding one another how much we appreciated each other.

By now, I am getting pretty good at throwing funerals if you ever need advice.

A year after that, my dear friend, mentor, and brilliant director Stuart Gordon of *Re-Animator* fame passed away, too. I was shocked and devastated that yet another person who had mentored and believed in me had passed. Damn folks, getting older is a bitch. How very lucky I was to have known Stuart. I'm not kidding you when I say, put this book down right now and call or hug someone you love or who has made an impact in your life. You never know when the chance to do so will go away. I really mean that. Tell those you love how much they mean to you. Get it while you can, as you truly never know when it's all going to change. Thank you, Johnny Vulich, Mr. Buechler, and Mr. Gordon. I appreciate you all more than you ever knew.

The best friend I have ever known

As I have spent the last year reading through my journals, writing this book, I am finally drawing these chapters of my crazy—sometimes funny, sometimes sad, but always blessed—life thus far to a close. I can't help but to feel so fortunate to somehow still be alive to write all of this down. There are a lot of miles on my odometer. If you made it all the way through this book, you'll realize that no one more than me knows that I have truly lived three full complete lifetimes. I happily lived life with my foot to the floorboard and took a huge bite out of the juicy peach that is my existence. I have seen and experienced things and people that so few have; maybe, few would want to.

The best part of my journey is the great friends I have made along the way.
Bill Mosley, Steve Johnson, Myself and Tom Savini

I somehow became a working actor with a dedicated group of fans who love me and treat me with unflinching kindness. I turned my love for all things horror into working on virtually every one of my favorite horror franchises as well as writing, producing, and directing films of my own making. I was lucky enough to become dear friends with so many talented and worthy people connected to many of those projects. I never had that many solid love relationships, but goddamn, the beautiful creatures I have canoodled with for stretches of time have been friggin' legendary. I attained a lifelong dream of working for the Walt Disney Company and am adored by what I dare say is the best family on the planet. I learned how to stop being self-destructive, dabbling in things I should not. And the dogs... oh, how I have been surrounded by lots of glorious, beautiful, loving dogs. Most importantly, I finally learned to grab that fucking parrot of doubt off my shoulder and strangle him until he squawked his last jab. No birdie. It's YOU that aren't fooling anyone.

The clueless fat kid with zero self-confidence and a fried green perm somehow figured a way out of Fresno, California, blindly following his bliss, making every single mistake you could make along the way, until he finally got it right and on his own terms, no matter how late in the game. I can write all I want in this book, but I truly cannot put into words how incredibly grateful I am. God or the universe, or whatever is out there, has somehow afforded me the marvelous luxury of this blessed, beautiful existence, traveling around the world to see so much of what it's truly all about, when I very easily could have ended up homeless or dead. Taking chances is everything in this life. You must do the same. You must. Like Tom Fox said, in the end, life is only about loving and finding your own bliss, and I know that now more than ever.

Billy Marquart and My Beloved Dogs

I am so thankful for the generosity that has been continually and most astonishingly bestowed upon me. And you, dear reader, are now a part of that generosity. Thank you for taking the time to read about my unlikely life and what a lucky dog I have truly been. No one is more astonished by that fact than me. Good times and bad, I honestly would not change a thing.

In closing, I am most happy to say I'm thankful to finally be completely content with who I am.

Somehow, in my mid-fifties, I have learned to no longer strive about being something I'm not. I am completely comfortable with the way I look, I'm no longer too fat, no longer too skinny, and I am finally content with my achievements on whatever level and do my very best to pay forward every ounce of good energy that is graciously put before me, and there has been a lot. I'm going to write when I feel like it, direct when I feel like it, and even act again when I feel like it. Most importantly, *with whom I want to do it.* I will no longer measure my self-worth on the achievements of those around me or spend any time worrying about people who don't consider me worthy or their particular cup of tea, and there are a few, some of which, I am willing to bet, are reading this book. Hi, there. I wrote a book and I truly wish you were in my life enough to be in it.

And as much as I have been forgiven for my own shortcomings and flaws, too numerous to mention, I also forgive anyone along my journey who made life tough for me and that includes forgiveness to my own biological father. I now believe you can't be truly content if you carry around too much angst from the past. Many of the rough times in my young life miraculously led me to some of my greatest moments, so maybe everything good and bad that happens to you is somehow a part of the plan for one's own enlightenment. Either that or I'm a very forgiving motherfucker. I'm sorry if anyone was hurt by this book. It's my truth. My memories. My experience. You keep living yours.

I like myself now. I highly recommend it.

So, here's to all of us living life to the fullest, finding our own bliss, and eventually telling our own story. Trust me: it's the best therapy money can't buy or earn apparently, as everyone keeps telling me there is no money in writing books. After this experience, I am unfortunately hooked and can't wait to do it again. With that said, would you please recommend this little darling to a friend? I have dogs to feed.

See? You can take the boy out of the carnival, but you can't take the carnival out of the boy.

BEAST WISHES

Your pal,
William Butler
Horror's (former) Boy Next Door

ACKNOWLEDGEMENTS

Loving Thanks and Acknowledgments to the following:

Connie and Robert Owens
Kimberly Williams
John Vulich
Jerrie Werkman
Kenny Meriedeth
Peter Garcia
Muffy Bolding
Leslie Jordan
Charles Band
John Carl Buechler
Mike Deak
Patti Lesser
Dana Cameron
Eric Covert
Mark Pinsker
Tom Fox
Tony Timpone
Mo Collins and Alex Skuby
Eryn Krueger Mekash
Viggo Mortensen
Exenne Cervenka
Tom Savini
Greg Nicotero
Ken Hall
David DeCoteau
Chris Gore
David Pearlman
The Membrains
Stephanie Denton
Maile Flanagan
Jessica Hughes
Colleen Camp
Todd Stites
Laura Jones
Jimmy James
Jill Hotchkiss
Carrie Sheldon
Nick Byassee
Gary Schwitzer

Kate Hodge
Ling Mah
Candi Milo
Jeffrey Sherman
Wendy Liebman
Hope Perello
Selene Luna
Margaret Cho
John Criswell
Robert Kurtzman
Jeff Farley
Thom Floutz
Pat Fraiser
Ellen Idelson
Billy Marquart
Paddy Perlaky
Will Gersh
Wendi McClendon Covey
Jonathan Hung
Lakeshore Entertainment
Melee Entertainment
Jim O'Heir
Melissa Peterman
Paul Vogt
Justin Jones
Howard Berger
Natasha Lyonne
Carrie Sheldon
Michael Patterson
Jody Komai
Rick Von Flue
Martha Brown
Aaron Strongoni
Rob Lucas
Brian Reams
Roy Nakamura
Selene Luna
Debbie Dion
Everette Burrell
Eddie, Henry, Walter, Yogi and Gibby
The Walt Disney Company
Rebecca Rowland and Louis Stephenson
Michael Aloisi for his hard work, belief and kindness

CPSIA information can be obtained
at www.ICGtesting.com
Printed in the USA
BVHW031947040521
PP12196000001B/1/J